Glory and Failure

Johann Helfrich Müller (1746–1830), a shadowy figure in the history of the difference engines. Silhouette of unknown origin, discovered by Dr. Ralf Bülow, Deutsches Museum, Münich.

Michael Lindgren

Glory and Failure

The Difference Engines of Johann Müller,
Charles Babbage and Georg
and Edvard Scheutz

Translation by Dr. Craig G. McKay

The MIT Press
Cambridge, Massachusetts
London, England

This book was printed and bound in the United States of America.

Library of Congress Cataloging-in-Publication Data

Lindgren, Michael.
    Glory and failure : the difference engines of Johann Müller, Charles Babbage and Georg and Edvard Scheutz / Michael Lindgren; translation by Craig G. McKay.

        p.   cm. — (The MIT Press series in the history of computing)
    Includes bibliographical references (p.   ).
    ISBN 0-262-12146-8
    1. Calculators—History. I. Title. II. Series.
QA75.L493   1990
681'.14—dc20   90-5944
                                                   CIP

To Barbro, Kerstin and Craig

History of Computing

I. Bernard Cohen and William Aspray, editors

Contents

Abbreviations

BL	British Library, London
BPL	Boston Public Library, Boston, U.S.A.
KB	Royal Library, Stockholm, Sweden
KTHB	Royal Institute of Technology, Stockholm
KVA	Stockholm University Library with the Library of the Royal Academy of Sciences, Stockholm
NM	Nordic Museum, Stockholm
PRO	Public Record Office, Kew, England
RA	National Archives, Stockholm
RS	Royal Society Library, London
SF	Society of Business Archives in Stockholm, Stockholm
SM	Science Museum, London
SML	Science Museum Library, London
SSA	Stockholm City Archives, Stockholm
TM	National Museum of Science and Technology, Stockholm

Acknowledgements

It was as an engineering student at the Department of Machine Design at the Royal Institute of Technology in Stockholm that I was first presented with the challenge of writing a thesis in the field of the history of technology. A department devoted to the latter discipline had been established at the Royal Institute of Technology in 1966 by the late Torsten Althin, and a teacher in the department, Svante Lindquist, suggested that I should focus my attention on the calculating machines of the Swedes Georg and Edvard Scheutz. I readily accepted this suggestion and at the same time, I was fascinated by the thought of entering a new field of research. My initial findings were summarized in short reports in Swedish. However, it soon became clear that there was a great deal of source material in the archives which was pertinent to the subject and which had been neglected. In December 1979, I managed to trace the 1843 Scheutz prototype machine to a depository of the Nordic Museum in Stockholm. The engine was duly restored and it was to be doubly significant, first of all, as an artefact which provided new knowledge and evidence of importance for the historian, and secondly, because the public interest occasioned by the rediscovery of the machine, paved the way for a deeper and more comprehensive study of the difference engines and indeed by so doing, made the present work possible. Through the good offices of Svante Lindquist, Stephan Schwarz, the Head Librarian of the Royal Institute of Technology and the late Anders Rasmuson, then Rector of the Royal Institute of Technology, I was given a position at the Department of History of Technology which allowed me to travel about, collect material and to write, for a period of eighteen months. Thus the original short report expanded and Craig McKay began to translate it into English in order to make it accessible to a wider public.

In 1980, the Department of Technology and Social Change, Tema T, was founded at the University of Linköping and it brought together a number of scholars with different backgrounds who were interested in analyzing technology and its role in society. This aim appealed to me and I joined the department as a research student in the autumn of 1981. For the next two years, I was mainly engaged in very stimulating full time studies which had a key role in broadening my perspective and my work on the difference engines proceeded slowly. However, eventually I was able to concentrate my full attention on it again. At the end of October 1984, I had the opportunity of being able to spend six valuable months participating in the Program in Science, Technology, and Society at M.I.T. and it was there that a large part of the present book was written. The visit also gave me the opportunity of exchanging views with various American scholars in the field.

I am greatly indebted to a large number of people for their generous help in the preparation of this work: to the late Torsten Althin, for his pioneer endeavours in developing the study of the history of technology in Sweden; to Svante Lindqvist, for his kind guidance in this field; to my official adviser in the field of technology and social change Per Sörbom and to Göran B. Nilsson, who have guided me in the craft of the historian; to Craig McKay, friend and philosopher, for carefully translating the manuscript; to Merritt Roe Smith, for his unfailing generosity in supplying helpful criticisms and suggestions; to Ulf Sandström and to Bo Sundin, for many valuable comments about the manuscript; to Stephan Schwarz for his inestimable support and understanding; to Nicolai Herlofsson for important assistance concerning the first version of the manuscript; to Ulla Riis and Lars Ingelstam, for crucial help; to Sune Zachrisson, for allowing me to take active part in the restoration work; to Per Westberg, poet and friend, for happy and memorable months spent together restoring the first Scheutz' engine; to Kerstin Andersson, Barbro Axelsson and Carine Hamrin, who have spent many hours skillfully and patiently typing the manuscript.

It is also a pleasure to acknowledge the help given to me at various stages of my research by Paul Armer, Christine A. Bain, Donald de Blasius Beaver, Anders Beckman, Svante Beckman, Göran Bergengren, Per-Olov Bjällhag, Elisabeth Björkman, Allan G. Bromley, Bruce Collier, Tore Frängsmyr, Jan Garnert, Owen Gingerich, Max Gorosch, Titti Hasselrot, Brooke Hindle, Thomas Parke Hughes, Sigrid Högberg, Ulrich Joost, Arne Kaijser, Hans Karlgren, Melvin Kranzberg, Martin Kylhammar, Åsa Lindgren, Torsten Lööf, Peter Mark, Uta C. Merzbach, Lars Norberg, Åke Norrgård, Bengt Nyström, Ola Palmér, Claudine Pouret, Alice Prochaska, Kalevi Rasilainen, Bo Sahlholm, Bernt Schiller, Staffan Smedberg, Jane Summerton, Roger Steuwer, Oliver Strimpel, Gary J. Tee and Alice Woods.

Research for this book has been greatly facilitated by the courtesy and cooperation of many librarians and archivists. I thank them all.

Two institutions, in particular, have provided the necessary conditions to sustain my work on this project and I am pleased to acknowledge their support and to express my sincere appreciation to the Department of History of Technology, Royal Institute of Technology, Stockholm and to the Department of Technology and Social Change, Tema T, University of Linköping. I am also grateful for the support given to me by the *Thord Gray Memorial Fund*, the American Scandinavian Foundation and *Tor-*

sten Althins Minnesfond, National Museum of Science and Technology, Stockholm.

I would also like to thank the photographers and staff at the Learning and Research Centre at the Royal Institute of Technology, for professional help with some of the illustrations in this book and I am grateful to the Trustees of the Science Museum, London, to the Royal Society, London and to the Nordic Museum, Stockholm for permitting me to reproduce illustrations.

A special word of thanks goes to IBM Sweden for generously funding the original publication of this dissertation.

Last but by no means least, I owe a special debt of gratitude to my wife Johanna for her continuing interest in the project and for her unfailing cooperation and good humour during the years I was married to Charles, Georg and Edvard.

Linköping, December 1986
Michael Lindgren

Preface to the Second Edition

The issue of a second edition of this book—an edition directly intended for an international readership—has allowed for several corrections to be made to the text. It should be noted that the book is exclusively concerned with the difference engines. As a result, a great deal from the history of calculating machines and computational tables has been omitted. In particular, nothing has been said about Charles Babbage's ingenious and original Analytical Engine, the direct mechanical predecessor of the digital computer.

Series Foreword

The MIT Press series in the History of Computing is devoted to the history of computers and information processing in the broadest terms. The series encompasses all aspects of modern computing—systems, hardware, and software—as well as the preliminary development of data processing and the mechanization of calculation. Historically based inquiries into the social, political, philosophic, and economic as well as the technical aspects of the introduction and use of computers and information processing fall within our purview.

The series includes both general works and specialized monographs. Some of the volumes concentrate on a particular development, such as magnetic memory, while others trace in full the technical history of an industrial company of significance in the computer industry. While most of the books in the series deal with the twentieth century, and particularly the most recent part of this century, others trace anterior developments. Thus the series includes a biography of Ada, countess of Lovelace, and another on Georg and Edvard Scheutz, both associated with the work in the nineteenth century of Charles Babbage. The series also includes autobiographical studies of key figures in modern computing.

I. Bernard Cohen
William Aspray

Introduction

This is a case study of invention.[1] It deals with an age when the word "computer" denoted a human being and not a machine. It is the story of a great invention. Great, not in the sense of being successful, but great because it embodied a remarkable and admirable idea, so grand in its conception that even today it can arouse the same feelings of respect and wonder that it did in the early 1820s. It was a creation of the industrial revolution, a product of man's striving to free himself from all monotonous and demanding labour. This is the story of the difference engine, an invention which was to bring its creators not only honour and fame, but which also presented them with many difficulties and left them without financial compensation. It is a tragic story of glory and failure.

This book presents a social and technical analysis of the first attempts to mechanize the production of numerical tables. The idea of having a machine to calculate and print tables originated with the German engineer Johann Müller in 1784. Müller's machine was designed but never built. In England, the mathematician Charles Babbage invented an engine based on the same principles in 1821. During the years 1823-1833, Babbage attempted to build the table engine with grants from the British government, but failed to complete it. In Stockholm, the Swedes Georg and Edvard Scheutz, father and son, were inspired by Babbage's work to build a difference engine. Georg and Edvard Scheutz managed to complete three engines − a prototype in 1843, one intended for regular use in 1853 and a copy of the latter in 1859. The latter two were marketed internationally and eventually sold and used.

With the exception of Müller, a great deal has been written on the originators of the difference engine and the reader is referred to the bibliography for details. My aim, which differs from that of previous writers dealing with the history of these machines, is to give a unified picture of the difference engines from Müller to Scheutz, with emphasis on two particular aspects. The first is to see the difference engine as part of the history of numerical tables. The second is to give as much prominence to the purely technical facts of the matter, i.e. to the engines themselves, as is given to personal and social aspects. I hope with this book to dispel a number of misunderstandings which have arisen about the men and their engines. Thus the portraits of Babbage and Scheutz which are presented here, in certain aspects differ markedly from those presented by previous authors and scholars.

The book is divided into two parts. The first part deals with the history and technology of the engines and with their inventors. The second sets out to provide an analysis of the material presented in the first part. The core of the book consists of three chapters: Chapter 1 deals with numerical tables, with Müller, Babbage and their engines, and the mathematical principles on which the engines were based; Chapter 2 is about Georg and Edvard Scheutz, about how they learned of Babbage's engine and about the design and mode of operation of their own machine and its history; Chapter 3 is principally concerned in providing the answers to why Babbage failed technically and why the Scheutzes failed commercially.

Something should be said about the way the book is organized. The first part, which is mainly descriptive, provides a review of new and known material in a traditional and uncontroversial form. Thus I accept − with certain exceptions − the established factual framework relating to the history of these men and their machines. In the second part, there is a change of perspective: I take a critical look both at what I myself have written in the first part and also at what other scholars have written about the difference engines. There I try to show how the same facts can be interpreted in quite another way, if the whole picture is taken into account. The result is that the structure of the present work is somewhat akin to a detective story. As the dénouement approaches, there is an accumulation of evidence and pieces of the puzzle which may have seemed mysterious, fall into place.

Certain sections of the book contain rather substantial technical descriptions. Their purpose is to pave the way for various arguments in the second part of the book, by providing the requisite technical facts. They also throw light on the inventors' way of thinking − whether right or wrong.

How was it possible for the teenager Edvard Scheutz to make a complete difference engine at a negligible cost and with the simplest tools in 1843, while Charles Babbage with the assistance of a skilled engineer, several workmen and an extremely well-equipped workshop and with a budget of more than 17,000 pounds, failed? How did the various sections of society react to the difference engine? Was incomprehension crucial when the inventors came to apply for governmental support? How was the financing arranged at a time when there was no organized method of financing inventions? These are some of the questions to be considered. Somewhat paradoxically from the standpoint of the institution where the major part of the writing of the present book was undertaken, the difference engine had no social consequences − apart from its effects on the lives of the inventors themselves. But the reader need hardly be reminded that the engine in another form − that of the modern digital computer − has transformed society.

PART I
HISTORY
AND
TECHNOLOGY

"Sweden has thus secured for herself
the glory of having been the first nation
practically to produce a machine for
Calculating Mathematical Tables by
Differences, and Printing the Results.
Wealthier and more powerful nations will
regret that the country of Berzelius
should thus have anticipated them, in
giving effect to an invention which
requires for its perfection the tools of
nations more highly advanced in
mechanical science."

Charles Babbage 1856

1. BABBAGE, MÜLLER, AND THE FIRST DIFFERENCE ENGINES

1.1 Numerical tables, a historical background

From a historical point of view, numerical tables reflect a world in change. In them are mirrored not only developments in science and technology over a period of more than 3,000 years but also the emergence of new fields of research, trade and labour, and thus social change in general. At another level, numerical tables contain the measurable evidence of man's endless quest for greater and greater precision and accuracy. Very little has been written about tables in more recent times and there is no book, whether old or new, which is entirely devoted to the history and role of tables in society. The articles which have been published in this century on the subject, have been narrow in scope and most often devoted to one specific table, discussing it in a scientific terminology that is difficult for the layman to understand. Nonetheless, some broader historical articles about tables have been written. The most important ones are the extremely detailed and exhaustive works by Charles Hutton (1785), Augustus de Morgan (1861) and James Glaisher (1873).[1] These together with the tables themselves have formed the basis of the general survey that is presented here. It does not claim to be exhaustive and should be considered an introduction to matters more fully analyzed later.

The purpose of this survey is ultimately to provide an analysis of the difference engines in their proper context, i.e. as machinery for the production of numerical tables. As will be shown in the second part of this book, this approach provides new knowledge about the market for these tabulating calculating machines.

A numerical table is a tool designed to save the time and labour of those engaged in computing work. A *table* can be defined as follows:

"*Table*. Any collection and arrangement (generally in parallel columns) in a condensed form, for ready reference, of many particulars or values, as of weights, measures, currency, specific gravities, etc.; also, such a collection or arrangement of a series of numbers following some law, and expressing particular values corresponding to certain other numbers on which they depend and by means of which they are taken out for use in computations."[2]

Numerical tables are defined somewhat more narrowly. They are tables containing only numbers, and not other particulars such as words or signs. The oldest tables which are preserved, were compiled in Babylon in the period 1800-1500 B.C.[3] They were intended to be used for the transformation of units and for multiplication and division, and they were inscribed in cuneiform on pieces of clay. The development of Babylonian mathematical astronomy reached its zenith around 300 B.C. During the first century B.C. Claudius Ptolemy in Alexandria studied the available statistics relating to solar and lunar eclipses in Mesopotamia. On the basis of these, he constructed his geocentric theories about the motions of the heavenly bodies in a work which later came to be known by the name of *Almagest*. The tables which the *Almagest* contained, were restructured and developed further by Ptolemy. They were to form one of the Ancient World's most important astronomical documents and they contained all the necessary tables for the calculation of eclipses as well as various kinds of ephemeris, that is to say tables which specified the positions of the heavenly bodies during a particular period, e.g. each day for a whole year.[4] Ptolemy's tables spread with Islam and eventually reached Western Europe. During the first half of the thirteenth century they caught the attention of King Alphonso the Wise of Castile. He then gathered together a great number of scholars in Toledo who were given the task of calculating a new collection of astronomical tables. The reason for this endeavour was said to be that King Alphonso, who was interested in astronomy, had discovered many errors in Ptolemy's tables.[5] The work began some time in the 1240s and took about ten years to complete. The tables produced were later known as the *Alphonsine Tables*. The vast costs involved were paid for by the king, whose name soon spread with the copies of the tables throughout the European scientific world.[6] Besides the Babylonian tables, Ptolemy's work and the *Alphonsine Tables*, a great deal of toil went into the production of many other numerical tables of different kinds during this period.[7]

With the introduction of the art of printing throughout Europe during the latter half of the 15th century, the first tables were printed. The *Alphonsine Tables* for example, were printed in Venice in 1483.[8] Up till then, books could only be reproduced by arduously copying them. Paper, which could be produced cheaply by this time, replaced papyrus and parchment. Two methods of printing were employed — block-printing and printing with movable types. The former meant that the symbols appearing in the tables were cut out in wooden blocks which then could be used for printing. A whole page of a table was cut in one block. An example of a numerical table produced in this fashion is *Das Bamberger Blockbuch*, printed circa 1482, see Fig. 1. It was a little collection of

1 mal	1	1 ist 1	3	6	18
2	2	4	3	7	21
2	3	6	3	8	24
2	4	8	3	9	27
2	5	10	3	10	30
2	6	12	4 mal 4		ist 16
2	7	14	4	5	20
2	8	16	4	6	24
2	9	18	4	7	28
2	10	20	4	8	32
3 mal 3		ist 9	4	9	36
3	4	12	4	10	40
3	5	14			

Fig. 1 Multiplication-table from the 15th century, produced by the method of block-printing. Table from Das Bamberger Blockbuch *printed in Munich around 1482.*

tables intended for the merchant.[9] The method of printing with movable types, invented shortly before the middle of the 15th century, yielded a number of advantages over the old block-printing method. Because the types were made of metal, they lasted much longer, they could be easily duplicated and produced a legible and standardized text. These improvements paved the way for an increase in the output of tables. The rise of capitalism and the voyages of discovery during the century also increased the importance of commercial tables. Special tables for the conversion of currency, volume, length and weight between the systems adopted in different places began to be produced. There were naturally tables for multiplication and division, but also for addition and subtraction. The latter tables were of great importance in daily life since with limited educational possibilities available, the general level of calculating skills was not high in most classes of society. Mathematicians, astronomers and other scientists formed obvious exceptions to this and their needs were mainly for different types of arithmetical and trigonometric tables.

Particularly at the end of the sixteenth century, several famous arithmetical and trigonometric tables were published. In 1592 in Venice, Johannes Antonius Maginus published his *Tabula Tetragonica*, containing a table of all squares of numbers from 1 to 100,000 together with tables of sines, tangents and secants. In 1596, another great collection of tables was published in Neustadt. It had been calculated by "the greatest of the table-computers", the Swiss astronomer and mathematician, Georg Joachim Rheticus, who for a time worked as an assistant to Copernicus.[10] Its title was *Opus Palatinum* and it contained the values of the trigonometric functions for every tenth second of the quadrant, reckoned to 10 decimal places.[11] Rheticus also calculated tables of sines to 15 decimal places, which were later included in the comprehensive collection of tables called *Thesaurus Mathematicus* which were calculated by the German mathematician Bartolomeus Pitiscus and published in Frankfurt in 1613.[12] *Thesaurus Mathematicus* and *Opus Palatinum* remained the unquestioned authoritative sources for the natural values of the trigonometric functions even up to the beginning of the twentieth century.[13]

At the beginning of the seventeenth century, there were two dominant number systems in Europe – the Arabic positional system with base 10 and the sexagesimal with base 60. The sexagesimal, which came originally from Babylon, was used in the measurement of time (hours, minutes, seconds) and in trigonometry (the partition of the circle into degrees etc.). The great general problem was multiplication and division, which took a great deal of time when these operations involved complex calculations with many decimals. In the case of certain earlier number systems like the Roman one, even the simplest operations had been difficult to perform. In order to simplify multiplication work, multiplication tables were published. One of the earliest and most comprehensive was the table of Herwart ab Hohenburg. It had 999 pages, contained products from 2x1 to 1,000x1,000, and was printed in folio in Munich in 1610.[14] However this type of voluminous table was expensive to produce, clumsy to use and rather rare. The solution to the difficulties involved in calculation came in 1614 with John Napier's discovery of logarithms.[15]

The word "logarithm" is derived from Greek and means "relationship between numbers". The logarithm of a number y, is the exponent x, to which another previously determined number a must be raised to give the number. The number a is called the base of the system. For example, the logarithm of 100 is 2 and the logarithm of 1,000 is 3 when base 10 is used ($10^2 = 100$, $10^3 = 1,000$). Mathematically speaking the relationship can be defined as follows: if $a^x = y$, then x is the logarithm of y, which can be written $x = {}^a\log y$. Various bases have been used. Napier's own system, or the system of so-called natural logarithms, has a base equal to $e \approx 2.718$. Henry Briggs who was Professor of Geometry at Gresham College in London, made the theory more practical by choosing base 10 instead. Briggsian logarithms are also called common logarithms or simply logarithms to base 10.

Logarithms came into their own as a tool of calculation. When there were no calculating machines available, the multiplication of two large numbers involved a considerable amount of work with pencil and paper and a sound knowledge of the multiplication table. With a table of logarithms at hand, the computational effort could be greatly reduced by means of the following laws.

$$\log A \cdot B = \log A + \log B \qquad \log \frac{A}{B} = \log A - \log B$$

$$\log A^B = B \cdot \log A \qquad \log \sqrt[n]{A} = \frac{\log A}{n}$$

Multiplication is reduced to addition, division to subtraction, and exponentiation and root extraction to multiplication and division respectively. An example will illustrate the practical significance of logarithms. Suppose we wish to multiply 203 by 365. We make use of the first of the foregoing logarithm laws and a table of logarithms. The logarithm (to base 10) of 203 is 2.30750 and of 365 is 2.56229. According to the formula, these are added to give 4.86979. It only remains to find out from the book of logarithms which number has that as its logarithm. We discover from the table that 4.86979 is the logarithm of 74,095 which is therefore the desired answer. Because of these practical properties, logarithms were to retain a special place as the handiest, cheapest and most widely used help to calculation well into our own century.

In 1617 Briggs published the first table of logarithms to base ten, from 1 to 1,000 with 14 decimal places.[16] Seven years later, he published a table, *Arithmetica Logarithmica*, containing logarithms of numbers from 1 to 20,000 and from 90,000 to 100,000, also with 14 decimals.[17] In addition, the complex calculations which were common in astronomy were greatly simplified by means of tables of logarithms of the trigonometric functions. Already in his *Mirifici Logarithmorum Canonis Descriptio* which was published in 1614, Napier had included a table of the natural logarithms for sine, and in 1620, Edmund Gunter, Professor of Astronomy at Gresham College, published the first logarithmic-trigonometric table to base 10.[18] The gap in Briggs' table for numbers between 20,000 and 90,000 was filled by the calculations of Adrian Vlacq, in his renowned set of tables *Arithmetica Logarithmica* which appeared in Gouda in Holland in 1628.[19] It contained the logarithms to base 10 of numbers from 1 to 100,000 (including those of Briggs) reckoned to 10 decimal places (667 pages) along with the logsines, logsecants and logtangents to a similar accuracy (90 pages). In addition, as in the case of its predecessor, it was furnished with differences, which meant that from the values appearing in the table the appropriate argument could be read off, even although the exact logarithm in question did not appear in the table.[20] An English translation of Vlacq's table was published in 1631 and there was also a version in French. In 1633, Vlacq published another famous collection of tables *Trigonometria Artificialis*, containing logarithmic sines and tangents to 10 decimal places, see Fig. 2-3.[21] The news about logarithms spread rapidly from country to country. Different

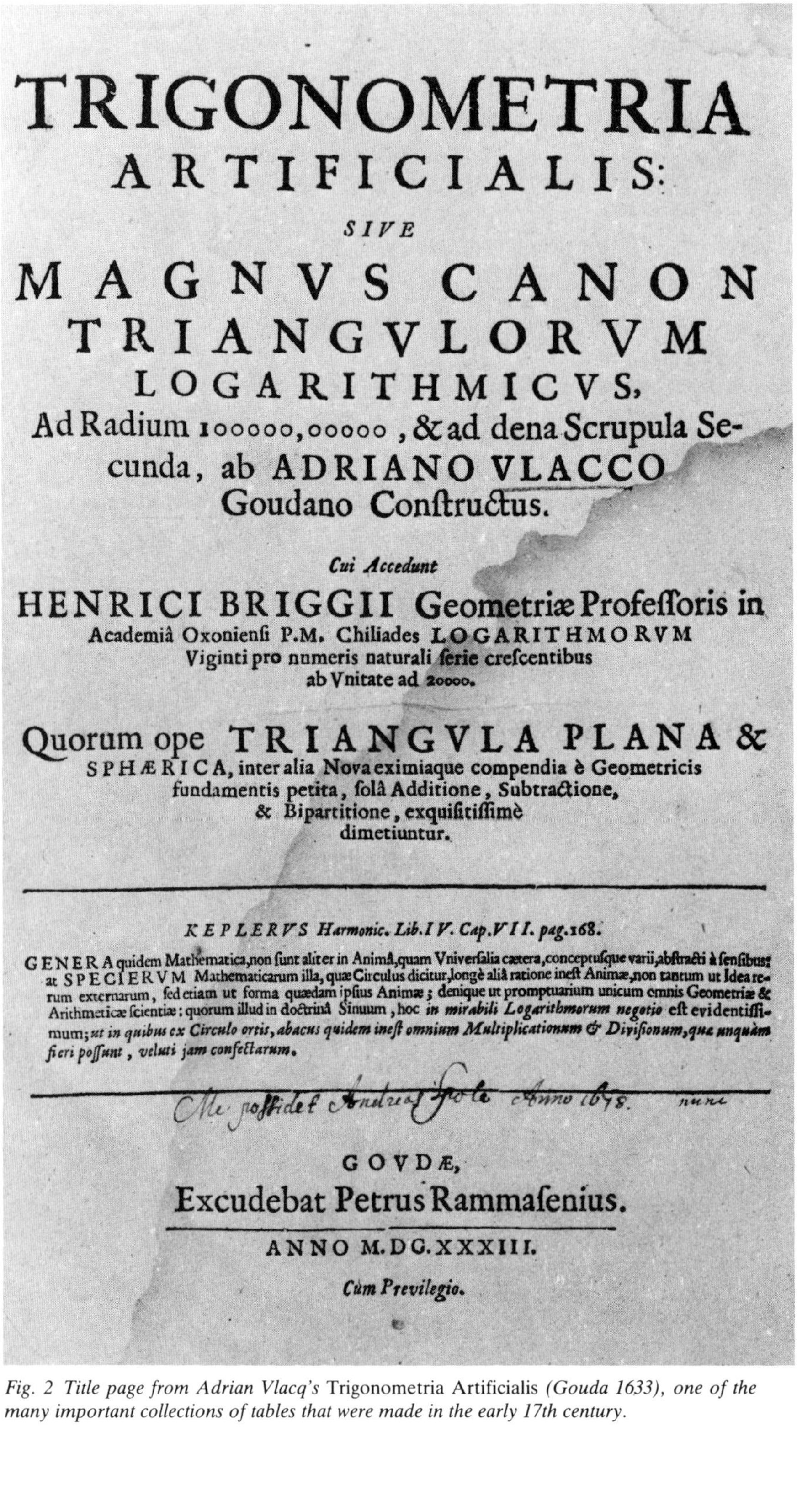

TRIGONOMETRIA
ARTIFICIALIS:
SIVE
MAGNVS CANON
TRIANGVLORVM
LOGARITHMICVS,
Ad Radium 100000,00000 , & ad dena Scrupula Se-
cunda, ab ADRIANO VLACCO
Goudano Conftructus.

Cui Accedunt

HENRICI BRIGGII Geometriæ Profeſſoris in
Academiâ Oxonienſi P.M. Chiliades LOGARITHMORVM
Viginti pro numeris naturali ſerie creſcentibus
ab Vnitate ad 20000.

Quorum ope **TRIANGVLA PLANA &**
SPHÆRICA, inter alia Nova eximiaque compendia è Geometricis
fundamentis petita, folâ Additione, Subtractione,
& Bipartitione, exquiſitiſſimè
dimetiuntur.

KEPLERVS Harmonic. Lib. I V. Cap. V I I. pag. 168.

GENERA quidem Mathematica, non ſunt aliter in Animâ, quam Vniverſalia cætera, conceptuſque varii, abſtracti à ſenſibus:
at SPECIERVM Mathematicarum illa, quæ Circulus dicitur, longè aliâ ratione ineſt Animæ, non tantum ut Idea re-
rum externarum, ſed etiam ut forma quædam ipſius Animæ ; denique ut promptuarium unicum emnis Geometriæ &
Arithmeticæ ſcientiæ: quorum illud in doctrinâ Sinuum, hoc *in mirabili Logarithmorum negotio* eſt evidentiſſi-
mum; *ut in quibus ex Circulo ortis, abacus quidem ineſt omnium Multiplicationum & Diviſionum, quæ unquàm*
fieri poſſunt , veluti jam confectarum.

Me poſſidet Andreas Spole Anno 1678.   nunc

GOVDÆ,
Excudebat Petrus Rammaſenius.

ANNO M.DC.XXXIII.

Cùm Previlegio.

Fig. 2 Title page from Adrian Vlacq's Trigonometria Artificialis *(Gouda 1633), one of the
many important collections of tables that were made in the early 17th century.*

professions began to make use of them and mathematicians and scientists who were impressed by the power of the system, calculated their own logarithmic tables. Thus for example in 1624, Johannes Kepler published a table of logarithms of Napier's type.[22] When his famous astronomical compilation − the *Rudolphine tables* − appeared three years later, he had introduced logarithms into his calculations and the work included in addition several tables of logarithms.[23] By the 1630s, logarithms were commonplace throughout Europe and logarithm tables had been produced in several countries.[24]

Two hundred years later, at the beginning of the 19th century, numerical tables were still the most important calculating aid in Europe. The sole alternatives were Napier's Rods (or Bones) which was a kind of adjustable table consisting of a number of rods, inscribed with numbers and made of wood, metal or bone; or else the slide rule which had been invented by Edmund Gunter during the first half of the 17th century. The latter was directly based on the potent principle of the logarithm. Mechanical calculating machines were extremely rare and at most a handful of very select individuals can ever have used them for serious calculations around 1800. Most of them were simply remarkable gadgets illustrating man's scientific progress, rather than genuine aids to calculation. For the normal calculator or scientist who had to carry out complex computations which demanded great accuracy, Napier's Rods and the slide rule were of little help. In effect, his tools were pen, paper and tables. The spectrum of tables that were available at the beginning of the nineteenth century, shows that their significance can not be underestimated. There were tables for mathematics, astronomy, navigation, physics and engineering. In the field of insurance, there were different types of statistical table, e.g. giving the life expectancy of men in a certain area of the country; in trade and finance, there were several tables to simplify interest calculations as well as tables for converting one currency to another; in the army, use was made of ballistic tables; and tables allowing one to calculate the volume of wood in a log of a certain profile were available for wood merchants. The following quotation from 1834 illustrates the importance of tables for large sections of the population.

> "The surveyor, the architect, the builder, the carpenter, the miner, the gauger, the naval architect, the engineer, civil and military, all require the aid of peculiar numerical tables, and such have been published in all countries."[25]

Mathematics and navigation are two areas in which the use of tables was indispensable at the beginning of the last century. Let me give two examples of how tables could be used in these fields. At the time, there was an astonishing variety of mathematical tables available. All the most common functions had been tabulated. Suppose that x has to be computed where:

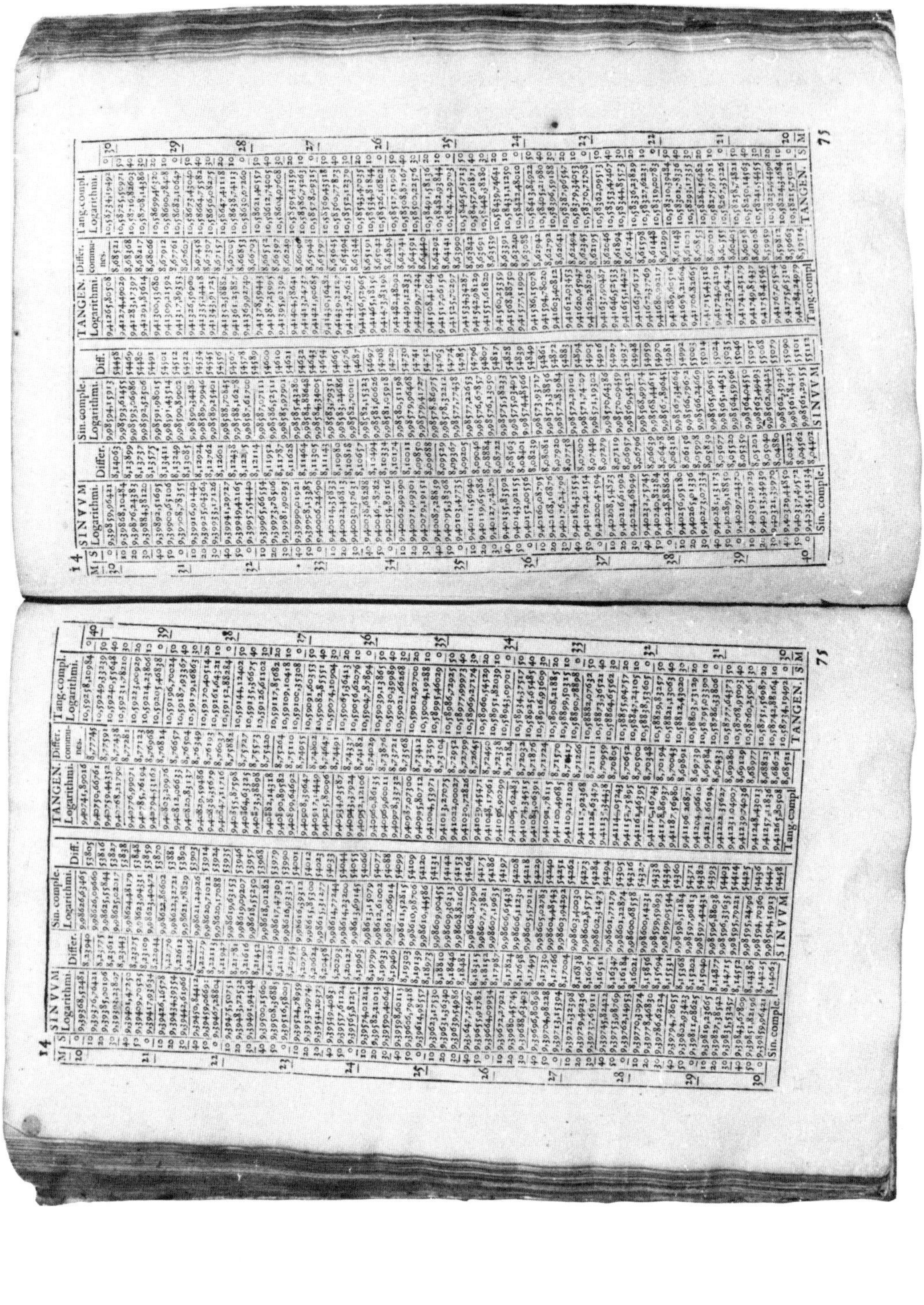

Fig. 3 Table of logarithmic sines and tangents computed and set with ten decimal places –
Vlacq's Trigonometria Artificialis *(Gouda 1633)*.

$$x = 3^{15} \cdot \log 1237 \frac{\sin \left(\frac{\pi}{4} \right)^9}{\tan 30°}$$

The tangent for 30 degrees (tan 30°) could be read off easily from e.g. the tables of Rheticus or Maginus, or one of their successors. Similarly the other functions (log, sin etc.) could be found in other tables. If one had a lot of such calculations to do, it was convenient to have a comprehensive set of tables which covered all the most common functions and their values for selected arguments. James Dodson's *The Calculator: Being correct and necessary tables for computation. Adapted to Science, Business, and Pleasure..."* (London 1747) was such a work.[26] It contained tables for the tangents, sines, logarithms and a table for the first 20 powers of the numbers 1 to 9. Thus 3^{15} and log 1237 could be looked up in it. Dodson's *Calculator* contained also a table where fractions of π could be found. $\left(\frac{\pi}{4} \right)^9$ could then be simplified with the help of logarithms, replacing the operation of exponentiation by multiplication. Finally all that remained was a computation of the type $x = A \cdot B \cdot C/D$ which, with the help of logarithms, was reduced to additions and subtractions and where one had the convenience of being able to look up logtan 30° and logsin $\left(\frac{\pi}{4} \right)^9$ in the tables. The computation could of course be carried out in other ways, but without a set of tables it would have demanded a great deal of time and patience. In Dodson's tables, the values were computed to an accuracy of between 5 and 7 decimal places. If greater accuracy was required, one could have recourse to other tables. Most of the larger scientific libraries in Europe had tables which provided accuracy to a greater number of decimal places. For reasons of production, tables demanding less accuracy were more usual, i.e. they required less work involving calculation, typesetting, proofreading and printing and were thus cheaper. Among the more notable and widely used collections of tables produced after the 17th century, there are *Sherwin's Mathematical Tables* (London 1706), which appeared in at least five editions during the 18th century, see Fig. 4; William Gardiner *Tables of Logarithms* (London 1742); Carl Johan Schultze *Neue und erweiterte Sammlung Logarithmischer, trigonometrischer und anderer [...]Tafeln* (Berlin 1778, 2 vols), and Georg von Vega's works *Thesaurus Logarithmorum completus* (Leipzig 1794) and *Tabulae logarithmico trigonometricae* (Leipzig 1797, 2 vols.).[27]

By 1800, seamen had long abandoned hugging familiar coastlines and had ventured out across the wide oceans. The great voyages of discovery in the 15th century and the consequent growth in international trade, had led to new and more certain methods of navigation. Using the compass as their main instrument, a definite course could be followed, but because of currents, winds and difficulties in manoeuvring the vessel, constant corrections were needed, when the ship's current position had to be determined. Already in antiquity, charts had been assigned coordinates by means of horizontal and vertical lines. This system was developed to

Num. 1 to 100, and their Log. with Indices.				N. 100 L. 00					
N.	Log.	N.	Log.	N.	Log.	N.	Log.	N.	Log.
1	0.0000000	51	1.7075702	100	0000000	150	1760913	200	3010300
2	0.3010300	52	1.7160033	101	43214	151	89769	201	31961
3	0.4771213	53	1.7242759	102	86002	152	1818436	202	53514
4	0.6020600	54	1.7323938	103	0128372	153	46914	203	74960
5	0.6989700	55	1.7403627	104	70333	154	75207	204	96302
6	0.7781513	56	1.7481880	105	0211893	155	1903317	205	3117539
7	0.8450980	57	1.7558749	106	53059	156	31246	206	38672
8	0.9030900	58	1.7634280	107	93838	157	58997	207	59703
9	0.9542425	59	1.7708520	108	0334238	158	86571	208	80633
10	1.0000000	60	1.7781513	109	74265	159	2013971	209	3201463
11	1.0413927	61	1.7853298	110	0413927	160	41200	210	22193
12	1.0791812	62	1.7923917	111	53230	161	68259	211	42825
13	1.1139434	63	1.7993405	112	92180	162	95150	212	63359
14	1.1461280	64	1.8061800	113	0530784	163	2121876	213	83796
15	1.1760913	65	1.8129134	114	69049	164	48438	214	3304138
16	1.2041200	66	1.8195439	115	0606978	165	74839	215	24385
17	1.2304489	67	1.8260748	116	44580	166	2201081	216	44538
18	1.2552725	68	1.8325089	117	81859	167	27165	217	64597
19	1.2787536	69	1.8388491	118	0718820	168	53093	218	84565
20	1.3010300	70	1.8450980	119	55470	169	78867	219	3404441
21	1.3222193	71	1.8512583	120	91812	170	2304489	220	24227
22	1.3424227	72	1.8573325	121	0827854	171	29961	221	43923
23	1.3617278	73	1.8633229	122	63598	172	55284	222	63530
24	1.3802112	74	1.8692317	123	99051	173	80461	223	83049
25	1.3979400	75	1.8750613	124	0934217	174	2405492	224	3502480
26	1.4149733	76	1.8808136	125	69100	175	30380	225	21825
27	1.4313638	77	1.8864907	126	1003705	176	55127	226	41084
28	1.4471580	78	1.8920946	127	38037	177	79733	227	60259
29	1.4623980	79	1.8976271	128	72100	178	2504200	228	79348
30	1.4771213	80	1.9030900	129	1105897	179	28530	229	98355
31	1.4913617	81	1.9084850	130	39434	180	52725	230	3617278
32	1.5051500	82	1.9138139	131	72713	181	76786	231	36120
33	1.5185139	83	1.9190781	132	1205739	182	2600714	232	54880
34	1.5314789	84	1.9242793	133	38516	183	24511	233	73559
35	1.5440680	85	1.9294189	134	71048	184	48178	234	92159
36	1.5563025	86	1.9344985	135	1303338	185	71717	235	3710679
37	1.5682017	87	1.9395193	136	35389	186	95129	236	29120
38	1.5797836	88	1.9444827	137	67206	187	2718416	237	47483
39	1.5910646	89	1.9493900	138	98791	188	41578	238	65770
40	1.6020600	90	1.9542425	139	1430148	189	64618	239	83979
41	1.6127839	91	1.9590414	140	61280	190	87536	240	3802112
42	1.6232493	92	1.9637878	141	92191	191	2810334	241	20170
43	1.6334685	93	1.9684829	142	1522883	192	33012	242	38154
44	1.6434527	94	1.9731279	143	53360	193	55573	243	56663
45	1.6532125	95	1.9777236	144	83625	194	78017	244	73898
46	1.6627578	96	1.9822712	145	1613680	195	2900346	245	91661
47	1.6720979	97	1.9867717	146	43529	196	22561	246	3909351
48	1.6812412	98	1.9912261	147	73173	197	44662	247	26970
49	1.6901961	99	1.9956352	148	1702617	198	66652	248	44517
50	1.6989700	100	2.0000000	149	31863	199	88531	249	61993
N.	Log.	N.	Log.	N.	Log.	N.	Log.	N.	Log.

Fig. 4 Table of logarithms computed to seven decimal places. From Henry Sherwin's: Sherwin's Mathematical Tables (London 1741).

cover the whole earth through its division into latitudes (parallel with the equator) and longitudes. The longitude for a particular place on the earth's surface is its distance in degrees from a predetermined reference meridian. Today this prime meridian is taken to run through Greenwich in England. However, around 1800, this convention had not been adopted and France had its prime meridian running through Paris, Holland through Amsterdam and England through London etc.[28] Since the earth rotates through 360 degrees every day, a difference of 15 degrees between two meridians corresponds to an hour. The problem of determining longitude was thus a problem of determining this time interval. For practical reasons, sailors looked on the earth as lying in the centre of a sphere to the inside of which were attached the stars. The basis of mathematical navigation was made up of these three ideas – the celestial sphere, latitude and longitude.

The position of a vessel at sea was determined by its latitude and longitude. As far as the former – the angular distance to the equator – was concerned, this could be determined by astronomical observations, such as observing the position of the stars at night (e.g. the Pole Star) or noting the position of the sun by day. This was accomplished by means of instruments like the quadrant, astrolabe, cross-staff or reflecting circle. The first navigational tables at the beginning of the 16th century contained tables for the Pole Star and tables of the Sun's declination.[29] The use of astronomical data for navigation increased in significance from about this time. The most prominent of the sea-going nations – the Portugese, the Spaniards and the English – published collections of tables the astronomical contents of which, go back to the *Alphonsine Tables* and thereby to Ptolemy himself.[30] The problem of determining longitude was much more difficult than that of determining latitude. In 1800, there were three methods in use. The first and oldest method was dead-reckoning where an estimation of course and distance by means of log and hourglass (and later on with the help of pocket watches with balance springs) gave the approximate longitude.[31] The second and dominant method was astronomical. By making use of tables providing predictions about certain astronomical events, the local time on the vessel and the time at the primary meridian could be determined simultaneously.[32] This gave the longitude. The third method was mechanical and was based on the employment of a marine chronometer which was a precision timepiece, the operation of which was unaffected by the motions of the vessel. The chronometer displayed the time at the primary meridian (say Greenwich) which meant that this did not have to be calculated. The local time on board the vessel, and thus the difference in time between it and the time at the primary meridian necessary for calculating the longitude, were determined in the usual manner by means of astronomical observations and tables. This was the simplest method of all but it was also the least used since, at the time, chronometers were still highly expensive and rare.

For stellar navigation, the use of tables was essential. The sailor required a nautical ephemeris, i.e. a collection of tables containing information about the sun, moon and stars' positions each day.[33] In addition, tables were needed to provide corrections for refraction, dip and parallax. Tables giving information about tides were also of importance. Finally, for the calculations involved, it was necessary to have tables of natural logarithms and of the values of the logarithmic trigonometric functions, so-called requisite tables.[34]

Numerical tables can be divided into three groups, depending on the circumstances of their production. First of all, there are those tables which were produced and financed wholly by individuals e.g. the tables of Napier, Briggs and Gunter. Secondly there are those larger collections produced by "government-financed" groups of calculators. Here the typical examples would be the *Alphonsine Tables*, computed by 50 astronomers and paid for by King Alphonso the Wise, and the *Opus Palatinum* of Rheticus which took 12 years work by a team of calculators under the direction of Rheticus, and was financed by the Elector Palatine Frederick the IV.[35] It was characteristic for this second type of table that it was specially commissioned and appeared only rarely. The third kind of organizational form responsible for the production of tables was a governmental office like the Nautical Almanac Office in London, which produced tables on a regular basis. Thus the Nautical Almanac Office published the popular and accurate collection of navigational tables *The Nautical Almanac and Astronomical Ephemeris*. This contained tables of astronomical events calculated on the basis of the Greenwich meridian for two to three years in advance. The first of these was produced under the direction of the Astronomer Royal at Greenwich, Nevil Maskelyne, which appeared in 1766 and dealt with the year 1767.[36] Similar kinds of ephemeris were produced by several of the prominent observatories, see Fig. 5. The Paris Observatory had published *La Connaissance des temps* from 1679 and *Ephemerides des mouvemens célestes* from 1701, both with Paris as the prime meridian; and Bologna Observatory had produced its *Ephemerides motuum coelstium* from 1715 with Bologna as the prime meridian. Long before this, however, various types of ephemeris had been produced privately, e.g. by Rheticus and Kepler.[37] In the case of the tables of the first type, the people who actually carried out the calculating work were usually mathematicians and astronomers. These were also the men who were responsible for supervising the work for tables of the second and third types, while the monotonous task of computation was left to human computers who had mastered the four basic arithmetical operations. An interesting and probably very unusual case was that of Michael Taylor who published his own collection of mathematical tables in 1792 − a volume of some 300 pages in folio − while at the same time being employed as one of Maskelyne's computers at the Nautical Almanac Office.[38] This was a remarkable performance which illustrates the immense dedication which appears to have characterized the indi-

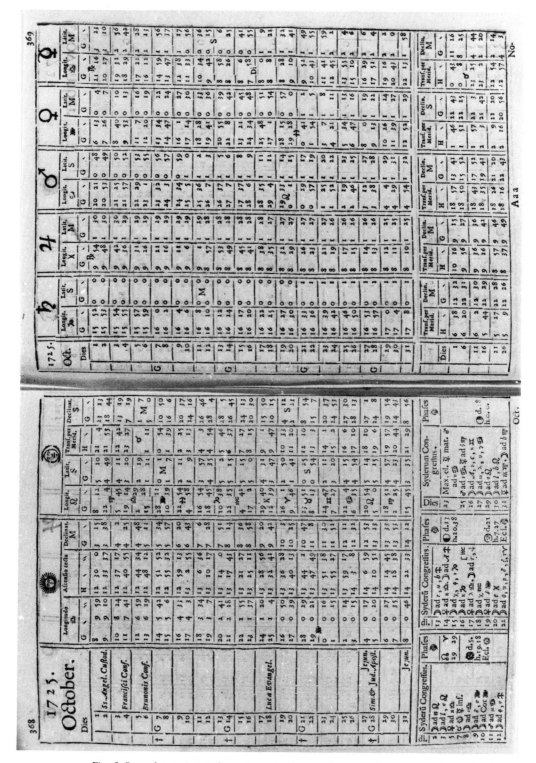

Fig. 5 Several prominent observatories in the world produced ephimerides for navigation and astronomy, showing the calculated movements of the celestial bodies. Since 1715 the Bologna Observatory published its Ephemerides motuum coelestium.

vidual authors of tables. Before this, moreover, Taylor had calculated a comprehensive sexagesimal table.

As in all areas of scientific endeavour, women were rare. However Glaisher in his account of tables mentions one such author of tables.[39] Mrs. Janet Taylor who ran a nautical school in the City of London, produced a collection of tables in two editions (1833, 1843), which besides the usual mathematical tables also contained a table specially intended for navigation (log versed sines).

How were tables produced? This can be illustrated by two historically important examples of tables, namely Prony's *Les Tables des Cadastres* and Babbage's table of logarithms. In both these cases, special measures were taken to produce error-free tables — in the case of the former at the calculating stage and in the case of the latter at the printing stage.

In 1784, the French government decided that new tables of logarithms and trigonometry for the centesimal division of the quadrant should be calculated. The work was assigned to the mathematician Marie Riche Prony, who had taken it upon himself to ensure that the resulting tables would be "constructed with such accuracy that they should form a monument of calculation the most vast and imposing that had ever been executed, or even conceived."[40] The work was carried out in a new way, namely, according to the principle of the division of labour which had been so fruitfully applied in manufacturing. The work-force was divided into three groups. Six mathematicians were selected who were responsible for devising suitable methods of calculation and afterwards for leading and checking the work. Eight calculators possessing some mathematical knowledge were appointed to superintend the eighty or so calculators who would carry out the basic computational work. This work was executed with the help of the method of differences, which is decribed in more detail in section 1.3. Every result was calculated by several people simultaneously and the answers were compared. The work took two years to complete and resulted in two copies in manuscript called *Les Tables de Cadastres*. They were bound in 17 folio volumes but were never printed because it was believed that this would introduce too many errors. One copy was deposited at the Paris Observatory, while the other, after Prony's death, went to his heirs. The tables were calculated to a great number of decimal places, the majority to 14, but some to 25.[41]

In 1827, the English mathematician Charles Babbage published a table of logarithms of the natural numbers from 1 to 108,000 to 7 places. With the object of producing error-free tables with a maximum of clarity, Babbage took special precautions when it came to printing. In the foreword to the third edition, he described the steps involved.[42] After the table had been set with movable types and printed, each entry was compared with other tables. First with von Vega's table up to 100,000, and the last 8,000 were compared with Francois Callet's *Tables portatives de Logarithmes* (Paris 1814). Then, the first 20,000 were again compared, this time with Vlacq's *Trigonometriq Artificialis*. Babbage then returned his table to the printers, where it was stereotyped (see below). After this, the proofs were read and the table checked with von Vega's up to 47,500, with the whole of Gardiner's table and with Taylor's logarithms. Finally, a different set of readers compared the table with Taylor's again. During this repeated proofreading process, several further errors in Babbage's table came to light at the last moment and were corrected. This long and laborious method also exposed a number of errors in the reference works – errors which up to then had passed unnoticed. Since Babbage's aim was to produce an error-free table of logarithms, he had visited Prony in Paris, where he had an opportunity to compare his table with *Les Tables de Cadastres* before the final printing. All these precautions had the desired effect, as was pointed out by Professor John Radford Young in his logaritm table, published in 1834: "In Mr. Babbage's table I could find no error, and I have no doubt they amply deserve the reputation for accuracy which they have obtained."[43]

Even if the production of Prony's and Babbage's tables can be considered as something of an exception, they nevertheless involved many of the characteristic methods which were used to reduce the number of errors. The errors likely to occur can be divided into four groups:

A. *Computational* errors.
B. Errors arising when *a copy of the table was being made* to be sent to the printer's.
C. Errors arising during *typesetting*.
D. Errors arising during *printing*.

It was difficult to avoid errors. Prony discovered, for example, that several different calculators, despite the fact that their computations of a particular tabular value agreed, had nevertheless obtained a result that was incorrect.[44] By far the commonest method of avoiding errors was that which was used by Babbage, namely to make a comparison with other tables. As a matter of fact, this was standard procedure in making mathematical tables. Every new published collection of tables contained an introduction which apart from explaining how to use the tables, and occasionally giving a historical summary about the history of tables, contained a list of the tables that had been used in the compilation of the new tables. If errors had been discovered in works of reference, this fact was mentioned. Good and also popular collections of tables appeared in several editions. Thus, for example, Babbage's table of logarithms was into its fourth edition by 1844. Moreover it had been published with an introduction and guide in German and Hungarian in 1834.[45] In other words, if errors were discovered, they could be corrected in later editions. The classical collections of tables, such as those of Briggs and von Vega, had been published in several editions and the errors had been successively reduced. Those errors which were discovered after printing were noted as in the case of ordinary books in lists of errata which enabled the reader to carry out the necessary corrections. A further check was provided by the fact that the tables were often reviewed in the learned periodicals (*Astronomische Nachrichten, Monthly Notices of the Royal Astronomical Society* etc.). Unreliable tables were thus weeded out by this process, at least to some degree. Such periodicals also published lists of errata. For the purchaser and reader, the typographical presentation of the tables was also of importance. The figures had to be clear and easy to make out, in relatively heavy type, the paper had to be tough and able to withstand hard usage and the general format had to make the tables easy to use. If the tables were difficult to read or were laid out in a manner tiring to the eye, reading errors were likely to occur. "It is well known that the number of errors of transcription is proportional to the distance the eye has to carry the numbers."[46]

By the end of the 18th century, stereotyping began to be used increasingly, which meant that errors of types C-D could be avoided to some extent. In stereotyping, when the printer had set a page of the table, he made an impression of this in a plaster mould, soft metal or in a damp piece of pasteboard.[47] When this so-called matrix had dried, molten metal (an alloy of lead and antimony) was poured directly into it. By then detaching the matrix, one obtained a plate or cliché which was identical with the page of the table that had been set by means of movable types. The method had several advantages. Before stereotyping, the printer was forced to wait for the first proof-copy to be read and corrected and a vast number of his types were assembled in galleys where they could not be moved. He was therefore required to have a large supply of types on hand, to be able to continue working while waiting for the proofs to be corrected. With the use of stereotyping, the printer could make use of his types while waiting for the corrected copy to come back from the proof-readers. If an error was discovered a new correct plate could be made. Plates were also cheap because they only weighed a tenth as much as the corresponding types and in addition they could be kept and used for a long time. This meant that once one had a set of correct plates for a book, they could be stored away, until it was time to print a new edition. Babbage had chosen stereotyping for his table and during the 19th century, the use of this highly practical method of printing spread throughout Europe. Stereotyping was in fact quite similar to the old method of block-printing. Once a plate or a block was correctly set, there was no possibility that an error could arise.

To sum up, it can be said that numerical tables at the beginning of the 19th century were familiar to many classes of society. Of particular importance for the development of science, technology and commerce were naturally the mathematical, astronomical and nautical tables. Some of the most important of them are listed in Fig. 6. It was also these tables, in contrast to the much smaller and less rigorous "trade tables", which placed the greatest demands on the table makers. Today, it is almost impossible to conceive the immensely demanding and monotonous work

ASTRONOMY AND NAVIGATION

Alphonsine Tables	around 1250	Toledo
La connaissance des temps	1679—	Paris
Ephemerides des mouvemens célestes	1701—	Paris
Ephemerides motuun coelestium	1715—	Bologna

MATHEMATICS: TRIGONOMETRY

Maginus, *Tabula Tetragonica*	1592
Rheticus, *Opus Palatinum*	1596
Pitiscus, *Thesaurus Mathematicus*	1613

MATHEMATICS: LOGARITHMS

Napier, *Mirifici Logarithmorum Canonis Descriptio*	1614
Briggs, *Logarithmorum Chilias Prima*	1617
Gunter, *Canon Triangulorum*	1620
Briggs, *Arithmetica Logarithmica*	1624
Vlacq, *Arithmetica Logarithmica*	1628
Vlacq, *Trigonometria Artificialis*	1633
Gardiner, *Tables of Logarithms*	1742
Taylor, *Table of Logarithms of all Numbers*	1792
von Vega, *Thesaurus Logarithmorum completus*	1794
Callet, *Tables portatives des Logarithmes*	1814
Babbage, *Table of Logarithms*	1827

MATHEMATICS: GENERAL

Sherwin, *Sherwin's Mathematical Tables*	1706
Dodson, *The Calculator*	1747
Schultze, *Neue und erweiterte Sammlung. . .*	1778
von Vega, *Tabulae logarithmico — trigonometricae*	1797

Fig. 6 Some of the most renowned numerical tables published before the year 1830.

involved in producing a collection of tables, in terms of calculation, checking, typesetting, printing, double-checking, proofreading etc. The difference between a good and bad set of tables could be reckoned by the relative number of errors they contained, errors which, in the opinion of some, might even mean that a piece of scientific research was delayed or a ship was set on a wrong course. Despite the most careful precautions, errors had the habit of creeping past the most conscientious and sharp-eyed proofreader. The number of errors could only be minimized by taking the most stringent measures during the production of the tables. This entailed that either the price was high or else, as in the case of *Les Tables de Cadastres*, they remained unprinted, known only to a minority of initiates. The problem of errors in tables appeared unsolvable. However around 1800, two scientifically interested men found the required solution by entrusting the mental computation to machines.

1.2 The "Utopian" invention

"This invention of Mr. Babbage's is one of the most curious and important in modern times: whether we regard the ingenuity and skill displayed in the arrangement of the parts, or the great utility and importance of the results. Its probable effect on those particular branches of science which it is most adapted to promote, can only be compared with those rapid improvements in the arts which have followed the introduction of the steam-engine; and which are too notorious to be here mentioned."[1]

The invention in question was the Difference Engine No. 1, a construction embarked upon by the English mathematician, Charles Babbage, in the year 1821, and which was to continue to engage his attention until 1833. The present section will deal with Babbage and his difference engine. It will also show how Babbage was anticipated by the German engineer, Johann Müller who invented a difference engine in 1784.

Charles Babbage was born on the 26th of December 1791 in London.[2] He was one of the four children of Benjamin and Betty Plumleigh Babbage. His father was a partner in a London bank. His mother came from a prominent Devonshire family. Young Charles was brought up as an Anglican and received his earliest education at home. His childhood was marred by chronic illness and around the age of ten he was sent to Devon to combine convalescence and study in suitable proportions. Once his health had improved, he moved to a school for boys outside London.[3] It was there that he discovered his great interest in mathematics and he began to read omnivorously about that subject.[4] He continued his education with a clergyman near Cambridge and also devoted some time to the classics with a tutor in Devon.

In April 1810, at the age of eighteen, Charles Babbage began his studies at Trinity College, Cambridge.[5] It meant new perspectives and he found the environment, the books and social life intensely stimulating.[6] Here he was to meet new friends who would remain close to him for the rest of his life. His days were spent in sampling the pleasures of undergraduate existence − parties with plenty of good food and drink, Sunday breakfasts with his friends after Church, chess and games of whist and trips on the Cam. There was a servant to take care of the routine chores and make Babbage's life all the more agreeable. All this was financed with the 300 pounds which Charles received as an annual allowance from his father.[7]

Among his new friends, John Frederick William Herschel soon took first place. He was the son of the German born astronomer William Herschel, who in 1757 had settled in England.[8] After studies at Eton and tuition at home, John Herschel had gone up to St. John's College, Cambridge in 1809.[9] With access to his father's observatory, books and scientific instruments and not forgetting paternal influence itself, John had

had a quite different background from that of his friend Charles, who was more or less the same age.[10] Together they began to devote themselves to mathematics.

Mathematics had a central position among the disciplines at Cambridge.[11] The undergraduate course reached its formal culmination in the final examination in the Senate House, when the candidates grappled with a number of teasing problems from various areas of mathematics. For the ambitious student, the aim was not simply to pass the examination and become a Bachelor of Arts of Cambridge University, but to acquit themselves well enough to fall within the ranks of those in the highest bracket − to become, in short, a "wrangler". This brought with it the chance of a college fellowship and a solid start to a career.[12] It is clear that Babbage and Herschel found the mathematical atmosphere at Cambridge highly stimulating and some of their correspondence consists entirely of mathematical formulae.[13]

In the spring of 1814, Charles Babbage received his B.A.[14] Shortly afterwards, in July of the same year, he married Georgiana Whitmore, the daughter of a wealthy Shropshire family.[15] According to what Babbage has related in his letters, the marriage was not welcomed by his father Benjamin and it would appear that the relations between father and son were far from harmonious.[16] It is clear that Charles ran the risk of losing his annual allowance and he wanted to become independent by finding employment.[17] In the autumn of 1814, he began actively to look for a position.

Although Babbage could imagine devoting himself to all sorts of work, his thoughts began to revolve around his second great interest, chemistry, and he had plans to enter the mining industry. Another possibility of quite a different character, was to enter the Church, but since all he could get was a curacy, this was ruled out on the grounds that the income was too meagre.[18] Most of all, he would have preferred to have worked with mathematics and in August 1814, he applied for the post of computer with the Astronomer Royal, John Pond, at the Nautical Almanac Office.[19] It is not known what sort of work Babbage had in mind there, but the greater part of the mathematics at the Office involved simply routine computations. Herschel advised him against applying, on the grounds that the position was not an attractive one.[20] This episode is the first occasion on which Babbage displayed a more or less conscious interest in the calculations of tables.

But Babbage was a man of many interests and none of these schemes came to anything. The most likely explanation is that he was waiting for some opening in mathematics to appear. His real bent was philosophical and speculative and during his time at Cambridge, he had not hesitated to enter into deep analyses of the most varied phenomena. He had become interested, for example, in developing a universal language and on many occasions he had discussed theoretical questions in physics, mineralogy and astronomy with Herschel.[21] The latter who had imbibed science from his earliest years, was to have a profound influence upon Babbage's development. Their friendship was marked by mutual trust and respect. When Babbage for example took it upon himself to construct a theory about the atmospheres of the stars and planets, his friend dismissed it with the words that it was "equally ingenious as impossible".[22]

There was only one domain which Babbage was unacquainted with in 1814 and that was engineering. Certainly he had made a number of minor inventions when he was growing up, and it is also true that he had come in contact with a lathe because Herschel possessed one; but that was more or less all.[23] At the close of 1814 Babbage invented a new type of lock which he was interested in having manufactured.[24] This was possibly his first serious excursion into that area of human endeavour, which was with time to cast its spell on him.

At the end of 1815, Babbage and his wife moved up to London. He had still to find some employment. For a year or so, he had been increasingly interested in the scientific world of the capital and had hopes of becoming a member of the Royal Society.[25] Soon he was invited to give a series of lectures about the history of astronomy at the Royal Institution and in the spring of 1816, he was elected a Fellow of the Royal Society.[26] More or less at the same time, he applied for the chair in mathematics at East India College at Hartford.[27] "I am happy to say I have a very good chance of getting it" he wrote to his friend Herschel.[28] But his hopes were soon dashed when another candidate was chosen instead.

In 1812, Babbage had founded a little association called "the Analytical Society".[29] Its purpose was to introduce continental mathematical methods into the conservative Cambridge. The reason was that English mathematics had stagnated in comparison with the development on the continent of Europe.[30] The whole issue had its origins in the famous priority controversy between Isaac Newton and Gottfried Wilhelm Leibniz concerning the infinitesimal calculus. Englishmen had sided with Newton and had chosen to use his synthetic methods and dot-notation while the continental mathematicians had followed in the footsteps of Leibniz and had adopted the latter's analytical method and d-notation.[31] In practice, the Leibniz approach was superior and this had contributed to the development of mathematics on the continent. In the beginning, the Analytical Society made little headway, mainly because few bothered about what a number of young and inexperienced undergraduates had to say. During his time at Cambridge, however, Babbage, Herschel and another member of the society began to translate a French textbook by Sylvestre Francois Lacroix, on the continental methods. Around Christmas 1816, this work was completed and it was to have decisive importance for the rebirth of British mathematics.[32] Babbage did not exaggerate when he wrote:

"In a very few years the change was completely established; and thus at last the English cultivators of mathematical science, untrammelled by a limited and imperfect system of signs, entered on equal terms into competition with their continental rivals."[33]

Thanks to the success of the Analytical Society, Charles Babbage became famous. But it was difficult at that time to have a career within mathematics. There were few posts and the competition was severe.[34] In 1819, Babbage once more applied for a professorship, this time at Edinburgh.[35] But despite all his recommendations from prominent French and English mathematicians, Babbage did not gain the position.[36] At the same time, he also applied for a seat on the Board of Longitude but this too ended in failure. In 1820, he made a new application but to no avail.[37]

At the close of 1820, Charles Babbage by now twenty-nine was still without any profession. For the previous six years, he had tried to find something suitable. He had carried out intensive mathematical research and had published a fair number of articles.[38] He had presented several of his findings in lectures at the Royal Society, among whose illustrious members he had managed to establish himself. He had also, once again, shown his predilection for reform by becoming one of the cofounders of the Astronomical Society in 1820. Several children were born to enrich the Babbages' life − three sons and a daughter.[39] In spite of everything, the family seemed to manage quite comfortably financially. Perhaps this was partly due to the fact that Georgiana's father had died in 1816 and had left a large sum of money.[40]

In contrast to Babbage, Herschel was soon on the road to success. He had remained in Cambridge until 1816. But he tired of the life of a don and gradually more and more began to follow in his famous father's footsteps.[41] His basically scientific temperament made him turn quite naturally to his father's astronomical experiments and continue them. Soon he was consumed by the subject, made many significant discoveries and in the course of time was to become one of his century's foremost astronomers.

The early 1820s saw a turning point in Charles Babbage's life and in his search for a profession. In August 1814, Herschel had advised him that "a practical knowledge of mechanics was of greater importance than any, except a very profound one of chemistry".[42] Four months later, Babbage had invented his lock.[43] There is little sign that he devoted more of his time to engineering after these events.[44] But it is obvious that Babbage, by means of some unknown mechanical achievement, had shown his friends that he possessed technical skills. In 1818, Edward Ffrench Bromhead, a close friend and one of the original members of the Analytical Society wrote to Babbage, saying that "your Genius is mechanical" and suggested that in order to be famous, he should invent something "strikingly useful".[45]

According to Collier, Babbage's ideas about the mechanical computation began around the end of the year 1821.[46] This is supported by a letter from Babbage to Herschel, dated the 20th of December 1821, in which

Fig. 7 Charles Babbage (1791–1871). Daguerrotype portrait from 1843. Photograph by courtesy of the Trustees of the Science Museum, London.

Babbage for the first time mentions his engine and says "I want to explain my arithmetical engine".[47] Babbage's first description of the sequence of events was recorded in the November of the the following year:

> "Being engaged in conjunction with my friend Mr. Herschel about the conclusion of the last year in arranging and superintending some calculations of considerable extent which were distributed amongst several computers, the delays and errors which are inseparable from the nature of such undertakings soon became sufficiently sensible...
>
> In the course of our conversation on this subject it was suggested by one of us, in a manner which certainly at the time was not altogether serious, that it would be extremely convenient if a steam-engine could be contrived to execute calculations for us, to which it was replied that such a thing was quite possible, a sentiment in which we both entirely concurred; and here the conversation terminated.

During the next two days the possibility of calculating by machinery (which I should never for a moment have doubted had I ever proposed it to myself as a question) recurred several times to my imagination; the idea appeared to possess that species of novelty which gives so much pleasure and makes so strong an impresson on the mind when for the first time we express in words some principle of or precept to which we have long tacitly assented. When we have clothed it with language, we appear to have given permanent existence to that which was transient, and we admire what was frequently only a step in the process of generalization as the creation of our own intellect.

Finding myself at leisure the next evening, and feeling confident not only that it was possible to contrive such a machine but that it would not be attended with any extraordinary difficulty, I commenced the task. The first point in the inquiry was to be fully aware of the power of the machine I wished to construct. In order to produce printed tables free from error I proposed the engine should be able to calculate any tables whatever and that it should produce a stereotype plate of the computed results, or at least that it should deliver a copper plate from which they could be printed...

In order to satisfy the condition that the calculating part should be capable of computing every species of tables, it was necessary to found it on some great and comprehensive mathematical principle; the method of differences is the only one that possesses this extensive range".[48]

In another later written account, Babbage states that the event described occurred when they were superintending calculations for the Astronomical Society.[49]

As can be seen in the quotation above, Babbage used the term *engine* for his invention. Soon he was to call it difference engine and calculating engine, a fact that is worthy of comment. The word "engine" is not the most natural expression for a calculating machine — nor was it so in Babbage's day. In fact, I have not been able to find any machine in the history of mechanical calculation before Babbage's, that has been called engine. The words most commonly used were machine, instrument or apparatus. After Babbage's use of the expression, the word was retained but used exclusively for difference engines. In the 1820's, the word engine was especially applied to the steam engine, also called the atmospheric engine, fire engine, water engine or simply engine.[50] *The Oxford English Dictionary* defines the word "engine" as "A machine, more or less complicated, consisting of several parts, working together to produce a given physical effect."[51] Among the examples given, is *calculating engine*.[52] In the entry relating to the latter, one example is given, namely "Charles Babbage, the designer of the well-known calculating engine".[53]

The fact that Babbage called his machine "engine" was naturally connected with that word's original connection with the steam engine and no doubt he envisaged his own machine as having the same profound and

PASSAGES

FROM

THE LIFE OF A PHILOSOPHER.

BY

CHARLES BABBAGE, ESQ., M.A.,

F.R.S., F.R S.E., F.R.A.S., F. STAT. S., HON. M.R.I.A., M.C.P.S.,

COMMANDER OF THE ITALIAN ORDER OF ST. MAURICE AND ST. LAZARUS,

INST. IMP. (ACAD. MORAL.) PARIS CORR., ACAD. AMER. ART. ET SC. BOSTON, REG. ŒCON. BORUSS.,

PHYS. HIST. NAT. GENEV., ACAD. REG. MONAC., HAFN., MASSIL., ET DIVION., SOCIUS.

ACAD. IMP. ET REG. PETROP., NEAP., BRUX., PATAV., GEORG. FLOREN, LYNCEI ROM., MUT., PHILOMATH.

PARIS, SOC. CORR., ETC.

" I'm a philosopher.   Confound them all—
Birds, beasts, and men ; but no, not womankind."—*Don Juan.*

" I now gave my mind to philosophy : the great object of my ambition was to make out a complete system of the universe, including and comprehending the origin, causes, consequences, and termination of all things.   Instead of countenance, encouragement, and applause, which I should have received from every one who has the true dignity of an oyster at heart, I was exposed to calumny and misrepresentation.   While engaged in my great work on the universe, some even went so far as to accuse me of infidelity ;—such is the malignity of oysters."—" *Autobiography of an Oyster" deciphered by the aid of photography in the shell of a philosopher of that race,—recently scolloped.*

LONDON:

LONGMAN, GREEN, LONGMAN, ROBERTS, & GREEN.

1864.

[The right of Translation is reserved.]

Fig. 8 *Title page from Charles Babbage's autobiography* Passages from the Life of a Philosopher *(London 1864).*

revolutionary social consequences as its power-source counterpart.

Thus by the end of 1821, Charles Babbage thought that it would be theoretically possible to build a machine for calculating and printing numerical tables. He had arrived at the idea while working on the calculation of tables and had perceived that only a machine could solve the problem of how to get rid of errors. He had also been encouraged to pursue this matter after noting the delays which the manual method involved. Mathematically, the engine was to be based on the method of differences, which had long been used in tabular calculation and which was particularly suited to mechanization. To illustrate its method in elementary terms, consider a table giving the price for various joints of meat at three pounds a kilo:

Weight	price
kg	£
1	3
2	6
3	9
4	12
5	15

This table can be calculated in two different ways.[54] One is to multiply the number of kilos by the price per kilo. The other, which reveals the basic principle of the method of differences, is to *add* the price (three pounds), to the price of the first kilo, and to continue to add three pounds to each succeeding kilo. Thus the method is based exclusively upon the operation of addition in accordance with a particular scheme.

Babbage also realised that the machine must print its results in some way and he contemplated letting it produce stereotypes. By making use of such a machine which correctly computed the tabular value and produced error-free stereotypes, all the errors of types A-D mentioned in the previous section could be eliminated.

This idea for a calculating machine differed markedly from previous notions. The difference engine was not designed to solve given problems (like the multiplication of two numbers), but instead to compute series of tabular values by following the method of differences.

The first known calculating machine was an adding machine made in 1623 by the astronomer Wilhelm Schickard of Tübingen in Germany. Its basic mechanical elements were incorporated in its successors.[55] The machine had gearwheels, with ten teeth each, one tooth for each of the numbers 0-9, and it was equipped with the necessary "carrying" mechanism. With that device, the numbers from the units were automatically carried to the tens, when the unit wheel turned from 9 to 0. Thus when 5 units were added to 7 units, the unit wheel would move forward 5 steps, thus passing the digits 8, 9, 0, 1 and would stop on the 2. When passing from 9 to 0 the wheel corresponding to the tens would be advanced one step, from 0 to 1, and the result displayed on the wheels would be 12. Carrying also took place from tens to hundreds and from hundreds to thousands etc., when this was required. However, the existence of Shickard's machine was unknown until the middle of the 20th century.[56] In Babbage's time, the first calculating machine known was the adding machine invented and built by the French mathematician Blaise Pascal in 1642, see Fig. 9.

The second and more powerful one, was designed by Leibniz in 1671. It was intended to carry out the four arithmetical operations (addition, subtraction, multiplication and division). Such a versatile machine might be called a universal calculating machine, as opposed to Babbage's special purpose difference engine. Leibniz' machine was followed by other, more or less successful attempts to build universal machines during the 18th century. One was built in Padua, one in Vienna and a couple in Germany.[57] But all of them were produced as single models or certainly in extremely small numbers. In all, it can be estimated that some thirty-five calculating machines had been built by the year 1800. Some of these had been built in England. In the early 1660s, Samuel Morland had invented at least three different type of calculating machines and in the 1770s two machines were constructed by the Earl of Stanhope.[58] As will be shown, Charles Babbage's knowledge about these or other calculating machines must have been very limited.

Babbage's machine was to consist of two parts – a calculating unit and a printing unit.[59] The operations of adding and carrying were to be performed in the calculating unit. The mechanics of these operations were known, although Babbage's own knowledge of them was limited. But the printing unit was something entirely new. No previous calculating machine had been able to print its results, or to deliver stereotypes for printing. Thus Babbage did not only intend to mechanize the monotonous labour of adding differences, executed by Briggs and the other table computers. Even more spectacularly, he wished to replace the skills of the printer, in setting up a couple of thousand movable number types. The printing unit in the difference engine was therefore – and it is important to stress this – an even more radical conception than the calculating part. Small wonder this idea was considered one of the most fascinating and remarkable ever conceived during the century.

In the spring of 1822, Charles Babbage began to turn his ideas into more concrete mechanical form. At the beginning of the year, his ideas had wavered between three different machines but he now decided to concentrate on a machine for the production of tables, in which the order of differences involved was ultimately constant (this will be explained in the next section).[60] According to his autobiography, he already possessed a lathe which he may well have purchased specially for the job of developing the machine.[61] He started to make drawings and perhaps he even built some of the parts himself. But he also needed professional expertise and machine tools, and this led him to get in touch with a skilled mechan-

ic.[62] Work on the engine proceeded and by the 10th of June 1822, the first difference engine was finished.[63] It was a working model or prototype. Little is known about this machine which is lost and no drawings or sketches appear to have survived. It could calculate with second order differences and was able to deal with six to eight digits.[64] The machine lacked the important printing unit but was nevertheless able to calculate simple numerical tables correctly. Babbage's own comment upon demonstrating the little difference engine for his friends and colleagues, was that despite defects in the workmanship, "it made no mistake and 'did as it was bid' ".[65]

How was the idea for the difference engine conceived? It was Babbage and Herschel jointly who had stumbled into this new field of calculating machinery. The key words that had given rise to the notion (if Babbage's account of the course of events is accepted) were "steam engine" and "calculations". A couple of years before, Herschel had mentioned to Babbage a system that could be used to arrive at new inventions and discoveries "for the good of science".[66] This was simply to open the index of a larger book and combine various words listed there at random. At that time Herschel was reading a book on the history of mathematics so that the idea of a difference engine could have been conceived earlier in this way. More probably the idea had other origins. As in the case of all inventions, a factor of importance was Babbage and Herschel's knowledge of the current state of technology in their society.

The much publicized steam engine, the rapid spread of mechanization and the fact that newspapers were daily printed (but not set) by steam, were all social features which must have played their part at the time the idea to mechanize table production was conceived. By 1800, the total number of steam engines in the United Kingdom has been estimated to have been no more than 1,000, with a rough aggregate capacity of 10,000 horse power. By 1815 this figure has been said to have risen to 210,000 horse power for Great Britain alone.[67] Steam engines of various kinds were used for draining and hoisting in mines and to supply power to flour mills, iron works, textile factories, breweries etc. But the steam engine did not remain stationary and as a means of providing power for transportation, it soon came to rival ancient power sources like the wind, rivers and the horse. Steam boats, first invented and tried in France and the United States during the last decades of the 18th century, could now and then be seen on the Thames by Babbage and his contemporaries. During the same period, the first steam road carriages were developed in France and England. When the steam locomotive was combined with the railway by Babbage's fellow countryman Richard Trevithick in the early years of the 19th century, a new era began. Although the steam engine was still rare as a prime mover for transport in 1821, it was indeed an established technology in its general applications. It was often viewed as something remarkable. Vast technical and social consequences followed wherever it was introduced. Its potentialities seemed boundless. Lord Byron reflected the spirit of the times in *Don Juan*:

"For ever since immortal man hath glowed
with all kinds of mechanics,
and full soon steam-engines will conduct him to the moon."[68]

Along with the increasing diffusion of the superior steam power came the rise and dispersion of mechanization. Repetitive and standardized manual jobs were successively handed over to newly invented machinery that was cheap and fast to operate. The first industry to be mechanized in England was the textile industry in the 1760s. By the turn of the century, the ancient style of building machinery in wood had begun to be replaced by cast iron and steel constructions, resulting in rigid and strong machines able to operate at higher speeds than ever before. Another important branch to be mechanized was the printing industry. In 1814, *The Times* had bought a steamdriven press for mass production, which was capable of printing four times as many copies as the old manual ones.[69]

Certain other factors were also of importance. First of all, Babbage was completely familiar with the method of differences. Perhaps he had already known about it before he went up to Cambridge, where this known method was included presumably as part of the curriculum. During the translation of Lacroix's book, Herschel had written his own supplement to the French original. This appendix contained 115 pages and had the title "On differences and series" and dealt with the method of differences and various methods of interpolation to be used in calculating logarithms etc.[70] Babbage had discussed this subject with Herschel and knew all about the principles involved. In addition there had been lectures at the Royal Society on the difference method and other methods of table production, which must have been noted by Babbage, given his interests in the subject. These were subsequently published in *Philosophical Transactions of the Royal Society* which he undoubtedly studied.[71] Secondly, Babbage had experience of numerical tables, partly as a user and partly because he had been involved in their computation. Later, he would become an active collector of numerical tables and had already by the end of 1821, when he conceived the idea of the difference engine, a number of tables on his bookshelves. Moreover, at the Royal Society was to be found the largest collection of numerical tables in England.[72]

In June 1822, the model engine was finished and Babbage had thus satisfied his curiosity about whether the thing was technically possible or not. Babbage announced the news by writing a few letters. The first was read at a meeting of the Astronomical Society on the 14th of June.[73] A second one − more exhaustive in character − was in the form of an open letter to Sir Humphry Davy, the Secretary of the Royal Society. It was dated the 3rd of July the same year. In it, Babbage stressed the importance of numerical tables that were accurate and absolutely free from error. Among the examples he gave, there was one showing how errors could arise during the process of printing.

"The quantity of errors from carelessness in correcting the press, even in tables of the greatest credit, will scarcely be believed, except by those who have had constant occasion for their use. A friend of mine, whose skill in practical as well as theoretical astronomy is well known, produced to me a copy of the tables published by order of the French Board of Longitude, containing those of the Sun by Delambre, and of the Moon by Burg, in which he had corrected above *five hundred errors*: most of these appear to be errors of the press; and it is somewhat remarkable, that in turning over the leaves in the fourth page I opened we observed a new error before unnoticed. These errors are so much the more dangerous, because independent computers using the same tables will agree in the same errors."[74]

Babbage continued by describing the working model and his ideas for the complete difference engine, with his first reference by way of analogy to Prony's system for producing *Les Tables de Cadastres*.[75] The machine could be used instead of the third group that Prony had employed, of sixty to eighty persons who were assigned the laborious task of adding. Furthermore, the results would be automatically ready for printing. The 96 calculators employed by Prony could be reduced to 12 or even considerably less, if a machine was employed for the same purpose. Babbage also discussed some of his other ideas for calculating machinery, something that Herschel thought was quite unnecessary.[76] At the end of the letter, Babbage showed that he was aware that he risked not being taken seriously and he ended the document by extending a cautious feeler for possible support:

"I am aware that the statements contained in this Letter may perhaps be viewed as something more than Utopian, and that the philosophers of Laputa may be called up to dispute my claim to originality. Should such be the case, I hope the resemblance will be found to adhere to the nature of the subject rather than to the manner in which it has been treated. Conscious, from my own experience, of the difficulty of convincing those who are but little skilled in mathematical knowledge, of the possibility of making a machine which shall perform calculations, I was naturally anxious, in introducing it to the public to appeal to the testimony of one so distinguished in the records of British science. Of the extent to which the machinery whose nature I have described may be carried, opinions will necessarily fluctuate, until experiment shall have finally decided their relative value: but of that engine which already exists I think I shall be supported, both by yourself and by several scientific friends who have examined it, in stating that it performs with rapidity and precision all those calculations for which it was designed.

Whether I shall construct a larger engine of this kind, and bring to perfection the others I have described, will in a great measure depend on the nature of the encouragment I may receive.

Induced, by a conviction of the great utility of such engines, to withdraw for some time my attention from a subject on which it has been engaged during several years, and which possesses charms of a higher order, I have now arrived at a point where success is no longer doubtful. It must, however, be attained at a very considerable expense, which would not probably be replaced, by the works it might produce, for a long period of time, and which is an undertaking I should feel unwilling to commence, as altogether foreign to my habits and pursuits.

I remain, my dear Sir,

Faithfully yours,

C. BABBAGE."[77]

Printed copies of this letter were distributed among Babbage's friends and acquaintances. A letter from Babbage to Herschel shows that Sir Humphry Davy had put forward his own views on the matter and in fact had helped Babbage with the formulation of the letter.[78] The lobbying for the construction of a larger engine had obviously begun.

A question arises at this point. It is clear that Babbage was offering a larger engine to some unspecified party, capable and willing to bear the large expenses involved. Why did he do this? Why was he not satisfied with what he had accomplished so far? In my view, at least three different factors were at work in encouraging Babbage to pursue his goal – practical, intellectual and social. The practical motive was that the difference engine solved the problem of getting rid of errors in tables and of producing tables quickly. Intellectually the engine was a challenge, combining so many of Babbage's interests – mathematics, theoretical problems, scientific systematization and philosophical speculation. These motives have been put forward before by other sholars.[79] In my opinion, the difference engine can also be regarded as another example in Babbage's long list of reform activities.[80] The social circumstances have been much neglected. I do not intend to provide a full analysis but rather to point out a couple of aspects which deserve further investigation. Babbage's wish had been to have a career in mathematics. At Cambridge, Herschel and another close friend, George Peacock, had been Smith's Prizemen and received College Fellowships.[81] Babbage won no such awards, which must have had a negative effect on his career possibilities in mathematics. When he wrote to Sir Humphry Davy in July 1822, he was still without a position. Not so his friends. It is clear that he did not wish to follow his father and become a banker.[82] Probably more for his own self-esteem than for economic reasons, he needed a position. I believe that he saw the larger difference engine as a way of satisfying that need.

John Herschel played an important role as Charles Babbage's closest friend. He had suggested that Babbage should devote himself to mechanics, and gave Babbage full support with the engine. Herschel may also have induced other colleagues to help out in various ways. Without the help and influence of John Herschel and his other friends, it is doubtful whether Babbage would have continued.

Later in life, Charles Babbage was on various occasions to regret bitterly that he had ever embarked upon the project. The very idea of calculating tables by machinery had opened up a new and vast field of technology, full of mathematical possibilities, which could be realized by a multitude of combinations of mechanical details. Babbage had no difficulties with the mathematics involved. But the down to earth, hard, practical work of designing the various mechanisms, now that he was considering building a complete engine, no doubt must have cost him much pain.[83] This is something that has been ignored by other scholars and that I will return to later. It must be emphasized that Babbage at this point was certainly not a trained or experienced engineer. Probably this was the prime source of his anxiety which began to manifest itself at an early stage. Exactly one month after the letter to Davy, Babbage wrote to Herschel saying that he preferred to work with chemistry and added: "I begin to be sick of the machine ..."[84]

A special cause for concern was the printing unit, which turned out to be more troublesome than the calculating part. Despite the fact that Babbage devoted much time and energy to building it, it was never completed. One of his initial ideas which he entertained for some time, was to let the engine arrange movable types in the manner of book printers.[85] He described how he proposed to make ten metal boxes, each containing 3,000 types of the same digit. One box would only contain the nines, another the eights etc. These types were to pass out one by one from the bottom of their boxes, when required by the computing part of the machine. Special devices were to prevent the engine supervisor placing the wrong type in a particular box.[86] Presumably Babbage was referring to the occasion when the boxes were to be loaded for the first time, since it might be presumed that the handling of types would have been completely mechanized in the finished machine. He also took precautions to prevent the types from being pulled out of their position once the whole table page was set.

There were few mechanical devices available in the 1820s which could have helped to guide Babbage on how to design the printing unit.[87] All tables and texts were set with movable types, before printing or stereotyping. The idea above, which shows a very low degree of technical sophistication, proves that Babbage in the design work on the printing unit had to deal with concepts far beyond his sphere of knowledge. He was to consider various mechanisms for this purpose in the years to come, but none of them were simple enough to be technically feasible.

In the autumn and winter of 1822, Babbage continued to publicize the engine by writing articles and giving lectures. One was published in *Brewster's Journal*, another was presented to the Astronomical Society.[88] Yet another one appeared anonymously in *The Edinburgh Philosophical Journal*.[89] Many articles of this kind were to follow. Babbage's article in *Brewster's Journal* concluded with the following interesting remarks:

"The more I examine this theoretical part, the more I feel convinced that it will be long before the novel relations which it presents will be exhausted; and if the absence of all encouragement to proceed with the mechanism I have contrived, shall prove that I have anticipated too far the period at which it shall become necessary, I will yet venture to predict that a time will arrive when the accumulating labour which arises from the arithmetical applications of mathematical formulae, acting as a constantly retarding force, shall ultimately impede the useful progress of the science, unless this or some equivalent method is devised for relieving it from the overwhelming incumbrance of numerical detail."[90]

The quotation shows that Babbage was aware that he had entered into a new and hitherto unexplored domain of human knowledge. Furthermore, his words reveal that this unique experience had led him to look forward and predict the importance of calculating machinery in years to come.

As Babbage had suspected, his difference engine met with varying reactions, even from his close friends. The opinion of the astronomer

Francis Baily, has already been noted at the beginning of this section. Although the physicist William Hyde Wollaston, according to Babbage's autobiography, was said to be favourably disposed, his first reaction on seeing the working model in June 1822, was quite the contrary.[91] "All this is very pretty, but I do not see how it can be rendered productive."[92] Given such comments (Babbage confided to Herschel) it was hardly surprising if he himself began to have his doubts.[93] Another friend, the mathematician, Olinthus Gregory entertained a different opinion:

"The application of machinery to the purposes of computation, in the way you have so happily struck out, is highly interesting, and cannot fail, I should think, to be exceedingly beneficial. I trust that our valued friend Mr D[avies]. Gilbert, and some other friends to science who possess influence in high quarters, will exert it cordially on this occasion, and obtain an adequate grant form the Government to complete and render extensively effectual the whole of your curious invention."[94]

Bromhead, who in 1818 had advised Babbage to invent something strikingly useful, was sceptical about the wisdom of Babbage devoting his powers to the difference engine. In August 1822, he told Babbage about his fears on this score. He suggested instead that Babbage should be satisfied with an article in the *Philosophical Transactions of the Royal Society* and added that "Napier and Newton did not increase their glory by making Rods and Reflectors."[95]

However the year 1823 marked the beginning of the building of the larger "Difference Engine No. 1", as Babbage was later to call it. Probably during the spring, Bromhead sent a letter to Babbage, in which he continued to raise objections to the project, but at the same time made suggestions about how it might be financed. Finally, he added that he was going to mention the matter to various friends with parliamentary connections.[96] After this, things moved swiftly.

The Vice President of the Royal Society, the mathematician Davies Gilbert, was not only a colleague of Babbage; he was also a member of Parliament and the representative of scientific interests in the House of Commons.[97] Through him, the difference engine and the question of its financing was brought to the attention of the First Lord of the Treasury, Sir Robert Peel. On the 8th of march 1823, Peel asked John Wilson Croker, the Secretary to the Admiralty, about the matter. Peel and Croker seldom took any important steps without conferring with one another and it is clear that Peel's view of Babbage's machine was not the highest.[98]

"My Dear Croker,
    You recollect that a very worthy seafaring man declared that he had been intimate in his youth with Gulliver, and that he resided (I believe)

in the neighbourhood of Blackwall. Davies Gilbert has produced another man who seems to be able to vouch at least for Laputa. Gilbert proposes that I should refer the enclosed to the Council of the Royal Society, with the view of their making such a report as shall induce the House of Commons to construct at the public charge a scientific automaton, which, if it can calculate what Mr. Babbage says it can, may be employed to the destruction of Hume. I presume you must at the Admiralty have heard of this proposal –

> "Aut hæc in vestros fabricata est machina muros,
> Aut aliquis latet error."

I should like a little previous consideration before I move in a thin house of country gentlemen, a large vote for the creation of a wooden man to calculate tables from the formula x^2+x+41. I fancy Lethbridge's face on being called on to contribute.

Ever affectionately,
ROB. PEEL."[99]

The Latin tag was entirely ironic and can be construed as "Either this has been built as an engine of war against your walls or some trickery lurks therein". It is taken from Virgil's *Aeneid* and refers in the original to the Trojan horse. (The original text says "our walls", something which Peel had changed).[100]

Croker's answer to Peel, dated the 21st of the same month, was more serious:

"Mr. Babbage's invention is at first sight incredible, but if you will recollect those little numeral locks which one has seen in France, in which a series of numbers are written on a succession of wheels, you will have some idea of the first principles of this machine, which is very curious and ingenious, and which not only will calculate all regular series, but also arranges the types for printing all the figures. At present indeed it is a matter more of curiosity than use, and I believe some good judges doubt whether it ever can be of any. But when I consider what has been already done by what were called Napier's bones and Gunter's scale, and the infinite and undiscovered variety of what may be called the *mechanical powers* of numbers, I cannot but admit the possibility, nay the probability, that important consequences may be ultimately derived from Mr. Babbage's principle. As to Mr. Gilbert's proposition of having a new machine constructed, I am rather inclined (with reference to his very superior judgment in such matters) to doubt whether that would be the most useful application of public money towards this object at present.

I apprehend that Mr. Babbage's present machine, which however I have not seen, answers the purposes which it is intended for sufficiently well, and I rather think that a sum of money given to Mr. Babbage to reward his ingenuity, encourage his zeal, and repay his expenses would tend eventually to the perfection of his machine. It was proposed at the Board of Longitude to give him 500l.[£] out of the sum placed at our disposal for the reward of inventions tending to facilitate the ascertaining the Longitude. But the Board doubted that the invention was likely to be practically useful to a degree to justify a grant of this nature.

I think you can have no difficulty in referring the matter to the Council of the Royal Society (of which although unworthy, I have the honour to be one), which by the assistance of its scientific members will give you the best opinion as to the value of the invention, and when that is obtained, it may be considered whether another machine should be made at the public expense, or whether Mr. Babbage should receive a reward either from Parliament or the Board of Longitude."[101]

As Croker had suggested, the Royal Society was asked by the Lords of the Treasury to give their opinion of the matter. On the 1st of May, 1823, that body issued a statement with the following conclusion:

"Mr. Babbage has displayed great talent and ingenuity in the construction of his Machine for Computation, which the Committee think fully adequate for the attainment of the objects proposed by the inventor; and they consider Mr. Babbage as highly deserving of public encouragement, in the prosecution of his arduous undertaking."[102]

The committee responsible for this verdict consisted of twelve men, most of them scientists and the majority of them Babbage's good friends.[103] One of the members of the committee, however, believed that it would be "far more useful" to invest their money in the funds and to apply the dividend to paying calculators.[104]

The matter of finance was settled shortly after this, almost exactly a year after Babbage's vague offer to Sir Humphry Davy. On the 13th of July 1823, Charles Babbage was awarded a gold medal by the Astronomical Society for the invention of his calculating machine − it was the first of its kind ever given by the Society.[105] Two weeks before this, he had met the Chancellor of the Exchequer Frederick John Robinson, who had promised that Babbage would be given 1,500 pounds, and more if necessary.[106] It was Babbage's opinion that the award of the Astronomical Society medal had played an important part in this.[107] It was in fact Herschel who had been the driving force behind the award of the medal, because Babbage wrote to Herschel that "He [Robinson] acquired the knowledge of the Astronomical medal two days since from [Davies] Gilbert, so that you got it for me just at the fortunate moment."[108] Consequently Babbage's friends had successfully acted behind the scene.

Babbage felt great relief and thought that the difference engine would be completed in two, or at most three years time.[109] In July 1823, the sum of 1,500 pounds was awarded to Babbage by the British government.[110] Babbage was certainly optimistic and declared to Herschel that "in a few years we shall have new [...] stereotype logarithmic tables as cheap as potatoes".[111]

No minutes of the meeting between the Chancellor of the Exchequer and Babbage were taken.[112] Nor was there any other written document or contract written, something which was to prove very unfortunate for the parties involved in the project. It was clear however, that it was the government's wish that Babbage should build a complete difference engine for calculating and printing numerical tables, obviously in accordance with what Babbage had suggested in his letter to Sir Humphry Davy and in the other articles.[113] As far as the mechanical design or the mathematical capacity of the machine was concerned, nothing was agreed.[114] Finally, it was Babbage's opinion that the difference engine would become the property of the government since it would pay for its completion.[115] The work on the engine could now get under way.

At Prospect Place, Newington Butts, in London, there was a workshop of a manufacturer of "small machinery requiring first-class workmanship".[116] Its owner, the draughtsman and engineer Joseph Clement lived in the office in the yard. He had set up this business on his own in 1817 and had become famous among his fellow craftsmen for his great skills as a draughtsman − a field in which he was unrivalled. He was also known for having invented various types of tool.[117] Indeed according to his biographer, nothing pleased Clement more than to have what he called "a tough job" − something that challenged his inventive faculty and which gave gave him the highest pleasure.[118] It was Joseph Clement who was to be chosen by Babbage to undertake the construction of the Difference Engine No. 1.

Clement was the son of a poor Westmoreland handloom weaver.[119] At an early age, he had been forced to help his father at the loom. When he was eighteen years of age, he changed his trade, due to the mechanization of weaving that was taking place, and became a slater. With a growing interest in mechanics, he had been able, with some help, to build his first lathe in his early twenties. With this machine, he made screws and musical and scientific instruments. Having thus made some progress in his field of interest, he got his first job as a mechanic at a power loom factory, where he made models (probably for casting) and he fitted the various parts of the iron looms.

In 1807, Clement moved to Glasgow in Scotland where he worked as a turner and learned to make drawings of machinery. Six years later, he went to London and as soon as his skills as a draughtsman had been discovered, he was hired at once. Such ability was rare at that time. In 1814, Clement was employed by one of the most famous British engineers of the era, Joseph Bramah. He appointed Clement chief draughtsman and superintendent of the Pimlico Works. There he also worked as a turner and his wages rose from one guinea to three guineas a week. He had worked for a year when Bramah died and Clement then joined the equally renowned engineer Henry Maudslay, also as chief draughtsman. He remained there until he had saved enough money to open his own business in 1817. What he had learned at Bramah's and Maudslay's was to influence the work on the difference engine project.

When Babbage hired Clement during the latter part of 1823, Clement had begun to display his skills for a wider public.[120] Many of the intricate drawings of machinery and instruments published in the *Transactions of the Society for the Encouragement of Arts, Manufacture and Commerce*, had been made by Clement.[121] In 1818, he had received the gold medal of the Society, for his invention of an instrument for drawing accurate ellipses.[122] Although his workshop was small, it included at least two machine tools. The first was a lathe, a very good one, which (in 1818) was equipped with a slide rest and means for self correction.[123] The second was a planing machine, which Clement used for planing the triangular bars of lathes and the sides of weaving looms.[124] In addition to this, he must have had precision hand tools, enabling him to do the odd jobs calling for the very accurate workmanship, which were his speciality.

Unfortunately almost nothing is known about the first stages in the development of Difference Engine No. 1. It might be imagined, however, that after Babbage had shown the model engine to Clement, that they together started to design the calculating part of the larger engine.[125] The possibility that the development of the machine was due to the joint efforts of both Babbage and Clement has not been previously considered.

Fig. 10 Charles Babbage's multi-purpose lathe, equipped with a compound slide rest, made by Joseph Clement in 1823–1824. This machine is now in the collection of the Science Museum, London. Photograph by courtesey of the Trustees of the Science Museum, London.

However, it must have required the contributions of *both* men and this will be further discussed in section 3.2. In my opinion the mathematician Charles Babbage was in no position to tell the technically experienced Joseph Clement how to go about finding solutions to detailed mechanical problems.

Apparently, the model engine had a design different from the one eventually chosen for Difference Engine No. 1.[126] Whether they therefore had to start from scratch or whether they were able to base the design of the new engine on the first one, is unknown. It is known that several drawings were made by Clement and other hired draughtsmen, at a later stage.[127] Perhaps these were based on the sketches made by Babbage.[128] Nor is it known how many workers Clement employed when work on the engine began. But in 1827, there were eight men working on it. In addition to this, Clement had another draughtsman to help him with the drawings.[129]

By the end of 1827, work on the engine had been going on for about four years.[130] Besides working on the engine, which was still unfinished, Clement had invented and made several new tools and had improved his machines. Many of them, like gauges, templates and fixtures had been made specially for the production of the difference engine. A drawing table for making large drawings, which was finished in December 1824, was probably used, if not specifically designed, for the work on the engine.[131] Six months had been devoted to making a compound slide rest for Babbage's own lathe.[132] It was the second of its kind, had three slides, and converted Babbage's lathe into a multi-purpose machine tool, see Fig. 10.[133] The first was Clement's own. The origins of this device can be traced directly back to the machine tools of Bramah and Maudslay. Furthermore, Clement had made experiments with taps for making uniform threads. By January 1827, he had started to make taps with a certain number of threads to the inch.[134] At this time, threads were not standardized and varied from one workshop to another. This meant difficulties when one workshop had to repair machines made by another maker of machinery. In this field too, Joseph Clement was a pioneer.

Babbage himself had invented a new graphical and symbolical method which he called the *Mechanical Notation*.[135] He claimed that by means of this method any machine and its mode of operation could be easily understood "almost without the aid of words".[136] It was conceived with the difference engine in mind, so that Babbage more rapidly could understand and recall the interpretation of the drawings.[137] As will be discussed more fully in the second part of this book, the mechanical notation had a great influence on the design of the difference engine.

On a personal level, the year 1827 was a very eventful one for Charles Babbage. In July, he lost one of his sons, Charles, and in the autumn his wife Georgiana died in childbirth.[138] In the spring, his father Benjamin Babbage had passed away, leaving Charles an inheritance of around 100,000 pounds.[139] But Charles had little time to think about this with the many tragedies that followed.[140] These sad events, together with his worries over the engine which by this time should have been completed, caused a breakdown in his health. He decided to make a long tour of the Continent, and at the end of the year, he set off.[141] Drawings and instructions were left with Clement so that the work on the engine could proceed.[142]

Upon Babbage's return to England, at the end of 1828, the difference engine was still unfinished. He had advanced considerable sums from his own pocket, and knew that the machine was going to cost a great deal more by the time it was ready.[143] The matter of the government's role and how far it was prepared to support the project had begun to worry Babbage all the more.[144] Since no contract had been signed, he was also anxious about the expected extent of his own commitments.[145] Babbage therefore contacted the government which in turn requested the Royal Society to investigate the state of progress of the engine. A committee was set up under the chairmanship of John Herschel and it reported to the government in February 1829.[146] In his statement to the committee, Babbage said that about 90 per cent of the drawings were finished, a figure which, in my estimation, does not say very much, despite the fact that it was also mentioned in the report that 400 square feet of drawings had been made.[147] It was left to the committee to estimate that around three-fifths of the whole engine, including the necessary tools, had been completed. A small portion of the calculating unit had been assembled for demonstration purposes, but little progress had been made with the printing unit.[148] The committee in a passage in their report, summarized the difficulties that had to be overcome in the project. It is worth repeating here:

"In the actual execution of the work they find that Mr. Babbage has made a progress, which, considering the very great difficulties to be overcome in an undertaking so novel, they regard as fully equalling any expectations that could reasonably have been formed; and that although several years have now elapsed since the first commencement, yet that when the necessity of constructing plans, sections, elevations, and working drawings of every part; that of constructing, and in many cases inventing, tools and machinery of great expense and complexity (and in many instances of ingenious contrivances, and likely to prove useful for other purposes hereafter), for forming with the requisite precision parts of the apparatus dissimilar to any used in ordinary mechanical works; that of making many previous trials to ascertain the validity of proposed movements; and that of altering, improving, and simplifying those already contrived and reduced to drawings; your Committee are so far from being surprised at the time it has occupied to bring it to its present state, that they feel more disposed to wonder it has been possible to accomplish so much."[149]

In conclusion, the committee was convinced that Babbage's engine was likely to fulfil the expectations of its inventor.[150] 1,500 pounds had been given to Babbage in 1823. Now, in April 1829, another 1,500 pounds was advanced towards the cost of the project by the government.[151] But it was not enough to cover the expenses. By May 1829, these amounted to around 7,000 pounds.[152] Babbage was neither able nor willing to spend his fortune on the difference engine.[153] The government's financial responsibility had not been settled despite several attempts by Babbage to clear this matter up. From Babbage's point of view, there was also another problem, namely Clement.[154] It was with some unease that Babbage viewed Clement's large fees and while waiting to have the bills examined by experts, he halted all payments to the engineer.[155] Clement responded by threatening with a stoppage of work. Babbage felt that he had Clement squeezing him on one side and the government prodding from the other.[156] All scholars who have studied the story of Babbage's difference engine have tended to see matters from Babbage's perspective. But the story is open to a quite different interpretation – one in which Babbage can be seen as Clement's great problem. This will be discussed further in section 3.2. On the 6th of May 1829, Babbage expressed his inner feelings about all the difficulties, to Herschel:

"Indeed I am at present ready to make any sacrifice provided it do not involve continued anxiety. – I believe I could give up the machine at once and smile at the world who would say it was impossible from the beginning..."[157]

A couple of days later, Clement stopped work on the engine.[158] Eventually the bills were found to be reasonable and new government money was injected, but the work was suspended for over a year.[159] In March 1830, it was continued again and Babbage was now of the opinion once more that the engine could be completed in three years' time.[160]

Although the difference engine occupied much of Babbage's attention, he managed to pursue other interests as well, after his return from his continental trip. In the spring of 1830, he finished and published *Reflections on the Decline of Science in England: and on Some of its Causes*.[161] It is beyond the scope of the present work to enter into the social and political background to the controversy which ensued with the publication of the book. For further information the reader is referred to the works of other scholars.[162] However, the foundation of the British Association for the Advancement of Science in 1831, in which Babbage was also involved, was one of the steps taken to remedy the poor state of science in the country.[163]

Despite the fact that Babbage undeniably made enemies through his criticism, he was nonetheless a popular figure in London society where his dinner parties became renowned. He attracted attention with his humour and irony and his interesting stories, not least about the difference engine. He met and corresponded with many distinguished people of the day from different classes of society and several of them were numbered among his friends. Among them were people like Alexander von Humboldt, the illustrious natural scientist, the famous English engineer Marc Isambard Brunel and his son Isambard Kingdom Brunel, and three other famous men called Charles – Darwin, the geologist Lyell and Dickens.[164] But Babbage was not only a sociable fellow in the scientific, political and cultural circles of London. He had also finally acquired an official position in society. From 1828 onwards, he could call himself Lucasian Professor of Mathematics at Cambridge.[165] This was Newton's Chair and although it was more of an honorary position than a financially well paid appointment, Babbage was deeply grateful for having been elected.[166]

Babbage's vaguely optimistic views about the project when it restarted in March 1830 were not to last long. At the end of the year, Babbage notified the government that additional space for the erection of the calculating engine had become an absolute necessity.[167] He even went further and suggested that the work should be transferred from Clement's workshop and carried on somewhere in the neighbourhood of his residence at No. 1 Dorset Street.[168] This would solve the organizational disadvantages that arose from having Clement's workshop some four miles from Babbage's home.[169] Babbage emphasized that this would contribute to a speedier completion of the engine.[170] Another reason given for the move was that the costly drawings and machine parts ought to be protected against fire.[171] Exactly what happened and who took responsibility for the costs involved, is unclear, but the available sources state that Lord Althorp, the new Chancellor of the Exchequer "accepted these proposals" and eventually a new fire proof building was erected in Charles Babbage's own garden.[172] The government had (in December 1830) declared that the difference engine was its property and was prepared to accept full responsibility for any further costs involved in its completion.[173] But the arrangements that were made were rather cumbersome. Clement's bills were to be examined by the engineers Bryan Donkin and Joshua Field, as they were sent in. If they were found to be correct, they were then transmitted by Babbage to the Treasury, which settled the account with Clement.[174] This was a complicated time consuming procedure as far as Clement and his workers were concerned. Although Babbage forwarded money from his own pocket, it is easy to understand Clement's feelings in this atmosphere of distrust. In addition, he was being expected to move the work on the engine, with all the men and tools involved, to Babbage's premises. In practice, this demand would have meant that Clement would have to move his whole workshop or divide it into two parts, one for the engine and one for his other jobs. Before he was prepared to move, Clement therfore demanded (in July 1832) an extra yearly sum in compensation for having his business divided.[175] According to Clement's biographer, Clement was "almost constantly in his workshop, in which he took great pride [...] and it was with difficulty he could be induced to leave the premises".[176] If this statement is correct, it explains Clement's personal reluctance to move. As far as the practical side of the matter was concerned, the engine was not the only item that made demands on both his workmen and his stock of tools and machine tools. Dividing the workshop would have meant that new machine tools had to be bought or built to keep the business running. This was of course impossible from an economic standpoint, but it helps to explain the monetary compensation which Clement had demanded.

The Treasury considered Clement's demands unreasonable and refused to pay up.[177] Perhaps this was what Clement was hoping for because he refused to budge despite various overtures from Babbage about ways of resolving the problem. It seems to me rather strange that Babbage had erected the buildings in the first place without first having an agreement with Clement about the matter. Be that as it may, Clement was definitely as tired of the whole business as Babbage. It also has to be made clear that Clement considered that the work on the difference engine yielded less than the average profit on ordinary contracts.[178] The whole business came to a head, when Babbage, who owed Clement money for an unpaid bill, decided on the 20th of March 1833 not to make any more advances from his own funds.[179] This triggered off a crisis and brought about the end of the project. Clement's response was to maintain that he was not hired by the Treasury but by Babbage himself and that it was Babbage who was ultimately responsible for the payment of his bills.[180] The following day, after some nine years work on the project, Clement dismissed the men and work on the Difference Engine No. 1 came to a standstill for good.[181]

It is not known how much of the difference engine was finished when the project came to a halt. On one occasion, Babbage mentioned that there were more than 10,000 pieces.[182] Collier who came across this piece of information, describes it as implausibly high, although it probably included every single screw. This leads him to the conclusion that nearly all of the parts of the engine must have been finished.[183] But against this, consider that besides a large percentage of screws, only a fraction of the 30,000 number types which Babbage at an early stage had planned to use, were included. This would indicate that far from the larger part of the engine being ready, only a small bit had been finished. In early 1833, a section of the calculating unit was assembled, see Fig. 11. It could deal with five figures and second order differences and was equal to approximately one seventh of the calculating unit of the greater engine which had been planned. This machine was, however, of little practical value. As will be shown in the following section, its limitation to two orders of differences and five figures, restricted its use to demonstration purposes only. Some other portions of the machine, capable of illustrating the chosen mechanisms for adding and carrying, were also put together.[184]

Fig. 11 The Difference engine No. 1. This is the part of the calculating unit that was assembled by Clement and his men in 1833. The machine is operated by means of the handle in the upper left corner. The right column represents the result, the middle column the first difference, and the left column the second and third difference. The engine is on display at the Science Museum in London. Photograph by courtesy of the Trustees of the Science Museum, London.

But no printing unit was ever assembled, and it is unknown how far it had been developed by the time Clement ceased working on the engine. A puzzling question remains. If Collier is right and such a large number of parts was actually completed, why was a larger machine not assembled? After all, the more that could have been put together, the more Charles Babbage's honour would have been vindicated. I am inclined to draw the conclusion that despite all the years that had been devoted to the construction of the engine, not much of it was actually finished.

The total sum spent on the difference engine by the British government, is said to have amounted to about 17,000 pounds.[185] When the project had started in 1823, Babbage had reckoned that the complete engine would cost no more than 6,500 pounds.[186] In addition, Babbage says that he had put up a similar sum (to that of the government) out of his own pocket.[187] This statement, however, is given in his autobiography and is not supported by any other primary source. 17,000 pounds was a truly exorbitant figure at the time. A comparison is useful here. In July 1831, America's first steam locomotive, the John Bull, made by the firm of Robert Stephenson and Company, was shipped from Liverpool. The cost of transportation across the Atlantic amounted to 19 pounds. The price of the locomotive was 784 pounds and 7 shillings.[188]

Many articles had been published about the project and more were to come. It is therefore hardly strange that public attention was drawn to the affair and that Babbage became the victim of accusations, from both the public and the government, that he had made a personal profit out of the deal. In 1834, it was stated by the Chancellor of the Exchequer in the House of Commons that not one shilling had ever gone into Mr. Babbage's own pocket.[189] However, I believe that he may have had some compensation in material terms, by being able to buy the unassembled parts for their scrap value, as well as several drawing boards.[190] It is also uncertain how much of the amounts mentioned was spent on the rebuilding of Babbage's own lathe. Nor is it anywhere made clear who actually paid for the new workshops adjacent to Babbage's home. Since he continued to develop other types of calculating machines in these buildings, they could not − at least from Babbage's point of view − be considered as a complete waste of money. Nevertheless, 17,000 pounds was indeed a very high price to pay for an unfinished machine of very little practical value.

Before I leave the story of Babbage and the Difference Engine No. 1, I would like to shed light on some other aspects of the project. I bring them up here, since they are important as background to the later discussion. They are concerned with how Babbage's knowledge in the three specific areas of numerical tables, calculating machines and machine design increased in the course of the project.

1) Numerical tables: as has been mentioned, Babbage became a collector of such tables. At the time of his death in 1871, his collection of tables amounted to 310 items.[191] These were of every kind and together they formed one of the most complete collections of tables in the world. Only the Royal Society perhaps was in possession of a larger collection.[192] Williams who has studied Babbage's library, has found that Babbage was most active in building up his collection of mathematical and tabular works during the period 1820 to 1830 or in other words, simultaneously with the work on the engine.[193] He bought as many as 70 to 80 items per year during this period.[194] What tables did Babbage acquire? It is astonishing to find that he managed to get such a variety of tables, from

the early "state financed and group-produced" *Alphonsine Tables* to "one man productions" like those of Michael Taylor.[195] With a couple of exceptions, he bought all of the important and famous tables mentioned in section 1.1. These tables were to form the basis for his research and investigations into the accuracy, structure and history of numerical tables.

In addition to collecting tables, Babbage himself started to make them. In 1824, when he was involved in the foundation of a new life insurance company, he prepared mortality tables.[196] At the end of the following year, he completed a comprehensive treatise on life insurance, covering most aspects of the subject from the calculation of the premium, to calculation of the payment of the sum assured to the nominee.[197] It included an appendix with various examples of tables, all printed with different layouts, a fact that indicates that he may have been making experiments in printing. After this, he embarked on a larger table project, namely the production of his table of logarithms. The way in which special measures were taken to keep the number of errors to a minimum, has already been discussed.

Babbage also expended much time on the typographical aspects of this question. One point to be decided was the colour of the paper and ink to be used. In order to find out which combinations of colour were the least fatiguing for the human eye, Babbage had two pages of his table prepared by the printers, for which *150* various colours of paper were chosen and upon which the tables were printed in inks of *ten* different colours.[198] Prints were also made with gold, silver and copper on vellum and various rich coloured papers.[199] Babbage even went as far printing with black ink on black paper and yellow ink on yellow paper.[200] These experimental and probably expensive tables were only made in one single copy bound into 21 volumes. It was finished in 1831. I have noted that the ordinary editions of Babbage's logarithm tables were in most cases printed with black ink on yellow paper, as this was found by Babbage to be the best combination for providing a distinct contrast.[201] A friend of Babbage's agreed that yellow paper was the best in daylight, but said that he preferred pink or blue paper when reading by candlelight.[202]

2) Calculating machines: Charles Babbage had at least three reasons for devoting attention to them. First, he started in the spring of 1822, to look into the history of calculating machines, for the purpose of answering any questions that might be raised when he had to discuss the matter of financing his own machine.[203] Secondly, he was eager to find out whether his ideas had been anticipated in any way by other inventors in this field.[204] Thirdly, Babbage must have become increasingly interested in the technical solutions and mechanisms embodied in these predecessors to the difference engine, now that he had been forced himself to tackle the problems of design. To satisfy his curiosity, he bought literature on the matter. As Williams points out, very little material had been published on calculating machines either before or during Babbage's

lifetime. Nevertheless, he was able to obtain 35 separate items dealing with mechanical calculation.[205] It is not known when each item was added to his collection but all reflect his interest in this subject. Among the items mentioned, there was material on Gunter, Napier, Morland and about Joannis Poleni, the inventor of a clocklike calculating machine in Padua in 1709, which was driven by gravity.[206] In addition to books and other written documents, Babbage personally examined machines from as early as 1822-1823.[207] At some point during his life, he also purchased some machines, namely the two of Samuel Morland and perhaps also three machines made by the Earl of Stanhope.[208] As a consequence, Babbage became increasingly familiar with the fundamentals of mechanical calculation.

3) Machine design: from around 1823 to the early 1830's, Charles Babbage visited a large number of workshops and factories in England as well as on the Continent.[209] It is not easy to say how far the experiences he thus gained affected the design of the engine. It is clear, however, that it was due to these thorough investigations that Charles Babbage was transformed from a pure mathematician into a man with a considerable general knowledge of engineering. It was most probably Clement and his men who played the most important role in improving Babbage's comprehension of the actual practical processes of designing and building machinery. I will return to these matters in the second part of the book.

It was Babbage's growing interest in machine design — a direct outgrowth of his work with the engine — which led him to take an interest in the field of industrial economics. In 1832, Babbage published his book *On the Economy of Machinery and Manufactures*.[210] It was originally intended to be presented as a course of lectures at Cambridge University, to which it was dedicated with respect and gratitude.[211] In this book, he presented a down-to-earth account of technology in industry, looking at its economic and technical advantages. He provided a thorough analysis of the significance of the availability of power, precision in manufacturing, the management of raw materials, large scale production and export. Various organizational questions were also discussed, such as the registration and control of production as well as questions relating to the workforce, the organization of work and automation. Like his predecessor Adam Smith, Babbage analyzed the way in which work was organized in a pin factory and thereby derived certain new conclusions about the relation between wages and the degree of the division of labour. This was to make Babbage one of the most significant authors on industrial economics during the Industrial Revolution. Babbage's name occurs not infrequently in the literature of economics today alongside such names as Adam Smith, David Ricardo and Andrew Ure. For both Karl Marx and John Stuart Mill, *On the Economy of Machinery and Manufactures* was a source of inspiration.[212] The book was published in several editions and was translated into French, Spanish, German and Italian.[213] Since it contained information about the difference engine, it also contributed to spreading knowledge about the invention internationally.

Driven by the demands of the engine itself, as well as from growing interest, Babbage carried out detailed investigations into numerical tables, calculating machines and machine design. The knowledge that he was to acquire about these matters was to prove useful as he continued to develop other types of calculating machinery, after the failure of the difference engine project.

After the work on the difference engine had been halted in the middle of 1834, Babbage conceived the idea of a new and highly complicated mechanical calculating machine − the Analytical Engine. I do not propose to enter into the history and technology of this machine. Some facts, however, are worth noting. The Analytical Engine was to consist (among many other parts) of an arithmetical unit where the calculation work was to be carried out, a memory where intermediate steps in the calculation could be stored, and a printing unit. The engine was envisaged being able to make its own decisions, depending on the outcome of the intermediate steps and it would be controlled by a program which would be fed in by means of punched cards of the Jacquard kind. Although Babbage was to devote the rest of his life to this engine, it remained, with the exception of a few parts, at the drawing board stage. Nevertheless by 1838, Babbage had notations and drawings for a complete version of the Analytical Engine ready. Recent research based on these documents has shown that the Analytical Engine could have been built and would have worked by 1838.[214] In terms of its underlying principles, the Analytical Engine constituted a direct predecessor of the modern computer, a fact that has drawn much attention to Babbage's work in recent years.[215]

Work on the Difference Engine No. 1 went on from 1821 to 1833, when only a fraction of the calculating unit had been assembled. It could calculate with second order differences and five digits. The printing unit was never built. The principles of the calculating unit were entirely understood however. The massive sum of 17,000 pounds had been invested by the British government and Babbage is said to have put up a comparable sum from his own pocket. Although the project was halted by Clement's action in 1833, Babbage continued to try and resume the work, by asking the government for further financial support. He was to wait many months for their final decision, which turned out to be negative. Babbage's difference engine never produced any error-free stereotyped tables, nor was it ever driven by steam as he had planned. Despite that, Charles Babbage's name spread over the whole world and his was the glory for having invented the Difference Engine No. 1. Although criticized at times, Babbage found his niche among his fellow scientists. Having chosen to dedicate his life to his calculating machines, he never ceased developing his ideas.

JOHANN HELFRICH MÜLLER

The idea for making a machine for calculating and printing numerical tables was not in fact new. It dates back to the year 1784, when it was first conceived by the German engineer and master builder, Johann Müller — a fact that has been neglected by historians.[216] Who was Müller and and how did he arrive at his idea?

According to his autobiography, Johann Helfrich Müller was born in Cleve in Germany, on the 16th of January 1746.[217] He received his initial education at little private schools and was then sent to study at the Grammar School in Darmstadt. In the Spring of 1762, he became a cadet in the Artillery Corps at Giessen, where his family had moved, and he began to attend lectures in mathematics and physics at the university. Lorenz Friedrich, Johann's father, who was in the building trade, wanted his son to carry on the family tradition, but Johann appears to have found certain other careers equally tempting. While still at the grammar school, he had wanted to become a painter; at the university he hoped to be a professor of mathematics and physics. Soon however he discovered that the profession of an engineer was the most interesting of all and he devoted much time to reading books on statistics, hydraulics and mechanics.

In 1769, the Artillery Corps was reduced in strength and Müller was forced to look for work elsewhere. Shortly afterwards, he was employed as an engineer by Prince Georg Wilhelm, the Governor in Giessen, and a man with wide interests in both civil and military engineering and architecture. In April 1772, Prince Wilhelm took Müller with him on a five month trip to Paris. There they visited and studied many of the marvellous buildings and machines in the city and at St.Cloud, Versailles and Marly. On his return from the trip, Müller devoted most of his time to architectural and mechanical design and various financial calculations for his master. In February 1774, Müller became building inspector in Darmstadt and three years later master builder with the responsibility for designing and maintaining buildings. He also was expected to act as an adviser in case of emergencies such as floods. Thus Johann Müller eventually ended up in his father's trade after all.

By the time Müller was thirty-five years old, he had established himself in society and was ready to settle down. On the 19th of August 1781, he married Johannetta Catharina von Westerfeld. Together they had five children — two daughters and three sons.

Johann Müller had a creative mind. His autobiography reveals him making inventions in his late twenties, among them a theatre equipped with optical and mechanical effects for the children of the Prince. It is plausible to assume that this ability manifested itself early, since unlike Babbage, he was used to strolling about building sites and mixing with his father's craftsmen. During the years 1775 to 1780, Müller used his spare time to make inventions, such as a large and powerful burning mirror. In contrast to Babbage, Müller was thus an engineer and an inventor with experience in machine design. On the other hand, Müller admittedly only possessed a limited knowledge of mathematics.[218]

It was in June 1782 that Johann Müller invented his first calculating machine.[219] This was not a difference engine, but was originally conceived to perform addition alone. The reason why he thought at all about using machinery for calculation, was because he had been asked by the local superintendent's office to check and recalculate some tables relating to the volumes of trees. To shorten this task he had come up with the idea of a machine for the purpose.[220] Soon he realised however that with a few small changes, he could get the machine to perform subtraction, division and multiplication as well. Rapidly one plan succeeded the other. At this stage, he came across an article about a universal calculating machine of his countryman, Philipp Matthäus Hahn which was to have an influence

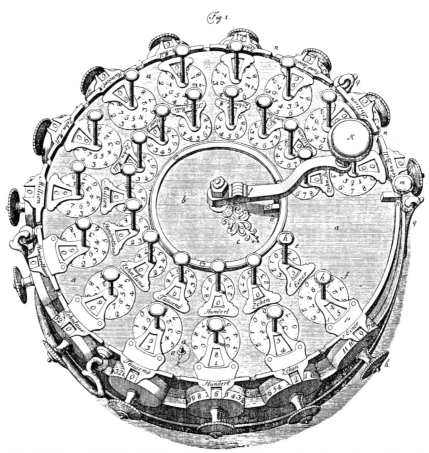

Fig. 12 Johann Helfrich Müller's universal calculating machine, invented in 1782 and finished on the 20th of June 1784. Eighty-one days later Müller presented his new idea — a printing tabulating calculating machine. Drawing from Philipp Engel Klipstein (ed.), J. H. Müllers Beschreibung seiner neu erfundenen Rechenmaschine; nach ihrer Gestalt, ihrem Gebrauch und Nutzen (Frankfurt and Mainz 1786).

on Müller's design.[221] After about three months of designing, he gave the drawings to a clockmaker, with the order to make the machine in metal. The work was taken over by a pair of journeymen in the same trade and on the 20th of June 1784, the machine was ready.[222]

Müller's universal calculating machine was in the form of a round box with a handle placed centrally and the number wheels concentrically arranged around the handle, see Fig. 12. It could calculate with 14 figures and its number and gear wheels could be altered to enable it to operate with non-decimal number systems. All 14 calculating mechanisms were identical. Mechanically, the machine was based on the ingenious stepped reckoners (Staffelwalzen) invented by Leibniz. In simple terms, they can be described as cylinders or gear wheels , with nine teeth with axially increasing length, so arranged that these teeth occupy about one fourth of the circumference. The machine was also equipped with a bell, which rang if the number wheels were set incorrectly or for instance if the operator tried to subtract a larger number from a smaller one.[223] The machine, which is still kept in the Hessisches Landesmuseum in Darmstadt, was 285 mm in diameter, 95 mm in height and weighed 15,4 kilos.[224]

While still working on his machine, Müller contacted his countryman Georg Christoph Lichtenberg in Göttingen. Lichtenberg was a famous physicist, known for his investigations in electricity as well as for his satirical writings. He was well established in the German scientific community and closely involved in the publication of a couple of scientific and literary periodicals. His institutional base was the University at Göttingen where he held a chair in physics. Clearly, Müller knew Lichtenberg. They had studied drawing together in their youth at the Grammar School in Darmstadt.[225]

On the 22nd of May 1783, Müller had written to Lichtenberg a long letter in which he described his invention and set forth his plans. This letter shows that Müller's ideas had developed rapidly and that he was an intelligent man who fully grasped the ideas involved in designing calculating machinery. He saw a chance to make a profit from the machine and informed Lichtenberg about his intention to make another copy of it, as soon as the first one was ready.[226] He also wanted to build a couple of simpler calculating machines for addition and subtraction only. Müller contacted Lichtenberg with the view to getting him to support these ideas. Müller stated that he was hoping to take the machines, including the simpler ones, to England. Before this, he wanted to show the first calculating machine to the members of the Academy of Sciences in Göttingen, in order to establish officially his priority in inventing the machine. Lichtenberg was the right man to contact. He had spent two longer periods in England and he was a member of the Academy in question. It should be noted that two of Müller's predecessors, as concerns calculating machines, namely Leibniz and Christian Ludwig Gersten, had shown their inventions at the Royal Society some decades earlier.[227] But Müller, who was apparently interested in mechanical calculation more for practical and economic reasons than for glory and fame, had another reason for talking about England. In another letter to Lichtenberg, dated 9th of September in the same year, he wrote that he had decided not to sell his machine for less than 1,000 guineas, and added − "This would not be too much for a great man or for a rich Englishman, who sometimes has more use for useless things".[228]

These words were written at a time when mechanical calculation was not much more than a curiosity, which is reflected in Müller's irony. Yet Müller knew that his machine could be of great use in making tables and noted − "How easy it would be, by this means, to correct and extend the tables of logarithms".[229] Despite the fact that the machine could not be compared with Babbage's powerful difference engine, it was quick to operate and Müller used it himself to calculate a set of tables: *Tafeln des Kubischen Gehalts des Bauholzes*, which was published in Frankfurt in 1788.[230] In Müller's creative mind, the idea of utilizing a machine for the production of tables was present when he started designing his adding machine in 1782. Whether at that point, he was familiar with the method of differences or not, is unknown. But his ideas progressed quickly. On the 9th of September 1784, 81 days after the machine was finished, Müller recorded a new thought for Lichtenberg in a postscript − a printing tabulating machine.

"P.S. If the calculating machine sells well, I would in the future make a machine, which would simultaneously print in printer's ink on paper any arbitrary arithmetical progression in natural numbers — or the units, together with the numbers of the terms and the lines in between — and which would halt of its own accord, when the side of the paper was full up.

After setting the first figures, all one has to do is to turn a handle and after stopping to turn over the paper or to put another sheet in its place. In this way, a sequence of 60 terms can be delivered in a minute."[231]

It is not certain whether the method of differences was to be adopted. However the basic idea of calculating and printing by machinery had been born, and Müller must be credited for having done this 37 years before Babbage. It should be noted that Müller's engine, invented before the invention of stereotyping, was intended to print tables directly on paper. Nevertheless the fact that they were to be printed, reduced the incidence of error considerably. Müller continued to develop the new machine. But since he was not convinced about its importance, he asked men of science for their opinion.[232] Their responses are unfortunately unknown. Johann Müller never built a machine of this kind. Instead the idea was further perfected and presented together with his universal calculating machine in a book published in Frankfurt and Mainz in 1786,

J. H. Müllers Beschreibung seiner neu erfundenen Rechenmaschine; nach ihrer Gestalt, ihrem Gebrauch und Nutzen.[233]

This 50 page booklet was edited by Müller's friend Philipp Engel Klipstein. It contained, besides an exhaustive description of the mode of operation and design of the constructed machine, also a discussion about its advantages over manual computation and a detailed account of the special security (correction) mechanisms incorporated. Finally, under the heading "Further inventions of superior calculating machines and an arithmetical printing machine" − the new machine was presented.[234] In these passages, it is made clear that Müller, perhaps at an even earlier date, had invented a difference engine for the rapid production of error-free tables, by means of "whole series of numbers" and by using "difference-numbers" (Differenzzahlen).[235] A description similar to that in the postscript to Lichtenberg is given of the printing part, which was supposed to print directly onto paper rather than produce matrices for stereotypes.[236] No mention is made of how the necessary mechanisms to accomplish this were to be designed. Nonetheless it is clear from this document that Johann Müller had conceived the idea of a difference engine by the year 1786.

One question cannot be avoided: was Müller's engine the source of Babbage's idea? In his autobiography, Babbage says − "The first Difference Engine with which I am acquainted comprised a few figures, and was made by myself, between 1820 and June 1822."[237]

Among Babbage's letters in the manuscript collection of the British Library I have come across a seemingly compromising document. It is a five page English translation of certain parts of Klipstein's book. It has been translated for Babbage by Herschel. It deals briefly with the matters mentioned above, but when Herschel gets to the description of the difference engine, he translates almost all of it − word for word.[238]

Did Babbage then know about Müller's machine when he invented the Difference Engine No. 1? This is not easily answered, because for one thing Herschel's translation is undated. Furthermore, the evidence which I have discovered, is by no means conclusive.

Collier has discovered that Babbage shortly after the conception of his idea, first started by considering the use of sliding rods, instead of the more natural use of wheels in the adding mechanism.[239] This kind of mechanism which was "new" in the history of calculating machines, gives rise to grave difficulties in the process of carrying, a fact which Babbage eventually realized. In fact this seems to have been such a revelation to him, that in November of 1822 he noted very solemnly that he had in future decided always to choose circular motion for this purpose.[240] This shows that Babbage must have known very little about machine design, mechanical calculating and the history of such machines at that time. It also indicates that he could not have read Herschel's translation, since it dealt among other things with number wheels. Having read this account, it would have been unlikely that Babbage would have persisted in designing rods, only to have realized later that wheels were superior.

Let me quote a letter from Herschel:

> "Dear Babbage. Bad news − I am sorry to have to tell you that some rascally Frenchman has been presenting to the Institute "A Machine for performing readily all the most difficult operations of Arithmetics and forming all sorts of tables" − D-n his Soul! The Inst. have, I am told, approved it. It does not however follow that it is the same as yours and everybody will at least swear to your independent invention of it."[241]

This letter is also undated. It is marked, obviously later, (in handwriting that is hard to decipher), December 1820. But in another letter, from Babbage to Herschel, dated 9th of April 1822, this piece of bad news is mentioned by a worried Babbage.[242] December 1821 might be the correct date. At any rate, it is undated and I have not, despite various attempts, been able to find out who this Frenchman was, nor anything about any French difference engine.[243] The letter clearly reflects the normal fear of an inventor, that someone else might have invented the thing before or is working on it simultaneously. Priority and honour were at stake.

Can etymology solve the problem? The fact that Herschel used the English word "engine" in his translation of Müller's text in Klipstein, indicates that the translation was made after the idea of the steam-power inspired British difference engine was conceived. However this argument is not entirely watertight since Herschel might simply have used the dictionary translation of the German word "Maschine" which is either "machine" or "engine" in English.

What conclusion can be drawn? Did Babbage get the "Utopian" invention from Müller or not? The question cannot be answered on the basis of the material presently available but it is better that the matter is at least considered rather than being disregarded by scholars as has been the case hitherto. Certainly it will not do to say (without further evidence or simply by reliance on Babbage's own words) that Babbage invented the engine independently of Müller, as some have done.[244] It should, however, be remembered that the key question is whether Babbage got the idea from Müller or not. The fact that at some point, he learned about Müller and his engine, is indisputable. The question about when this took place, remains to be answered. I will return to that question in the second part of this book.

To sum up, *either* Müller and Babbage invented their difference engines independently *or* Müller's work was the origin of Babbage's own idea − a question still unanswered. They both wanted to solve the problems with the errors and delays involved in computing tables by hand. In Babbage's case, the highly publicized steam engine appears to have influenced the idea, instantly leading to the concept of a difference engine. For Müller, the process seems to have been more of a step-by-step one.

He started mechanizing the four basic mathematical operations by building an ordinary calculating machine which he used for making tables and only after this, did he realize that the process of table production could be mechanized further. Perhaps Babbage was inspired by the tradition of Thomas Newcomen and James Watt in steam engineering, while Müller drew his inspiration from the strong German tradition of machine calculation, which had been initiated by Leibniz. Babbage was a mathematician and not an engineer: Müller was an engineer and not a mathematician. Babbage, the man of science, analyzed the theoretical possibilities in depth and believed that the thing was mechanically possible. Müller, the down to earth practical man, investigated the mechanisms and their operations and was then convinced that it could be made.

In the final passages of Klipstein's book, Müller offered his universal machine for sale. He continued to say that if a buyer were found, he would be able to go on and build a difference engine, if someone was interested in that.[245] It is evident that he encountered difficulties in finding a buyer. Eventually, Müller's machine was bought by a German count who incorporated it in his collection of scientific instruments.[246] Johann Helfrich Müller never got round to building a difference engine, despite the fact that his offer was widely publicized and even found its way to England.

1.3 The method of differences

The method of differences, the mathematical principle embodied in the difference engines, can be used for the computation of most mathematical and other numerical tables. By this method intermediate tabular terms can be interpolated, by the use of differences, when some terms of a series at equal distances within an interval are known. In other words, a table of e.g. logarithms may be calculated by addition only, once the start values are known.

Little has been written about the history of the method of differences. It was probably known already in ancient times, although tradition says that it was first developed and used by Henry Briggs in 1624 in his construction of logarithms and other numbers.[1] Other table computers adopted the method and it was presented in a new form in 1687 by Isaac Newton in his *Principia*.[2] In 1711, Newton's friend the mathematician William Jones published his *Methodus Differentialis*, and in 1730 appeared another book with the same title, written by James Stirling.[3] But, despite mathematical and notational variations, the basic principles of the method were nevertheless the same. The method of differences was successfully adopted by a number of producers of numercial tables in the following decades. The present section will present the basic ideas of this mathematical principle.

Let me begin with a simple example. Suppose we wish to make a table showing the values of the polynomial $f(x)=x^2$. We begin by calculating the function for a number of integers x.

x	f(x)
1	1
2	4
3	9
4	16

From this tiny bit of the table, the differences between successive function values f(x), the so-called *first differences* $\Delta 1$ (delta one) can be calculated. When this has been done, we can proceed to compute the *second differences* $\Delta 2$, that is to say the differences between successive values $\Delta 1$.

x	f(x)	$\Delta 1$	$\Delta 2$
1	1		
		3	
2	4		2
		5	
3	9		2
		7	
4	16		

Observe that the second difference is constant, and equal to 2, for the polynomial $f(x)=x^2$. We can now by using the above *difference scheme* calculate as much of the table as we desire — and this by addition alone. In actual fact, only the underlined numbers above, the *start values*, are required. Addition is then carried out according to the arrows in the following scheme.

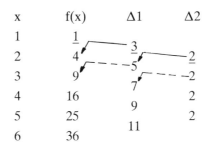

x	f(x)	$\Delta 1$	$\Delta 2$
1	1		
		3	
2	4		2
		5	
3	9		2
		7	
4	16		2
		9	
5	25		2
		11	
6	36		

The simple basic idea of the method is to use certain start values, which first must be computed, to calculate a series of tabular values by means of addition. It is this second part of the work, the sequence of additions according to a pattern, which is mechanized in a difference engine.

The method is ideally suited for polynomials, because these always have a constant difference. In the case of a polynomial of degree two, the second difference is constant, in the case of a polynomial of degree three, the third difference is constant and so on. Sometimes, the differences for a given function are negative. By making use instead of the number's arithmetical complement, addition alone can still be used. For manual calculation with the method this is not important, because subtractions can be quite easily done. But this possibility simplifies a difference engine to a large extent, since the mechanisms for subtraction become obsolete. An example involving a negative number shows how this works.

$$768$$
$$-351$$
$$\overline{417} \quad \text{Answer.}$$

The arithmetical complement to the number 351 is 649; that is to say 649 = 1000−351. Now let us instead add the complement to 768.

$$768$$
$$+649$$
$$\overline{1417} \quad \text{Ignore the first digit,}$$
$$417 \quad \text{Answer.}$$

The operation might be also explained like this: 768−351 = 768+1000−351−1000 = 768+649−1000 = 417. In other words, the result of this two stage operation, is a subtraction of the number 351. In a difference engine this can be achieved very simply by letting the engine lack the wheel corresponding to (in this case) the third power of ten.

Let me give another example of the advantages of the method. Consider the difference scheme corresponding to the polynomial $f(x)=4x^4 + 3x^3 + 5x^2 + 8x + 1$.

x	f(x)	Δ1	Δ2	Δ3	Δ4
1	21				
		104			
2	125		246		
		350		258	
3	475		504		96
		854		354	
4	1329		858		96
		1712		450	
5	3041		1308		
		3020			
6	6061				

The method of differences allows us by changing the sign of the odd differences (Δ1 and Δ3, underlined) to "work backwards" and thus calculate the start values we began with. This is useful when using a difference engine for checking whether the start valus were put in correctly at the beginning. But as will be shown below, this possibility has a more general application. The result of such a backward calculation is shown in the following difference scheme, where only the signs of the odd differences have to be changed, once the calculation is completed.

72

x	f(x)	Δ1	Δ2	Δ3	Δ4
6	6061				
		−3020			
5	3041		1308		
		−1712		−450	
4	1329		858		96.
		−854		−354	
3	475		504		96
		−350		−258	
2	125		246		
		−104			
1	21				

The most interesting functions, for which tables are required, are however not polynomials but transcendental functions, such as the logarithmic and trigonometric functions. These do not possess constant differences. Nevertheless, they can be calculated by the method of differences. This is done by approximating the transcendental function in a given interval by a polynomial. The preliminary work of finding the required polynomial takes place "outside of the engine".[4] It lies beyond the scope of this book to enter into the mathematical details of the method of differences but the following basic facts should be mentioned. Suppose first of all that the transcendental function to be tabulated, call it f(x), can be approximated by a polynomial of degree four:

$$f(x) = k + ax + bx^2 + cx^3 + dx^4$$

The problem is to determine the coefficients k, a, b, c and d. This is done by solving a set of linear equations.[5] The polynomial thus obtained only approximates the transcendental function in the given interval. For a different interval, a different polynomial can be obtained.

The kernel of the method is to be able to interpolate, i.e. to compute the values of a function at certain selected points within the given interval. A final example will show how Briggs and his fellow table computers might have used the method. Imagine that the task is to compute a table of logarithms to the base 10, for the interval [1, 10], to five decimal places. Also imagine that we are limited to differences of the fourth degree. (As will be discussed later, Scheutz' second and third engine had a mathematical capacity limited to differences of the fourth degree). In order to be able to start at some point in the table, the logarithms for five equidistant values have to be found. We may choose to start with the ones for x=2.6, x=2.8, x=3.0, x=3.2 and x=3.4, calculated to seven places of decimals. These can easily be obtained with the logarithmic rules (p. 21), once certain initial values of logarithms are known, or have been calculated according to some mathematical method. Having the five necessary functional values, we can write up the difference scheme below.

x	f(x)	Δ1	Δ2	Δ3	Δ4
2.6	0.4149733				
		0.0321847			
2.8	0.4471580		−0.0022214		
		0.0299633		0.0002868	
3.0	0.4771213		−0.0019346		−0.0000520
		0.0280287		0.0002348	
3.2	0.5051500		−0.0016998		
		0.0263289			
3.4	0.5314789				

From the scheme we obtain:

$$f(3.0) = 0.4771213$$
$$\Delta 1_{f2.8} = 0.0299633$$
$$\Delta 2_{f2.8} = -0.0019346$$
$$\Delta 3_{f2.6} = 0.0002868$$
$$\Delta 4_{f2.6} = -0.0000520$$

These are the differences which are necessary for calculating the polynomial which will be used for approximating the logarithmic function in the interval [2.6, 3.4]. Once this is done, the start values for interpolation e.g. with step 0.005 can be obtained:

$$f(3.000) = 0.4771213$$
$$\Delta 1_{f2.995} = 7.244172204 \cdot 10^{-4}$$
$$\Delta 2_{f2.995} = -1.206418361 \cdot 10^{-6}$$
$$\Delta 3_{f2.990} = 4.085156252 \cdot 10^{-9}$$
$$\Delta 4_{f2.990} = -2.031250001 \cdot 10^{-11}$$

With these start values and the application of the difference method, 80 logarithms for x in the interval [3.0, 3.4] are obtained.

x	f(x)	Δ1	Δ2	Δ3	Δ4
		$7.244172204 \cdot 10^{-4}$		$4.085156252 \cdot 10^{-9}$	
3.000	0.4771213		$-1.206418361 \cdot 10^{-6}$		$-2.031250001 \cdot 10^{-11}$
		$7.232108020 \cdot 10^{-4}$		$4.064843752 \cdot 10^{-9}$	
3.005	0.4778445		$-1.202353517 \cdot 10^{-6}$		$-2.031250001 \cdot 10^{-11}$
		$7.220084485 \cdot 10^{-4}$		$4.044531252 \cdot 10^{-9}$	
3.010	0.4785665		$-1.198308986 \cdot 10^{-6}$		$-2.031250001 \cdot 10^{-11}$
		$7.208101395 \cdot 10^{-4}$		$4.024218752 \cdot 10^{-9}$	
3.015	0.4792873		$-1.194284767 \cdot 10^{-6}$		$-2.031250001 \cdot 10^{-11}$
		$7.196158547 \cdot 10^{-4}$		$4.003906252 \cdot 10^{-9}$	
3.020	0.4800069		$-1.190280861 \cdot 10^{-6}$		
		$7.184255738 \cdot 10^{-4}$			
3.025	0.4807254				
etc.					

74

By changing the signs of the odd differences and by going backwards, (that is adding in the normal way), the remaining 80 logarithms for x in the interval [2.6, 3.0] are produced.

Thereafter by calculating new start values for a new partition of the interval we are able to get in a similar fashion another piece of the required table. By making forward and backward computations, the complete logarithm table for [1, 10], can be obtained correctly to five decimal places and in steps of 0.005.

This is, in brief, the practical procedure for operating with the method of differences, whether it is done manually or by machine. It should be noted however, that the process of calculating the start values involving several digit numbers (>15 decimals) is both cumbersone and time consuming. Since a numerical series is generated, one of the advantages of the method is that a computed function value can be picked out at random and compared with a known value. If there is no discrepancy, this means that all the previously computed values are also correct. An example is when five positions of a star are known through observations made at five evenings in a row. A table showing the position of the star for every hour can be made with the help of the method of differences. If this is done, and the initial and the final position of the star in the table are identical to the observed ones, then the whole calculation has been carried out correctly.

Certain other facts about the method should be noted. First, the higher the order of differences that is available, the greater the number of correct digits that can be obtained in the answer. Secondly, if it is wished to have more correct digits in the answer, a shorter interval of interpolation has to be chosen. If a large number of correct digits is required, but the machine lacks high-order differences, this can still be accomplished by inserting new start values more often.

In spite of the fact that the method of differences facilitated the production of tables by reducing the basic operations involved to addition, it is clear that with only paper and pencil at one's disposal, the monotonous work of calculation remained. The production of a table page, see Fig. 4, according to the method required in itself more than 1,000 additions involving several digit numbers. (Here the preparatory calculation of the start values is not included). Both Müller and Babbage realized that the method could be mechanized. Only Babbage, however, had the motive and opportunity to continue the project further – "to throw the process of thought into wheel work".[6]

1.4 The Difference Engine No. 1

"Pray, Mr. Babbage, if you put into the machine wrong figures, will the right answers come out?"[1]

This question, which was put to a somewhat astonished Babbage on two occasions by members of Parliament, serves to introduce a discussion of the technology involved in the Difference Engine No. 1. The mode of operation and design, will be further analyzed in section 3.1. Here, two aspects are primarily dealt with. First, the part of the calculating unit assembled in 1833 will be described, mainly to explain its underlying mathematical principles. Secondly, something will be said about the projected large engine which was never completed.

The part of the difference engine that was put together has been preserved and is shown in Fig. 11. The machine is on display in the Science Museum in London. Despite the fact that it was only a fraction of the calculating unit, it is still referred to as the (complete) engine. As the picture shows, it was a beautiful piece of machinery, made in shining bronze and steel. Its weight can be estimated at around 200 kilos. It is 650 mm high (including the wooden base), 440 mm broad and 300 mm deep. The diameter of the number wheels is 60 mm and their height is 35 mm. In other words, it is quite a large machine, and although not complete, it was the largest calculating machine hitherto made.

When Babbage and his men assembled the engine, they apparently did so with the idea that it would serve as a kind of summary or indication of the complete projected engine. For demonstration purposes, the engine was equipped with certain special adjustment possibilities, which probably would have been omitted from the complete engine. The machine was divided into three columns, each one containing six compartments for the number wheels, as can be seen in Fig. 13. These wheels were numbered from 0 to 9 and could be positioned by hand. The left column represented the second difference, the column in the middle the first difference, and the column on the right the result f(x). In the illustration all the wheels are set at zero. For the moment, the reader can neglect the bottom number wheels in the columns at the right and in the centre.[2] The three uppermost wheels in the column at the right were not coupled to the engine, but could be set in an arbitrary fashion to function as a memory device. Finally, the three uppermost wheels in the left column, were so connected to the engine that they functioned as a counter for the argument x, i.e. they showed the number of calculations that had been carried out.[3] There remain three wheels in the left column for the second difference, five wheels in the middle column for the first difference and five wheels in the column at the right, for the result. The number indicated by the number wheels is read by starting at the top and going down; in other words, the lowest power was situated at the bottom.

From the hand lever, which can be seen in the upper left corner of the

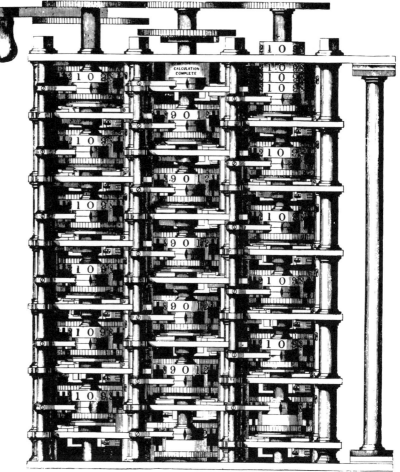

Impression from a woodcut of a small portion of Mr. Babbage's Difference
Engine, No. 1, the property of Government, at present deposited in the
Museum of King's College, Somerset House.

It was commenced 1823.

This portion put together 1833.

The construction abandoned 1842.

This plate was printed, June, 1853.

*Fig. 13 Drawing by Babbage's son Benjamin Herschel Babbage showing the position of the
number wheels in the Difference Engine No. 1. This drawing was reprinted in Babbage's*
Passages from the Life of a Philosopher.

woodcut, the motive force was transmitted via gears, so that the engine
operated in four steps. Compare them with the difference scheme shown
on page 71:

1. The first difference was added to the result column.
2. Carrying took place in the result column.
3. The second difference was added to the first difference.
4. Carrying took place in the first difference.

77

Babbage had designed the engine in accordance with two main principles. The first was that it should be highly reliable i.e. work smoothly without jamming. Secondly, the mechanical resistance in the engine, which arose for example when a number wheel was rotated, should be minimal. To achieve these ends, the internal workings of the engine had been supplied with special mechanisms. Great reliability was guaranteed by building the engine very carefully with very fine tolerances and an extremely high surface finish. A special system ensured that the number wheels could not be set at a point between two numbers. A second system corrected such an error in the event of it still occurring. If this second system failed to perform as intended, the engine locked. A catch finally prevented the number wheel from rotating in the wrong direction. In order to minimize the forces, which was an important consideration in the larger engine, the mechanical resistance was distributed. Thus the addition, for example, of a three-figure second difference to the first difference took place sequentially, one figure at a time, beginning with the lowest power. As a consequence only one addition from one wheel to another, occurred at a time. The idea behind this was to prevent an increase in mechanical resistance that might arise if several numbers were added. In adding one column to another, carrying occurred later. Here again the forces were reduced by carrying the appropriate unit from one number wheel to the wheel situated directly above it, and only then to the wheel above the latter. Babbage's idea of serial or step-by-step addition was new. As far as its application to carrying goes, it was a matter of necessity since carrying had to take place successively from the lower to the higher powers.

The calculating unit of the Difference Engine No. 1 also contained a number of refinements. Bells rang when a wheel passed from 9 to 0. This was useful because it signalled when it was time to insert a new start value. The bells could also be used to indicate zeros in the solution of equations or to draw attention to a change of sign. It was also to some extent possible to couple the number wheel in one column to the number wheel next to it, in the column on its left. Addition could then take place from right to left in Fig. 13, i.e. from the lower difference to the next one above (i.e. from $\Delta 1$ to $\Delta 2$). In the section of the engine displayed in the figure, this capability has been used to show that the engine could calculate with three differences. Here the bottom wheel in the centre column has been coupled to the left column. The engine thus acquired a single-figure third order difference which was then added to the second order difference simultaneously with step 1 in the foregoing engine cycle.

The engine was supplied with an extra kit consisting of a pair of vertical axles, with cogwheels which could be mounted at the front of the engine, see Fig. 11. This was intended to be used to demonstrate a mathematical formula that Babbage had discovered, relating to the fact that for certain tabular functions, the second difference was not constant but was a function of the tabular function. The additional kit allowed one to calculate such functions, by supplying the second difference with the result.

The calculating unit in the complete Difference Engine No. 1, would probably have only differed in minor respects from the part assembled in 1833, with regard to the basic principles involved but it would have been capable of calculating with higher orders of differences, and with a larger number of digits. In purely physical terms, the complete engine would obviously have been much bigger, but its work cycle would have been identical to that of the smaller unit. Only a reformulation of the four steps is required:

1. Odd differences are added to even ones and to the result.
2. Carrying takes place in the even differences and in the result.
3. Even differences are added to the odd.
4. Carrying takes place in the odd differences.

It appears as if Charles Babbage did not initially determine the mathematical capacity of the engine. He only describes it as being intended as "a larger engine". Shortly after his letter to Sir Humphry Davy, a close friend of Babbage wrote that the engine was being made to calculate with four orders of differences.[4] The number of digits was not mentioned. In 1829 the machine was said to be able to operate with sixth order differences, 12 digits, and to print 16 digits in the result (allowing for probably four in the argument).[5] At some point Babbage settled for six orders of differences, but the number of digits continued to vary, depending on the author. 18 digits are mentioned in 1834 and as an old man Babbage himself said that the whole engine would have been capable of calculating with 20 places of digits.[6] Perhaps this increase in capacity over the years, reflects a growing awareness of the relationship between the number of differences and the amount of digits, necessary for the optimum performance of a difference engine.

Fig. 14 shows a drawing of the complete difference engine, made in 1830. It provides a good illustration of the probable appearance of the projected large engine.[7] To the left is the calculating unit and to the right, the printing unit and parts of the power transmission system. In the calculating unit there are seven vertical axles, with the sixth order difference farthest to the left and the result at the right. From top to bottom this machine contains 16 compartments, with a number wheel in each, which would suggest yet another intended digit capacity. The size of the finished engine, as it is seen in the drawing, is roughly 2,600 mm high, 2,300 mm broad, and 1,000 mm deep.[8] Its weight would have been over 2 tons. The calculating part alone would have been 7 times larger than the little unit that was assembled.

The matrices for the stereotyping of the tables would have been produced in the printing unit. The result was to be taken from the result column in the calculating unit and transferred to the printing unit. There, eleven steel punches were supposed to print the result and argument in a

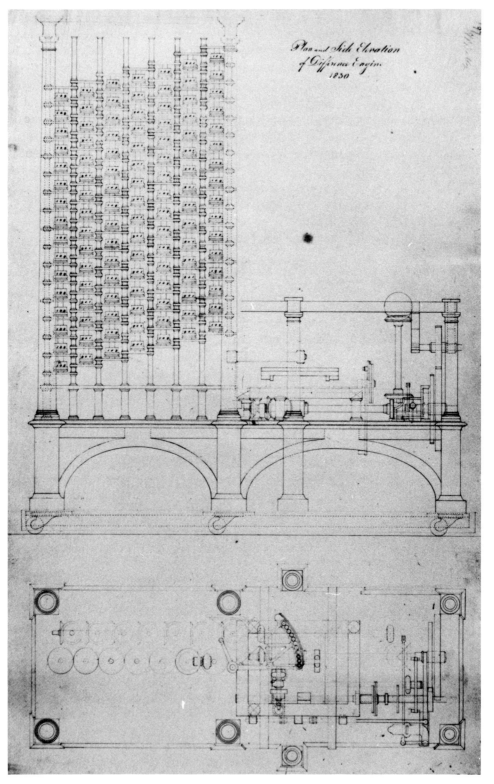

Fig. 14 "Plan and Side Elevation of Difference Engine 1830". Drawing of Babbage's complete engine, with 16 figures and six orders of differences, and the printing unit. Original drawing kept in the Babbage collection in the Science Museum Library, London. Photograph by courtesy of the Trustees of the Science Museum, London.

copper plate.[9] The punches or types, were intended to be mounted on a circular sector, which can be seen in the figure. Thus the crude idea of having 30,000 types in boxes, had finally been abandoned. A coordinate board under the types was able to move the copper plate in two orthogonal directions in its plane. Using this design, a numerical table page of normal appearance could be obtained. It is not known whether Babbage envisaged having some of the number wheels perform the task of advancing the argument, or if he planned to have a special device for this in the printing unit. In some way or other, the argument was to have emerged and have been printed beside the function value.

In reality, no printing unit and not even all of the finished calculating mechanisms were ever put together. To Babbage's enemies, the assembled fraction of the engine became the embodiment of the Utopian in his ideas. To his supporters, the engine stood as a great monument over man's ingenuity and ability to mechanize all kinds of labour. The idea was too important and exciting to be forgotten. Babbage's exertions brought in their wake considerable publicity, which was an important factor in keeping the idea alive. Another factor was naturally the problem itself. A handful of inventors, all with different backgrounds, were to try during the course of the 19th century to build difference engines according to their own ideas. One of these was Pehr Georg Scheutz.

2. SCHEUTZ AND THE SWEDISH DIFFERENCE ENGINES

2.1 Georg Scheutz, auditor, journalist and inventor

During the 1820s and almost at the same time as Babbage, Georg Scheutz turned his attention to technology. He had spent some time as a political journalist in opposition to the status quo. Now technology was to become his main weapon in his struggle to develop and improve Swedish society. His role was to be that of a disseminator of technology in his native land which, comparatively speaking, was still underdeveloped as regards its industry. To this end, he read all that he could about the rapid changes in the field and presented the most useful foreign ideas to the Swedish public in books and technical journals which were the first general magazines of their kind in the country.

Pehr Georg Scheutz was born in Jönköping on the 23rd of September 1785. His father, Fredrik Christian Ludvig Schieutz, was born in Copenhagen of German parents.[1] Together with his wife, Johanna Christina Berg, he ran the popular inn and wine merchant's business Fortuna in Jönköping.[2] Besides the inn, Fredrik Schieutz was responsible for providing refreshment for the guests at Medevi Spring, the most frequented spa in the country at that time. In the summertime, some 250 to 300 guests had to be served daily. Since Jönköping lay on the main road between southern Sweden and Stockholm, great numbers of Swedish and foreign travellers of every class of society passed the Schieutz inn on their way, and not a few spent a night there. It was in this stimulating, cosmopolitan spot at the southern end of Lake Vättern that Georg Scheutz, his parents' only son, grew up.

When he was about seven years old, Georg Scheutz began to receive instruction at home from G. V. Alander the associate headmaster of Jönköping's elementary school. This consisted mainly of accompanying Alander who was both interested and well read in natural science, on his various trips about the town and its surroundings. There were several foreign craftsmen living in Jönköping, among them an engraver of seals, a plaster cast maker and a maker of barometers. It was by visiting them, that the young Georg was initiated into the secrets of craftsmanship as well as the rudiments of physics and chemistry. Since his father was also involved in various engineering projects in the town it is clear that Georg was brought into contact with technology in various forms at an early age.

In 1796, when he was eleven years old, Georg Scheutz entered Jönköping elementary school. There he followed the normal course of instruction, which included theology, history and political geography and in addition he made the acquaintance of the classical authors. His school performance was by no means exceptional and he himself maintained − no doubt with a certain modesty − that he just managed to keep up with his companions. Afterwards Scheutz moved on to the Gymnasium in Wexiö where the subjects on the curriculum were much the same as before. However his interest in languages which had been awakened by Alander now received fresh stimulus. He read the New Testament in Greek and even picked up − somewhat outside the normal routine − a fair amount of Hebrew. Botany and mechanics were also studied, but to a lesser extent. The main emphasis of Scheutz' schooling was on languages and the humanities and this was to be of great use to him in his future career. It is also certain that he read a great deal about other subjects in his spare time. His wide interests and love of reading distinguished him at an early stage from his companions. One of his friends wrote:

"Already as a boy, he was something of a peculiar phenomenon among the rest of us, because his games usually took the form of physical experiments in which he made use of optics, electricity and chemistry."[3]

Scheutz matriculated at the University of Lund on the 12th of December 1794.[4] But he first began to study there in the autumn of 1803. Scheutz' intention was to take a law degree as a preparation for *bergsexamen* − the qualification required for more senior posts in mining − for this had become his main goal. He soon discovered, however, that the University of Lund was not the right place for training as a mining engineer. He nevertheless stayed on at the university and passed his examinations with flying colours, finally obtaining his law degree in 1805. His studies had included algebra and of course Latin. In 1800 his father had died and in order to pay his way, Scheutz had been compelled to tutor junior students. Before the estate was finally settled, Scheutz' mother was short of money, but she did what she could to help him by sending clothes.

Instead of immediately proceeding towards bergsexamen, Scheutz devoted himself to the law. In 1805, when he was around twenty years old, he became probationer at Göta Hovrätt in his home town. At various times, he also served as deputy actuary, provisional magistrate and on one occasion as mayor in Ulricehamn. After five years of legal work, an opportunity arose to take bergsexamen in Uppsala. He satisfied the entrance requirements but since he lacked the means to live in Uppsala for a longer period, he asked if the preparatory part of the course might be

Fig. 15 Pehr Georg Scheutz (1785-1873).

shortened.[5] After Scheutz' knowledge had been tested, the professors in mathematics and physics were prepared to go along with his request. The assistant in chemistry took the same line but his professor refused to budge and even refused to allow Scheutz to be examined in order to test his competence in the subject. When Georg Scheutz looked back on this episode in 1847, he noted that "it was the worst piece of misfortune to befall him; he had experienced deeper sorrows that had shaken him to the core, but none had been more bitter and irrevocable than this".[6] If there had been the Mining School in Falun or the School in Marieberg to turn to (he wrote) he would have sought admission there.

The partly state-subsidized Mining School in Falun was not inaugurated until 1822. In contrast to the universities, it was more practical in its approach to mining engineering.[7] The Artillery School at Marieberg in

Stockholm which dated from 1818, was a military school of well known international type, which provided instruction in technical and scientific subjects. It was opened to civilian applicants in 1842, but the intake was restricted to four per year. They were trained as civil engineers, responsible for the building of roads and dams.[8] In other words, if Scheutz had been able to choose, he would have chosen the career of the more practical type of engineer.

In 1811 Scheutz moved to Stockholm where he was employed in the chancellery of "Justitie-Revisionen för Sjöärendena", the body charged with the preliminary investigation of Supreme Court cases dealing with maritime affairs. His mother had died of consumption in the winter of 1809 and around Christmas 1811, two aunts who had been close to him, also passed away – circumstances which led him to return to Jönköping to sell off various properties.[9] He soon found a buyer, who was willing to pay 5,758 riksdaler banco for the house.[10] He also sold three acres of land and movable property for 588 riksdaler banco.[11] In total, Scheutz inherited about 1,000 pounds.

From these sales, after various debts had been paid off, Scheutz acquired an initial capital which would later be put to good use. In 1812, he served as deputy actuary in his native town, but he longed to return to Stockholm. "I am being worn down in this boring small town", he wrote.[12] At the close of 1812, he left the place of his childhood and moved to Stockholm.

Stockholm, the capital of Sweden, was of course the country's political and administrative centre. In this old town, perched on the Baltic and Lake Mälaren, Scheutz was to find not only stimulus but also his livelihood. Here too were all the necessary preconditions, whether social, political, scientific, technical or cultural, for ensuring that his interest in designing a table printing engine would find an outlet. Stockholm was the seat of the King and *Riksdag* – the Swedish Parliament. Every few years, the four Estates – the Nobles, the Clergy, the Burghers and the Peasants – met to discuss in closed debate, issues affecting the internal and external policy of the realm.

Though considerably larger than any other town in the country, Stockholm was with its 72,000 inhabitants, a small city by international standards. Only some three kilometres from north to south, all the administrative and prominent buildings were concentrated in an even smaller area. Among the institutions located in the city was the Royal Academy of Sciences. It had been founded in June 1739, in imitation of its English and French predecessors. Among its more internationally famous members were numbered Carl von Linné, Per Wilhelm Wargentin and Anders Celsius.[13] Right from the very start, the Academy published *Swenska Wetenskaps Akademiens Handlingar* (Proceedings of the Royal Swedish Academy of Sciences) which covered a great range of subjects from purely scientific contributions to essays on the most utilitarian of topics. These were studied carefully by Scheutz who also attended the

Academy's yearly series of lectures where the latest ideas in astronomy, geology, physics, chemistry and other subjects were taken up for discussion by its members.[14] On a hill in the city was situated the Academy's Observatory, which had been inaugurated in 1753.

The rapid technical and organizational changes, which decades before had radically altered British trade and industry, had still to reach Sweden. Three quarters of the population worked on the land, and urban life was still dominated by the guilds. Even in the field of textile manufacture, there was nothing comparable to the industrial production then current in England.[15] The greatest changes did not take place until after 1870, but the whole of the nineteenth century was characterized by an increase in industrial growth.[16] During the first decades of the century, the enterprises were small and the methods employed, those of craftsmen. In 1811, there were 456 "industries" in the Stockholm region. In all, they employed some 1,925 people – in other words, an average of four people to each.[17] In the same fashion, according to the statistics there were 35 "clock factories" with a total of 48 employees.[18] Nevertheless it was a time of change when Scheutz arrived in Stockholm. In 1785, the engineer Charles Apelquist, who had received part of his training in England, had founded one of Stockholm's first mechanical workshops. In it, machines of iron, wood, steel and brass, including for example lathes, were made to order.[19] In 1809 the workshop premises were taken over by the Englishman Samuel Owen, who some years before had come to Stockholm with four steam engines from England. It had not taken long before Owen was known throughout the city, because he began to build – among other things – steamboats at his foundry and workshop. The first Swedish steamboat, "Amphitrite", made its maiden voyage on Mälaren in 1818.[20]

The city had much to offer in the way of culture as well. There were the Opera and "Kungliga Mindre Teatern", for which there were no counterparts in Scheutz' home town. Moreover, with the end to the royal monopoly over theatrical production, Scheutz had further opportunities for developing his artistic gifts. In Stockholm's Palace were to be found the rich collections of Kungliga Biblioteket (Royal Library), which was Sweden's national library. There, Scheutz was able to retreat to peace and quiet. Its librarian, the journalist Per Adam Wallmark, provided him with both advice and support and became with the passage of years a true friend.[21]

Yet Stockholm had also its negative sides. The town was very dirty and had enormous problems in public hygiene arising from deficiencies in sanitation and sewage, and the supply of clean drinking water. Mortality was high – higher than most of the cities in Europe – and it was not until the end of the 19th century that the city's death statistics dropped to more normal levels.[22] It was only through the continuous inflow of people from other parts of the country, that Stockholm was able to preserve the size of its population.

Scheutz was appointed second auditor with the Svea Artillery Regiment and in November 1814, he received "Royal authorization as Auditeur". This type of post carried with it more honour than money, which led Scheutz on the 5th of June 1816 to resign. He had given eleven years of his life to the Law and now he left it for ever.

In politics, Scheutz, like Babbage, was early drawn to Liberalism, an ideology which drew its support from the ranks of journalists, writers, lawyers, industrialists and financiers.[23] The new and growing middle class was attracted by notions such as individual freedom, free competition and the promotion of education and culture. Those ideas had caught the imagination of the young Scheutz who in the course of his legal career had seen the abuses of power and privilege at first hand. Now he sought to counteract the ruling conservatism and began to propagate for free trade, the right to a choice of work, the diminution of the powers of the state and increased public insight into matters of law and legislation.[24] Above all, he was interested in education, culture and practical knowledge.[25] His weapon in the struggle for his ideals was to be the press.

In 1816, the author and printer Fredrik Cederborgh had begun to publish the newspaper *Anmärkaren* (the Remarker). At the time, Stockholm had around ten newspapers and Cederborgh's was known for its criticism of the Establishment. Right from the start, Scheutz had been interested in it and had also been actively involved in it. Because of his legal experience and liberal ideals, he had perceived the possibilities of the press. Thanks to the money he had inherited, he was able to buy Cederborgh's printing press — one of Stockholm's eighteen printing

Fig. 16 In November 1820 Georg Scheutz published the first issue of Argus: Political, Literary and commercial Newspaper. Argus had one of the largest circulations among contemporary Swedish newspapers. It was Scheutz' preoccupation with politically oriented newspapers, like Argus, that lead him eventually to publish Sweden's first general technical magazines.

presses in private hands – and on the 11th of October 1817 he became joint owner-cum-editor of *Anmärkaren*.

With Scheutz as editor and columnist, *Anmärkaren* rapidly became popular. Its circulation trebled during 1817-1820. His articles on the Wermdö case (which involved police violence), and other examples of the legal abuse of power, became renowned. However, despite this success, there were problems. The new laws of 1812 relating to the freedom of the press gave the authorities the right to withdraw the publisher's licence. In practice, this meant that the freedom of the press was severely curtailed. If the Court Chamberlain considered that a newspaper contained something unsuitable, he could withdraw the publisher's licence. Journalists soon discovered however, that they could get round this by changing the name of their newspaper and by taking out a new licence, in a new name. When in January 1820, the Chamberlain intervened against *Anmärkaren* because it had become too sharp in its criticisms, Scheutz was prepared. Two days later, the newspaper was back on sale under the name *Anmärkarne* (the Remarkers).[26] *Anmärkarne* was more openly critical than its predecessor, and in it Scheutz directed his main attack against protectionism. In November 1820, it changed its name to *Argus: Politisk, Litterär och Commersiell Tidning* (Argus: political, literary and commercial newspaper). *Argus* had one of the largest circulations among contemporary newspapers.[27] Scheutz worked on it, first as editor but latterly only as publisher, until 1836.[28] Thereafter, his career as a political journalist gave way more and more to his technical and scientific interests. This interesting period in the history of Swedish newspapers cannot, however, be considered in detail here. On the role of Georg Scheutz, a contemporary journalist had the following to say:

"Georg Scheutz was the first Swedish newspaper publisher after 1809, to emerge with a definite political stance, and to pursue not literary or economic goals but a clear political one."[29]

The purchase of Cederborgh's press marked a new phase in Scheutz' life. His career had become one of printer and journalist. This was to be relevant to the history of the Swedish difference engines in three ways. First, his preoccupation with *Anmärkaren* and its successors, led him eventually to publish Sweden's first general technical magazines. This pioneer work compelled him to keep abreast of technical developments in Europe and America. Secondly, it meant that on an everyday level, he had to master all the aspects of printing technology – the machines, tools and methods that were involved. This led him to make his own inventions. Thirdly, his liberal anti-Establishment critique was to have important repercussions for the financing of the Swedish difference engine.

Scheutz' striving to improve training and practical skills in the country is evident in the technical magazines which he published. The work involved with them, gave a fresh impulse to his innate leaning towards technology and science. From May 1825 to December 1826 and from January 1833 to December 1834 he published, on his own initiative and at his own expense, the monthly *Journal för Manufakturer och Hushåll-ning*.[30] This magazine contained descriptions of useful inventions and discoveries in physics, chemistry and technology, which could be simply put to practical use by the intended readers — cottagers and tradesmen. Both domestic and foreign ideas were presented in an elementary but thorough fashion. There was a great deal of work behind every article, since Scheutz made a point of reading a large number of European technical magazines, among them *London Journal of Arts and Sciences*, *Mechanics Magazine* (London), *Gill's Technical Repository* (London), *Repertory of Arts, Manufactures, and Agriculture* (London), *Journal des Connaissances Usuelles et Practiques* (Paris), *Journal de Physique* (Paris), and *Dinglers Polytechnisches Journal* (Augsburg).[31] Foreign books also provided substance for Scheutz' articles. The pieces which appeared in *Journal för Manufakturer och Hushållning* covered a wide spectrum of topics, from improved steam engines and spinning machines, to practical hinges and French polishing. Scheutz carried out all the work involved himself. It was he who tracked down and read the articles, determined what use they could be put to, checked their correctness and finally made the translations.

After the twelfth number of *Journal för Manufakturer och Hushållning* in December of 1834, Scheutz discontinued publication. The reason for this was that the Swedish Industrial Association, which had been founded in 1832, decided to publish its own journal — *Svenska Industriföreningens*

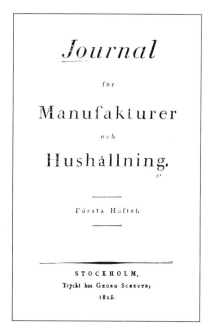

Fig. 17 At his own initiative and expense Georg Scheutz published his monthly Journal för Manufakturer och Hushållning. *It was in this journal, in November 1833, that the Swedish public were first introduced to Charles Babbage's difference engine.*

Tidskrift.[32] This, at any rate, was the way Scheutz himself explained matters. But it is plausible that he had more to do both with the founding of the Association and the new journal than he reveals. He duly became editor and publisher and was in addition chosen, in January of 1836, to be the Association's permanent secretary.[33] The first issue appeared in December 1834, and the journal continued publication on a monthly basis. In character, it was similar to its predecessor but it also contained reports on the development of Swedish industry, as well as information about new legislation of importance for industry. With the support of the Association, Scheutz was able to make use of the finest paper in the country for the publication of the journal.[34]

The fact that something like the Swedish Industrial Association had been formed in the first place, deserves comment. It illustrates the increased interest, shown by Scheutz and others in industrial production. Very little is known about the Association but according to its statutes, its purpose was to further the growth and improvement of Swedish industry, in part by bringing together the country's industrialists and manufacturers, and in part by disseminating knowledge of domestic and foreign ideas about production methods, machinery etc.[35]

The Association met every Tuesday. Among its 158 members in 1834, there were officers, doctors, professors, merchants and engineers, all with a common interest in industrial production. The old order of mill owners and guildrymen rubbed shoulders with the emerging class of manufacturers and "owners of Mechanical Factories". It was a microcosm of the change taking place in Swedish society. Those engaged in textiles formed the largest group while there were very few representing mechanical workshops (approx. 3%). The vast majority carried on their business in the city.[36]

The first major step taken by the Association to bring itself to the public's attention, was to arrange an exhibition in Stockholm in 1834, "to provide a survey of the present state of Swedish Industry".[37] Similar exhibitions were common in France and England, but apart from a more modest experiment in Stockholm in 1823, the Association's exhibition was the first of its kind in the country.[38] The results however, were disappointing. Despite the fact that advertisements to prospective participants appeared thirteen months before the opening day, in June 1834, less than 250 manufacturers had answered positively. This figure can appear high, but according to Scheutz and his colleagues, it was quite deceptive. It had only been achieved after repeated advertisement and by extending the final date of application. Everything had been devised to win a good response from people in industry: a palace in Stockholm which was without a doubt the best site in the country, had been chosen to host the exhibition and the exhibition had been timed to coincide with a sitting of the Riksdag.[39]

According to Scheutz, the exhibition failed to catch on for two reasons – "prejudices of various kinds, and a certain Swedish national characteristic". Among the former was the fact that many people connected with industry looked on the very idea of exhibiting, as a kind of "boast" and either did not participate at all, or else avoided putting their name up on a plaque, something that would have been incomprehensible abroad.[40] As for the national characteristic, Scheutz maintained that the Swede in general lacked "the known talent of *bringing his goods to the market*, which the foreigner usually possesses to a high degree and which we, however, alas to our ruin, almost despise".[41] Scheutz developed this thought further:

> "A Swedish craftsman who has carried out a good piece of work, often believes that it is enough to have done it. He knows that the product is good, but he often does not care if others know it. Instead of 'bringing his goods to the market' in a purposeful way, so that he receives not only reward for his industry or his ingenuity but also what is of chief importance, the stimulus to fresh endeavour, he vegetates impotently in the shade, unnoticed, unpaid, often struggling with embarrassment, and sometimes even with harsh poverty itself; and the skills he has acquired, the ideas he has put forward, and all the inventions due to him, are often lost to the trade or perish and are forgotten with his passing."[42]

It is clear that there were real problems in getting manufacturers to exhibit their products. The Stockholm industrial exhibition of 1828 arranged by the Royal Technological Institute had been even more of a fiasco.[43] With 20 days to go before opening, no applications had come in from prospective exhibitors. The final date of application was extended with little result. The whole thing was called off when it became clear that only 13 exhibitors had responded. The Industrial Association continued its activities, and the indefatigable Scheutz published its journal until December 1839, when for some unknown reason the journal suddenly ceased.[44] In November of the following year, Scheutz began to publish a new magazine series of the same kind. It was called *Tidning för Näringarne*. As its predecessors, it was printed at the Scheutz press, but one alteration had been made. Instead of appearing every month, it came out every week, which meant that it was able to react more swiftly to events, and to include readers' contributions and public announcements. *Tidning för Näringarne* was a continuation of *Svenska Industriföreningens Tidskrift*, wrote Scheutz, but he stressed that he alone was responsible for the journal and its choice of articles.[45] It ran for thirteen months altogether.

In seeking to spread knowledge about science and technology, Scheutz published not only magazines and newspapers but also quite a number of technical handbooks. This began in 1819 with *Handbok för så wäl enklare som mera konstig Blekning...*, and between then and 1832, he published some twelve handbooks in all, which were collected in a series entitled "Library for Art, Handicrafts and Applied Science".[46] Two other items in this series were *Handbok för helsans bevarande* (Handbook in preserving health), and *Handbok i ritkonsten* (Handbook in the art of drawing), both of which appeared in 1832. The former had been translated and edited by Scheutz, while he was the author of the latter. The series also included handbooks dealing with turning, technology, surveying, mechanics, algebra, vinegar manufacture and brewing. The original idea had been to publish fifty titles at least, but presumably the sales did not live up to expectations. Among those projected, had been handbooks dealing with astronomy, printing, forming and casting, fireworks, music, macaroni- and starch-making.[47] Although in the majority of cases, these books had been translated and arranged by Scheutz, they illustrate both his wide interests and his sound technical knowledge, without which they would have been impossible.[48]

In exactly the same way as in *Anmärkaren* and its successors, Scheutz had created a means for bringing about social and political change, so by means of his technical magazines and books he sought to influence the country's technical and economic development. The differences in the rate of industrial expansion, and in industrial and economic maturity, between the relatively backward Sweden and other countries – particularly England – were obvious to him. But with more enlightenment and increased information, progress was indeed possible. *Journal för Manufakturer och Hushållning* was Sweden's first general technical journal.[49] Scheutz' role as a technology disseminator is undeniable. It remains to investigate the practical effect of his technical journalism and writing.

Apart from Scheutz' general journals, there were a few specialized technical journals published in the country. Thus in the period 1833-1835, the mill owner could find articles of interest in *Tidskrift för Bruksegare och Bergsmän*. The practical mining engineer had *Tidskrift för Bergsmän* (1841-42), or *Tidskrift för den Svenska Bergshandteringen*, which took up metallurgy, mining engineering, geology and forestry. The latter appeared in the period 1843-1845.[50] For advice about what was going on in technical chemistry at the country's two Technical High Schools, one could refer to *Tekno-kemisk journal* (1847-48).[51] All these publications, as can be seen, were short-lived. There was no market for such publications and the owners and editors could not continue to publish them over a longer period, given the meagre financial recompense involved.[52]

In 1847, Georg Scheutz wrote of himself:

"Meanwhile he has made a considerable number of inventions, of which some have been patented, some have been described in print and some have remained unknown or are simply proposals in the inventor's portfolio."[53]

The creative side to Scheutz' nature was not content simply to read and write about technical matters. The technical problems he encountered at his press, led him to make improvements and it was there that he was to make his own first inventions. A major one was to occur only a few years after he had left the legal profession. Around the end of 1819, he applied for a twenty-year patent, or as it was then called, a "privilegium exclusivum", for a number of improvements connected with printing.[54] This was to be the prologue to an interesting episode in Scheutz' career as an inventor.[55] The normal procedure then employed in printing, was to ink the types by hand, lay the sheet of paper in the press, and print. If one wanted to print on the other side of the paper, one had to wait till the ink had dried, and then the procedure was repeated. In his patent application, however, Scheutz speaks of a number of machines combined into a single unit, which inks the types, feeds the paper into the press, prints, feeds out the paper again, turns it over and prints on the other side. In other words, it was a machine which was highly advanced for its time and which set out to mechanize a series of manual operations. At that time in Stockholm, there were some ten newspapers and their circulation was constantly increasing. There was every reason to anticipate an interest in new, faster methods of printing.[56] The Society of Book Printers in Stockholm, which was responsible for vetting inventions in this area, was in general positive towards Scheutz' invention even if it was not convinced that there was any great need for it.[57] Scheutz, however, continued to develop his press and in 1823 he submitted a new patent application. This time the foot-operated machine was equipped with a cylinder and the inventor requested not only a monopoly on the manufacture of the machine but also on its use.[58] This was a tactical mistake. He had gone too far. The Society of Book Printers of which Scheutz was himself a member, was more or less united against him. It was particularly opposed to the idea that he should have a monopoly on the use of the machine.[59] It was considered that this might prevent other printers from being able to import cylinder presses from England. One member even feared, that if the patent were granted, other printing presses would become superfluous and the Society would be economically threatened.[60] For the next few years, Georg Scheutz was kept in a state of uncertainty, while his patent application was being considered.[61] It was clearly a sensitive issue and certain people refused to have anything to do with it.[62] In 1831, Scheutz made yet another application, from which it is clear that Kommerskollegium − the authority which was responsible for the granting of patents in the country − had finally compelled him to make certain technical improvements.[63] The latter were merely a pretext, however, since according at least to Scheutz himself, even the presses which printed *The Times* lacked such refinements.[64] But Scheutz solved these problems and the patent regarding the manufacture of the machine was finally granted.[65] In its original form, he had devised the press so that it could be used for printing *Argus*, but he did not succeed in getting it ready in time, due to the fact that he could not find a suitable workshop to build it.[66] In the 1820s, there was a lack of mechanical workshops in Stockholm and all that he had managed to achieve was a relatively incomplete prototype.

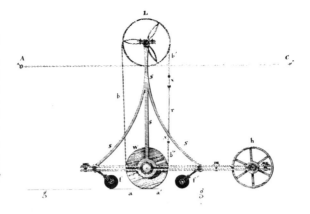

Fig. 18 Drawing by Georg Scheutz from circa 1831. Showing part of his cylinder press, for which he on several occasions tried to get the exclusive rights of manufacture and use. The original drawing is kept in RA, Kommerskollegie Huvudarkiv, Acta Privatorum, EXVII d:2, vol 403. No 45. Photograph by courtesy of the National Archives, Stockholm.

Even the finished machine was not able to print as fast in practice as Scheutz had promised.[67] But irrespective of these technical failings, this episode has much to reveal about Scheutz and his time. First, it displays Scheutz' farsightedness and initiative, which have given him the honour of having invented Sweden's first fast press. Secondly, it shows how a conservative sector of industry and trade fears technical and social changes.

Georg Scheutz' press never found a purchaser. A contributing factor was that Kommerskollegium had taken so long to make up its mind and in the meantime modern printing machinery had been introduced into the country. In 1829, the first English fast press had been imported into Sweden by Nils Magnus Lindh of Örebro, an ingenious printer and also a friend of Scheutz.[68] The year before, the first Stanhope press had reached Stockholm. The design was copied and the press was produced in comparatively large numbers at Theofron Munktell's workshop in Eskilstuna, which was founded in 1832.[69] In comparison with these solid and stable machines, Scheutz' press must have appeared odd, see Fig. 18. Scheutz also made an attempt to invent a grinding machine for printer's ink, but without achieving any satisfactory results.[70] In 1838, he devised an etching instrument for letters of the alphabet, which was put to use in producing *Svenska Industriföreningens Tidskrift*.[71]

Scheutz made inventions in other fields as well. Many of the ideas were improvements of those due to other people. It reveals his desire to improve and develop existing technology. His experience as a disseminator of technology disposed him to see the shortcomings of existing technology, rather than to develop radically new solutions in the course of his own practical work. Just as for Babbage, the steam engine was for Scheutz the high technology of the era and was frequently mentioned in his journals. But it also gave rise to accidents and around 1835 Scheutz invented a safety valve for steam engines, which was manufactured and successfully used in at least one factory in Stockholm.[72] Five years later he applied for a ten year patent on "using steam to bring about a rotary motion" − in other words, for a simple type of steam turbine.[73] With this invention, he joined the long line of inventors, who from classical times had attempted to put the idea into working practice. It is worth mentioning some of the other inventions he tried to patent. In 1825 he sought a patent for *"Ett Hydrauliskt Instrument"* which in principle was a piston in a cylinder which could be used in various ways.[74] In 1832 he applied for a fifteen years privilegium exclusivum on the manufacture and sale of " *Alun, hvars kristallform är kubisk"*.[75] According to Scheutz, alun with cubical crystals, as opposed to the usual octahedral ones, had certain advantages in dyeing. They were also easier to manufacture industrially. His invention concerned the industrial process, for which there was nothing similar in the country. Another of his inventions was an optical instrument used for copying called *"Portfeuille Iconografique"* for which he sought a patent in 1841.[76] It was based on an invention of William Hyde Wollaston, among others, but was designed along quite different lines. The following year, Scheutz applied for a patent for a drawing instrument which he called *"Sinus-delare"* ("Sine divider"), and in 1850 he applied for a patent for *"metod att bränna Tak- och Murtegel"* ("method of baking tiles and bricks").[77] The former appears to have been an original invention due to Scheutz, while the latter was a method discovered abroad, for which Scheutz wished to obtain monopoly rights in Sweden. These facts show how the older patent statistics have to be taken with a pinch of salt and that each case has to be checked carefully. All of Georg Scheutz' patent applications were granted.[78]

For some of his inventions, Georg Scheutz did not bother to seek a patent. Some of these remained only "described in print". Since Scheutz wrote all the articles and reviews in his technical journals anonymously and without mentioning any particular inventor's name, it is difficult to trace these inventions. However, a couple of them are known and they illustrate the fact that Scheutz was primarily an inventor of improvements on existing techniques. Consider, for example, his article on aerial cableways, so-called "flying wheelbarrows", which appeared in *Journal för Manufakturer och Hushållning* in 1825.[79] The article was presumably based on some foreign account, and in it Scheutz presented a number of alterations to the original invention.[80] He proposed replacing the counterweight with another basket, adjoining several baskets to the cable and designing the baskets so that they could be emptied automatically.[81] In Scheutz' technical journals, it was the simple practical solution which had pride of place. This can be illustrated by what he has to say in the article on aerial cableways. Scheutz wrote − "By means of this neither difficult nor costly device, workmen are able to avoid wheeling their barrows backwards and forwards, which can be difficult, even impossible, where the ground is uneven and stony. The whole contraption can be constructed wherever there is a country blacksmith and turner, and it can be moved with the greatest ease from one site to another as required."[82]

According to one scholar the improvements suggested by Scheutz in this article were widely adopted.[83]

A more obvious example of Scheutz' leaning towards improvements, and one which illustrates his lifelong interest in physics and chemistry is the following. Although the roots of photography can be traced back to the middle of the 16th century, it was first in 1839 that it became really practical in the form of the daguerrotype, developed by Louis Jacques Mande Daguerre and Joseph Nicéphore Niépce. The knowledge about the sensitivity of silver salts to light and their use in simple photography had been around for more than a hundred years, when in 1832 an anonymous translation of a French book on surveying was published in Stockholm.[84] The author of the original work was Silvestre Francois Lacroix. The publisher of the Swedish edition of Lacroix' book added his own description of a photographic method of determining a place's meridian, with the help of camera obscura and salts of silver.[85] Later on, Georg Scheutz revealed that it was he who had been responsible for this addition.[86] This addition, which also shows Scheutz' interest in the new art of "painting with light", crops up quite anonymously in the middle of the translated text. The book itself, *Handbok i landtmäteriet* (Handbook in surveying), was part of the series "Library for Art, Handicrafts and Applied Science".

The two foregoing examples illustrate two of Georg Scheutz' typical characteristics — his constant urge to improve inventions and his inclination to make anonymous contributions. There are no doubt many more examples of these qualities to be found in his extensive journalistic and publishing production.

Pehr Georg Scheutz — the son of a innkeeper — was an auditor, printer, journalist and editor, political commentator, spokesman for technology, translator and inventor. However, he had two other strings to his bow as well. From his earliest days, he had loved literature — whether poetry or prose.[87] His own literary efforts were many and various and they often appeared in the newspapers and journals of other editors.[88] The majority of his pieces were anonymous.[89] It would certainly be worthwhile making a thorough investigation of Scheutz' literary production.[90] Here it will be sufficient to give only a brief summary.

His writings — leaving aside the newspapers and magazines he edited — can be divided into two categories: original works on the one hand and arrangements and translations on the other. Scheutz had a wide knowledge of foreign languages — among them English, German, French, Italian and Latin. It is very probable that he also knew Greek and Hebrew. His first known translation dates from the period before his move to Stockholm and was of a German book about Brazil.[91] This was to be succeeded by an imposing collection of literary works, which he translated and on occasion rearranged, abbreviated or extended.[92] Most of them were printed at his own press. Among some of the titles to appear, were *Guiscardo och Sigismonda* (1818) by Giovanni Boccacio, *Italiensk läsbok, med tillhörande ordbok och språklära* (1819) by Morten Sommer, *Julius Caesars kommentarier öfver Galliska kriget* (1828) after the Latin original, and Xenophon's *Cyri härfärd och de tiotusendes återtåg* (1829). The later translations of Scheutz included Justus Liebig's *Kemiska bref* and Victor Hugo's *Napoleon den lille*. The former appeared in 1853 and the latter in 1852.[93] In Sweden, Scheutz was much praised for his translations of Shakespeare's *Julius Caesar* (1816) and *Köpmannen i Venedig* (The Merchant of Venice) which appeared in 1820. In the autumn of his life, he was awarded the Carl-Johan prize which was considered a great distinction, for these translations. He also translated King Lear which was performed on a private stage in Stockholm but the translation was never published.[94]

What sort of man was Georg Scheutz? All the available sources speak well of him. He was a good employer and an accomplished and respected colleague. At the same time he was a modest man who avoided the limelight and who took no pains to claim the credit which he often deserved. He preferred instead the role of anonymous author, perhaps privately rejoicing at the use his work was put to. In this respect, he was very different from Charles Babbage who did not hesitate to solicit openly both the praise of others and official recognition.[95] To Scheutz' modesty was added a fundamental altruism. Consider the 1825 article on his "Hydraulic Instrument".[96] There he tells the reader that he had taken out a ten year patent on his invention but for reasons quite other than personal gain. The purpose of the patent was to provide a proof of the invention's worth, since many people demanded such a certificate before they were prepared to manufacture and make use of an unfamiliar machine or technique. Having said this, he then continued his article by describing in great detail the basic idea, with accompanying drawings and even a list of all the conceivable areas of application.[97] Perhaps a similar train of thought lay behind those articles where he anonymously presented other inventions of his own for the benefit of all.[98] An exception was his printing press which he nowhere described in his journals. It is plausible that he regarded this invention as a potential means of livelihood and as a way of securing his future, which he did not wish to lose. The printing press also illustrates another of Scheutz' psychological traits − he did not give up in spite of reverses. Last but not least, Scheutz was essentially a very practical man. Whenever he translated foreign technical articles and books, it was invariably with the aim of carrying over something to Sweden that was practically useful. When he invented or improved something, it was to solve practical problems. It is clear that Scheutz was very practically oriented in his way of designing machinery too, relying on the method of "trial and error" and simple drawings. In a letter written in 1838, he points out the fact that one can reach various conclusions by theory or practice, and he emphasizes the importance of experience as opposed to "mere theories".[99] Babbage the theorist − Scheutz the practical man. This is the fundamental distinction between the two men, which led them to tackle the difference engine in such different ways.

2.2 The transfer of technology

Among all those technical ideas and inventions which Georg Scheutz in his role as a disseminator of technology had occasion to examine in the course of the years, there was one invention in particular which was to rivet his attention. It was around the year 1830 that he heard for the first time about Babbage's engine. At the time, he was still busily engaged with *Argus* at his press. Despite the fact that his work with *Journal för Manufakturer och Hushållning* ceased between 1827 and 1832, he continued to read foreign journals with the same enthusiasm, not least to help him with his handbooks. In November 1833, he published an article on Babbage's difference engine in *Journal för Manufakturer och Hushållning*.[1] The introduction to this article sets out his views on the matter:

> "*Babbage's Calculating Engine*
> There has been such frequent reference in the periodical literature of recent years to the invention due to the present Secretary of the Royal Society, and its highly important implications, that a more detailed account of it would probably interest more than one of our readers, even although the invention does not properly fall within the scope of the present journal and demands for its implementation such complete accuracy and vast capital that it could only be carried out in England, where even there, several years' work has been needed − work which is still going on. The small scale engine which has already been built, shows however that the project is in no way a wild fancy. Even if the larger and more complete engine were to remain the only example of its kind, it would suffice for the needs of the whole world; for England cannot monopolize its fruits, and once the calculations had been carried out, they would soon become the *common* property of civilization. The following information about this remarkable invention is to be found in *Mechanics Magazine*, (No. 488), borrowed from an article in *Partington's "British Encyclopaedia"*, which in turn is based on information from Babbage himself."[2]

Scheutz had come to the conclusion that Babbage's engine was sufficiently remarkable and interesting to be described in *Journal för Manufakturer och Hushållning*. In this particular case, it was very much a matter of his own personal interest since he could hardly claim to his readers that the difference engine was of "immediate practical use" for cottagers and craftsmen which was the avowed aim of the journal.[3]

The remainder of Scheutz' article was an almost word for word translation of the original English text, in which the following paragraph occurred.

"Great as the power of mechanism is known to be, yet we venture to say that many of the most intelligent of our readers will scarcely admit it to be possible, that astronomical and navigation tables can be accurately computed by machinery; that the machine can itself correct the errors which it may commit; and that the results, when absolutely free from error, can be printed off without the aid of human hands, or the operation of human intelligence."[4]

These words illustrate how enthusiastically the difference engine was received almost without exception in the daily press and technical journals. The errors and misunderstandings which had been introduced by one writer, survived in subsequent articles as evidence of the engine's remarkable properties. In Scheutz' translation, the passage "that astronomical [...] without the aid of human hands" is placed in italics, which shows that he wished to place particular emphasis upon this central part of the content of the text.

Both the original and Scheutz' translation gave an account of Prony and his tables and described the method of differences with the help of a couple of examples. It was suggested that the calculating unit was almost ready, but that problems with the printing unit remained − an observation calculated to arouse Scheutz' curiosity still more. In the article one could also read that Babbage intended to get the engine to transfer the results onto plates for one whole page at a time, so that the finished tables would have the usual appearance. Undoubtedly Scheutz, as an experienced printer, must have had reason to reflect on these words. In the English text which he translated, there was not a word about stereotyping which must have given him further cause to wonder. Nor did the article contain anything about the engine's technical design. Finally, there were some remarks about how fast the engine could work. This in substance is all that Georg Scheutz knew of Babbage's difference engine in November 1833. If he had known more − which seems plausible because he speaks of having read several times about the engine − he would, as a matter of course, have supplemented his information. In fact, Scheutz did add one reflection to his translation, but of a different character. In a note, he discusses the article's illustration of the method of differences in a way which shows that he himself had devoted some time to thinking about the mathematical principles of the engine.

"One discovers that the same arrangement of machinery, with the help of a quite insignificant adjustment, can be employed to carry out the most diverse calculations; the whole idea is, in short, utterly simple like all really great and fruitful ideas. The consequences of Babbage's

important invention could only with difficulty be perceived in advance; one of the most beneficial is the emancipation of human thought from the grinding work of table-making which, hitherto, it has been unable to avoid. But there is also a host of problems which are important in a purely *analytical* sense and to which science possesses the key, but which must nevertheless be set aside, because the use of the key would involve such a labour of calculation as to defy all human perseverance; the solution of such problems should no longer occasion any difficulty since the necessary mechanical work can be left to a real machine."[5]

It is clear that Scheutz was impressed by Babbage's invention. At this stage, Scheutz considered the engine equally well adapted for the computation and printing of tables as for mathematical calculation.

Georg Scheutz kept his eyes open for more information about the difference engine. Undoubtedly he studied Babbage's *Economy* extra carefully in the hope of finding something new about it. One chapter was entitled "On the division of mental labour" which dealt with Prony's work in *Les Tables de Cadastres*, and ended with a short description of how the difference method could in an anologous way be mechanized.[6] Babbage illustrated this by means of three mechanical clocks so connected to function as a difference engine. Although this description was quite superficial, Scheutz no doubt found the presentation novel and stimulating. In the June number of *Journal för Manufakturer och Hushållning* in 1834 he wrote a paragraph which indicates that he had studied *Economy* with the greatest interest, looking for further information about the engine. The paragraph occurs in an article based on Babbage's book, which deals with punching in copper plate with steel types. Scheutz perceived that Babbage was speaking about the printing unit to his engine and set forth some of his own thoughts on the subject in a note:

"These attempts seem to have been made with the intention of bringing into being the table printing unit of the Author's illustrious calculating engine, [...] and from the foregoing description, it could be deduced that the tables so produced either are intended to be printed in copper plate, or that the copper plates are to be used as moulds for stereotypes. There would seem to be no longer any question that a genuine composition of the tables, in the printer's sense, could be brought about by means of this machinery."[7]

Scheutz perceived – quite correctly – that Babbage's *Economy* was not a systematic treatise and as such was more suited to being quoted and summarized than being translated in full into Swedish.[8] It is worthwhile to give Scheutz' conclusions about the contents of *Economy*, since they reveal the differences that existed, in Scheutz' view, between Sweden and the rest of Europe.

"The quite exclusive *English* viewpoint from which the Author not infrequently deals with his subject, deprives his opinions of all application outside of England and at the same time he presupposes both in industry and trade, and in the governmental view of economic matters which depends on them, a development which dates back a century in the case of Great Britain and at least several decades in the case of France and Germany, but which in our case is still far too insignificant."[9]

Babbage's *Economy* was actually translated and published in both France and Germany but never in Sweden where Scheutz believed that it would not enjoy the same success.[10]

In summary, it is clear that Scheutz in June 1834 knew only the broad outlines of Babbage's engine. In the course of the years, he had been able to supplement his knowledge but his sources of information lacked the details of technical design that he was interested in. He was still unaware at this time that work on Difference Engine No. 1 had been at a standstill for a year. Quite the contrary impression had been created in his mind, for Babbage had written in the third edition of *Economy*, which Scheutz had studied with such great care, in a new note, that − "The ease and precision with which it [the assembled machine] works, leave no room to doubt its success in the more extended form."[11]

Georg Scheutz was now forty-eight. For the past two years he had devoted himself more and more to technology and allowed his political interests to take on a secondary role. In 1832 after much labour, he had published handbooks on algebra, surveying, drawing and a further three on chemical subjects. In the same year, he had also completed *Handbok i teknologien* and the following year *Handbok i mekaniken*, both of which were edited versions of foreign works. At the same time he was busily at work again with the *Journal för Manufakturer och Hushållning*. The news about Babbage's engine thus reached Scheutz just when his contributions to technical journalism and popularization had increased significantly. It should be noted that in these works that have been mentioned, Scheutz displayed the profound and fully developed three dimensional thinking characteristic of the engineer. He was now a man of considerable experience and much more skilful than the self-taught designer that he had been when he invented the press in 1819. Above all, he had a sound knowledge of all aspects of printing and an interest in mathematics. All this has to be borne in mind in assessing his reaction to the news about Babbage's engine.

An interesting proof of Scheutz' interest in mathematics is to be found in his little pamphlet *Portatif räknemachin i form af en liten bok* (Portable calculating machine in the form of a little book), which was published in Stockholm in 1834, see Fig. 19.[12] This invention was one of Scheutz' own and constituted an improvement of John Napier's Rods. Scheutz writes that he himself had used the calculating rods to great advantage but he

*tionis promptuario. Quibus accessit & arithmeticæ localis liber unus.   Auctore &
inventore Joanne Nepero, Barone Marchistonii, &c, Scoto"* .*

Att räknestafvarne, oaktadt deras användbarhet vid multiplikationer och di-
visioner, särdeles med många siffror, sedermera råkat nästan i glömska, torde
dels kunna tillskrifvas logaritmernas allmännare bruk, dels den obeqvämlighe-
ten, att dessa små stafvar — ursprungligen ett slags aflånga tärningar med samma påteckning som de här befintliga små bladen eller remsorna — voro skilda
ifrån hvarandra, och således både medförde svårigheter att i hast sammanleta
och ordna, och, en gång ordnade, lätt kunde genom en stöt, en skakning på
bordet, o d., råka i oordning.

Utgifvaren af närvarande lilla arbete hade vid åtskilliga tillfällen med för-
mån begagnat de Neperska räknestafvarne, men dervid äfven som oftast erfarit
nyssnämnda olägenheter; till deras förekommande ärnade han stundom anbringa
ett antal af 10 stafvar, från 1 till 9, på band, utspända bredvid hvarandra, helst
emellan dubbelt så många på två axlar uppträdda trissor; än teckna siffrorna o-
medelbart på kanten af ett antal runda eller mokantiga trissor, uppträdda på en
axel; och ehuru begge dessa tillställningar lyckas ganska väl, så har den så-
lunda sammansatta räknemachinen likväl det felet att intaga plats, och vara
tung samt alltför litet portatif. Slutligen påfann utgifvaren en tredje inrättning — den närvarande — hvari han trott sig träffa de önskade egenskaperna
förenade, eller att Nepers räknestafvar genom den blifva både lätta att uppsöka
och ordna, samt så portativa, att de kunna medföras i bröstfickan eller planboken.

Man kan emedlertid med detta mindre instrument ej beräkna tal som bestå
af mer än 10 siffror, d v s som uppgå till fullt tiotusen millioner; men för
de flesta fall torde det ändå vara tillräckligt. Behöfver man likväl räkna med
större tal, så kan det ske med tillhjelp af två eller flera räknemachiner, lagda
bredvid hvarandra; sifferantalet kan då i samma förhållande få vara fördubbladt
eller flerdubbladt.

G. S.

*) Vi ha blott haft tillfälle att begagna den i Leyden 1626 utgifna upplagan.

Fig. 19 Portatif räknemachin i form af en liten bok *(Stockholm 1834) is an example of
Georg Scheutz' interest in mathematics and aids of calculation. The strips of paper by means
of which the calculation is performed can be seen the lower part of the photograph.*

points out they are difficult to arrange and keep track of in the calculation. He suggests that this fact, along with the general use of logarithms
as an aid to calculation, had led to the rods being more or less forgotten.
Scheutz had therefore constructed some calculating machines in which
the rods had been mechanized by means of "shafts, belts and pulleys".[13]
Because these machines had turned out to be cumbersome, he decided to
try a different approach and finally produced calculating rods in the form

of paper strips. By an ingenious arrangement of Napier's Rods in the form of these strips, pasted into the covers of the book, the *Portatif räknemachin* (which in essence was a kind of adjustable table) constituted a handy computational aid. In the *Portatif räknemachin* Georg Scheutz says that he had not only been irritated by the difficulty involved in using the calculating rods, but had consequently set to work to overcome the problem. Thus about the same time that he became aware of Babbage's engine, Scheutz had himself been engaged in building mechanical calculating machines.[14]

What was there for Georg Scheutz to compare the difference engine with? One's first thought suggests universal calculating machines. Those of Pascal and Leibniz had become famous within the world of science and it is highly probable that Scheutz had known about them for a long time. He had also read about them in the article in *Mechanics Magazine*, where other were also mentioned. But it can be assumed that his knowledge about these devices was very superficial and almost certainly he had never seen a calculating machine in reality. For Scheutz, it was tables, Napier Rods and perhaps slide-rules which were the best known devices for assisting calculation. In general, however, calculations were quite simply performed with pen and paper. Given these facts, it is hardly surprising that Scheutz reacted with a certain amazement to a machine which not only calculated but which also, somehow or other, was able by itself to print error-free numerical tables.

It is plausible to suppose that Scheutz associated the difference engine with clocks. But his knowledge of Babbage's engine was far too meagre to lead anywhere. The steam engine had become all the more common in Swedish industry and the mechanization of manual procedures was another kind of parallel which must have arisen in Scheutz' mind. But most of all, his thoughts must have revolved round printing itself. He had long been familiar with stereotyping which had been introduced into Sweden in 1832.[15]

But what did he know of the trials and tribulations of printing tables? An investigation of the printed tables for interest, mathematical calculations and other purposes which are preserved in the Royal Library in Stockholm, throws some light on this. There is no example of a table printed by Scheutz in the collection. However, in *Handbok i algebra* (1832) he added a number of tables for "Squares and Cubes, Square and Cube Roots", which were not included in the French original.[16] A sample of the table entries shows that Scheutz had taken great trouble to eliminate errors arising in composition and no errors have been discovered. In a number of *Argus* which appeared in 1823, there is a rather substantial statistical table which Scheutz may have arranged and proofread.[17] In other words, it is reasonable to suppose that he was acquainted with "the grinding work of table-making". His older colleague, the prominent printer Nils Magnus Lindh in Örebro, had in the course of the years printed a number of tables which proved highly popular and were published in several editions.[18] Lindh had taken care of Scheutz' move to Stockholm and seems to have been something of a Nestor for Scheutz as regards printing.[19] The printing fraternity in the capital was a small one and everyone knew everyone else. In combined terms, they published a comparatively large number of tables, most often transformation tables of various kinds and small tables of interest providing different percentages. It is interesting to note that tables of logarithms and trigonometric functions were very rarely produced at these presses. Presumably those who needed them, made use of foreign publications. At the beginning of the century, interest and transformation tables had been printed at the Marquard press in Stockholm. Johan Peter Marquard, appears to have been a valued printer of tables. The following episode illustrates that the difficulties involved in printing error-free tables were well known in the Swedish capital.

Hans Jacob Seseman, a teacher of mathematics at the Elementary School in Vadstena, spent a long time compiling a comprehensive set of tables of interest. In 1808, the actual printing had got under way in Stockholm. At the end of his table collection, which appeared in 1811, Seseman wrote as follows.

"Thus the printing of this time-consuming work is brought to completion. It was first undertaken at the close of 1808 by the Diligent and Venerable Printer and Director Anders J. Nordström, who was little willing to provide me with as many proofs as were necessary to ensure that the Work was devoid of error; and, according to my contention that it is the duty of every Printer (if the Work shall be free of error) to deliver to the Author or Corrector as many proofs as he may require, I was compelled to write on the Proofs which he gave me the following signed statement: *I am not prepared to allow printing before I have received a Proof which is free from error and of which I have no criticism to make.*"[20]

In 1809, one year later, there were still only 59 pages ready. Seseman turned to "the Accommodating and Upright Printer" Marquard, and by April 1810 the remaining 77 pages had been printed. However the book did not appear until 1811 which would suggest that Seseman read the proofs after printing. The book contains no list of errata so that the work must have been carried out meticulously.

During the first three decades of the 19th Century, there were at most some 40 tables printed in Stockholm.[21] For the rest of the country as a whole, the figure must have been comparable, perhaps somewhat lower. Even although the production of tables was not a common assignment for the capital's printers, the problems it posed and the time and labour it demanded, were no doubt subjects of discussion for Scheutz and his printer friends.

Some time during the latter part of the summer of 1834, the informa-

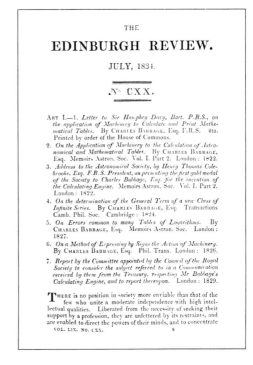

THE

EDINBURGH REVIEW.

JULY, 1834.

N° CXX.

ART I.—1. *Letter to Sir Humphry Davy, Bart. P.R.S., on the application of Machinery to Calculate and Print Mathematical Tables.* By CHARLES BABBAGE, Esq. F.R.S. 4to. Printed by order of the House of Commons.

2. *On the Application of Machinery to the Calculation of Astronomical and Mathematical Tables.* By CHARLES BABBAGE, Esq. Memoirs Astron. Soc. Vol. I. Part 2. London: 1822.

3. *Address to the Astronomical Society, by Henry Thomas Colebrooke, Esq. F.R.S. President, on presenting the first gold medal of the Society to Charles Babbage, Esq. for the invention of the Calculating Engine.* Memoirs Astron. Soc. Vol. I. Part 2. London: 1822.

4. *On the determination of the General Term of a new Class of Infinite Series.* By CHARLES BABBAGE, Esq. Transactions Camb. Phil. Soc. Cambridge: 1824.

5. *On Errors common to many Tables of Logarithms.* By CHARLES BABBAGE, Esq. Memoirs Astron. Soc. London: 1827.

6. *On a Method of Expressing by Signs the Action of Machinery.* By CHARLES BABBAGE, Esq. Phil. Trans. London: 1826.

7. *Report by the Committee appointed by the Council of the Royal Society to consider the subject referred to in a Communication received by them from the Treasury, respecting Mr Babbage's Calculating Engine, and to report thereon.* London: 1829.

THERE is no position in society more enviable than that of the few who unite a moderate independence with high intellectual qualities. Liberated from the necessity of seeking their support by a profession, they are unfettered by its restraints, and are enabled to direct the powers of their minds, and to concentrate

VOL. LIX. NO. CXX.   s

Fig. 20 The July issue of the Edinburgh Review for 1834 contained the article that Georg Scheutz had been waiting for. It was entitled "Babbage's calculating engine" and its author was Dionysius Lardner who had written it in collaboration with Babbage. This photograph shows the first page of the article where the references to the seven published papers that also formed basis for the article are given.

tion about Babbage's engine which Scheutz hoped for, became available. It was to be found in the article "Babbage's calculating engine" by Dionysius Lardner, which appeared in the *Edinburgh Review*. It was an exhaustive piece of work and, according to the text, had been written with three aims in mind:

> "*First*, To show the immense importance of any method by which numerical tables, absolutely accurate in every individual copy, may be produced with facility and cheapness. This we shall establish by conveying to the reader some notion of the number and variety of tables published in every country of the world to which civilization has extended, a large portion of which have been produced at the public expense; by showing also, that they are nevertheless rendered inefficient, to a greater or less extent, by the prevalence of errors in them; that these errors pervade not merely tables produced by individual labour and enterprise, but that they vitiate even those on which national resources have been prodigally expended, and to which the highest mathematical ability, which the most enlightened nations of the world could command, has been unsparingly and systematically directed.
>
> *Secondly*, To attempt to convey to the reader a general notion of the mathematical principle on which the calculating machinery is founded, and of the manner in which this principle is brought into practical

operation, both in the process of calculating and printing. It would be incompatible with the nature of this review, and indeed impossible without the aid of numerous plans, sections, and elevations, to convey clear and precise notions of the details of the means by which the process of reasoning is performed by inanimate matter, and the arbitrary and capricious evolutions of the fingers of typographical compositors are reduced to a system of wheel-work. We are, nevertheless, not without hopes of conveying, even to readers unskilled in mathematics, some satisfactory notions of a general nature on this subject.

Thirdly, To explain the actual state of the machinery at the present time; what progress has been made towards its completion; and what are the probable causes of those delays in its progress, which must be a subject of regret to all friends of science. We shall indicate what appears to us the best and most practicable course to prevent the unnecessary recurrence of such obstructions for the future, and to bring this noble project to a speedy and successful issue."[22]

This article, which was written in collaboration with Babbage and based on seven published papers on the engine, was to have decisive importance in the subsequent course of events, see Fig. 20.[23] It was the first time that the difference engine was described as a material object with attention paid to the principles involved in its design.[24] According to Georg Scheutz' own testimony, it was this article which inspired him to build a difference engine.[25]

The *Edinburgh Review*, which had appeared from the beginning of the century, was the main organ of the Whigs. That was one good reason why Scheutz, who was also engaged in the struggle for liberal reforms, took an interest in the journal. Another reason was provided by the popular articles on science and technology written by the former Trinity undergraduate Lardner, which were published in the *Edinburgh Review* and elsewhere.[26]

A summary of the three major sections in Lardner's article gives an account of what Georg Scheutz found out about the Difference Engine No. 1. First of all, after having given a comprehensive enumeration of the significance and multitude of numerical tables as a calculating aid in diverse walks of life, Lardner got to the real problem − the occurence of errors in tables. He stressed the gravity of the situation with several examples.

"A few years ago, it was found desirable to compute some very accurate logarithmic tables for the use of the great national survey of Ireland, which was then, and still is in progress; and on that occasion a careful comparison of various logarithmic tables was made. Six remarkable errors were detected, which were found to be common to several apparently independent sets of tables. This singular coincidence led to an unusually extensive examination of the logarithmic tables published both in England and in other countries; by which it appeared that thirteen sets of tables, published in London between the years 1633 and 1822, all agreed in these six errors. Upon extending the inquiry to foreign tables, it appeared that two sets of tables published at Paris, one at Gouda, one at Avignon, one at Berlin, and one at Florence, were infected by exactly the same six errors. The only tables which were found free from them were those of Vega, and the more recent impressions of Callet. It happened that the Royal Society possessed a set of tables of logarithms printed in the Chinese character, and on Chinese paper, consisting of two volumes: these volumes contained no indication or acknowledgement of being copied from any other work. They were examined; and the result was the detection in them of the same six errors.

It is quite apparent that this remarkable coincidence of error must have arisen from the various tables being copied successively one from another. The earliest work in which they appeared was Vlacq's Logarithms (folio, Gouda, 1628); and from it, doubtless, those which immediately succeeded it in point of time were copied; from which the errors were subsequently transcribed into all the other including the Chinese logarithms."[27]

The consequences of successive copying were stressed in another example:

"The *Opus Palatinum*, a work published in 1596, containing an extensive collection of trigonometrical tables, affords a remarkable instance of a tabular error; which, as it is not generally known, it may not be uninteresting to mention here. After that work had been for several years in circulation in every part of Europe, it was discovered that the commencement of the table of co-tangents and co-secants was vitiated by an error of considerable magnitude. In the first co-tangent the last nine places of figures were incorrect; but from the manner in which the numbers of the table were computed, the error was gradually, though slowly, diminished, until at length it became extinguished in the eighty-sixth page. After the detection of this extensive error, Pitiscus undertook the recomputation of the eighty-six erroneous pages. His corrected calculation was printed; and the erroneous part of the remaining copies of the *Opus Palatinum* was cancelled. But as the corrected table of Pitiscus was not published until 1607, − thirteen years after the original work, − the erroneous part of the volume was cancelled in comparatively few copies, and consequently correct copies of the work are now exceedingly rare. Thus, in the collection of tables published by M. Schulze (1778), the whole of the erroneous part of the *Opus Palatinum* has been adopted; he having used the copy of that work which exists in the library of the Academy of Berlin, and which is one of those copies in which the incorrect part was not cancelled."[28]

Computational, typesetting and printing errors were equally thoroughly discussed by Lardner, with examples taken from mathematical, nautical and astronomical tables. The difficulties involved were illustrated by Prony's work and the errors which even he had been unable to avoid. Babbage's own table of logarithms was used to show that despite the special precautions taken, errors had still managed to slip through. Attention was drawn to the fact that there was often a great number of errors in the list of errata so that sometimes one had to add a list of errata of the errata to the tables. Lardner also of course pointed out several errors that had been discovered in known numerical tables. He also showed that highly costly attempts had been made in vain to eliminate these errors. This was indeed the first time that the seriousness and dimensions of the problem were fully revealed to Georg Scheutz.

In the second part of the article, Lardner described the method of differences. This contained nothing new as far as Scheutz was concerned. It was the third and most comprehensive part that was the most interesting for him. It contained a detailed description of the principles involved in the engine and its design. This section was the most important one, because it allowed Scheutz to form his own opinion of Babbage's design and encouraged him to develop his own ideas.

Lardner began first by describing in broad outline the calculating unit.[29] His account was based on Babbage's projected engine, i.e. with 18 digits and six differences. Although the work had come to a standstill in 1833, Lardner gave a description of the complete engine as though it was ready. Scheutz learned that the calculation process consisted of two steps, addition and the carrying of tens, and that the engine was assembled from a number of identical engine components. This latter fact implied that to cope with a larger number of differences, all one had to do was to supply some additional components of exactly the same kind. Lardner mentioned the order in which adding and carrying occurred and noted that these did not occur simultaneously.

The description then went on to deal in more detail with the calculating unit.[30] Each number wheel was engraved with the ten digits 0 to 9 so that they could be read with ease. If one of the wheels was set at the digit 0, addition did not take place. Lardner explained, without any figures or illustrations, the mechanism that was needed to a accomplish this. He also explained how a single carrying-operation could give rise to the need for several others, and he set out how this problem was solved mechanically. "This peculiar contingency is provided against by an arrangement of singular mechanical beauty...".[31] The mechanism in question operated not only by dealing with the carrying-operation but also by distributing the mechanical resistance which the carrying operation gave rise to due to the fact that it occurred in succession from the lower to the higher power. The same distribution of the resistance was incorporated in the adding mechanism. Lardner summed up the above mechanism's properties as follows: "... equalizing the resistance, economizing time, harmonizing the mechanism, and giving to the whole mechanical action the utmost practical perfection".[32]

In order to increase the engine's reliability, Babbage had devised a system which corrected small deviations from the correct positions which could arise in the parts of the calculating unit. The system was so designed that if the deviation (for example due to wear and tear) was considerable, the whole calculating unit locked: "... the impelling power would necessarily lose all its energy, and the machine would stop."[33] Lardner described various detail solutions in this "supplementary system". Scheutz could also read how the engine's number wheels were connected to bells which rang when the wheels indicated a certain number which had been set earlier. Another similar possibility was that if one was dealing with a function, where the highest difference was constant only within a certain interval, one could get a bell to ring when it was time to change this difference. An important detail was that the calculated tabular values had to be rounded off correctly before printing. If the first omitted digit was greater than four, the last significant digit had to be increased by one. Babbage's engine did this automatically. How this was done was not mentioned.

Lardner also described some other properties in the engine. A difference of arbitrary order could automatically be added to another arbitrary difference. This could take place in both directions, from a low difference to a higher one and vice versa. Scheutz learned that the purpose of this feature was to be able to calculate certain special functions.[34] Another property was that when a table involving differences of an arbitrary order had reached a certain argument value, a certain alteration took place in the constant difference. In this way, tables could be computed automatically in which the "constant" difference altered periodically. In the case of these two somewhat remarkable refinements Lardner gave no indication of how the mechanical problems involved had been solved.

The readers must have marvelled in particular at certain paragraphs in the article. It is clear that the difference engine constituted a major step in the development of calculating machines. Babbage himself had been struck by the possibilities which his initial ideas had revealed. He and many others regarded the difference engine with respect and even awe. But despite the fact that he was always very pleased to demonstrate and carefully explain the principles of the engine for those who were interested, he was simultaneously not slow to embark on more abstract speculations. The following paragraph from Lardner's article is a typical example. In essence, the words are Babbage's own.[35] There is little doubt that Scheutz found them as exciting as they were obscure.

"Equations have already been tabulated by the portion of the machinery which has been put together, which are so far beyond the reach of the present power of mathematics, that no distant term of the table can be predicted, nor any function discovered capable of expressing its general law. Yet the very fact of the table being produced by mechanism of an invariable form, and including a distinct principle of mechanical action, renders it quite manifest that *some* general law must exist in every table it produces. But we must dismiss such speculations: we feel it impossible to stretch the powers of our own mind, so as to grasp the probable capabilities of this splendid production of combined mechanical and mathematical genius; much less can we hope to enable others to appreciate them, without being furnished which such means of comprehending them as those with which we have been favoured. Years must in fact elapse, and many inquirers direct their energies to the cultivation of the vast field of research thus opened, before we can fully estimate the extent of this triumph of matter over mind."[36]

Lardner's article provided relatively clear technical descriptions but at the same time there was a recurring note of mystification. He spoke of "this astonishing mechanism", "its wonders" etc. and the word "remarkable" often occurred. In this way, the technical description was hidden in something of a metaphysical fog which only served to make Scheutz' task of understanding the mechanics of the engine more difficult.

Nevertheless Scheutz also obtained insight into how the engine could be used for the solution of equations, about which Lardner had this to say: "Among a great variety of curious accidental properties (so to speak) which the machine is found to possess, is one by which it is capable of solving numerical equations which have rational roots."[37] The description of the calculating unit closed with a reminder that although the unit had only 18 number wheels on each axle, and therefore appeared to allow only calculations involving numbers of up to 18 digits, it could in fact deal with numbers of up to 30 digits. This was possible by means of two successive calculations. Scheutz had proposed a similar procedure in the case of the *Portatif räknemachin* where calculations with large numbers were involved. He thus had a useful frame of reference.[38]

The properties and construction of the printing unit were presented by Lardner, just as in the case of the calculating unit, as though it had been completed and was working.[39] He was brief in his discussion of this important part of the engine but at the same time provided sufficient information to give Scheutz some notion of the design of the printing unit which Babbage had chosen. The unit consisted of two main parts — the type sector and the coordinate board. Lardner said that the type sector, which had the form of a circular sector, contained ten number punches, 0-9. A cam was connected to every number wheel in the result row of the calculating unit. The cam consisted of a metal plate with ten different radii corresponding to the digits 0-9 on the number wheel. Lardner pointed out that this cam was not unlike the part in an ordinary clock that is called *the snail*. By means of an arm, the snail could adjust the type sector to the number shown on the wheel corresponding to the snail. A bent arm was then straightened out and pressed the spring-loaded steel type against a copper plate, so that a digit was punched in the plate. Thereby the last digit in the result was printed. The coordinate board then moved the copper board to the right. The snail, which corresponded to the penultimate digit, then adjusted the type sector, and this was printed and so on. When a complete tabular value with argument had been printed, the calculating unit set about calculating a new value, while 'simultaneously the coordinate board moved the copper plate in two orthogonal directions in its plane to allow the new tabular value to be printed beneath the previous one. It was not essential, Lardner finally added, for the calculating and printing unit to work alternately.

Although this description was quite detailed, and in general more detailed than has been indicated here, many important facts were omitted. Lardner did not, for instance, clearly say whether the machine printed a whole page, or only part of it, all at once. Nor did he mention that an eleventh punch for the decimal point was necessary. Perhaps these things were considered obvious. It was of course normal book printer's practice to make a whole page at once. Nevertheless, little questions like these must have aroused Georg Scheutz' curiosity, made him wonder and guided his mind along new avenues of thought.

In concluding this summary of the description of the engine in the *Edinburgh Review* it should be mentioned that Lardner revealed that for pedagogical reasons, *he had transposed rows and columns* in his description of the calculating unit.[40] He said that the powers were ordered in columns so that they could easily be read in the usual fashion from left to right, while the differences were arranged in rows with the highest order of difference furthest down. In Babbage's engine the construction was the exact reverse.

To sum up, Georg Scheutz first of all was presented with new arguments about the importance of error-free tables, which also claimed that the difference engine was the only solution to the old problem. Secondly, he got to know about the mechanical construction and operation of the

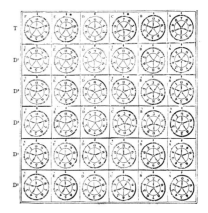

Fig. 21 This was the only type of illustration in Lardner's article in the Edingburgh Review. It was incorrect, since Lardner for pedagogical reasons had transposed rows and colums — something that was to have affect on the design of the Scheutz engines.

machine. Lardner's partly diffuse article wavered between general remarks and detailed descriptions of the parts of the engine, which must have entailed that Scheutz got an imperfect picture of Babbage's machine. Moreover, with the exception of the schematic sketch in Fig. 21, *the article lacked illustrations*, although the reasoning involved was often highly complicated so that much was left to the imagination. Thirdly, he at last was able to confirm that the machine was intended to produce matrices for stereotyping, as he had suspected. Finally, he learned that Babbage's work had come to a temporary halt, and that no less than 15,000 pounds had been spent by the government on the project.[41] This was in 1833 equal to 205,000 riksdaler banco.

What was Scheutz' reaction to the information in Lardner's article? Undoubtedly he read the piece several times in order to try and visualize the engine that was described. Perhaps he went on and obtained the writings which Lardner had based his article upon. It may be assumed that he created drawings of the machine — drawings which had little in common with the actual engine and which were influenced by Scheutz' own experience of technical matters. In actual fact, Lardner's article was written in such a way that it would have been possible to design and build ten engines, all quite different and yet all perfectly consistent with Lardner's description. It would take nine years of hard labour before Georg Scheutz' own difference engine was completed. Yet the article was the spark that lit once and for all the flame of Scheutz' enthusiasm. It was not because the difference engine was an inventor's invention — the summit of contemporary technology, as Babbage himself tended to see it. Nor was it directly because the work on it had come to a halt. Scheutz' motive was quite another. Ever since he had critically read the article, he had come to the conclusion that — "even with all England's technical expertise, it would be impossible to advance further, as long as one followed the same plan".[42] These were strong words from a man who had the greatest respect for England's technological skills.

2.3 Edvard Scheutz and the first engine

Georg Scheutz satisfied his first curiosity by some provisional models in wood, pasteboard and wire. Then he postponed further developments in expectation of what was going on abroad.[1] But his ideas of an improved difference engine would probably never had been realized without the interest, intervention and skill of his son Edvard Scheutz. In contrast to the multidisciplinary achievements of his father, Edvard's contributions in the fields of publishing, politics and the public area of life were much more modest. His only surviving literary work is a comedy — *Vackra flickor finnas äfven i Sibirien* (There are also pretty girls in Siberia) — which was set and printed in a limited edition by Edvard himself at the

Fig. 22 Edvard Raphael Scheutz (1821–1881). The photograph is probably taken in London during the late 1850's. Photograph by courtesy of the Trustees of the Science Museum, London.

age of fifteen.[2] Even as a qualified engineer, Edvard Scheutz never achieved any substantial fame. It is entirely because he managed to build the first complete difference engine in the world that his name has survived. However, being first is not the important thing in this case. Indeed, the circumstances are what deserve attention and this section will focus upon them. While Babbage and Clement had failed despite all the money and "high technology" at their disposal, the teenager Edvard Scheutz, without any of the seemingly good conditions of the Englishmen, surmounted the problems encountered – and this at negligible cost.

Edvard Georg Raphael Scheutz was born on the 13th of September 1821 in Stockholm.[3] His mother, Anna Margaretha Schaumann was twenty-five at the time.[4] Very little is known about her apart from the fact that she, like Georg Scheutz, was a native of Jönköping. The couple had intended to marry, but Anna Schaumann died on the 16th of March

1823 from breast fever after having given birth to a daughter, Hildegard Amalia Georgina Scheutz.[5] The child lived for only one day.[6] Georg and Anna became formally engaged as she lay dying.[7] Since according to Swedish law this was considered equivalent to having entered the state of marriage, Edvard Scheutz was entitled thereafter to consider himself his father's "legitimate" son. A close bond united father and son from the latter's earliest years. Edvard began his studies at the New Elementary School, but was forced to discontinue on account of a leg injury.

In November 1835, Edvard Scheutz matriculated at the Royal Technological Institute in Stockholm, the major institution in its field in the country.[8] He was thus only fourteen years of age. His relative youth in this respect may be explained by the fact that at the Institute, no minimum age was prescribed. Pupils of all ages, from ten upwards, were brought together in the same class room, a circumstance hardly conducive to good discipline.[9] Under the direction of Gustav Magnus Schwartz, the Royal Technological Institute, which had been founded in 1827, took on a special character. According to its statutes, the aim of the Institute was "to acquire and communicate skills and knowledge which are necessary for proficiency in the exercise of handicrafts or of what is usually called a trade or industrial occupation".[10] A further statute ruled that the teaching should be more popular and practical than strictly scientific in its orientation.[11] Schwartz had made a point of interpreting this stipulation quite literally. The teaching emphasized practical rather than theoretical considerations and critics of Schwartz spoke of his "almost pathological aversion to everything theoretical".[12] This fact was to be the cause of continuous battles, first between him and the teachers and the board of management, and in due course between him and the general public and the Riksdag. It ended with Schwartz's dismissal, in 1846.[13] During the whole of Edvard's time at the Institute, however, this practical outlook still dominated.[14] The classes ran from seven in the morning to seven in the evening, during weekdays and Saturdays (with some variations).[15] In all, there were some 100 students and six teachers.[16]

As a little boy, Edvard liked to play in his father's printshop, and as a printer's apprentice he learned all that there was to know about the trade. The bond between him and his father also contributed much to awaken his interest in all aspects of technology. It is unclear how young Edvard came to be enrolled at the Technological Institute. Perhaps Georg simply wished him to have the technical education he himself would have so dearly loved.[17] Georg Scheutz was certainly aware of the Institute's general orientation and presumably therefore had few fears about Schwartz' emphasis on the practical; indeed it is likely that he fully endorsed it. He was well informed about what sort of technical education was available in the country, not least through his colleagues and friends in the Industrial Association. On the board of the latter sat Jonas Samuel Bagge, a teacher of physics at the Technological Institute. Among the other board members, there was the Professor in Chemical Technology at the Institute, Joachim Åkerman. Both of these were to become Edvard's teachers. In addition, Georg Scheutz was on good terms with Professor Carl Palmstedt, the head of Chalmers Technological School (Chalmerska Slöjdskolan) in Gothenburg, which was considered the second most significant centre of technical training in the country. Palmstedt was also a committee member of the Industrial Association. It was through correspondence with him that Scheutz gained yet another perspective on education at the Royal Technological Institute.[18]

Edvard Scheutz had been given the chance of attending one of the few institutions for higher technical education then existing in Sweden. There is little doubt that this was to play a very significant role in the decades that followed. He matriculated as an ordinary student which meant that his studies were intended to be fulltime. The entry requirements stipulated a knowledge of the Christian religion, the ability to read and write Swedish, some competence in arithmetic and last but not least the necessary financial support.[19] However in practice, the requirements were often relaxed which led to problems, for example, when students were unable to count.[20] Edvard belonged to those who possessed the necessary entry qualifications. In addition, he had read a book on geometry, he was able to manipulate decimal fractions and he could speak German.[21]

During the first term, autumn 1835, Edvard Scheutz participated in courses on technical drawing.[22] In the spring term of 1836 the pace increased, and he studied chemistry, mathematics, technical drawing and modern languages ("lefvande språk"). The latter allowed the pupils to study German or English, and it is evident that Edvard at least chose the latter. When the next academic year 1836-37 got under way, he had completed the course in technical drawing, but continued with the other subjects. There was also a new course − craft skills ("handarbeten"). Since there were a metal turning shop, a woodworking shop, several filing shops, a forge and a casting shop on the premises, this must have been a highly practical discipline.[23] Indeed, the majority of the rooms in the building were workshops of various kind.[24] Construction projects involving metal work were part of this, and Edvard participated among other things in the preparation of "a telegraph of French invention". After two years of study, he hade acquired a good theoretical and practical training which would serve as a secure foundation later on in grappling with technical problems. The books used in the courses were good and were for the most part written by the teachers themselves. Today they seem advanced for a fifteen year old.[25] Edvard's interests are reflected in his exam results. In the spring term exams of 1837, as on earlier occasions, he received good marks. In chemistry, he was first in the class. He was also praised for his results in craft skills and he received a medal for his achievements in chemistry.[26] Doubtless Georg was pleased with his son's performance.

After the summer holidays, Edvard continued with his studies in the autumn. He relaxed the tempo and concentrated on two subjects −

modern languages and craft skills. However, his results at Christmas were less satisfactory. In the spring term of 1838, he took courses dealing with physical and technical topics and continued with his mathematical studies. As will be shown, this change in tempo and in choice of subjects, was occasioned by his work on the difference engine. According to the official results, his knowledge of languages was good, but he fared less well in other subjects. In the autumn term of 1838, he took part only in the courses dealing with practical craft skills. This subject embraced mechanics and he was awarded a medal for his progress in that discipline.[27]

In the beginning of summer 1837, three years after the article in the *Edinburgh Review*, Edvard Scheutz, then fifteen years of age and inspired by his newly acquired practical skills, offered to build a fully functioning difference engine made of metal. It was designed to give concrete shape to his father's ideas, which had remained on paper.[28] The design which Georg Scheutz had chosen, differed sharply from Babbage's and was according to Scheutz both "substantially simpler and less expensive".[29] The project, without a doubt, fascinated Edvard, and the only condition he made for carrying out the work, was that he should have access to a workshop at home which contained a lathe, a vice and other necessary tools. Georg was happy to agree and Edvard immediately set to work.[30]

By the end of summer, Edvard had made so much progress with his work, that it seemed perfectly feasible to produce a complete engine.[31] A couple of months later, on the 3rd of October 1837, Georg Scheutz sent a long letter to the Royal Academy of Sciences. This letter, which has hitherto escaped attention, is very similar to Babbage's letter to Sir Humphry Davy. In it, Scheutz set out his ideas for the first time. However, Scheutz was more direct in his approach. He began by stating that he had discovered a simpler and cheaper design for a difference engine than Babbage had done. Scheutz then offered to build such an improved engine, which − inclusive of the stereotype printing unit − would be 19 times smaller than Babbage's! While Babbage's engine had cost 15,000 pounds in 1829 "and was still unfinished", Scheutz (so he claimed) was able to build an engine for 20,000 riksdaler banco (circa 1,638 pounds) within an estimated time of one to two years at most.[32] Since he lacked financial means of his own, he pointed out, he would require an advance against security. Because the machine would be much smaller in size, it could be moved around like a piece of furniture and put to use wherever it was needed. Scheutz did not explicitly ask for government money for the project, although given the large amount involved, this was virtually the only possible source. Nor did he mention to whom he was offering the engine in his letter. As shall become clear, he had his reasons for mentioning neither the King nor the government. However, he did have one suggestion for financing the investment in which he had placed his hopes. This was that the money might be raised by a public loan ("ett publikt förlagslån") some of which were interest-free. What kind of loan Scheutz had in mind is uncertain. Both the Academy of Sciences and the government awarded financial grants in support of inventions. These were usually for small amounts and were non-repayable. The fact that Georg Scheutz was prepared to repay any sum that he was given, was therefore highly unusual. Scheutz would build and retain the engine and then print with pleasure any tables which the Academy of Sciences might desire.[33] These could then be published in the Academy's *Handlingar*. In his view, tables of logarithms were the first priority. This was an entirely reasonable assumption since no comprehensive logarithm-table had been produced in Sweden.[34]

Whereas Babbage, as he had explained in his letter to Davy, had been reluctant to get involved in the business because it was altogether foreign to his habits and pursuits, Scheutz had doubts on account of the money and time involved. However, there was an even more essential difference between the two letters. The more practical Scheutz believed that the difference engine was technically quite feasible and this aspect caused him no worry at all. On the other hand, he was not in a position to judge if there was a real need for such a machine — and he therefore asked the Academy for their view of this important question. Was the difference engine "an artefact, which from the lofty pinnacles of Science appeared as a mere mechanical toy devoid of practical interest"?[35] Compared with this question, the matter of finance was a secondary affair. It is interesting to note that despite the fact that he had read a great deal about errors in tables in several articles on the difference engine, he was not himself convinced that there was a real need for this mechanism. In posing this question to the learned men of the Academy, Scheutz like Müller before him, tried to settle this key issue before daring to embark on the construction of a printing calculating engine. As far as Babbage had been concerned, the answer to the question had been "yes" from the outset.

In his eleven page letter to the Academy, Scheutz did not provide any details about the design of the projected engine. Instead he devoted more than four pages to a mathematical proof, showing that the number of differences needed is equal to the degree of the polynomial used to approximate the function to be calculated. Thus it requires three differences to compute a table for the cube function. In a humorous aside about his lengthy proof, Scheutz remarked that "in all probability, it would have been much shorter for a greater talent than my own, but since I have nothing else to rely upon, it only remains for me to apologize for the probably unnecessary length".[36] From this proof followed a number of corollaries which demonstrate that his knowledge of mathematics and of the difference method in particular, was in fact highly limited. He asserted namely — and this explains the small dimensions of his engine — that only *one* difference sufficed for tables of logarithms since the second difference (in the case of logarithms) became negative and it was most convenient to calculate with positive numbers. In actual fact, one difference would have been completely impossible. In addition, he considered that the engine should calculate with 10 digits and print 20 in the result, an erroneous idea that was incorporated in the first Swedish engine.[37] But despite the fact that Scheutz' knowledge of mathematics was limited, he had nonetheless managed to understand the larger part of Lardner's technical description, to which he had added his own ideas and modifications. In time, both his own and his son's knowledge of the necessary technology and mathematics involved, would grow so that their engines would indeed be more comprehensive than Babbage's.

The estimated cost which Scheutz had given in the letter, was based on the price which Swedish instrument makers and engine-builders took for making analogous components.[38] Undoubtedly he had checked up on these matters with his friends in the Industrial Association. Since the design of the engine at this stage is unknown, the information quoted by Scheutz tells unfortunately nothing about the differences between Swedish and English workshop technology. The only thing that is known, is that the entire engine, with the possible exception of the steel types in the printing unit, could be built in Sweden.[39] Georg Scheutz concluded his letter to the Academy with the following summary:

"Thus it lies beyond my capacity to occupy myself more with this idea, than I have already done, no matter how eager I might be to see it realized, without in some sense being assured of support for the additional time that I must lavish on it. I have, moreover, been long prepared to content myself with the knowledge that I have attained, especially since, as was mentioned right at the beginning, I do not know with the same certainty what importance such machinery can in general possess. But before I entirely consign the whole idea to limbo, I thought it my duty both to Science and Country to try in some way to achieve its continuation and realization, to the extent that it deserves.

I, therefore, in all humility, make bold to request that the Academy of Sciences deliver their judgement in this matter, having previously resolved in the light of that judgement, to bring to fulfilment what I have begun, as far as opportunity allows, or calmly to set it aside for ever.

Stockholm, the 3rd of October 1837

Georg Scheutz"[40]

On the 11th of October, Scheutz' letter was taken up for discussion at a meeting of the Academy of Sciences in Stockholm. A committee of four was appointed to investigate the matter and to deliver its judgement.[41] It was to take until the 14th of February 1838 before their deliberations were completed. From their statement, it appears that Scheutz had been unwilling to provide the necessary information so that the Academy committee could judge how far Scheutz' engine was simpler and cheaper than Babbage's.[42] The reasons for this are unclear and nothing is said about them in the statement itself.[43] But, at any rate an answer was given to Scheutz' main question, albeit in still very general terms. In the view of the committee, such an engine "must possess a great value for practical calculation".[44] In addition, it was said that the price Scheutz had quoted was "relatively cheap", but "too much for a country like Sweden with its limited resources". The comparison drawn here was with the "much richer England".[45] It was also pointed out that despite all the money which had been spent on Babbage's engine, it was still unfinished. Nonetheless, the committee did not doubt Babbage's genius, and was confident that he would bring his engine to completion. The report ended as follows: – "Moreover we believe that the time which may be required for this, cannot in any notable way, delay the progress of the mathematical sciences, all the less so since the delay will be richly compensated by the fact that a single Babbage engine, once invented, will be sufficient not simply for the country where it is invented, but for the whole world."[46]

Undoubtedly it was Georg Scheutz himself who had put these words in the mouth of the Academy's committee members. But despite this failure to obtain financial support to build a difference engine, he did not let the matter rest there as he had suggested. Now he knew that that there was a need – in his enthusiasm he must have been easy to convince on this point – and he let Edvard continue with his project, trying out each promising idea as it arose. For Edvard, the whole thing was much more of an absorbing game. Georg was driven on by other motives. There was Babbage's apparent failure and the need for error-free tables. On a later occasion he was to say that it was sufficient that science itself gained from the enterprise.[47] There was also another aspect to be considered. By building such a machine, his son Edvard would be assured of a promising career as an engineer.[48] No doubt other motives were at work as well. I believe that it must have been a particularly stimulating challenge for him to try to construct the printing unit which would produce tables automatically. The possibility of replacing one of his compositors by a mechanical device must have fascinated him. The mere fact that Babbage had grappled with the engine but had been unable to complete it, was a great challenge in itself. If he could succeed where Babbage had failed, Scheutz would have proved to himself that he was a talented engineer who had been prevented only by unfortunate circumstances from following his true calling. It is unlikely that Scheutz was interested in winning fame through the invention. When he had invented his automatic fast press, he had thoughts of building a company round it but fame did not enter the picture. Nor did it do so with his plans to inaugurate the world's first fully mechanized press for printing tables. Neither was Scheutz concerned to rise in the social ladder, as will be shown. Yet it would be naive to believe that he thought of building an expensive difference engine without some form of financial compensation. Presumably he anticipated either eventually being able to sell the engine, or else its products, whether in the form of the stereotype plates or the finished tables in

Sweden or abroad. Stronger, however, than this economic motive, was Scheutz' desire to solve once and for all the serious problem of errors in tables and to get rid of the monotonous preparatory work involved.

The work on the Swedish difference engine proceeded without any publicity in the peace and quiet of the Scheutz home. Father and son worked closely together in happy cooperation, a not unimportant consideration given the difficulty of the work. It happened quite often that Georg thought up various solutions regarding components in the engine, which turned out to be impractical. It was then the turn of the imaginative Edvard to work out an alternative solution, which would allow the work to continue.[49] The Swedish difference engine thus developed by a process of trial-and-error. It is also clear that Edvard's knowledge and skill increased as the work on the engine proceeded.[50] Closely following Lardner's words, Georg and Edvard Scheutz chose to design the calculating unit as follows: columns were to correspond to powers and rows were to corrspond to differences, which was the exact reverse of the arrangement adopted in the English difference engine, but at the same time wholly in accordance with Lardner's exposition.

Edvard devoted all of his spare time to work on the engine, but it demanded more and more. When the spring term 1839 began at the Technological Institute, Edvard Scheutz was not numbered among the students. For the following three terms, his attention was entirely devoted to the difference engine and he did not resume his studies again until the autumn of 1840. It is interesting to note that during this final year, he specialized primarily in mechanics. His skill did not pass unnoticed and he received his third medal.[51]

Meanwhile, during the autumn of 1838, Georg Scheutz tried to sell a difference engine to France.[52] His reasons for looking abroad were in the main economic, and were naturally influenced by the negative reaction of the Academy of Sciences. The choice of France was made perhaps from a certain uncertainty about how Babbage and his fellow Englishmen would react. The Swedish ambassador in Paris, Count Löwenhielm, had been of great assistance in forwarding Scheutz' invitation.[53] On the 17th of December 1838, a short announcement from Georg Scheutz was read out at a meeting of l'Academie des Sciences "about a Calculating Machine, said to be simpler and consequently less costly than that of Monsieur Babbage".[54] Unfortunately the details of Scheutz' offer on this occasion remain unknown.[55] But according to Georg Scheutz the astronomers François Jean Dominique Arago, the Secretary of l'Academie des Sciences, and Théodore Olivier who were given the task of considering the matter, demanded to inspect the machine themselves, preferably in Paris.[56] Indeed, this demand was hard to satisfy since the machine was very far from being ready. Bringing the finished machine to Paris was difficult too, because of Georg's limited finances. In 1847 he wrote – "As this condition was hard to satisfy, the offer still awaits a decision".[57]

If Scheutz did not want to reveal to Babbage what he was up to (as

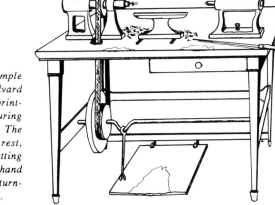

Fig. 23 It was on a simple lathe like this one that Edvard Scheutz built the first printing difference engine during the years 1837–1843. The lathe lacked a slide rest, which meant that the cutting tool had to be held in the hand as in the case of wood-turning. Drawing by author.

there is reason to believe), there would have been little he could have done about it, once the news was sent to the scientific society abroad. Arago was one of Babbage's close friends on the Continent, and they had remained in touch with each other since Babbages' trip to Paris in 1819.[58]

In Stockholm the work on the difference engine progressed slowly. One reason for this was the simple tools that Edvard had at his disposal, which made each part a difficult task on its own.[59] Parts were sawn out of sheet metal with an ordinary hacksaw, filed to final size and form, and soldered, riveted or screwed together with other finished pieces. Edvard's lathe was a chapter in itself. Although it was the pride of his workshop, it was of the simplest kind – a far cry from the extremely modern and sophisticated machine tools used by Clement and Babbage. Unfortunately, no document has survived that can throw any light on the exact progress of the development work on the engine.[60] However, some facts are known. Georg Scheutz states that on the 19th of April 1840, after many trials and changes, the calculating unit was "so far completed [...] that it correctly calculated series with terms of *five figures*, and *one difference*, also of *five figures*".[61]

Two years later, on 29th April 1842, the calculating unit had been extended to take care of the second and third order differences.[62] The Scheutzes had at last understood that one difference was not sufficient if the engine was to do some serious work. With the help of his simple lathe, Edvard had been able to make the 15 addition elements, which served to perform the operation of addition. It was a singularly impressive piece of work, given that the lathe in question lacked a slide rest, which meant that the cutting tool had to be guided and held by hand, see Fig. 23.[63] As the various parts were made, they were mounted in the wooden frame which formed the body of the machine.

The printing unit was not yet ready, although the Scheutzes must have worked on it simultaneously with the development of the other parts.[64]

121

Clearly Georg Scheutz must have given the printing unit particular attention. It was right in the centre of his field of interest and knowledge, and furthermore, they had to produce a printing unit in order to get a useful machine, and to be able to prove that their plan was superior to the one Babbage had chosen.

Part of the autumn of 1842 Georg Scheutz devoted to writing an article on the method of differences. He hoped that it would appear in the series: *Vetenskapsakademiens Handlingar*, and on the 12th of October he submitted his eleven page manuscript to the Academy.[65] It was entitled "Praktisk Differensräkning för *Geometriska* Serier", and dealt with how one could with the help of the difference method extract roots of arbitrary degree, something that was indeed possible but was not the principal purpose of the method. The Academy passed the article to two of its members for refereeing.[66] In their judgement, the article was not suited to the Academy's series of learned papers.[67] Georg then asked for the article to be placed in the Academy's archive, which appears to have been done.[68] The article is of interest, because it is in fact an attempt to spread knowledge of the difference engine, although in a special and modest way. At the end of the article, its existence is noted. But it was an attempt to publicize the engine nonetheless, perhaps even a part of some general strategy. Scheutz noted that it was scarcely possible for anyone who had tried out this mathematical method, in the manipulation of numbers involving many digits, to find something quicker or more adequate – "in particular when one can employ any calculator one likes, provided that he possesses the mechanical skill of adding and subtracting integers quickly and correctly".[69]

Where did Edvard Scheutz learn to use tools, and above all the lathe, with such precision and confidence? No doubt his father had an interest in lathe technique as is shown by the fact that he had written many shorter articles and notices, as well as published a book, on this subject.[70] Georg might thus have served as a good teacher. The very practical training at the Technological Institute under Gustav Magnus Schwartz also contributed its share, if not the major one. An inventory of the workshops at the institute from 1846 sheds further light on the practical orientation of the training.[71] At this time, there were four metal lathes, one screw cutting engine and four wood turning lathes in the building.[72] In addition to this there were many other machines for metalwork as well as hand tools. On the premises, there were also shops for casting, forging, sheet metal work and carpentry.[73] In other words, it was a very well equipped ordinary workshop. It might very well be supposed that the majority of these tools and machine tools were present when Edvard was a student at the Institute.[74] It is possible that he even made some parts of the engine there. The famous Swedish inventor and engineer Christopher Polhem's *Mechanical Alphabet* also had an impact on Edvard's work on the difference engine.[75] This alphabet consisted of some 80 wooden models, each one representing a mechanical movement or part, and which

Fig. 24 Model of a mangle wheel mechanism built by some unknown student of the Technological Institute during the first part of the 19th century. Original model kept in the National Museum of Science and Technology, Stockholm. TM no 1.642, model marked A.II.G.b.I. Photographed by Rigmor Söderberg, TM.

Fig. 25 Front view of Georg and Edvard Scheutz first difference engine, finished in 1843. It was the first complete difference engine in the world. Photograph by courtesy of the Nordic Museum, Stockholm.

were used in the training at the Institute. With these models as examples and sources of inspiration the Polhem tradition was carried on. Students like Edvard made their own mechanical models as part of the education. Many of these small size machines and mechanisms from the Technological Institute have been preserved, see Fig 24.[76] They all display remarkably great craftmanship and reflect the very practical emphasis which prevailed during Edvard Scheutz' time at the Institute. After the years 1846-48, due to Schwartz' resignation and the later reorganization, the focus gradually changed towards more theoretical subjects.

Finally, after numerous hours of labour, Edvard Scheutz finished the difference engine at the end of the summer 1843.[77] Six years had elapsed since the work had started. Father and son were probably as proud as they were happy and relieved over their successful venture. They had brought a seemingly impossible project to completion with the simple tools at their disposal. Their engine, although a modest prototype, included the very important printing unit and thus marked the construction of the first complete difference engine in the world, see Fig 25.

The Academy of Sciences which previously had been unable to judge if the Scheutz engine was simpler and cheaper than Babbage's, could now see and test the finished product. With a view to getting a certificate testifying to the engine's performance, Georg Scheutz asked some members of the Academy to inspect it. He must also have been eager to get a dated statement to the effect that he had invented the machine. Such a document would be useful if the priority of the invention was questioned by some other inventor, or in the nationalistic debate that was likely to follow. After several tests and experiments on the machine, executed shortly after it was finished, a certificate in Swedish was duly issued. Moreover, a French version, with some additions, was also composed. It was presumably intended for Arago and Olivier.[78] The three men responsible for the inspection were the Secretary of the Academy, Jöns Jacob Berzelius, the astronomer Nils Haqvin Selander, and the lecturer in physics, Carl Bertil Lilliehöök. Their certificate, translated from the Swedish original, is here given in full.

"The undersigned take leave to issue the following statement concerning a calculating and printing machine, which they were requested to inspect and which was conceived by the Auditor Mr. Georg Scheutz and brought to a finished form by his son Edvard Scheutz, a student at the Royal Technological Institute, who also has invented several important parts of the machine.

The general purpose of the machine is to provide a solution to the same problem for which the English Calculating Machine constructed by Babbage was designed, namely to present in tabular form and to print in stereotypes the successive terms of arithmetical series. It can thus be used for the construction of tables where the difference of a certain order becomes constant. The machine in question consists of three parts:

1st — *The Calculating unit itself*. This is certainly unable to deal with arithmetical series of a degree higher than the third, and it cannot give complete terms, where more than five digits are called for, but there is nothing in the nature of the mechanism to prevent one from extending its performance to include series of arbitrary degree and terms with as many digits as required. To accomplish this, it is only necessary to supply additional machine-parts, similar to those already existing, i.e. the machine's height and length are increased. In its present state, he [sic] can nevertheless, under certain circumstances, print 10-digit numbers. The last five digits are already given correctly and provided the terms do not grow too rapidly, the 6th together with all the digits to the left of it, are increased by 1 or alternatively, several of the subsequent terms become constant. This mechanism of the machine was supplied with another device, which allowed the missing digits in terms greater than 99,999 to be displayed. In our presence, specific terms were correctly presented for five different series of the third degree, supplied by us. Here it may be observed that in the case of decreasing series the machine gave not the negative terms themselves, but their complements relative to 100,000. However, if the machine is halted at the term where the series changes from positive to negative and the com-

124

plements to the differences, arising from that point onwards, are inserted, the negative terms and not their complements result.

2nd − *The Printing unit.* Each term supplied by the calculating unit is presented in the form of printed digits, arranged in rows close to one another, as in a printed table and the rows are immediately printed in some material, which allows galvanoplastic or stereotype copies to be made. The printing is accomplished by means of ordinary printer's type, which, however, in the case of a larger machine or where the digits had to be printed in copper, would require to be made of steel or some other hard metal, and the rows are set with great accuracy, one beneath the other in the same vertical column. In the test carried out, the digits were printed in a thin layer of lead.

3rd − *The Numerator.* The printing unit is combined with another mechanism, which before each term prints its corresponding argument.

The machine is operated by turning a handle by means of which, without any additional measure, one can carry out both the calculation, arrangement and printing of the digits and rows. In its present form, it occupies a case 2 feet 8 inches long, 2 feet wide and 8 inches high. When placed on a table large enough to support it, it can be lifted and moved, together with the table, by two persons.

Finally, it may be noted that the machine, being merely a model, has been built without access to those mechanical tools required for more accurate metal work and it does not therefore possess that perfection which a larger scale model, designed for actual use and executed in more favourable circumstances, would and must possess. Nevertheless, in its present form it is capable of evaluating certain classes of mathematical formulae when the variables involved receive steadily increasing definite values.

Stockholm 18th September 1843
Jac. Berzelius
Secretary to the Royal Academy of Sciences

N. H. Selander
Astronomer to the Royal
Academy of Sciences,
Professor

C. B. Lilliehöök,
Lieutenant Commander. Lecturer
in Physics at Marieberg"[79]

For the prospective buyer, this statement contained a great deal of interesting information. The mathematical capacity of the engine was mentioned and it was somewhat greater than what Babbage had managed to accomplish. Several series had been calculated with the help of the engine quite correctly and in addition printed in the matrix material with great accuracy. It also contained a mechanism which advanced the argument successively, something which Babbage's engine also required but which he had never mentioned. The size and weight of the engine were

Fig. 26 The Secretary to the Swedish Royal Academy of Sciences, Jöns Jacob Berzelius (1779–1848). At the end of the summer of 1843 Berzelius and two other Swedish scientists tested the performance of the first Scheutz engine. With the statement they signed in September 1843 as reference Georg Scheutz turned to England offering a the Englishmen a complete engine in metal able to calculate with 7 orders of differences and 17 digit numbers. Photograph by courtesy of the Stockholm University Library with the Royal Academy of Sciences, Stockholm.

also small, which suggested that the design differed markedly from Babbage's. It was also possible to extend the mathematical capacity of the engine as desired. Finally although the statement made clear that it was a prototype engine that was being considered, it was suggested that a larger engine built along similar lines would function satisfactorily.[80]

The most remarkable aspect of this statement of Berzelius was that it was not an official pronouncement of a committee of the Royal Academy of Sciences, which has been asserted repeatedly.[81] It was the private judgement of three members of the Academy, one of whom happened to be its Secretary. There is no mention of this inspection in the archive of the Academy, and in the statement itself there is nothing to suggest that it was carried out on behalf of the Academy.[82]

Ever since Scheutz had first presented his idea in 1837 to the Academy of Sciences, Berzelius had been informed of the matter.[83] It is even possible that Scheutz and he knew one another. At any rate they had a number of acquaintances in common. It had been an Italian instrument maker called Joshua Vacano, who had taught the young Georg his trade and opened his eyes to the wonders of physics and chemistry.[84] Berzelius, who was Scheutz' senior by six years, had had the same man as his teacher.[85] Both Scheutz' friend Ludvig Borgström and the director of Chalmers, Carl Palmstedt, had worked with Berzelius.[86] Palmstedt and Berzelius were close friends.[87] In 1832, Berzelius had been called to comment on Scheutz' cubic alun.[88] In 1838, Berzelius had been a member of the grand jury in the trial of Scheutz' best friend, Magnus Jacob Crusenstolpe when he was charged with sedition.[89] So even if they were not personally acquainted, it is clear that that they knew a great deal about one another, not least through their books and articles. What is more, Berzelius was probably personally acquainted with Babbage and knew about his engine. During his travels in Europe at the end of September 1828, the Englishman had participated in the great congress of natural science in Berlin. One of the guests of honour had been Berzelius and in a letter to John Herschel, Babbage's mother proudly relates how her son had spent an evening in conversation with Berzelius and three other famous scientists.[90] No doubt at some point the difference engine entered the conversation. It is even possible that Berzelius had got to hear about it earlier. In 1812 he had visited London and become acquainted with Davy, Wollaston and Thomas Young with whom he continued to correspond.[91]

Given these circumstances, it is reasonable to suppose that Berzelius must have been especially interested when he heard that Scheutz had plans to build an improved table printing engine in the Swedish capital. Count Löwenhielm in Paris was, like Arago and Olivier, a good friend of Berzelius as well as of Palmstedt.[92] It seems more than a mere coincidence that Scheutz offered France the engine and that just these people were involved in the matter. It is my conjecture that Berzelius was personally active in promoting the Scheutz calculating engine and was happy to consent to take part in the desired inspection. The Scheutz engine was not only the first complete difference engine. It was also, as Merzbach emphasized, the first printing calculating machine.[93] Last but not least, for reasons of national honour, it was also the first Swedish calculating machine.[94]

Nils Haqvin Selander had professional reasons for taking an interest in the engine. Since 1837 he had been the Academy's astronomer.[95] Like Scheutz, he was the son of an innkeeper but he had succeeded in coming to Uppsala where he studied mathematics and wrote his dissertation on astronomy. In the 1830s he had trained himself in practical astronomy at the Observatory at Åbo in Finland and at Königsberg in Prussia. As the Academy's astronomer, he was responsible from 1838 onwards for the composition and publication of he Swedish Almanac for the four horizons of Lund, Gothenburg, Stockholm and Haparanda, a work which required the same accuracy as the production of numerical tables. In the history of the Academy, there are a number of examples of errors which crept into the Almanac, both during the calculation stage and later at the printing stage.[96] In addition the Academy also published from time to time an astronomical calendar. *Astronomiska calendern* also called *Sjökalendern*, was a nautical astronomical collection of tables on the lines of the French collection *La Connoissance des Temps*. No steps had been taken to issue this Swedish ephemeris on a regular basis.[97] Perhaps this thought struck Selander when he first heard about the Scheutz engine. He had closely watched the development of the Swedish table machine project from the very beginning, and as the Academy's permanent assistant secretary, he was, in one sense, Berzelius' closest associate. When Scheutz had sent in his application in 1837, Selander had been a member of the committee which had to decide if there was a need for such an engine, as well as trying to answer Scheutz' other questions.[98] When Scheutz sent his article to the Academy several years later, Selander was one of the two referees appointed to judge the paper.[99] Scheutz knew about Selander and had listened with interest to his lecture on the latest findings in astronomy at the Academy's celebration on the 31st of March each year.[100]

Of the three men, Carl Bertil Lilliehöök, was the youngest and the least well known. His scientific merits were also the most modest. His training and career had originally been in the Royal Swedish Navy.[101] After a three year course at the Artillery School in Marieberg, he had accompanied the French scientific expedition to northern Scandinavia and Spitzbergen, which took place in 1838. When he returned from this long trip he was appointed lecturer in physics at Marieberg and he was elected a member of the Academy in 1844. Very little is otherwise known about him but it can be assumed that it was because of his knowledge about navigation and physics that he was chosen to be one of the three men.

With Berzelius' statement as their reference, Georg and Edvard Scheutz immediately set about trying to sell their invention. On the 31st of October 1843, Georg Scheutz wrote to England offering to sell a difference engine.[102] There were two factors at work behind this move. First of all, he was convinced that one engine was sufficient to satisfy the world demand for tables. Secondly, it would have been a waste of money for any other country to invest in such an engine, in the event that Babbage succeeded.[103] Unfortunately the details of Scheutz' offer and the related documents have been destroyed.[104] Nevertheless, some things are known. According to Scheutz himself, he offered a complete engine in metal, that would calculate and print tables with 7 orders of differences and 17 digit numbers.[105] In order to prove that he could in fact do this, he enclosed an English version of Berzelius' statement.[106] Through the good offices of Count Magnus Björnstjerna, the Swedish ambassador in London, this was forwarded to the Home Secretary, Sir James Graham, who appointed a committee to investigate the matter. It included the Surveyor to the Navy, the naval architect Sir William Symonds, the Astronomer Royal, George Biddell Airy, together with another unidentified professor at London University.[107] On this occasion Count Björnstjerna had been very eager to give Scheutz all kinds of help for which the latter was very grateful.[108] It is probably more than a coincidence that Björnstjerna was a member of the Swedish Academy of Sciences and a colleague and friend of Berzelius and Palmstedt.[109] Furthermore, Björnstjerna had been present at the meeting in February 1838, when the committee reported on Scheutz' first letter about his plans to build an engine.[110] However, according to Georg Scheutz, his offer was turned down by the Treasury on the grounds that Parliament would be unlikely to support a foreign invention of the same kind as the English difference engine, which had already cost the country so much money.[111]

By the time Scheutz offered his difference engine to England, Babbage had long been immersed in the design of the superior Analytical Engine.[112] For over a year, he had been free to apply his mind to how to use his own money to construct this engine at the workshops at his house at No. 1 Dorset Street. Now aged fifty-five, he worked for ten to eleven hours a day, surrounded by his own draughtsmen, workmen and at least one assistant and a servant.[113] The preceding years had been something of a trial. From March 1833, when the work on the Difference Engine had been discontinued, he had been uncertain about whether the project had been abandoned by the government or not.[114] On countless occasions, he had demanded an answer but without success. The general public, the newspapers and scientific societies had demanded either that he and the government should be held responsible for the failure, or else that he should carry through the project to its completion.[115] These disputes had not afforded him any rest. However, there was also a further problem. Babbage was not particularly interested in resuming his work on the Difference Engine, unless he was actually forced to do so.[116] He was wholly taken up with the Analytical Engine. Already at the end of 1834, he had enquired, albeit cautiously, if the government would allow him to build that engine instead.[117] Thereafter this engine was always part of the picture. On the 4th of November 1842, the First Lord of the Treasury, Sir Robert Peel, finally gave Babbage his verdict. The government had decided to abandon the Difference Engine, on the grounds of expense.[118] Babbage, for his part, was not prepared to let it go at that and demanded to see Sir Robert personally. On the 11th of November they met and according to Babbage's version, there was soon a clash of wills. Babbage, in a final attempt, offered the government a "New Difference Engine", based on some of the more simple contrivances he had invented for the Analytical Engine.[119] Peel turned this down. Babbage then changed the subject and suggested that he should receive some recompense for his years of work on the difference engine, which had helped the advancement of science. Airy, the astronomer, had for example an annual pension of 1,500 pounds plus a house to boot. George Peacock, another of Babbage's friends, received 1,800 pounds annually. Peel retorted that Babbage was not entitled to any remuneration and rubbed salt in his victim's wound, by pointing out that Babbage had "rendered the Difference Engine useless by inventing a better".[120] The exchange grew more and more acrimonious, and when Babbage suggested that these pensions were not professional rewards, Peel became furious. As for Babbage, he considered that he had been treated with great injustice and rising to his feet, he took leave of Peel: − "If these are your views, I wish you good morning."[121]

With this painful ending, the history of the English difference engine came to a close. In January 1843, the machine and its drawings were consigned, on government instructions, to the Museum of King's College, London.[122] It was on the 23rd of November 1843 that Georg Scheutz' offer concerning his difference engine reached the Home Office in London − that is almost one year after Peel had told Babbage that the project was abandoned.[123] Peel was still at the Treasury and therefore given what had happened, it is hardly surprising if the English reaction to Scheutz' offer was frosty. Georg Scheutz, however, maintained that the committee which was set up to look into the matter delivered a not unfavourable report.[124] Although nothing is known about this report, it will be useful to say a little more about one of the members of the committee, George Biddell Airy. Like Babbage, he had studied at Trinity College but had been both Senior Wrangler and First Smith's Prizeman, subsequently becoming Fellow of Trinity.[125] In 1826, he was elected Lucasian Professor of Mathematics and in 1828 Plumian Professor of Astronomy and director of the Cambridge Observatory. By 1835, he had reached the summit of his career. He became Astronomer Royal and was responsible for the Observatory at Greenwich. Airy is an important figure in the history of the difference engines, since he is one of the few who was called upon to give his opinion about these machines. Although in time, he would become known for his rash judgements and his tendency to become embroiled in scientific controversies, I do not believe that his opinions, as the man responsible for the production of tables at Greenwich, can be neglected. In 1837, he is said to have remarked of Babbage's difference engine that "the thing is a humbug".[126] When the Chancellor of the Exchequer, Henry Goulburn, had asked for Airy's professional opinion of the engine, he had replied that "It was worthless".[127] His views of Scheutz' first engine and its possible use in England seem not to have survived. But as will be shown, Airy came to play an important role in Georg and Edvard Scheutz' ensuing efforts to sell their invention.

Georg Scheutz' hopes about selling his engine to England had been crushed but he was an optimist and considered that the attempt alone had been worthwhile. Through Björnstjerna, he had come by important information, which showed that the mere fact that a committee had been set up to look into the matter, was a positive sign. Georg now thought that no less than 30,000 pounds (363.750 riksdaler banco) had been lavished on Babbage's engine and that the plans for any future subsidies had been cancelled.[128] Instead of looking on this as a final defeat for the difference engine, Georg Scheutz now decided to apply to the Swedish government for financial support.

On the 31st of August 1844, Auditor Scheutz went to the Royal Palace and delivered a letter addressed to the King.[129] It was no accident that he had waited till this date. On the 8th of March in the same year, Karl XIV Johan had died and had been succeeded by his son, the Crown Prince Oscar, who now ruled over the Union of Norway and Sweden. Karl XIV Johan had been a French general, who in 1810 had been chosen for political reasons to be Sweden's Crown Prince. During his reign, he had shown little interest in the country and had been principally notable for his conservatism. Among those who belonged to the powerful group which opposed his "autocratic" leanings, was Georg Scheutz and he and other liberal journalists were to play an important part in the struggle. The opposition first made its breakthrough in the 1830s. The July Revolution in France helped to encourage them. Georg Scheutz had been editor and publisher of *Argus* and about the middle of the decade, he published for a short time another opposition paper called *Spegeln*, which made a point of directing many of its barbs against the King.[130] It was also in 1840, that Scheutz published a political essay *Slägtvälde och idévälde, eller det som var och det som kommer* (The power of family inheritance and the power of ideas, or what was and what is to come).[131] This little book of 122 pages had been published anonymously at his press, but in certain copies it appears that he had set out his own name.[132] In the book, Scheutz had boldly attacked the aristocracy and had prophesied that their days in power were numbered. The privileges of birth could no longer take precedence over knowledge and "within a century or so, it [the aristocracy] would be made up of nothing but useless idiots".[133] The Constitution of 1809 came under attack, and thereby Karl XIV Johan, as a bulwark of the old conservatism.[134] It was advocated that the Estates should be replaced by popular representation and the country should be run in accordance with the ideas of liberalism.[135] Nor did two other Estates escape criticism — the Clergy and the Peasants — and the latter were informed that they had been transformed from rich peasants to "easily led, ignorant countryfolk".[136] Such was the message of the tract. Scheutz also continued his political opposition in the pages of *Aftonbladet*. For two years, he had written for this — the most potent — organ of the Swedish opposition.

These circumstances help to explain why Georg Scheutz had refrained up till then from applying for official support for his engine. It is unclear how Karl XIV Johan would have reacted to such an application. But in any case he was the last man whose support Scheutz would have solicited. On the other hand the new successor to the throne, King Oscar I, took an interest in the country and was more liberally inclined, even to the extent of eventually having contacts with the liberal opposition. During his reign, many progressive changes would take place. It was for this reason that Georg Scheutz chose now to apply for government finance for a new difference engine.

What did Scheutz' application contain? After an introduction devoted to errors in numerical tables and Babbage's costly failure, Georg described the improved engine which he and Edvard had built and explained how he had offered an extended version of this engine to England. One such engine was sufficient to meet the world demand for tables and England was the only conceivable purchaser for such a machine. This was because the original decision to build such an engine had been taken there and it would be a waste of money for any other country to put its money into such a scheme, if Babbage had a chance of ultimately succeeding. However, England had turned down his offer and furthermore all government support for the Babbage project had been discontinued. This latter fact had a positive consequence, namely "it disposed of the risk that the money otherwise invested in it, would be superfluous".[137] Scheutz asked the government to provide money so that his son could make an engine with a capacity of 7 differences and 17 digits. The costs had been calculated to amount to 8,980 riksdaler banco. For this figure, a complete engine which "was ready for immediate use and was strong and durable" could be built, within a year and a half.[138] At the same time, Scheutz made a reservation. If more men had to be employed on the project, or if the work ran over two years, it would be dearer. For this reason, he asked for 10,000 riksdaler banco, approximately 825 pounds. The application ended with an eloquent tribute to King Oscar, in which mention was made of the economic benefits which might flow from the printing of new logarithm and other tables, with the help of the engine. In addition His Majesty had the opportunity of being the first to supply the world with error-free tables.[139] And so Scheutz' submission ended with a pertinent historical example:

> "The annals of Royal learning still preserve in grateful memory the renowned Alphonsine Tables as being a more illustrious and imperishable monument than any other..."[140]

The Department of Education and Ecclesiastical Affairs took charge of the matter and it was remitted for expert judgement to the Academy of Sciences. On the 11th of September, at a meeting of the members, a two man committee consisting of Professor Selander and Baron Fabian Jacob Wrede was appointed to look into it.[141]

Fabian Wrede had displayed his talent for mechanics and physics already in childhood. He had served as a professional soldier in the Swedish Army but was drawn to science. In 1835, he became a Member of the Royal Academy of Sciences and also the head of the Artillery School at Marieberg, thus later becoming Carl Bertil Lilliehöök's superior. Wrede taught mathematics and physics. He was particularly interested in invention and had devoted himself to this art.[142]

After having contacted Scheutz and looked at the engine, Selander and Wrede were ready to make their report. It was delivered on the 13th of November to Berzelius, Lilliehöök and the other members of the

Academy.[143] The draft of their statement makes it clear that it was Selander who was mainly responsible for the conclusions drawn and the arguments adduced.[144] What he had to say, was in glaring contrast to the earlier statement he had signed about the Scheutz invention. First of all, he considered it was doubtful if Scheutz could build a larger, extended engine on the basis of an "incomplete model".[145] The engine would be too technically complicated if it was expanded to cope with so many digits and differences. Secondly, even if the technical design problems could be overcome, the significance of the engine should not be overestimated.[146] He then specified what he meant, more closely:

> "Logarithmic, trigonometric and other tables, which are purely mathematical in character, and do not rely on information from experimental results or observation, have already been computed with such accuracy that they leave little to desire; the improvement of astronomical, physical and similar tables depends primarily on access to more exact observational data."[147]

Selander's conclusion was obvious:the application should be rejected.[148] To these noteworthy views, Wrede added his own more positive, but somewhat meaningless commentary. In his view, the Academy should "favourably praise what is beautiful and ingenious in Aud. Scheutz' invention, which in a country with greater resources would be certainly considered worthy of encouragement and support".[149] How could he assert this, given Selander's remarks about the limited interest of the engine? The explanation was that Wrede had been interested in the Scheutz engine from the beginning. In time, he would become one of the Swedish engine's most enthusiastic proponents. Why had Selander altered his opinion? He had endorsed the positive answer given to Scheutz in the spring of 1838 about the need for a difference engine. Five years later along with Berzelius and Lilliehöök, he had testified that the engine could be extended by simply adding engine parts similar to those already employed. One theory is that Selander had suppressed his own judgement initially out of respect for Berzelius and the others. He was newly established as astronomer at the Academy, and perhaps chose to act with circumspection. But later, when his position was more secure, he could afford to put forward his own views based on experience. Another view might be that Selander had simply become wiser with the passage of time, and was more aware of the issues involved in the printing and provision of tables. Whatever the real reason, the outcome was to be expected. On the 3rd of December 1844, the Swedish authorities decided against supporting Georg Scheutz' application, partly on the grounds set out by the Academy of Sciences and partly because there were no funds available.[150]

Just like his colleague George Biddell Airy, Nils Haqvin Selander had maintained that the difference engine was a technical invention of little practical significance. Selander had said that all standard mathematical tables were already sufficiently accurate and that what astronomical and other tables relating to the experimental sciences required was more refined observational methods. King Oscar and his advisers had taken note of these words. But they were also the last to do so. Georg Scheutz' reaction to the Academy's statement is unknown. Either he did not learn of Selander's opinion or else he quietly forgot about it. In the future, he would act as though he knew nothing about it and his autobiographical article makes no mention of Selander's views, although it does cite Wrede's opinion.[151] In the battle of opinions, Wrede was to emerge as the victor. After his negative judgement of the difference engine in the winter of 1844, Selander was to vanish from the story for good.[152]

Unlike the wealthy Charles Babbage, Georg Scheutz lacked money to continue with the project. In consequence, the matter was put to one side. In 1847, he wrote in a tone of resignation, that "the solution to the problem, so long sought in England and at such great cost, has been found, and sooner or later, it must find practical application".[153]

It must have been incomprehensible to Scheutz and most of his contemporaries that the engine was worthless. If it had been, the British government and Babbage would surely never have wasted so much money and time on it. Despite these negative reactions, Scheutz took great care from the very beginning to keep his invention as secret as possible. It is nowhere mentioned in his journals or books, nor for example in the popular daily newspaper *Aftonbladet* which one might have expected, given his close association with that newspaper.[154] He was afraid that his invention might end up in the hands of unscrupulous people and this, however strange it might seem, was why he did not take out a patent.[155] Nor indeed had Babbage.[156] Perhaps the latter believed that it was unlikely that anyone would have embarked on such a demanding project and even if they did, that it was improbable that his own priority would be contested. It is also conceivable that Scheutz kept quiet about the engine for fear of Babbage. There is an article by Georg which explains clearly why the Swedish difference engine's secret was guarded so well.

The title of the article was "Öfversigt af de egentligen industriella Staternas Patentlagar" (Survey of the Patent laws of the genuinely industrial States). It was published in *Tidning för Näringarne* and dealt with the patent question with reference to England, France and America.[157] Georg Scheutz began by stating that it could be profitable for a Swedish inventor to apply for a patent on his invention abroad, particularly in England. A patent there could provide more financial reward than the sale of the invention itself in Sweden. The reason was naturally the status and comparatively large security which accrued from an English patent. However, Georg Scheutz also gave a warning in words which revealed the grounds of his own worries and suspicions. He related that in England there was a special class of industrialists, who made their money from other people's inventions. According to Georg, these men tirelessly read foreign journals, reports etc. They also had special agents who studied the patent offices and workshops in foreign countries. In the English patent applications, it was sometimes admitted that such activity had been employed. More often, said Scheutz, it was disguised with the tactful phrase that such and such, had *"been communicated by a friend abroad"*. He concluded with a cautionary example and stressed that one really has to watch out for such things in England, if one invents something.[158]

Georg Scheutz' worst fear was that someone might take out a patent on the difference engine. Is it not a trifle ironic that this warning came from Scheutz who himself was engaged in essentially the same kind of dissemination of technology and who moreover had patented a number of foreign inventions in Sweden? Had he not even "borrowed" Babbage's idea?

On the 26th of June 1841, Edvard Scheutz completed his studies at the Technological Institute.[159] During his four and half years of study under the supervision of Schwartz, he had been trained as a qualified engineer.[160] Although his training had been highly practical, he also had a knowledge of mathematics, physics, chemistry and foreign languages, which set him apart from the ordinary Stockholm metal worker. But he also knew how to operate lathes and other machine tools and had become a skilful filer and draughtsman. One school had been the Technological Institute, but the difference engine had been another equally important one. For some reason it was not until the 1st of October 1845 that Edvard Scheutz received his final certificate. In comparison with those few of his fellow students who had completed the training, he had acquitted himself excellently.[161] But he represented a new class of citizens, the academically trained mechanic and work was apparently hard to find. His father's idea about him making a living from the difference engine, was impossible at the time and Edvard was forced to work as a printer.[162] In February 1843, Georg Scheutz had arranged for Edvard to take over the ownership of the press.[163] But not long after, the family sold the press and Georg left the printing trade.[164] (However, this was not to be a definitive step.) It seems that Edvard remained in the trade, possibly working for a time for the new owner.

In December of 1842, Georg Scheutz had joined the editorial staff of *Aftonbladet*. His duties were to follow the foreign press and to write popular articles on cultural matters, economics, science and technology.[165] For this he received a monthly salary of 100 riksdaler banco.[166] It was a position which suited him perfectly and he held onto it until his death. *Aftonbladet* had the largest circulation among Swedish newspapers, and was owned and run by Lars Johan Hierta. In his youth, he had taken both a law degree and a doctorate at Uppsala with the intention of pursuing a career as a public official.[167] In 1822, he had begun on this career in earnest in Stockholm. In 1819, however, he had read Scheutz'

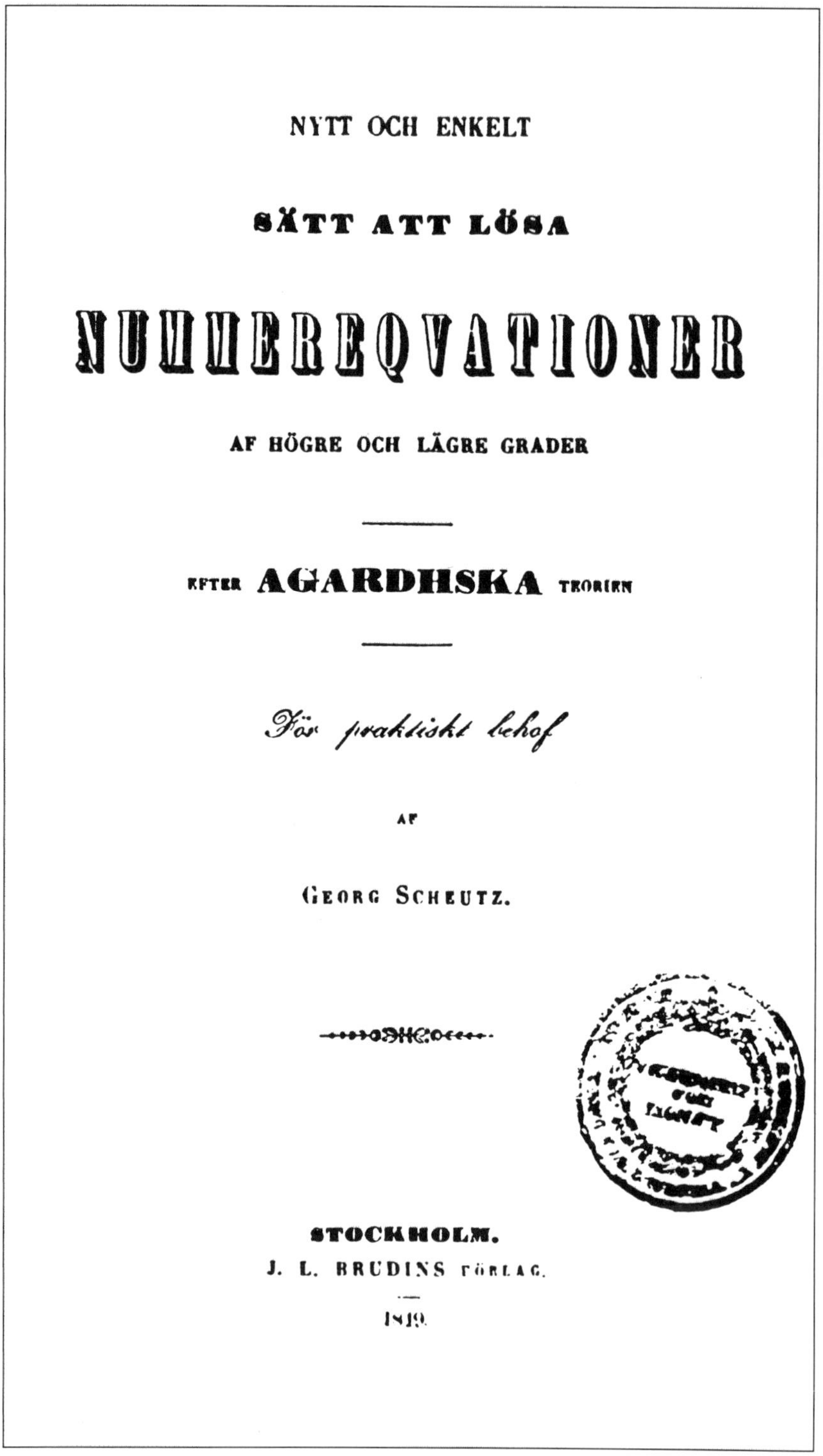

NYTT OCH ENKELT

SÄTT ATT LÖSA

NUMMEREQVATIONER

AF HÖGRE OCH LÄGRE GRADER

———

EFTER **AGARDHSKA** THEORIEN

———

För praktiskt behof

AF

GEORG SCHEUTZ.

————⊙❋⊙————

STOCKHOLM.

J. L. BRUDINS FÖRLAG.

—

1849.

Fig. 27 *Georg Scheutz' book* Nytt och enkelt sätt att lösa nummereqvationer *(Stockholm 1849), dealt with methods of solving equations by the method of differences. In an addendum Scheutz presented his difference engine for the first time in print.*

74

Tillägg.

De svårigheter vid den här beskrifna metodens tillämpning, som omförmälas i § 38, s. 61, skulle naturligtvis försvinna, om analysten, sedan han gifvit sina problemer tjenlig form att behandlas i siffror, kunde anförtro det mödosamma och tidsödande sifferarbetet åt någon *biträdare*, som *aldrig tröttnade, aldrig förvillades,* och *lika skyndsamt och säkert* behandlade *högre* graders sifferutvecklingar, som dem för *1:a graden.* Då äfven sådana sifferexpressioner, som icke i verkligheten ega någon konstant differens, t. ex. *rötter, kretsfunktioner, logaritmer,* o. s. v. skilja sig så litet i sina högre differenser, att dessa, för ett stort antal termer, kunna antagas som konstanta, så skulle man med detta slags biträde kunna konstruera *tabeller* af dylika sifferexpressioner, *absolut felfria* inom en viss, på förhand och godtyckligt bestämd gräns för tabellen; hvilket hittills icke varit möjligt. — Ett sådant biträde finnes emedlertid; det är en *tabellmachin,* uttänkt af författaren till närvarande skrift, i förening med hans son, *Edward Scheutz,* som utfört densamma i modell 1843. — I förmodan att det kunde interessera allmänheten att se ett vedermäle af uppfinningen, bifogas här ett sådant, nemligen en tabell, grundad på eqvationen

$$x^3 - 3x^2 + 90037x = \frac{u}{x}$$

Tabellen är af modellen samtidigt beräknad och intryckt i matrisämne, i närvaro af Notarius Publicus i Stockholm, Herr J. H. Ritterberg, hvilken officielt vitsordat operationen; och aftrycket återgifves här omedelbart från den på matrisen tagna stereotypen.

x	$\underbrace{u}_{x}$
1	90035
2	180070
3	270111
4	360164
5	450235
6	540330
7	630455
8	720616
9	810819
10	901070
11	991375
12	1081740
13	1172171
14	1262674
15	1353255
16	1443920
17	1534675
18	1625526
19	1716479
20	1807540
21	1898715
22	1990010
23	2081431
24	2172984
25	2264675

Fig. 28 This little table of a polynomial of the third degree was made by the first Scheutz engine. It is the oldest existing example of a table calculated and printed by a difference engine. The page is from Georg Scheutz Nytt och enkelt sätt att lösa nummereqvationer (Stockholm 1849).

137

articles on the Wermdö Case, which had revealed to him what the press could accomplish by influencing both the public and the authorities.[168] He had seen how the behaviour of the judge and of various public officials had been exposed for the first time. Later, as a supernumerary clerk in the House of Nobility, he had gained an insight into how the nobles interpreted the law and the constitution. This led him to follow in Scheutz' footsteps and on the 6th of December 1830, he published the first number of the liberal *Aftonbladet*.[169] The newspaper soon achieved wide circulation and kept the Lord Chamberlain busy. Politically, it was much more violent in its tone than Scheutz had been and for this reason Scheutz had withdrawn from Hierta's political group. But in 1842, Scheutz had no longer any misgivings.[170] Once Hierta had attacked Scheutz' cylinder press in an almost malicious fashion, which Scheutz can hardly have liked.[171] But all this was in the past and in his memoirs, Hierta presents Scheutz as his admired forerunner.[172] The good relations which grew up between the two men, would ensure that still another difference engine, despite all the obstacles, would be built in Sweden.

"Unfortunately for himself Mr. Scheutz was fascinated by the subject, and impelled by an irresistible desire to construct an engine for the same purposes".[173] Thus wrote Babbage in a later pamphlet. He had the second Scheutz engine in mind but the judgement has a general application. Like the Englishman, Scheutz was under the spell of the engine. He returned to his project once more with renewed vigour. His own words in the article about the Industrial Exhibition in 1834, on the Swede's hopeless inability to market his products, no doubt revealed something about his own disposition, after these years which had witnessed no new attempt to sell the engine. However, he went about matters in his characteristic, cautious fashion, making use of much the same method he had employed previously when he had sent an article on calculation by means of differences, to the Royal Academy of Sciences.

He wrote a book, which was published in 1849, entitled *Nytt och enkelt sätt att lösa nummereqvationer af högre och lägre grader efter Agardhska teorien: För praktiska behov.* (A new and simple method of solving numerical equations of higher and lower degree with the help of Agardh's theory: For practical purposes). In it he gave an exposition of the method of solving equations by the method of differences, which the professor of botany, mathematician and latterly bishop Carl Adolph Agardh had presented in 1809.[174] In an addendum, he remarks that while the method is excellent, it is time consuming when used on equations of high degree. He then adds that this disadvantage could be removed if one "could assign the laborious and time consuming figure work to some *assistant*, that *never tired*, *never made an error* and dealt with the numerical calculations for the *higher* degrees as *swiftly* and *certainly* as those for the first degree".[175] Georg Scheutz notes that such an assistant does in fact exist and he gives an example of a stereotyped table calculated and printed by the first engine, see Fig. 28. The table shows that Scheutz still was fascinated by the machine's capability to solve equations. But more important, this table is the only existing illustration of what the Scheutz prototype engine could do. It is also the oldest automatically made numerical table in the world, which has been preserved.[176] It is indeed a remarkable little table, standing like a hitherto unnoticed milestone, between the great works of Maginus and Rheticus, and any ordinary tabular listing produced by a modern digital computer.

By 1850, seven years had elapsed since the completion of the first engine. Father and son Scheutz' attempts to either sell or obtain backing for a larger engine had been fruitless. Georg was now an old man, sixty-five years of age. Edvard was twenty-nine. No alterations had been made to their difference engine since 1843. In their home in Stockholm, it remained "quite untouched" in its case.[177] But despite this lull, it was at this point that the story of the Scheutz engine was to begin in earnest.

But before the history of the first engine is put aside, some things have to be said about the machine itself.

MODE OF OPERATION

How had Edvard and Georg Scheutz solved the technical problems involved in their 1843 difference engine? How did it differ from Babbage's great engine, and in what respect was it an improved version of the same design? How did the Scheutz prototype engine operate and what were the engineering ideas on which it was based? These questions can now be answered for the first time. The engine was never exhibited outside of Stockholm during the whole of the 19th century. No articles were written about it and no illustrations of it appeared. At the end of the 1870's, it was for a short time put on public display, but up to then the only people who caught a glimpse of it, were those who paid a visit to the Scheutz home. For a long period, it seems to have been quite forgotten. First in December 1979, it was rediscovered among the collections of the Nordic Museum, where it had laid undisturbed in a depository since 1881.[178] The aim of the present section is to provide a technically detailed description of the engine's physical construction, reflecting Edvard and Georg Scheutz' way of thinking and confronting the reader with the problems they had to solve.[179] These matters will be further developed in the following section, under the heading *design*, where the actual construction of the engine, the choice of materials etc. will be discussed.

Scheutz' first difference engine may be divided into three major units − *the calculating unit*, *the transfer mechanism*, and *the printing unit*, see Fig. 25 and 29.[180] The engine could cope with five digits and three orders of differences. It could print five digits in the result f(x) and five digits in the argument x. In certain circumstances ten digits could be printed in the result. Printing took place by pressing the calculated tabular value into a matrix of soft material, which was then used to make the stereotype plate

Fig. 29 Scheutz' first difference engine. The picture shows the back side of the machine with the transfer mechanism to the left and the printing unit to the right. Photograph by courtesy of the Nordic Museum, Stockholm.

Fig. 30 The calculating unit in Scheutz' first difference engine. Photograph by courtesy of the Nordic Museum, Stockholm.

140

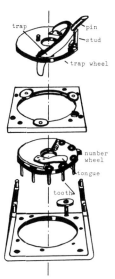

Fig. 31 The components in the addition elements in the first Scheutz engine. Drawing by author.

used for printing on paper. The engine was operated by cranking a handle, which operated upon the three units through a system of gears. Wood and metal were the materials used. Wood was employed exclusively to support the movable metal parts and had no mechanical function. The black-painted engine frame composed of rectangular rods determined the engine's size, with a height of 500 mm, breadth of 740 mm and depth of 510 mm. Its weight is estimated to be about 70 kg, excluding the mahogany case intended for transport and protection.

The calculating unit, the core of the engine, contained 15 *addition elements* and a carrying mechanism. These were grouped in four horizontal rows and placed on wooden shelves, see Fig. 30. Starting from the bottom, these represent Δ3, Δ2, and Δ1 respectively. The uppermost row corresponded to the result f(x). Beginning at the left, the five vertical axles corresponded to ten thousands, thousands, hundreds, tens and units. Addition took place from one row to the row above it in the calculating unit.

The addition element was an interesting technical idea, which allowed for the possibility of building additional units onto the engine, see Fig. 31-32. Apart from certain minor features, all 15 elements were identical. Each contained a *trap wheel* and a *number wheel*. Both of these could rotate freely and were not connected to the vertical axle. The number wheels were marked with the numbers 0-9 and were fitted with ten teeth on their underside. The addition of a number from one element to another placed directly above it took place as follows. The trap wheel was turned by a pin fixed to the vertical axle. If the associated number wheel was set at a number different from zero, *the trap* was lifted up by *the tongue* as the axle turned. The *pin* on the trap then moved in between two teeth of the number wheel belonging to the addition element situated above and moved it round the required number of units. When this was taking place, the trap rested on a stud, see Fig. 32 a. Thereafter the stud was withdrawn and the trap returned to its lower position, see Fig. 32b. If the number wheel in the addition element was set at zero, the trap remained unaffected and rotated freely beneath the teeth of the number wheel above it. This was the way in which the trap wheels were acted upon by the rotation of the five vertical axles in the process of carrying out addition.

Fig. 30 shows that the uppermost row in the calculating unit representing f(x) consisted of number wheels only, to which numbers were added from the row beneath, Δ1. The addition elements in the bottom row Δ3, representing the constant difference, could be locked in different positions 0-9.

The calculating unit also had carrying mechanisms, one for each of the respective rows Δ2, Δ1 and f(x). This was unnecessary in the case of row Δ3, because it was set at a constant difference. Carrying took place when a wheel moved from 9 to 0. It took place sequentially, moving from the lowest to the highest multiple of ten, i.e. from the right to the left in

Fig. 32a Addition element with trap in upper position, with the trap resting on the stud. Photographed by author during restoration.

Fig. 32b Addition element with trap in lower position. Photographed by author.

Fig. 33 Carrying mechanism and adding elements in the first Scheutz engine. The photograph shows the second difference while the engine was taken apart during its restoration in 1981. Photographed by author.

142

Fig. 30. Mechanically it was accomplished by means of a link mechanism, which was operated by the number wheels see Fig. 33.

Because of its very special design and because it reveals something of the underlying ideas, it is worthwhile giving a more detailed description of this carrying mechanism. Consider the example in Fig. 34. Carrying occurs in three stages. In *stage 1*, two number wheels, are shown from above. In the course of an addition, they rotate clockwise. The wheel on the right represents the units and that on the left, the tens. The tens wheel is set at 0 while the units wheel is set at 9. The purpose is to add a one to 9 to give us the result 10. Between the two wheels in the figure there is a link mechanism. It is mounted on two axles a in the number wheel shelf. In addition there are three riveted joints b which allow the link mechanism to move in the plane of the paper. On the pin c, which is fixed to the link mechanism, there is a metal tongue d, which can be rotated around c. Fixed to the number wheel shelf, there is a guiding cam e, against which the movable hook f's arm g can slide. The link mechanism is free to move along the dotted arrows and is operated by the gear wheel h, which engages the carry rack k. On its underside, the gear wheel has two arms i_1 and i_2, which in the course of the rack's motion, make contact with the link mechanism at points j_1 and j_2 respectively. In stage 1, the rack has reached its return position on the left and the arm i_1 is in contact with the hook f at the point j_1. The hook's arm g is therefore at its stop position on the right, nearest the units wheel. The metal tongue d is at rest upon the upper side of the tens wheel on tooth number 2. This is a description of the disposition of the parts prior to addition.

In *stage 2* one unit has been added from the shelve below to the units wheel causing it to be turned on clockwise by one unit so that it is now set at 0. The tens wheel is also set at 0, just as before. A cog l on the units wheel has, in the course of the wheel's rotation, engaged the hook f and drawn the link mechanism along with it and upwards a distance x in the figure. The metal tongue on the tens wheel has descended between tooth number 2 and tooth number 3. The rack remains unaltered in its return-point at the left.

In *stage 3* the following sequence of events has taken place. The rack has moved to the right, turning the gear wheel so that its other arm i_2 has taken hold of the hook f at point j_2 and drawn the link mechanism donwards with it. As a result, the metal tongue which rested against tooth number 2 has in the course of its motion, turned the tens wheel forward one unit. To avoid the hook acting upon the units wheel via the cog, the hook was steered by the guiding cam e during the movement. Both wheels taken together, now show 10 and the carrying operation is completed. Finally, the rack returns to its return-position on the left and thus to stage 1, but this time with the tongue between tooth number 3 and tooth number 4 of the tens wheel.

Cogs were not fitted to the carry rack all the way along but only at four different, long stretches, see Fig. 33. Similarly, the gear wheels did not

143

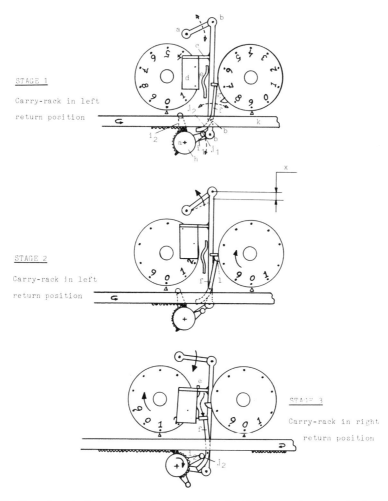

STAGE 1

Carry-rack in left
return position

STAGE 2

Carry-rack in left
return position

STAGE 3

Carry-rack in right
return position

Fig. 34 The three stages in the operation of carrying in the first Scheutz engine. Drawing by author.

have cogs all the way round. Due to this, carrying took place sequentially from right to left, i.e. first with respect to the tens wheel, then the hundreds wheel and so on. There was also another reason for the arrangement of cogs, namely to ensure that the link mechanism always brought forward a whole unit. This was done by making the two black cogs on the rack and gear wheel respectively, larger than the other cogs on the same gear wheel, so that they served to block the link mechanism's downward motion, see Fig. 34, stage 3. If the units wheel in Fig. 34 did not stop at 0, or passed over 0 during addition, no carrying took place. In this case, since the cog on the units wheel did not engage the hook and pull the link mechanism along with it the distance x, stage 2 was omitted in Fig. 34. The metal tongue remained positioned above tooth number 2 and at stage 3, the tongue simply glided over the tooth, without pulling the tens wheel with it.

144

The above description of the carrying mechanism in Scheutz' engine, reveals that it was extremely complicated. At the same time, it shows that the opposite is also true — namely that in a way it was simple! The interesting point with the carrying mechanism is the light it sheds on Georg and Edvard Scheutz' thought processes during the actual development work. Obviously, it is out of the question to describe the precise sequence of their thoughts but the following conjecture is plausible. Somehow or other, they had to use the units wheel to operate the tens wheel, so they began by putting a cog on it, see Fig. 34, stage 1. To bridge the gap between the wheels, they devised a link mechanism, which afterwards had to be modified in the light of difficulties. At this point, the guiding cam came into the picture. Seeing that carrying had to take place sequentially, they were led to develop the rack and the gear wheels. In saying that this mechanism was simple, I mean that no great degree of abstraction was involved: the mechanism's movements and design corresponded directly to the intuitive ideas of the inventors. All this is borne out by the absence of detailed drawings and by the down to earth trial-and-error methods that were employed.

The calculating unit was designed to operate continuously in a four-stage sequence in a manner similar to Babbage's engine, see Fig. 30. In stage 1, even differences were added to odd ones ($\Delta 2 \rightarrow \Delta 1$). In stage 2, carrying took place with respect to row $\Delta 1$. Stage 3 involved the simultaneous addition of odd differences to even ones ($\Delta 3 \rightarrow \Delta 2$, $\Delta 1 \rightarrow f(x)$). In stage 4, carrying took place with respect to rows $\Delta 2$ and $f(x)$. In operation, all the trap wheels belonging to $\Delta 2$ rotated anti-clockwise (as seen from above), while the trap wheels $\Delta 1$ and $\Delta 3$ remained still. When, on the other hand, the trap wheels $\Delta 1$ and $\Delta 3$ rotated clockwise, the trap wheels $\Delta 2$ remained still. In keeping with this, the number wheels $\Delta 1$ and $\Delta 3$ were numbered anti-clockwise, while $\Delta 2$ and $f(x)$ were numbered clockwise. In other words, the arrangement was entirely analogous to that adopted in the Difference Engine No. 1. In order to carry out these movements, the five vertical axles in the calculating unit of the Scheutz' engine went through two motions — a rotation through 350° forwards and backwards, and an up-and-down motion. In summary, addition involved two movements, orthogonal to one another, taking place in the engine's calculating unit, see Fig. 30. First, there was the operation of addition itself that involved a vertical motion from the bottom upwards. Secondly, there was the operation of carrying, which involved a horizontal movement from right to left.

Via the *transfer mechanism* the result $f(x)$ was transported to the printing unit. When the tabular value had been calculated, it had to be printed. Each of the five number wheels in the uppermost row of the calculating unit (which together represented the number $f(x)$), see Fig. 30 was connected to a *snail*, see Fig. 35. The snail consisted of a horizontal toothed volute cam divided into ten sectors 0-9 with uniformly decreasing radii. To every snail there corresponded a stepped tooth cam, which was

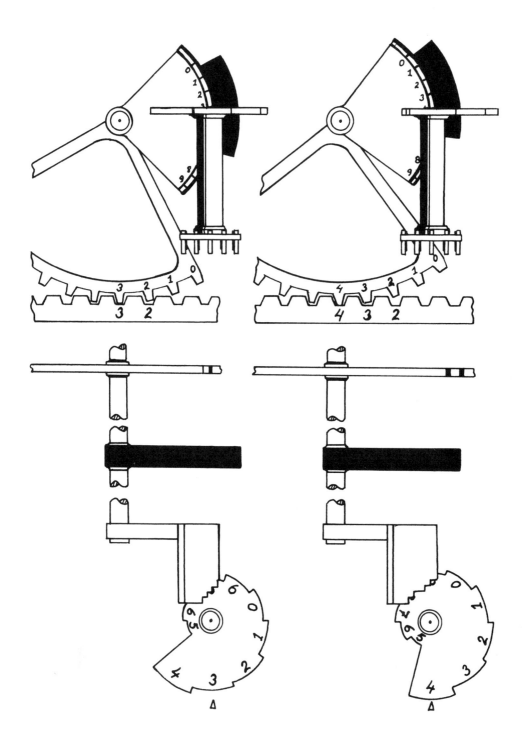

Fig. 35 The components of the transfer mechanism − the snail, the stepped tooth cam, the lead weight (black), the toothed segment and the rack. In the left figure a 3 is transmitted. In the right the snail has turned to 4, the stepped tooth cam has *risen* by one unit and the 4 is transmitted to the printing unit. Drawing by author.

146

so designed that it would sink one step (as the axle was turned) for every new digit displayed on the associated snail, when this was turned clockwise from 9 to 0. On the axle of each of the five stepped tooth cams, there was mounted a toothed segment and a triangle shaped lead weight. The toothed segment was engaged with a rack. These five racks ran side-by-side along the calculating unit to the printing unit, see Fig. 29.

The *printing unit* consisted of three major parts – the type wheels, the numerator and the printing table. The 15 *type wheels* were ingeniously designed as gear wheels with ten cogs, fitted with number types 0-9, see Fig. 37. The type wheels were mounted on a common axle, on which they were able to move freely. The five transfer mechanism racks engaged the cogs on the five type wheels, which are to be seen in Fig. 36 farthest from the reader. During the computation of a tabular value by the calculating unit, the stepped tooth cams were not in contact with the snails but were positioned above them. This was achieved by having the transfer mechanism racks pushed to the left by a roller at their short side, see Fig. 29 and Fig. 36. This roller derived its force from a lead weight via a cord, see Fig. 29. When a tabular value had been printed, the roller was pushed beneath, so that the torque induced by the triangle-shaped lead weights on their axles, turned the step toothed cams in contact with the snails. The toothed segments then adjusted the racks, which in turn set the five type wheels to the result f(x).

The *numerator* was the mechanism which ensured that the argument x increased by one unit at a time (1, 2, 3...).[181] The argument was printed by the five type wheels nearest to the reader in Fig. 36. Without going

Fig. 36 The printing unit of the first Scheutz engine. Photographed by author.

Fig. 37a Type wheel of brass with lead types in the printing unit of Scheutz first engine. Photographed by author.

into the detailed design of the numerator in the Scheutz engine, one can say that it consisted of a number of cams and a system of links. As in the case of the carrying mechanism, it was highly complicated, but somewhat more sophisticated in its underlying ideas.

The numerator was also responsible for the special feature incorporated in the engine, which Berzelius had alluded to when he mentioned that the engine "can nevertheless, under certain circumstances, print 10-digit numbers".[182] What he had in mind, was that if the true result f(x) was more than 99,999, the numerator could go on to 100,000. The remaining five of the fifteen type wheels were designed for this. Thereafter the engine could continue to calculate values up to 999,999 whereupon the numerator increased the 6th power of 10 column by one unit, and so on. It is clear that the idea behind this device was to demonstrate that the engine could print many digits, which was certainly of interest. But in practice, this method only yields a correct result provided the first difference is less or equal to 99,999. Selander, Lilliehöök and Berzelius had submitted a report which was clear and technically correct in all but this point. No one on the committee had noticed that the engine contained a mechanism which made it calculate wrongly after a certain time. The Public Notary in Stockholm was later officially to witness a printed calculation by the engine, the one shown in Fig. 28, without registering this fact. Had the calculation been continued a bit further, the results would have been erroneous. Consider Fig. 28. When x=60, the correct

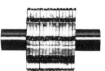

Fig. 37b The fifteen typewheels on their axle. A compact and reliable mechanical solution employed by the Scheutzes in their engines. Photographed by author.

148

Fig. 38 The slide in the printing unit upon which the matrix material was fixed. Photographed by author.

functional value is u=5607420. The engine would however have printed u=5507420. All the subsequent values would also have been wrong.

The *printing table* was located beneath the printing unit, see Fig. 36 and Fig. 38. It was fixed on a hinge and provided with a slide, which could slide on rails along the printing table. The matrix material was fixed securely in the form of a strip to this slide, before the engine was put into operation. When the type wheels registered the argument x and the result f(x), the corresponding types were turned to face the matrix material's upper side. The type wheels were locked in this position with the help of a wedge which went in between the cogs of type whels and ensured that the row of digits was straight. The force exercised by the wedge came from the lower lead weight in Fig. 29. The printing table was then lifted up so that the tabular value along with the argument was pressed into the matrix. At the same time as the printing table lifted up, a new table row was released by two hooks operating on a ratchet so that the slide was moved a bit to the left in Fig. 36.

If instead of printing out the result with five digits, one only wished to consider the first four of these, the result could be rounded off by means of a simple adjustment. To begin with, the engine was allowed to calculate the first tabular value. But before both printing and carrying in the result row took place, the result row's units wheel was turned forward five units by hand. The units wheel's stepped tooth cam was locked manually and the engine proceeded to print the correctly rounded-off four digit tabular value. The number wheel was equipped with extra-long teeth on the upper side (see Fig. 30) to facilitate its adjustment.

All the units and movable parts in the Scheutz difference engine were operated by hand by means of a crank, see Fig. 25. The force applied was transmitted by a system of gears to the cams, arms and racks that operated the calculating unit. Beneath this were two carriages (one of them on wheels), which ran along rails, which were suitably curved to give the five vertical axles their up and down movements. The printing table in the printing unit was acted upon by a crank mechanism, see Fig. 38.

The calculation of a table was carried out in four stages:

1. The start values of the table in question were calculated manually.
2. The number wheels in the calculating unit were set at the start values with the help of a special tool.
3. A piece of matrix material, wax, pasteboard or lead, was fastened to the slide on the printing table. Then the slide was pushed in, until the feeding hooks reached the first notch of the ratchet. The numerator was set at zero.
4. The handle of the engine was cranked and after every 6th revolution, a result was printed.

When one had once made a matrix with the engine, a metal cast was made of it. This could be done if the matrix was made of lead or specially prepared pasteboard. When the matrix was in wax, one had first to make a more robust matrix in another material e.g. plaster, The metal cast (cliché) was afterwards mounted in a press and the tables were then

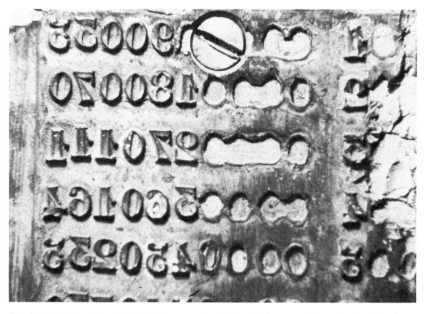

Fig. 39 Cliché made by the first Scheutz engine. This cliché was used to print the table shown in Fig. 28. Unnecessary zeros has been removed before printing. Photographed by author.

	lower carriage	upper carriage	rack for vertical axle motion	carry rack	Δ1	Δ2	Δ3	f(x)	printing table	operation
1	⤺	∩	−	⤺	−	−	−	−	↑	NEW TABLE ROW
2	−	−	→	−	○	−	−	−	↑	Δ1=Δ1+Δ2
3	−	−	⊃	−	−	−	−	−	∩	PRINTING
4	→	↓	−	→	−	−	−	−	↓	CARRY Δ1
5	⊃	↻	−	⊃	−	−	−	−	↓	−
6	−	−	←	−	−	○	−	○	↓	Δ2=Δ2+Δ3 / f(x)=f(x)+Δ1
7	−	−	⤺	−	−	−	−	−	↻	−
8	←	↑	−	←	−	−	−	−	↑	CARRY Δ2, f(x)

Sequence of motions in Scheutz' first difference engine.
Stages 1 to 8 corresponding to six revolutions on the
handle.

→ moving in direction of arrow
⊃ return position
− no motion
○ turning

Fig. 40 Sequence of motions in the first Scheutz difference engine. Stages 1 to 8 corresponding to six revolutions on the handle. Drawing by author.

printed, column by column, on the paper, as in Fig. 28. Note how the numerator has advanced the result f(x) one step every time it has gone beyond 99,999. In this case, everything works out satisfactorily because the first difference does not exceed the number 99,999. The table lacks the zeros pressed into the matrix material between the argument x and the result f(x). These were unnecessary and were removed from the cliché prior to printing, see Fig. 39.

The various motions taking place in the engine have been described as though they were independent of one another; in actual fact, they were naturally linked to one another and occurred in a particular sequence. A table exhibiting these motions is to be found in Fig. 40. It summarizes the mode of operation of Scheutz' first difference engine.

DESIGN

What was the impact of the Difference Engine No. 1 on the Scheutz engine? In what way did other existing mechanical concepts or traditions influence the design work and choice of mechanisms of the Scheutzes? What were the contents in Edvard's tool-box and can anything be said about his skill in using them?

Certain aspects of the engine coincided with those which Lardner had described in his article in the *Edinburgh Review*. Which were these and what had Georg and Edvard Scheutz borrowed freely from Babbage? The Scheutz engine carried out addition and carrying in two separate steps, and carrying took place sequentially, moving from lower to higher powers. The number wheels were engraved with the digits 0-9, and if they were set at 0, no addition was carried out. The transfer mechanism contained the snails that Babbage had proposed using. Finally, the calculating and printing units worked simultaneously. These were the properties that the Scheutz engine had in common with the engine envisaged by

Babbage in its completed form. Apart from the snail, no specific detailed mechanical solutions were adopted – only principles, which anyone building a difference engine would sooner or later arrive at. Nonetheless, Lardner had provided Georg and Edvard Scheutz with a set of answers that Babbage and Clement had reached after much labour. It meant that the Scheutzes got off to a flying start since part of the necessary basic research had already been done.

Lardner's article induced Georg Scheutz to follow his own hunches, when it came to providing mechanical solutions. Thus his engine turned out to be a completely new design. The only detail which the Scheutzes borrowed from the Babbage engine was the snail. This had been invented in the 1670s by Edvard Barlow and was a common component in a clock's striking mechanism, see Fig 41.[183] Curiously enough it was the one part of that engine that Babbage himself had not invented! The Englishman later acknowledged these facts:

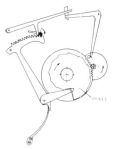

> "Mr. Scheutz's engine consists of two parts, – the Calculating and the Printing; the former being again divided into two, – the Adding and the Carrying Parts. With respect to the Adding, its structure is entirely different from my own, nor does it even resemble any one of those in my drawings. The very ingenious mechanism for carrying the tens is also quite different from my own. The Printing part will, on inspection, be pronounced altogether unlike that represented in my drawings; which, it must also be remembered, were entirely unknown to Mr. Scheutz. The contrivance by which the computed results are conveyed to the printing apparatus, is the same in both our engines: and it is well known, in the striking part of the common eight-day clock, which is called 'the snail'."[184]

Fig. 41 The only detail which the Scheutz borrowed from Babbage was the snail. The snail was a part common in the striking mechanisms of clocks. It was, invented in the 1670's and made the clock strike the number of strokes that corresponded to the actual time of the day. The figure shows such a mechanism. Cf. Fig. 35. Drawing by author.

Examples of innovatory detail are found in the addition element of the Scheutz engine, with its trap wheel and in the very special carrying mechanism – solutions not to be found in any earlier calculating machine. The very use of gear wheels that do not have cogs all the way around the periphery, together with similarly designed racks, can be traced back to Christopher Polhem. He was particularly fond of this kind of contraption which was incorporated in several of his Mechanical Alphabet models. The fact that Polhem's original Alphabet models were used in the training at the Technological Institute, combined with the unusualness of this particular device in the history of technology (undoubtedly caused by its unreliability) is interesting, and certainly more than a coincidence.

The real novelty in Scheutz' engine was the printing unit which involved a wholly new technique. The way the Scheutzes had solved this, perhaps Babbage's most difficult problem, was very elegant. By letting the machine only make one column of a table at a time and not a whole page, the printing had been drastically simplified. This idea probably

Fig. 42 Scheutz' printing unit was a concious or unconcious synthesis of other inventions. The figure shows a revolution counter invented by the Englishman Bryan Donkin Sr in 1819, a device similar to the type wheels of the Scheutz engine. Photograph taken from: [anon], A Brief Account of Bryan Donkin F. R. S. and the Company he founded 150 Years ago (Chesterfield 1953).

originated in the mind of the experienced bookprinter Georg Scheutz who many times must have set pages with movable types, a handicraft presumably quite far from Babbage's world of experience. With this solution, (and combined with the type wheels), many movements which Babbage had had in mind, became obsolete. The matrix did not have to move in two orthogonal directions but in one. The types did not have to move across the matrix to get into position but only to rotate, which was much easier to achieve. Scheutz' printing unit could therefore operate much faster, not least because the types were always in position to print.

But despite the fact that the printing unit was a new machine in the history of printing, it was in fact a synthesis of other inventions. It is very possible that the Scheutzes were not aware that a couple of things they had invented, already existed. One was the numerator. Devices for the same purpose had been invented before. One example is the revolution counter conceived by the Englishman Bryan Donkin Sr. in the year 1819. This counter was employed in the manufacture of stamps and bank-notes, to keep track of the number of items produced, see Fig. 42.[185] With respect to the numerator, I am convinced that they did not know of any similar contraption. One reason is the very special way it is designed,

153

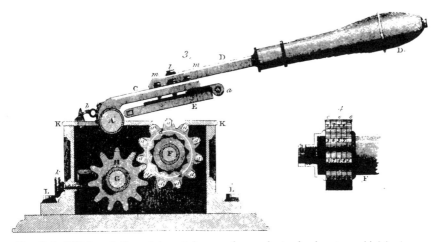

Fig. 43 In 1806 Joseph Bramah invented a press for numbering bank-notes, which is shown
in this figure. The wheels in this press show a striking similarity to the type wheels of the
Swedish difference engine. Photograph taken from: James Moran, Printing Presses: History
and Development from the 15th Century Modern Times (London 1973).

showing Scheutz' typically low degree of abstraction. Another reason is
its name. The word numerator is not used in Swedish for any other
purpose than in connection with the Scheutz engine. If Scheutz had
known of Donkin's counter, he would probably have used the word
counter as well. As regards the type wheels, there is a striking similarity
between them and the corresponding wheels in Joseph Bramah's press
for numbering bank-notes, invented in the year 1806, see Fig. 43.[186] This
press was used at the Bank of England, and it is conceivable that Georg
was aware of its existence and appearance when the printing unit was
made. Otherwise, the first Scheutz difference engine contained no additional details borrowed from other machines.

Making use of his father's basic ideas, it was Edvard who alone built
the engine, while the detailed solutions adopted were the result of a
cooperative effort on the part of father and son. One or two details in the
engine are superior to the others (have a finer finish etc.), and these can
be presumed to have been taken from other machines. The crank is an
example. Otherwise, the engine was hand-made by Edvard with the help
of a few simple tools.

The materials used in making the engine, were wood and metal. The
idea of building machinery consisting of a wooden frame in which operating metal parts are mounted, is an old tradition. It was standard procedure to build e.g. textile looms and lathes this way everywhere until
around the end of the 18th century when machines made entirely in metal
started to appear in England and in France. The Scheutzes chose to build
their machine this way for practical reasons. But it may also be that this
choice was influenced by the state of technological development in Sweden. In most technical areas, Sweden had not reached the same level as

154

the rest of Europe. Wooden machinery may still have been much more common in Sweden than machines made entirely of metal. One fact which lends support to this theory, is that printing presses made of metal were rare while wooden presses were still predominant in Sweden in the 1830's. These had oak frames and their design had remained largely unchanged for 300 years, see Fig. 44.[187]

The woods employed in the engine were pine, birch and oak, which were coated with black oil paint. A number of the metal parts had been similarly painted. The majority of metal parts were made of brass. Steel and iron were used for axles, links and cams. In the calculating unit, there were also components made from zinc and copper. To allow for various adjustments to be made after the engine had been mounted, great use had been made of paper and plate wedges. The majority of the metal components had been riveted together and for example the addition element was composed of riveted units which could not be taken apart. Use was also made of nuts, screws and soldering.

To guard the engine against dust and damage, there was a protective cover which could be fitted over the engine and screwed to the base. This

Fig. 44 The Swedish lottery press was built in the second half of the 18th century and the first Scheutz engine was built in very much the same engineering design tradition. Photograph by courtesy of the Nordic Museum, Stockholm.

155

Fig. 45 During the building of the difference engine Edvard encountered a number of problems. Thin sections fell apart and he was forced to make repairs. This photograph shows a link mechanism of the carrying mechanism that has been repaired with two very small rivets (diameter 0.5 mm). Photographed by author.

was made of Honduras mahogany fitted together by means of glue and dovetail joints. It was equipped with four brass handles. Judging from the quality of the work, it was made by a cabinet-maker.

The execution of the various parts of the engine has been carried out with the help of ordinary tools. Apart from these, Edvard Scheutz had the use of a simple lathe. This was probably foot-operated, see Fig. 23. The lathe lacked a movable support, which meant that the cutting tool had to be held in the hand as in the case of wood-turning from which the method originated.[188] This is difficult, but despite this, Edvard achieved a very good result. On Clement's lathe the cutting tool was fixed on a movable support which in turn moved automatically. The majority of the components were sawn by hand from sheet or larger bits of metal. Edvard had, therefore, great use for a metal saw and files with which he was able to make all the gear wheels and racks. A countersink, taps and dies, soldering iron and chisels must also have been included in his tool-box. These simple tools and the lack of precision machine-tools led to a comparatively rough finish. This does not, however, apply to the surface of the bearings. My conclusion is that the engine's performance took precedence over its appearance.

As the calculating unit was built up from the bottom, improvements were made in the shaping of the addition elements. It is also interesting to note how the quality of the turned components, improved with time. The addition elements $\Delta 3$, which were finished in April 1840, have an inferior number wheel bearing than the later made elements $\Delta 1$ and $\Delta 2$.[189] The

Fig. 46 Cracked number wheel repaired with sheet metal strips riveted to the wheel during the building of the engine by Edvard Scheutz. Photographed by author.

best of all are those in $\Delta 1$ which were ready in April 1842. During the course of the work, Edvard encountered a number of problems. One that came up frequently was that involving thin sections ($\leqslant 1$ mm) which fell apart. Probably he made new parts but on occasions he was forced to make repairs, see Fig. 45-46. Another example, which also points to difficulties encountered, is the fact that several of the parts, which have been marked with number punches or engravings, have been altered.

In 1843, Berzelius and the others had written that the engine did not possess the perfection that an engine built with the aid of the appropriate machine tools, would have. These words were naturally applicable to the engine as a whole. But in point of fact, there were only a few components that were open to criticism. First, there were the ordinary book printers' lead types. They were, as had been specifically mentioned in Berzelius' statement, far too soft for printing in a lead matrix (the material which gave the best impressions). In 1837 Scheutz had said in his letter to the Academy of Sciences that all of the parts of the engine could be made in Sweden, except perhaps the steel types. His choice of lead types was thus an economically motivated compromise. Secondly, the rack which operated the calculating unit's five vertical axles, was made of a thin brass sheet and consequently underdimensioned. Thirdly, the Polhem influenced racks for the carrying mechanisms, with their short intervals of cogs, were unsuitable since the gear wheels could easily be displaced due to vibration. The wrong cog could then be put into operation with the result that carrying failed to take place. These deficiencies entailed that

157

the engine was not one hundred per cent reliable. But the operators, i.e. the Scheutzes, were aware of this and were able to take appropriate precautions to ensure that the engine performed in a satisfactory manner. Reliability was not one of the main desiderata. The important point was that the engine was complete with both a calculating and a printing unit and that it worked.

When Georg Scheutz informed the Academy of Sciences that he could build a difference engine, he said that he had checked up with various professional mechanical engineers about the matter. In 1837 there were in Stockholm several workshops which dealt with mechanical engineering of different kinds. There were 17 "workers in bronze and metal" who employed the services of 48 men, and 32 "clock manufacturers" with a total of 60 employees.[190] In addition, there were 9 "mathematical instrument makers" with a staff of 26 men in all, 2 "makers of meteorological instruments" and workshops specializing in engineering work in iron and steel, which employed 90 men. The expansion in this sector of interest can be seen from the fact that whereas in 1811 the total production had been valued at 2,660 riksdaler banco, in 1837 it was estimated at 213,903 riksdaler banco — that is 80 times as much.[191] The principal cause of this change was the contribution of the English-inspired general workshops such as Owen's (101,775 rdr bco) and Amach's (61,028 rdr bco). Thus there is little doubt that both quantitatively and qualitatively there was no hinder to having a working difference engine built by professional craftsmen in Stockholm in 1837. But the Academy of Sciences had refused its financial support and instead it was left to Edvard to complete the project by building an engine himself. However, bearing in mind Babbage's own failure, I am prepared to argue that the Scheutzes were fortunate that things turned out as they did. For otherwise, it is by no means improbable that they might have ended up with the same difficulties as Babbage when he relied on a professional workshop. It is clear that when Georg Scheutz contacted the Academy, he was very far from having a complete engine, even on paper. This is evident from the engine itself. Because they were forced to build the engine themselves, the Scheutzes were released from the external pressure of time and money and they could take their time to make use of the skills they had acquired — in the case of Edvard, during his education, and in the case of Georg, during his career as self-taught inventor. The methods they used were quite different from those which Babbage had employed in the construction of his first model and the large engine. The Swedes were able to feel their way forward by trial and error, to arrive at a superior design solution. They did not hesitate to strip down the machine and replace one part by another. It eventually became clear that Edvard was able to do everything that their purpose required. The costs of the project were restricted to material and tools. As a result, the final cost was negligible compared with the enormous sums that had been expended on the Difference Engine No. 1.

Despite what Selander had said about the engine, it could in fact easily be extended with regard to the number of digits and differences it could cope with. This was possible by installing the desired number of identical addition elements. The frame of the engine was built to allow for the digit capacity to be increased by one digit, see Fig. 30, where the row f(x) has a bit of pasteboard covering the space intended for this. Such an extension would in due course take practical shape, but in another engine.

2.4 The second engine

In 1850, sixteen years had passed since Lardner's article in the *Edinburgh Review*. From newspaper reports it was now clear that Babbage's difference engine would never be completed. Awareness of this fact, coupled with the need for error-free tables, induced the Scheutzes to apply again for a government grant. This time a new strategy was adopted.

On the 26th of December 1850, a committee of the Royal Academy of Sciences was sent to make a fresh examination of the first engine.[1] It once again consisted of Baron Fabian Jacob Wrede accompanied by the new head of the Technological Institute, Lars Johan Wallmark. No alterations had been made to the engine since it had been built in 1843.[2] On the 28th of January 1851, Georg Scheutz submitted his application to King Oscar, seeking support to build a second difference engine.[3] After having given a summary of the application of 1844, he proceeded to explain that there had been no advance in solving the problem with tables, whether by difference engine or otherwise, during the intervening years. He stressed that the work on the difference engine in England had come to a halt and he concluded his application as follows:

"For this reason, I now humbly apply for a gracious contribution of three thousand three hundred and thirty three riksdaler 16 skilling banco, to allow me partly to devote myself to the construction of a sufficiently complete prototype of the invention, which has been successfully produced in this field, that it might serve as a guide in the production of the machinery in question, in whatever amount is desired, and partly to undertake a journey abroad to demonstrate the prototype, especially at those institutions concerned with the annual preparation of nautical and astronomical tables, where the employment of such machinery would offer savings of time and money, as well as the security of error-free results, which hitherto have been sought in vain by other methods."[4]

It is important to underline that Scheutz on this occasion asked to be allowed to build "a sufficiently complete prototype [...] that it might serve as a guide in whatever amount is desired ...". In contrast to his application of 1844, he had not only reduced the sum requested by two-thirds, but also changed the aim of the project from producing a complete engine with the same capacity as the English engine, to producing a prototype. Furthermore, the required amount (which was equal to approximately 283 pounds) was also intended to cover travel expenses.[5] In accordance with normal practice, the matter was on the 6th of February, duly referred to the Royal Academy of Sciences, for its expert opinion. In the statement which was sent to the King on the 12th of February 1851, and which was based on the Academy's, or more exactly Wrede and Wallmark's examination of the first engine carried out the previous month, there are a number of noteworthy remarks.[6] First of all, it is stated that "it [the Royal Academy] had only become acquainted with an incomplete prototype [in 1844], which gave no guarantee that it could be extended to the requisite size and capability ...". This clearly contradicts the wording of Berzelius' statement (see p 124). Secondly, upon mentioning this former application by Scheutz, the Academy quoted only Wrede's positive view on the matter. Not a word was mentioned about Selander's negative opinion of the usefulness of the engine. Thirdly, the Academy layed stress on an important alteration:

> "to this, is added the important fact that the present engine although it is only experimental in character, calculates, sets and prints tables where the third difference is constant, and is so firmly based on a thorough and comprehensive analysis, that it can, with ease, be extended to the requisite size and capability ..."[7]

Yet, there is no question of there having been some new prototype built. Interestingly enough, the Academy testified to Georg Scheutz' contribution as a journalist and writer and noted that he had been responsible — quite without government support — for disseminating knowledge in Sweden about foreign technology. They also pointed out that the sum he requested, amounted to no more than one per cent of the money that had been granted in England towards the development costs of Babbage's engine. Finally, the Academy recommended that the engine that was to be built with the help of the grant, should be the property of Scheutz, as recompense for the amount of time and trouble he had invested in it.[8] This made the Scheutz difference engine project different from the British example in yet another way.

Indeed, there were some strange things afoot. First, it is curious that the Academy had asked Wrede and Wallmark to examine the engine *before* Scheutz made his application to the King. They all knew that the King would ask the Academy for their professional opinion. Secondly, Wrede and Wallmark's opinion was misleading. It was exactly the same engine that Wrede had examined with Selander in 1844. But those who knew this did not react. Why? Berzelius had died in 1848. Lilliehöök was by now an established navy officer in the town of Karlskrona, far from Stockholm and the Academy.[9] Last, but not least, the astronomer Selan-

Fig. 47 Supporter of the Scheutz engine: Baron Fabian Jacob Wrede (1802–1893). Photograph by courtesy of Stockholm University Library with the Library of the Royal Academy of Sciences, Stockholm.

der was still attending the meetings at the Academy but for some unknown reason he was no longer part of the scene. His written opinion about the engine had been entirely replaced by Wrede's. I believe that Wrede, the great enthusiast for Scheutz' engine, perhaps together with Scheutz, Wallmark and even other scientists, were involved in some tactical scheme.

Nevertheless, on the 29th of April 1851 the King, together with his ministerial advisers, turned the application down on the grounds that no funds existed for the purpose.[10] If any other reason was behind this decision, it is nowhere stated in the available archival material.

It might be noted that an application of this kind was in fact unusual since requests for support for inventions were rare. At the same time the State was practically the only conceivable source of funds, because the banking system, which fairly soon afterwards would have the capacity to finance the industrialization of the Swedish society, was just in its initial phase.[11]

Georg Scheutz refused to be dissuaded by this decision and pointed out in a letter to the new Secretary of the Royal Academy of Sciences, Peter Fredrik Wahlberg, that because "the outcome had been determined by external circumstances, having nothing to do with the matter in question, it is still possible to try again ...".[12] It would soon become clear that someone, perhaps Georg himself had some scheme at the back of his mind and he continued: "For this purpose, I would especially require the Statements in extenso from both the Academy and the Department [of Education and Ecclesiastical Affairs] ...".[13] Scheutz asked Wahlberg, therefore, for copies of these documents. When the King's decision came up for discussion at the meeting of the Royal Academy of Sciences on the 18th of June of the same year, one of its members, Johan Theophil Nathorst proposed that some alternative way of raising support for Georg Scheutz' invention should be found. He suggested that a committee should be formed, which would then invite the general public to subscribe to the cost of the project. Because the members of the Academy were about to go on holiday, the decision about the matter was deferred until September.[14]

Up till now, Scheutz had made two unsuccessful attempts to solicit the King's support. There was in fact another way still untried. This was via the four-Estate Riksdag. Scheutz had chosen to approach the King, probably because if the King had granted the money, then the Riksdag would have had little to say against it. The application could also have been presented to both the King and the Riksdag. But with the Academy of Sciences' strong support, Scheutz probably did not expect that the matter would be turned down. In order to get the Riksdag to consider a request, a motion would have had to be introduced by some member of the Estates. Furthermore, this had to be done by December when the Riksdag began their sessions. It was not until April 1851 that Scheutz learned about the negative decision of the King. By then, it was too late to act. It was only in the event of matters of importance, like war, failure of the crops etc., that a motion normally could be introduced in the Estates during the current sessions.[15] Thus, to approach the King was one way. To introduce a motion in December was another. Only, in special cases, could a motion be introduced later. This was the remaining alternative. The King's rejection would have been final under normal circumstances. But the circumstances were not normal and the third way was in fact given a try.

Somewhat simplifying matters, one could say that in the Riksdag, the upper Estates – the Nobles and Clergy – were conservative and supporters of the King. The lower Estates contained more of a political mixture. This was especially true for the Estate of Peasants, where besides liberals and conservatives, there was a large group which was politically unaligned. The Estate of Burghers, however, was the stronghold of the liberal opposition, and mirrored most closely the opinions of Georg Scheutz.

Subsequently, on the 12th of July 1851, an event took place which eventually was to make the Academy's suggested subscription superfluous. A representative for the Burghers, the radical politician Anders Magnus Brinck presented the members of his Estate with a motion, calling for the four Estates to deal with the matter of a grant towards Scheutz' engine, since this had been rejected by the King for purely economic reasons.[16] This motion was thus introduced late and not quite according to the rules. For the first time, the fate of the Scheutz engine was in the hands of the politicians.

"During the present Riksdag, [said Brinck] a case has occurred where the King 'due to lack of funds for the purpose in hand, has been prevented' from giving his approval to an application, which has been approved with '*the highest*' recommendation by the Royal Academy of Sciences in its report, namely for a grant towards the completion of a Swedish invention, which in the view of the Academy 'will indubitably benefit science and bring honour to its native land'; I refer to the machine invented by Messrs. *Scheutz*, father and son, which calculates, sets and prints mathematical tables.

This invention will provide several advantages to navigation and applied mathematics which, hitherto, could be achieved neither so cheaply nor, in particular, so certainly by other means; this fact has induced the British Parliament to supply to a similar English project, which is now suspended, as is made clear in the Royal Academy's report — a hundredfold more in financial support, than the sum which the Academy has recommended for the completion of the Swedish invention, which the Academy has inspected and found to be useful for that purpose, the fulfilment of which was sought in vain in England."[17]

Brinck continued by specifying the sum that Georg Scheutz had asked for. He added, that it was desirable that the business should be expedited as soon as possible, particularly because an international meeting of scientists would shortly take place in Stockholm. These scholars would then have their attention drawn to the invention and "to this new proof of the generosity of the Estates in encouraging the sciences and general learning".[18] Brinck therefore suggested that his motion should be dealt with by the Estates, by having the matter remitted to the Standing Committee (Statsutskottet). The demand was made that the motion be shelved, whereupon Brinck repeated his request. Once again it was demanded that the motion should be shelved but this did not meet with general approval. Up to this point, the matter was no different from any other. But now Johan Tore Petré, another member of the Burghers, spoke up. He said that the King in fact had at his disposal sufficient funds for the project and that there were probably other reasons for the rejection. According to him, the King's decision had made "a great stir" at the Royal Academy of Sciences.[19] Petré thus suspected that the rejection was a result of lack of "fair play", and concluded:

"If matters are as they seem to be, the Estates ought not to neglect, as far as they are able, to offer redress for what the other organ of Government [the King] has failed to do."[20]

Petré was the leader of the opposition in the Burgher Estate and therefore a very powerful man. His intervention transformed the matter from being simply a technical issue to being a matter of politics. It was now not simply a question of an invention and its fate, but it had become part of something that greatly interested the opposition in the Estates, namely the struggle between them and the King. If Petré had not bothered to politicize the issue, it is not impossible that it might have been decided there and then. But now matters developed along the lines suggested by Brinck and his motion was, according to the procedure passed on for consideration by the Standing Committee.

The four Estates were equally represented on the Standing Committee. It was unable to give its unconditional approval to a grant, but instead proposed that the four Estates should place the sum of 3,333 riksdaler 16 skilling at the King's disposal and thus provide the King with the money he lacked.[21] But a condition was added; the money would be paid out to Georg Scheutz, only after a proper examination of the finished engine had been carried out.[22] Four of the members of the Standing Committee objected to this proposal. One of them, Nils Strindlund, the voice of the conservatives in the Estate of Peasants, argued:

"that the Academy of Sciences, in its report concerning the utility of the calculating machine in question, has really only pronounced that it *has reason to assume* that the machine is useful."[23]

No such statement had been made by Wrede and Wallmark in their report. But Strindlund was perhaps referring to the Academy report from 1838 and was perhaps also aware of what Selander had stated in 1844.

The Standing Committee had considered the motion and had delivered their report. This meant in practice that they had considered the matter too important to be refused on the grounds that the motion had been introduced too late.

In the middle of August 1851, the matter came up for discussion in the four Estates, which had to make the final decision. If three of them were of the same opinion, then the matter was settled. In the debate in the Estate of Nobles, Count Carl Göran Detlof Mörner, who belonged to the old conservative group, opposed the grant. He argued that the Scheutzes had only presented an idea and that it was rather uncertain whether a complete engine could ever be made.[24] Mörner was one of those in the Standing Committee who criticized the proposal. It is evident, however, that he had not seen the prototype engine himself. He added that the idea of letting the engine become Scheutz' property, in case a grant nevertheless was given, was to allow things to go too far.[25] Another member of the Nobles, Baron Rudolf Cederström was of a quite different opinion:

"After having read through the Select Committee's report which has now been submitted, I, for my part, have not the slightest hesitation in giving my support, since the Royal Academy of Sciences has felt called upon to endorse completely Messrs. Scheutzes' request, and their invention is deemed not only to benefit science, but also to bring honour to their native land. When one considers these pronouncements by an authority which ought to enjoy every right to issue an expert statement about this matter, when one, as I say, sets those pronouncements beside the other factor which must be taken into consideration — namely the governmental funds available — and when one considers the paltry sum involved and the cautious conditions which are to be attached to its payment [...] then I believe that it would be wholly right for the Estates, as the elected representative of the people, to grant the money in the manner suggested by the Standing Committee. Sweden ought to maintain its reputation as a cultural nation; and since the invention in question has been pronounced by competent judges to be of great value, it would not be right to deny sufficient funds to bring it about."[26]

While Cederström thus had full confidence in the professional opinion of the Royal Academy of Sciences, Count Anton Gabriel Gyldenstolpe, took up the matter of the money: — "there could hardly be such a shortage of funds that the sum of 3,333 riksdaler and 16 skilling could make a difference", adding at the same time that if this were the case, then the money could be supplied from customs duties.[27] The Estate of Nobles supported the proposal of the Select Committee, although a minority voted against it.[28] In the Estate of Burghers, from which Brink's motion had originated, the proposal was accepted unanimously.[29] The same thing happened in the Estate of the Clergy.[30]

The Peasants, however, were against the proposal. What happened there was that Nils Strindlund, the conservatives' man among the Peasants, started the debate by advocating refusal, on the ground that the motion had been introduced too late and was thus not quite in accordance with constitutional law. A debate followed, in which seven of the Peasants spoke and all agreed with Strindlund's opinion. When it was clear that the majority was on his side, Strindlund asked that another argument should be used when the matter was referred back to the Standing Committee for opposing the proposal, to wit, his opinion about the unproven practical importance of the engine.[31] The members agreed and the proposal to support Scheutz was accordingly rejected.

It is beyond the scope of this book to enter into the contemporary political situation in detail. Some facts, however, are of interest. Strindlund had kept the members of his Estate in place by pointing out that the motion had been proposed too late. In fact this was not much of an argument; given that the Standing Committee had dealt with the matter, it was formally approved. But it was an argument which carried some weight in the Peasants' Estate since its members were less well-versed in the rules of procedure and simply accepted what Strindlund said. He knew, however, that the argument would hardly do for the Standing Committee as a reason for a rejection. Therefore Strindlund had requested that his second argument should be included instead, in the statement from the Estates. His second argument is interesting. Is it possible that he was not in fact convinced about the utility of the difference engine and knew that the Academy was not wholly convinced either, at least in the beginning? If Strindlund had put forward this argument to the Estate of Peasants, it would have been difficult to have mustered support. Politically, few of them were steadfast conservatives and moreover the Academy of Sciences had approved the project. The opposition leader Petré had politicized the issue and his conservative opponent could not just allow the issue to pass without comment. In general, the Estate of the Peasants was noted for its emphasis on frugality when it came to dispensing public funds and it was very seldom prepared to support financially any cultural or other project which was not of immediate practical use. This undoubtedly helped to unite the Estate on this question. Perhaps there were even personal feelings involved, and Strindlund as well as the other members of the Estate of Peasants, did not want to support Scheutz on the grounds of his critical writings. In *Slägtvälde och Idévälde* (1840), he had called the Estate of Peasants "easily led, ignorant country folk". It is quite possible that they did not want to prove that he was right. However, the only Estate of the Riksdag of 1850-1851 that voted against the Scheutz difference engine, was also alone in more or less conciously calling attention to an important argument which no other estate had even raised.

Since the proposal now had been supported by three of the four Estates, it was duly carried.[32] On the 20th of August 1851, the King was informed by the Estates that the sum of money in question was being made available from the National Debt Office (Riksgäldskontoret).[33] The condition, that the Standing Committee had included in their proposal, remained. The money was not to be paid out to Scheutz until the King, after examination and tests of the finished engine, considered that it fulfilled its purposes. The reason for including this condition arose from the fact that the Estates had "not doubted the utility of the machine in question", but they had "been unable to judge reliably the value of this invention".[34] This seemingly contradictory statement, could only mean that they had not been able to judge whether the 3,333 riksdaler and the 16 skillings perhaps was more than necessary for building the engine. Despite the condition attached, from the viewpoint of the Scheutzes the decision was encouraging.

Because they had no capital of their own, Georg and Edvard were unable to get down at once to work on the second engine and in the autumn of 1851 Georg Scheutz was forced to appeal to the King for the whole sum to be paid out in advance.[35] Apparently conceding the logic of Scheutz' request, King Oscar announced on the 24th of October 1851 that the money would be paid out to the Royal Academy of Sciences. Instructions were given for it to be paid out in smaller sums to Georg Scheutz, against securities approved by the Royal Academy of Sciences.[36] In addition, a new condition was imposed by the King. The engine had to be ready in working order before the end of 1853. It was a crucial condition. Without such a time limit, this project could have become just as protracted as the English one. Perhaps someone had realized this risk. It was the responsibility of the Royal Academy of Sciences to see that all these conditions were met.

At the meeting of the Academy on the 10th of December 1851, the members were apprised of the contents of the King's statement. The Executive Committee of the Academy realized that Scheutz would have difficulty in finding guarantors willing to underwrite the full amount and therefore they decided that he would be permitted to draw out smaller sums of money (but not less than 100 riksdaler), provided that the Academy was satisfied that earlier payments had been allocated to their proper purpose. For each such part-payment Scheutz was to provide an approved security and moreover he was required to fill in a form. In this form, Georg Scheutz was bound over to repaying the whole of the money already received, immediately, in the event that the conditions relating to the engine's completion and functioning before 1854, were not fulfilled.[37]

The bureaucratic machine had completed its work and the result, despite the harsh conditions, was positive. Wrede and the other supporters had won their tactical game. When the King unexpectedly had turned the application down, a new strategy had been adopted. First Brinck had introduced his motion in the Estate of the Burghers in which the opposition were well represented, despite the fact that it was introduced abnormally late. Next the opposition leader Petré had turned the whole matter from being a technical issue into one of politics by maintaining that the motives behind the King's decision had not been entirely "fair". Thereafter the Standing Committee had dealt with the matter and had proposed that the project should be supported. In Brink's motion, the money was to come from the Estates, while according to the recommendation of the Standing Committee, money was to be placed at the King's disposal. In this way, the conservative members on the Standing Committee were able to preserve the King's preeminent authority in the matter. Shortly thereafter, King Oscar used that authority to introduce certain extra conditions.

The conclusion to be drawn from this political interlude is crucial. If there had not been a gulf dividing the King and the Estates, the matter would never have become political. If Georg Scheutz had not been politically linked to the opposition through his pioneering writings, he would never have received any assistance. Among the liberals, he was not just anyone. With the help of the difference engine, he had managed to help those who shared his political view − with Petré, chief among them − to win some political capital. If Scheutz had been simply another inventor, he would have had to wait to the next Riksdag (1853-54). But instead, he was now given an unique extra chance.

Thus apart from the intrigues in the Academy of Sciences, Scheutz' invention became a political issue. If it had not been for the contributions of these men together, no further difference engine would presumably have ever been made.

During the winter of 1851, Georg and Edvard Scheutz were finally able to seriously set about building a second difference engine. Edvard, who had now been a fully qualified engineer for a number of years, was given the task of making the technical drawings.

By the 1st of February 1852, Edvard was ready with the first design drawings.[38] The second engine was to be a direct offshoot of the first. All the parts that Edvard had made so patiently by hand for the first engine, would now be professionally manufactured, according to the highest standards of precision. Wood would be replaced throughout by metal; the design would be improved. But who was to manufacture the engine?

The man who was given the responsibility of building the Swedish difference engine was Johan Wilhelm Bergström, Fig. 48. He was born in Stockholm in 1812, the son of a carpenter at Samuel Owen's workshop. Bergström had started work at the age of twelve as a glass-blower's apprentice, worked his way up to become a master, and had opened a glass manufacturing business in the late 1830s. His interest in science had led him to study mechanics, physics and chemistry, with the help of some eminent professors. In 1843, he had started to make the new and popular daguerrotypes, and soon became famous for his achievements in this field. Three years later, he expanded his glass business into a mechanical workshop. Thus, in this building, not far from the home of the Scheutzes, Bergström cut crystal, made "light-paintings" and manufactured light-ning conductors for the roofs of Stockholm, goldplated chandeliers for King Oscar and bombs for the government of Sardinia. He had been sent by the King on a trip to study mechanical workshops on the Continent in 1849; he had received a gold medal from the monarch for his successful improvements of the Swedish exhibits at the Great Exhibition in London 1851; and the same year the products of his shop had dominated the successful industrial exhibition in Stockholm.[39] By 1851 he was a promi-nent Stockholm figure. No doubt, Georg Scheutz must have known Wilhelm Bergström. They shared interests in industrial affairs, were both pioneers in daguerrotyping and Scheutz had written about Bergström in at least one of his journals.[40] Even his Majesty may have had Bergström in mind when he decided that the engine should be finished within little over two years. Furthermore, Bergström's teacher in physics name was Fabian Jacob Wrede.[41]

Beginning in the 1820s, a workshop revolution had taken place in England which had resulted in increased production, lower prices and superior quality. This was due in part, to the development of already existing machinery, but also in part, to the introduction of completely new types of machine. Influenced greatly by what had taken place in England, Swedish workshops underwent a similar revolution.[42] Although they did not have the same resources as their English counterparts, they nonetheless had access to similar tools and equipment to those used by Babbage and Clement.

Fig. 48 The daguerrotypist and mechanical workshop owner Johan Wilhelm Bergström (1812−1881), who in 1852 started to bild Georg and Edvard Scheutz' second difference engine. Photograph by courtesy of the National Museum of Science and Technology, Stockholm.

The construction of the engine at Bergström's workshop began some time during the summer of 1852, under the direct supervision of Edvard Scheutz.[43] Georg Scheutz had managed to find guarantors with sufficient faith in the difference engine and in his own and his son's technical ability, to be willing to underwrite the scheme. Fifteen men came forward to help Georg Scheutz and it is of interest to know a little more about them.[44]

First and foremost, there was Bergström himself. His interest in the project was obvious and the fact that he was prepared to act as a guarantor, was a good sign. Six of the fourteen remaining men formed a coherent group. They were Lars Johan Hierta, Carl Fredrik Bergstedt, Sven

169

Gustaf Lallerstedt, Per Adam Siljeström, Per Erik Svedbom and Jonas Gustaf Wahlström. These men all belonged to the liberal circles in which Georg Scheutz moved. Furthermore, they were all, like Scheutz, journalists and men of letters. It was natural for Hierta, as Scheutz' friend and employer, to give him his support. Four of these men also belonged to the group which in 1852, after Hierta's departure, took over the editorial control of *Aftonbladet*. Bergstedt, who later would write Georg Scheutz' biography, became the chief editor of *Aftonbladet* in the same year and thus Georg Scheutz' employer. Another common denominator of this liberal group, was that they all had been educated at Uppsala university. Both Bergström and in fact also Hierta, were businessmen and factory owners. In that capacity they were joined by two other men – the factory owners Carl Gottfrid Crasselt and Per Wilhelm Lundgren. Crasselt had a closer personal relationship to the Scheutzes, since Edvard Scheutz was the godfather to his daughter.[45] Another man of business was the retailer Napoleon Grafström, who also seems to have been close to father and son Scheutz. In England, Babbage had been supported almost exclusively by men of science. Among Scheutz' guarantors, only two were professional scientists. One was Teodor Fredrik Berg, a physician and a statistician. In 1850, he had been appointed to the Royal Commission on Tables (Kongl. Tabell Kommissionen), and had given up his medical career to devote himself to statistical work of various kind. Later he was to become one of the driving forces behind the foundation of The Central Statistical Office (Statistiska Centralbyrån, founded in 1858), which corresponded to the General Register Office in London. The other scientist was Sven Ludvig Lovén, a zoologist. Interestingly enough, he and Svedbom had attended several of the meetings of the Academy, where they were members, when the Scheutz engine had been discussed. The first occasion had been in September 1844, when Scheutz had asked for support from the King. It is not a wild guess to assume that they were part of the Wrede-Wallmark-group at the Academy. Another guarantor was Berndt Otto Nycander, who was a teacher at the Royal Technological Institue and who shared his profession with both Siljeström and Svedbom, who also were teachers. Finally, there were Jonas Falkenholm, chief inspector of Customs, and a certain unidentified Eklund.

These fifteen Stockholm citizens supplied the necessary security. The extent of their individual financial liability is not known.[46] But perhaps the fact that they were fifteen in number, indicates both that the risk to each individual was minimized and also that Georg Scheutz had difficulties in finding one or two guarantors for the whole sum. About half of the group were liberal journalists and the rest scientists, factory owners and teachers. More importantly, several were Scheutz' close friends.

Very little material dealing with the construction of the second engine has survived. However, in a letter from Georg Scheutz to a colleague in Örebro, dated 1st of October 1852, Bergström was said to be engaged on the calculating unit which was expected to be ready by Christmas. The

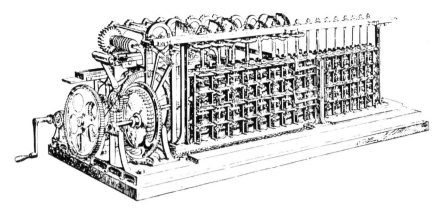

Fig. 49 Scheutz' second difference engine. It was ready in october 1853 after almost two years of work. It could calculate with four orders of differences and 15 digits. Drawing from Specimens (1857).

printing unit was not to be ready before the end of April in the following year. The work was proceeding swiftly and with great precision. Georg Scheutz noted that the funds received for the table-printing engine were to be used only for their appointed purpose. The Academy of Sciences kept a close watch on the project, checking up on how the money was spent and on the parts of the machine that were successively produced.[47]

Bergström was not the sole manufacturer of parts for the second engine. In the ledger of Bolinder's Engineering Workshop in Stockholm, for the period of 1853, there is an entry to the effect that Johan Wilhelm Bergström had received "a plate for a calculating engine" on the 20th of January 1853.[48]

Before the close of October 1853, the second Scheutz difference engine was ready.[49] Georg and Edvard Scheutz, with the help of the skilled workers at Bergström's workshop had not only managed to build the engine on time. "The very first occasion it was assembled, it worked so well that no adjustment was necessary."[50] The engine could calculate with four differences and 15 digits, of which eight were printed. It was made completely of metal and was equipped with several refinements which will be discussed in more detail below.

Shortly after the engine was ready, Georg Scheutz requested that the representatives of the Academy of Sciences should come to Bergström's workshop to make their final inspection. The men appointed to carry out this examination were once again Fabian Wrede and Lars Wallmark.[51] In their judgement, the engine was entirely satisfactory and much more than a "mere guide" for the development of similar engines of much greater capacity.[52] But this was exactly what Scheutz had asked to make and had received a grant for. Furthermore, Wrede and Wallmark pointed out that the grant was not sufficient to cover even the production costs, which meant that there were no funds left to cover the costs of travel involved in publicizing the engine, as had originally been intended.[53] These findings were communicated in the Academy's final report to the King, dated 9th November 1853.[54]

In the view of the King and his ministers, Georg and Edvard Scheutz had fully satisfied their side of the agreement and they were willing to increase the amount of the original grant.[55] On the 13th of January 1854 the King proposed that a further 3,333 riksdaler and 16 skilling should be paid out to the Scheutzes as compensation and reward. Indeed, it was a fair compensation, although the actual sum spent on the engine, was not mentioned. In the King's view the engine "ought to be of special benefit to science and an honour to our native land".[56]

King Oscar's proposal was supported by the Standing Committee which argued that Georg Scheutz had devoted many years to the development of the difference engine, at considerable personal cost. Moreover, he had contributed to the progress of industry — without any financial reward — over a long period of time, by his writing and journalism.[57] Just as had been the case when the application for the grant had been debated by the Estates during the Riksdag session of 1850-1851, the Peasants once more voted against the proposal.[58] The other three Estates, however, were for it.[59] In 1851, the business had become a matter of national importance so there was little reason to refuse now. On the 1st of July 1854, it was finally voted that Georg and Edvard Scheutz should receive the additional sum of 3,333 riksdaler and 16 skilling recommended by the King.[60] In the middle of August 1854, the Scheutzes were officially informed about the matter.[61]

It seems plausible that Georg and Edvard Scheutz made use of this extra grant to pay off debts incurred during the construction of the engine. This hypothesis is consistent with the fact that they themselves did not pay for the cost of the trip abroad, which will be described later.

It had taken the men at Bergström's nearly two years to build the complicated machine. One possible explanation for this comparatively long period is that Edvard and Georg Scheutz' work on development and design may have been carried out while the engine was being built. It is also very possible that the amount of filing work involved in the construction work, was a contributing factor. Little, however, can be said about the actual building of the engine mainly due to the fact that no manuscripts, ledgers or other papers have been preserved from Bergström's workshop. Nevertheless, whereas the first engine had taken around six years to complete the second was finished in two. 6,666 riksdaler and 32 skilling had been granted by the Swedish government towards the invention. Compared with Babbage's 17,000 pounds, this sum amounted to a paltry 566 pounds.[62]

The Scheutzes began to entertain hopes of selling the engine abroad. On the first of November 1853, shortly after the machine had been completed, Georg and Edvard signed a contract. It stated that since Edvard had made the second engine almost by himself (without much of Georg's assistance), Edvard was to consider it from then on as his property. This meant that he could sell it, without consulting Georg, should a buyer be found. Furthermore, the contract stipulated that, if the engine was sold, Georg was to get one third of the money and the remaining two thirds were to go to Edvard.[63]

Thus the long rocky road from the making of the first parts of the prototype engine to the first cranking of the handle on the finished metal machine, had been travelled. The 1843 engine had served as a workable model for its successor and had perhaps been used during the construction work at Bergström's. The Scheutz second engine was in fact entirely based on the first engine. The essential difference was that the second engine was built by skilled workmen equipped with modern machine tools; in other words, it was built very much under the same basic technical circumstances as Babbage's engine. But the second engine was also mechanically different from the 1843 machine in several respects.

MODE OF OPERATION

The Scheutz second engine, like the first, consisted of three major units: *the calculating unit*, *the transfer mechanism*, and *the printing unit*, see Fig. 49.[64] The engine could deal with 15 digits and four differences. It was thus capable of calculating logarithms with the formulae given on page 73. Of these 15 digits, eight corresponded to the result, f(x), and five to the argument, x. Once more the engine was operated by cranking a handle, but the system of gearing for transmitting the force to the various units, was different from that in the first engine, see Fig. 55. The engine was 1600 mm long, 520 mm broad, and 450 mm high. It was made entirely of metal and weighed around 400 kilos.

In *the calculating unit*, there were 15 vertical axles corresponding to the 15 digits that the engine was able to calculate with, see Fig. 49. The number wheels were arranged in five horizontal rows, the uppermost corresponding to f(x) and those underneath corresponding in turn to $\Delta 1$, $\Delta 2$, $\Delta 3$, and $\Delta 4$. The construction of the addition element was quite different in this engine − the trap wheels and number wheels were not mounted in the same unit, see Fig. 50. The number wheels were mounted in shelves fixed to the frame. They consisted of cylindrical rings with the digits 0-9 engraved round their edges. Depending on the difference involved, the digits were arranged clockwise or anticlockwise.

In contrast to the solution adopted in the first engine, the trap wheels were fixed to the vertical axles. During the engine's operation, all the trap wheels revolved once in one direction and then once in the opposite direction. But they did not move up and down as they had done on the first engine. Georg and Edvard Scheutz had in fact discovered that the traps were only operated in one rotational direction. In the opposite direction, the trap pushed down the tongue (see section 2.3) without the

Fig. 50 Addition elements in Scheutz' second engine. This engine is now at the National Museum of American History, Smithsonian Institution, Washington, where it is exhibited. Photographed by author.

trap lifting up. As regards trap wheels and number wheels, there was no difference between the first and second engine. The Scheutzes had fixed the trap wheels to the axles, which simplified the engine since it was no longer necessary to have the axles move up and down.

The number of teeth on the number wheels varied, depending on which number system was to be used. Besides wheels for the usual decimal system, with ten teeth, the engine also had wheels and snails with six teeth. These were designed to be used when one was working with a sexagesimal system e.g. hours, minutes and seconds. This refinement had been suggested by Fabian Wrede who thus played a role even when it came to the mechanical details of the machine.[65]

The carrying mechanism was greatly improved in the second engine. To enable a comparison to be made, the method of operation of this mechanism in detail will be described. Consider Fig. 51, which shows a drawing of two shelves with a number wheel mounted in the right-hand shelf. This wheel represents a lower power than that placed to its left. It was fitted with a cog q. When the wheel was set at the digit 0, the cog pushed the arm st so that it ended up in the position shown in the figure. On the arm there were two cams − a vertical one t_1 and a horizontal one u. On both sides of the calculating unit, there was a milled and polished track, see Fig. 49 and 52. In each of the tracks, a gland with a pillar ran backwards and forwards. On each of the pillars, there was a pair of latches, see Fig. 52-53. The latch y was intended for carrying to the result-

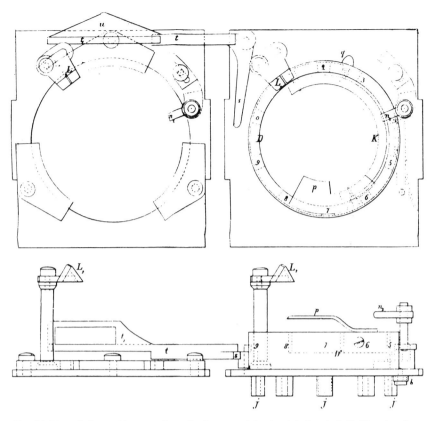

Fig. 51 Two shelves with a number wheel mounted in the right-hand shelf. Drawing from Scheutz' patent application: Letters Patent *(London 1855).*

row f(x), and the latch y_1 acted similarly in the case of row $\Delta 1$ etc. Since Δ 4 was constant, carrying to this row was superfluous. The latches normally took up the position shown in Fig. 50, but if a latch on its path along the calculating unit encountered an extended arm st (Fig. 51), the following sequence of events took place. Consider Fig. 51 and Fig. 53. At the end of the latch, there was a friction roller z which could mount the cam t. The tooth z_1 of the latch then caught hold of a tooth on the adjacent number wheel and rotated it forward one unit.[66]

Thereafter, the latch fell back down and the arm st was pushed back by the horizontal cam u. The carrying operation thus took place successively, going in turn from the lower to the higher powers, as the pillars were moved in one direction. They were then able to return to their initial position without acting upon the number wheels.

The Scheutzes had clearly perceived that the carrying mechanism which they had designed for the first engine, was inadequate. It was complicated and because of the tolerances involved in the first engine, unreliable. They, or perhaps Edvard alone, had therefore evolved this

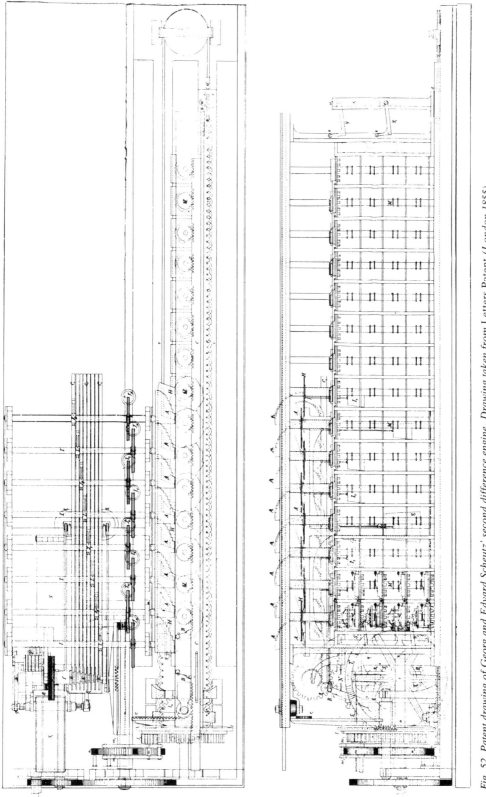

Fig. 52 Patent drawing of Georg and Edvard Scheutz' second difference engine. Drawing taken from Letters Patent (London 1855).

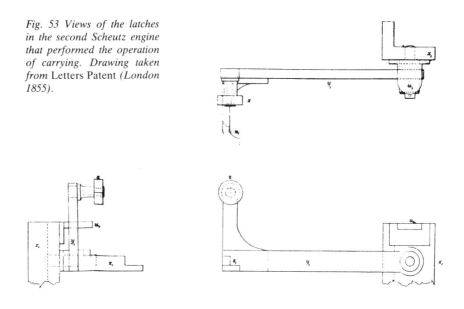

Fig. 53 Views of the latches in the second Scheutz engine that performed the operation of carrying. Drawing taken from Letters Patent *(London 1855).*

new and more reliable design. It is clear that they had matured as inventors and that their thinking had become sophisticated and profound. They no longer went cautiously forward, piecing together the whole system from the individual components, but were able to stand back and view the problem from a higher level. Edvard's training at the Technological Institute was reflected in the design, although of course Bergström, may also have played his part, as Clement had done in the case of Babbage's engine.

The calculating unit worked in a four-stage cycle, just as had been the case in the first engine. However, in the second engine, there was an additional difference $\Delta4$. The first step was therefore to add the even differences to the odd ones ($\Delta4 \rightarrow \Delta3$, $\Delta2 \rightarrow \Delta1$). Then carrying took place in rows $\Delta3$ and $\Delta1$ (by means of the latches on the rear pillar). The third step was to add the odd differences to the even ones ($\Delta3 \rightarrow \Delta2$, $\Delta1 \rightarrow f(x)$). Lastly, carrying took place in rows $\Delta2$ and f(x). In other words, it worked exactly like Babbage's great engine would have worked.

The transfer mechanism was analogous to that in the first engine. The sole difference was that the triangular lead weights on the stepped tooth cam axles were replaced by pulleys, wires and brass weights, see Fig. 54. Of the 15 digits with which the engine calculated, to achieve great accuracy, only the first 8 digits of the result were transferred to the printing unit.

The printing unit was also of a similar type to that in the first engine, apart from certain new refinements. The eight transfer racks were located in the printing unit, each one engaging its respective gear wheel, see Fig. 52 and 55. These wheels were mounted at the end of their respective tubes, which were telescoped within each other, and they

Fig. 54 Part of the transfer mechanism in Scheutz second engine. In the figure the snails, the stepped toth cams, the pulleys, the wires and the brass weights can be seen. Photographed by author.

could all rotate around a common axle, see Fig. 56. At the opposite end of each of the tubes, there was a gear wheel. These eight gear wheels engaged the corresponding type wheels involved in the result f(x). This telescope axle arrangement allowed for a washer to be inserted in between the type wheels, with the object of increasing the distance between the printed figures in the table row, without any of the gear wheels losing its ability to engage. These washers could be fitted with different types of signs, such as comma, hyphen or full-stop. The typographical possibilities were further increased by allowing for the use of type wheels with different styles of types.

The argument x was advanced by *the numerator*, which was essentially the same as it had been on the first engine. Five type wheels in the printing unit were responsible for seeing that the argument x was printed before the result f(x). The first engine had possessed the dubious advantage of permitting the numerator to progress to further powers in the result f(x) if this exceeded the calculating unit's maximum capacity. This possibility was removed in the second engine, for the simple reason that it must have been realized that it eventually led to incorrect results. It was sufficient that the second engine could correctly round off and print eight digits from the 15 that it could calculate with.

In contrast to what had been the case with the first engine, each typewheel belonging to the result f(x), was fitted with 11 cogs. Besides the digit-types 0-9, there was also an 11th cog which was blank and therefore made no impression in the matrix. Series often occurred where the initial terms contained only a small number of digits, but where the number of

Fig. 55 Scheutz' second engine from 1853. Through this transmission system the power from the crank was distributed to the calculating and the printing unit. The printing unit is located in the upper left corner in the photograph. To the right is the mangle wheel. Photographed by author.

Fig. 56 The printing unit seen from above, with the racks and gear wheels of the transfer mechanism. Each rack was engaged by a gear wheel, which was mounted on a tubular axle. At the opposite end of the axle another gear wheel was attached, which engaged a type wheel (to the left in the photograph). Photographed by author.

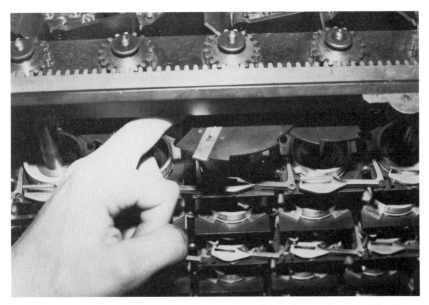

Fig. 57 Spring-loaded slide mechanism on the snails in Scheutz' second engine. This device, combined with a blank 11th cog or type on the type wheels, eliminated the superflous zeros that otherwise would have been printed before the results. Photographed by author.

digits in subsequent terms increased. The Scheutzes added the 11th cog to eliminate the unnecessary zeros, which preceded such a tabular value. By fitting the snails with a special mechanism which raised the stepped tooth cam so that the 11th cog was turned away from the printing table, one was able to avoid the labour of removing these superfluous zeros from the prepared cliché. This mechanism consisted of a little spring-loaded slide, which could be drawn out at the side of the snail, see Fig. 57. This gave the snail an 11th radial segment that was somewhat longer and which was able to act upon the stepped tooth cam. As soon as the digit at this place was different from zero, this mechanism ceased to operate, allowing the digits 0-9 to be printed in the usual manner.

When it came to printing, the engine was able to cope with double the length of matrix strips (approx. 180 mm.), possible with the first engine.

As already mentioned, the actual driving forces of the engine were organized and transferred in an entirely different manner from that pertaining in the first engine. In order to enable the operator to keep the engine working smoothly, there was a system of gear wheels which served to effect an initial, substantial "change-down" in the number of revolutions performed by the crank, see Fig. 55. The forces were thereafter distributed via the gear wheels to the calculating unit and the printing unit. The *mangle wheel*, see Fig. 58-59 is an orginal idea. This wheel was fitted with a ring of pins which engaged a smaller gear. At one point in the ring, some of the pins were missing. This had the effect of causing the smaller, driving gear wheel to traverse alternately the inner and outer

180

Fig. 58 The mangle wheel in Scheutz' second engine. It bears the engraved text "Inventerad af G. & E. Scheutz/ Förfärdigad hos J. W. Bergström/Stockholm/1853". Photographed by author.

perimeters of the ring, see Fig. 59. As a result the mangle wheel was rotated backwards and forwards. Connected to the mangle wheel, there was a toothed segment which transmitted to the 15 vertical axles their alternating rotations via a rack above the calculating unit, see Fig. 49 and Fig. 52. Both of the glands with pillars employed in carrying, were also driven via gear wheels and a chain, by means of the mangle wheel. The printing unit received its operative force via gear wheels and four cams. Just as on the first engine, the transfer racks were held in place by a roller actuated by two lead weights. One of the cams was responsible for pushing in this roller and releasing the racks so that the type-wheels were set to the calculated tabular value. Once the type wheels had been set in this way, two other cams were responsible for acting upon the wedge which entered between the cogs of the gear wheels corresponding to the type-wheels and held the types in place during printing. The fourth cam gave the printing table its up and down motion.

Fig. 59 Mode of operation of the mangle wheel in Scheutz' second engine. The driving gear, which engages with the pins on the mangle wheel, is mounted on a movable arm which allows the driving gear to traverse alternately the inner and outer perimeters of the ring of pins. Drawing by author.

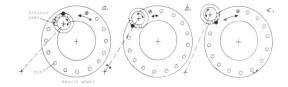

Scheutz's second engine was factory built that is to say hand-made within an industrial context. This meant that its overall detailed finish and reliability was much superior to that of the first engine. Skilled workmen with modern equipment had assisted the Scheutzes and this ensured that the result was satisfactory. Almost certainly, use was made of drawings, templates and jigs. Since the engine numbered over 2,000 parts (leaving aside screws and nuts), it would have been impossible for Edvard Scheutz to build it unaided within a reasonable time-span. One feature of the engine was that it involved several series of identical parts (e.g. traps) which were amenable to serial production. Such parts were interchangeable, since they were made to fine tolerances. The engine frame was a stable construction, cast in brass or bronze, and was mounted on a strong base plate of steel. This plate in turn rested on a mahogany-veneered base, consisting of a table with four legs that had been turned on a lathe. The engine also had a protective cover. Just as had been the case with the first engine, the second engine was easily extendable. In the calculating unit, the number wheels were silver plated and were engraved with digits in black enamel.[67] In contrast to the first engine, none of the parts were underdimensioned. The cogwheels, for example, were very strong and all the bearings were made of bronze to great accuracy. The majority of joints in the engine were made with screws, although soldering and riveting also occurred. In various vulnerable spots where precautions had to be taken against possible dismantling, screws with a special head requiring a special tool, had been used, see Fig. 60. In the printing unit, a great improvement was made by engraving the types on the type wheels in steel, instead of using lead types as in the first engine. It is quite clear, taking account of the techniques then available, that this must have entailed great difficulties. The results, however, were good, see Fig. 61.

The surface was treated in a variety of ways. Some parts had been painted dull black, while others had been black-finished. Some parts

Fig. 60 Special head screws in the second Scheutz engine, used in various vulnerable spots to prevent dismantling. Photographed by author.

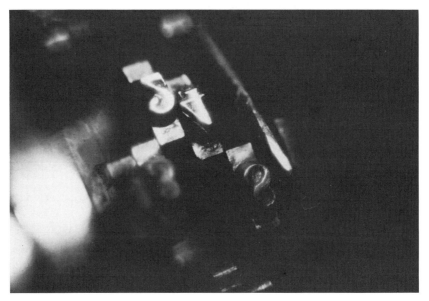

Fig. 61 The engraved steel types in the second Scheutz engine. These were difficult to make, but gave a good result and lasted of course much longer than the lead types the Scheutzes had been forced to employ in the first engine. Photographed by author.

made in the copper alloy were untreated. The brass was somewhat darker than it had been in the first engine and either presumably contained a larger amount of copper or was bronze chosen for casting.

One curious feature is that nearly all the parts in the second engine were numbered. This is understandable in the case of two bearing-halves that have been cut to fit a specific axle. However, I have been unable to find some plausible reason why screws and nuts were also numbered Perhaps this was a tradition from the days when fitting by hand was dominant in the engineering industry and the threads were filed by hand. It is also quite plausible that the numbering was part of an administrative system.

Another notable feature is the lack of material in the appropriate dimensions, illustrated by the fact that in various places Bergström's workmen were forced to make joints. One example is the upper rack (see Fig. 52), which is skillfully joined in two places, see Fig. 62. The use of such dovetail joints to bind together parts seems to have been relatively common during the 19th century.

Finally, the most apparently "new" part in the second engine was the mangle wheel. Its origin is evident from its name − it was to make the cylinders of a mangle for linen alternate in rotation, while operating the handle continuously in one direction only.[68] It is almost certain that Edvard Scheutz got the idea of using this rather ingenious device at the Technological Institute. Among the many models of mechanisms that were made by the pupils and used for illustrative purposes, there was at least one mangle wheel. I have already used the model in question as a general example in Fig. 24. Although an uncommon mechanism from the 20th century point of view, it was probably not as unusual during the last century, when e.g. the famous British engineer James Nasmyth at his firm in the 1850's produced planing machines for metal work equipped with mangle wheels for the back-and-forth motion of the metal piece to be cut. Thus the difference engine of 1853 embodied mechanical solutions, that had their origins in at least three different branches of production — the snails from the clockmakers, the mangle wheel from the textile workers, and the type wheels from the bank-note printers.

Was the second engine really a prototype or a model? This problem will be discussed in section 3.1, but it should be stressed that it certainly was not a model in the sense of being a simple forerunner to a later, more definitive design. On the contrary, the design was perfectly definitive, and the engine's capacity could be extended as required, just as had been the case with the first engine. The difference lay in the fact that the second engine was made of stable metal parts and therefore functioned in a more reliable manner.

*   *   *

In 1854, a new chapter began when Georg and Edvard Scheutz turned their attention to marketing their new engine. According to Georg Scheutz' application and to the conditions pertaining to the award of the

Fig. 62 Lack of material in the appropriate dimensions forced Bergström's men to make skilful joints like the one seen in this photograph. Photographed by author.

Fig. 63 Count Pehr Ambjörn Sparre (1828–1921). Photograph by courtesy of the Post Office Museum, Stockholm.

grant, the engine was to be put on display abroad. The first country chosen was England.

On the 30th of September 1854, Georg and Edvard Scheutz arrived in London with their engine.[69] Their fare and the cost of their stay in London was paid by the Swedish Count and engineer Pehr Ambjörn Sparre.[70]

Pehr Ambjörn Sparre was to play a particularly important role in the marketing of the Swedish Difference engine. Sparre who was seven years older than Edvard, had completed his school studies in Uppsala in 1847.[71] The three following years, he had spent at Motala Engineering Works, Sweden's largest mechanical engineering workshop which had been founded in 1822 in connection with the building of the Gotha Canal. There he received an excellent general technical training. He had also acquired special knowledge of printing and paper manufacture and in 1857 he became acting superintendent of the Estates' Paper Works at Tumba, outside Stockholm, where the country's bank-notes were produced. Sparre held this position until the summer of 1853 when the post of permanent superintendent was filled. Concurrently with his interest in the Scheutzes' engine, he was also plainly trying to assume responsibility for the printing of Sweden's first postage stamps. Postage stamps had been discussed for some time, and a decision from the Post Office about government issue stamps, was first made during the Riksdag of 1854.[72] In his search for good presses and other machinery necessary for the printing of stamps, Sparre had contacted a number of engineers and machine-builders in England.

On the 17th of October 1854, Georg and Edvard Scheutz made a formal application to take out a patent in England and on the very same day they signed a very remarkable contract with Ambjörn Sparre.[73] From the contract it is evident that Scheutz and Sparre had already come to an agreement in Sweden, whereby they would travel to England with a view to obtaining a certificate of recommendation from various famous scientists and engineers, to the effect that the engine was reliable and well-made. Sparre was prepared to pay for everything on the one condition that if a customer for the engine was found, then he was to have, for 4,000 pounds Sterling, (equivalent to the very large sum of 46,667 riksdaler banco), the engine ownership rights and the patents.[74] From the 4,000 pounds, 800 was to be set aside for Admiral Christian Adolf Virgin, to recompense him for the costs and trouble that he had encountered in the matter.[75] 800 pounds Sterling was the equivalent of 9,333 riksdaler banco and in comparison with the total grant made by the Swedish government, it was also a very large sum. What Virgin did to deserve this reward, is unfortunately unknown. In the winter of 1854, however, he was appointed the Swedish envoy in London. Moreover, in the contract the Scheutzes agreed to take out patents in Belgium, Prussia and Austria, and when the patent rights had been assured, to put the engine on show at the general exhibition of industry and arts in Paris in 1855. Such were the contents of the contract that Georg and Edvard Scheutz entered into with Sparre on the 17th of October 1854. On the 30th of the same month, Sparre paid out the money to cover the costs of the Scheutzes' foreign travel and residence.[76] This document is of the greatest interest because it was largely to dictate the ensuing course of events.

The contract with Sparre is also interesting for another reason. It implies in principle that Sparre bought the engine in the belief that it had commercial possibilities. The only condition he attached to sealing the purchase, was that a customer turned up. In the event of this happening, it is unclear whether Sparre intended to sell both the engine and the patent rights. What is clear, however, is that the contract meant that the Scheutzes consigned the fate of the engine to Sparre. Their reasons were financial. 3,200 pounds was certainly not a sum to be despised at that time. It was nearly seven times as much the total grant that they had received from the Swedish government. According to the first agreement between the Scheutzes, two thirds was to be given to Edvard. On the assumption that the Scheutzes had financial problems and were not in a position to contemplate the expensive marketing operating involved, their course of action seems perfectly natural.

Through Sparre, Georg and Edvard Scheutz were introduced to the engineering firm of Bryan Donkin & Company and the engineer William Gravatt.[77]

Bryan Donkin Sr. was an engineer who in the early decades of the 19th

Fig. 64 The British engineer William Gravatt (1806– 1866), F. R. S. He became a great supporter and promoter of the Scheutz engine. Photograph by courtesy of the Royal Society, London.

century had become famous by having constructed the first successful machines for producing paper. By 1854 about 200 of these machines which rapidly replaced the method of making paper by hand, had been made end erected by Donkin and his sons, also in other countries. Bryan Donkin Sr. had also introduced improvements in printing machinery, like the revolution counter shown in Fig. 42, and had worked on methods and machinery for printing stamps in two colours to prevent forgery, in 1820. Although a very old man, eighty-six years of age, his wellknown company at Bermondsey in London, now run by his three sons, flourished.[78]

William Gravatt who was born in 1806, had also devoted his life to engineering.[79] He had been employed by the Donkins and had worked on the Thames Tunnel as assistant to Isambard Kindom Brunel. Later, while building railroads, Brunel had taken on Gravatt who had become one of his most trusted men.[80] In 1833 William Gravatt had been elected a Fellow of the Royal Society and when Georg and Edvard Scheutz met him, he was a man with an established reputation for his mechanical inventions, as well as a knowledgeable civil engineer.

The engine was taken to Donkin's workshops in Bermondsey where it was examined by Gravatt who took a very keen interest in the machine. On the 16th of November 1854, a note from him was read at the Royal Society, announcing that the Scheutz engine was now in London.[81] Shortly afterwards, the engine was transferred to the Royal Society, where it was demonstrated for the Fellows and other interested parties.

Fig. 65 Pehr Georg Scheutz at old age, still auditor, journalist and inventor. Photograph by courtesy of the Royal Library, Stockholm; source unknown, (signum Fc).

Among the visitors who saw it on display there, were the celebrated scientists George Gabriel Stokes, Michael Faraday and Charles Wheatstone.[82]

It was Wheatstone who provided Georg and Edvard Scheutz with a letter of introduction to Charles Babbage.[83] The first meeting between the Scheutzes and Babbage probably took place on the 30th of November 1854.[84] It must have been an exciting moment for all three of them.[85] Although united by the same desire to build difference engines, they were quite different personalities. Edvard, now thirty-three years of age, was a trained engineer. Georg and Charles, sixty-nine and sixty-two years old respectively, were autodidacts in the matter of technology. Nevertheless, they were highly experienced men in the field, no less knowledgeable than young Edvard. Georg belonged to the lower middle-class and was sensitive to economical set-backs. Babbage was a wealthy man's son. They were both authors who still frequently wrote and published books and articles. Georg was the practical man and the humanist, while Babbage was the theoretical scientist, little interested in the works of Homer and Plato.[86]

188

Indeed, there were deeper hidden contrasts between the two inventors. Georg Scheutz despised the English gentleman's way of life. In an article published in 1840, he had written that "the theories of Adam Smith were so dominant in *England* that it is *not enough to own enough*; there, one has to own *things in abundance* – one has to be *rich*. Anyone in England who is not rich, has neither a reputation or can hope to be trusted by others and cannot be happy. From childhood onwards, the Englishman has been so used to confuse riches, pleasure and honour, that he cannot imagine one without the other."[87] Although Scheutz was not altogether fair to Adam Smith, it is clear that he put forward simpler ideals, such as enough food for the day, simple clothes etc.[88] Babbage, who was economically independent and had servants to help him change his attire – "not too gay for the morning, and not too dull for the evening" – must have fitted Georg Scheutz' description of the typical English gentleman perfectly.[89] Babbage, on the other hand, described Georg Scheutz as "a person of the greatest simplicity and modesty".[90]

Apart from the difference engine, Babbage and the older Scheutz had other things in common which they must have talked about. In their youth they had been politically active and drawn to liberal beliefs. While Scheutz had acted as one, if not the leading, figure of Swedish oppositional journalism, Babbage in the early 1830s had been a candidate for Parliament, although he was unsuccessful.[91] Interestingly enough, in *Slägtvälde och idévälde* (1840) Scheutz had unrestrainedly attacked the ignorant nobles in the position of inherited power and in 1833 Babbage had published *A Word to the Wise; Observations on Peerage for Life*, being a quite similar work to Scheutz', although milder in its tone.[92] Both had tried to improve their societies also in other ways – Babbage as a reformer of science an industrial economy and Scheutz as a promoter of culture and technology. But they did have the engine in common too and Georg and Edvard Scheutz were plainly surprised by the friendly reception that Babbage gave them.[93] Babbage who showed the Scheutzes his house, workshops and engines, was greatly interested and devoted two whole days to investigating Scheutz' engine for which he had much praise, especially for the way they had succeeded in building it with the funds at their disposal.[94] From this moment onward, the Scheutzes had the support of two people – Charles Babbage and William Gravatt – who would devote themselves to demonstrating the engine and making it known throughout Europe. In addition Bryan Donkin Jr., who was only nineteen years of age, became the Scheutzes' agent in London.[95]

On William Gravatt's initiative, the difference engine remained at the Royal Society.[96] At the end of 1854, it was inspected by a committee under the chairmanship of the physicist George Stokes and consisting of the physicist Charles Wheatstone, the crystallographer and mineralogist William H. Miller and Robert Willis, professor of mechanics. All this was in accordance with the conditions specified in the contract with Sparre, whereby the engine was to be inspected by a number of well-known scientists and engineers. The committee presented its report to the Royal Society on the 21st of January 1855 and stated that:

"The machine works with the greatest freedom and smoothness. The parts move with the utmost facility, in fact, quite loosely. On this account no amount of dust which it would reasonably be expected to receive in any moderate time seems likely to interfere with its action. Besides, it can easily be taken to pieces and examined, if need be. Those motions which are not the direct consequences of the revolution of the handle acting through a train of rigid bodies are performed in consequence of gravity, no springs being employed in the whole construction except two, the office of which is quite subordinate. When the parts are moved, they remain in their new places either from their weight or from friction, there being nothing to disturb them. This circumstance, which renders a wilful derangement of the machine exceedingly easy, permits of great simplicity and consequent cheapness of construction; nor does the machine seem likely to get out of order if reasonable care be taken of it."[97]

The mode of operation of the engine was described and the mathematics involved were discussed in detail with examples. With respect to the utility of the machine, the committee concluded:

"It must be confessed, however, that except in the case of mathematical tables like those of sines, cosines, logarithms, &c., it is not ordinarily required to tabulate functions to intervals at all approaching, in closeness, to those in the example selected. Hence it is mainly, as it seems to us, in the computation of mathematical tables, that the machine of M.Scheutz would come into use. The most important of such tables have long since been calculated; but various others could be suggested which it might be worth while to construct, could it be done with such ease and cheapness as would be afforded by the use of the machine. It has been suggested to us too, and we think with good reason, that the machine would be very useful even for the mere reprinting of old tables, because it could calculate and print more quickly than a good compositor could set the types, and that without risk of error."[98]

Presumably due to lack of money, Georg and Edvard Scheutz returned to Stockholm sometime during the first months of 1855. The engine was left in the custody of Gravatt and Donkin. On the 9th of March 1855 the Scheutzes signed the papers, approving the English patent, in Stockholm.[99] Sparre, who was careful to see that the patent was guaranteed according to the contract, acted as witness. On the 13th of April, the patent was sealed.[100] The engine was still at the Royal Society and at the end of June it was demonstrated for His Royal Highness Prince Albert by

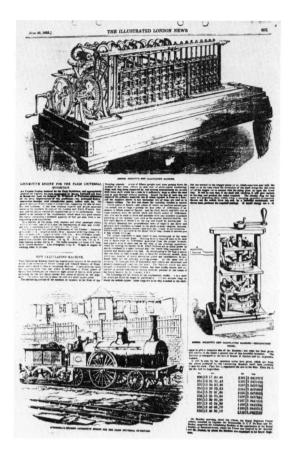

Bryan Donkin and William Gravatt.[101] Some days later a large front page article with illustrations of the "New Calculating Machine" appeared in *The Illustrated London News,* Fig. 66. It began by bringing attention to the "great interest" the machine had created in the scientific world and continued with a description of the engine, with words such as "beautiful stereotype moulds", "this beautiful invention" and "how perfectly it does its work".[102] The tone used in this article was to be adopted in other publications during the following years. About a month after this, a translation to Swedish of this article was published in *Illustrerad Tidning.* In contained some interesting additions. In it, it was stated that the model shown in Fig. 66, had been made for demonstration purposes by Gravatt and Donkin.[103] The anonymous author, who probably had consulted the Scheutzes (and may even have been one of them), also said that the engine was operated by a crank. "This does not require great power, and the machine could be kept in motion by a little dog, of the kind that is used in England as motive power for roasting-spits".[104] In a note it was added that "Like a squirrel, the dog walks around in its little cage, the

191

rotation of which is transferred to the spit".[105] It is indeed ironic that the great British difference engine of Charles Babbage was, at least symbolically, intended to be driven by the glorious steam engine, while now, in accordance with the spirit of the modest Georg Scheutz, a little dog was enough to do the job.[106]

Sometime at the beginning of 1854, Gravatt or Donkin had demonstrated the Swedish difference engine for two famous British astronomers, namely Herschel and Airy.[107] Unfortunately, nothing is known about their opinion of the machine.[108]

According to the contract with Sparre, patents were to be taken out in certain European countries. In May 1855, George and Edvard Scheutz were informed that applications for patents had been made in Belgium and France.[109] The applications had been made by Sparre's friend Count Nils Barck in his own name, something that would prey upon the minds of the Scheutzes in the future. The man in question − Nils Ferdinand Barck has been described not only as a count but also as "an adventurer". During the 1840s he lived in London and engaged in financial speculations.[110] It is clear that the Scheutzes had good reason to be worried.

During the spring of 1855, Charles Babbage got down to the task of making the Scheutz difference engine better known. This took concrete form when Charles' son Henry Prevost Babbage was given the task in April 1855 of devising mechanical notation for the second Scheutz engine.[111] It was an extensive piece of work which turned out to require the whole summer for its completion.

From the end of 1846 Babbage had not devoted much time to the Analytical Engine, and in June 1855 he wrote to Stokes that he had no plans to build a difference engine again.[112] According to Collier, however, Babbage in 1846 had suddenly switched his attention to the difference engine, and had in fact started to design a new improved version of it.[113] He had called it the New Difference Engine, and later the Difference Engine No. 2. Why this happened is unclear, although Collier suggests that it might have something to do with the fact that Peel's Conservative government had been replaced by a Whig administration.[114] In 1848 or 1849 Babbage had had the drawings and notatons for the new engine ready but the machine was never built.[115] The Difference Engine No. 2 was supposed to calculate with six or seven orders of differences and perhaps as many as 31 digits.[116] Several drawings of the engine and its printing unit still exist. From them, it is evident that Babbage, at least theoretically, had solved the problems involved in designing the printing unit. It was a complicated device. Like Müller's machine, it could print directly on paper, apparently with two different sizes of types. It also produced stereotypes simultaneously, with types in two sizes.[117] The coordinate board, introduced in the first engine, had been retained, showing that Babbage still obviously intended to print a whole table page at a time, instead of strips or columns like the Scheutzes.[118] The adding and carrying would apparently have been similar to the design in the Difference Engine No. 1.

Babbage offered his new engine to the British government in June 1852.[119] This time the engine was supposed to be built by a mechanical engineer at a fixed prize.[120] In his submission Babbage wrote that his motive for offering the engine was to fulfil the original expectations that he should produce a difference engine for the government, and to discharge whatever *"imagined"* obligation that may rest on him.[121] He ended the letter − "I feel, in laying this representation before your Lordship, and in making the offer I now make, that I have discharged to the utmost limit every implied obligation I originally contracted with the country".[122] It is likely that Babbage by then knew what the Scheutzes were up to and wanted to defend himself in case they arrived in England, offering an inexpensive printing engine.

As Babbage had expected, the government's answer turned out to be negative.[123] The reason was that "Mr. Babbage's projects appear to be so indefinitely expensive, the ultimate success so problematical, and the expenditure so large and so utterly incapable of being calculated, that the Government would not be justified in taking upon itself any further liability."[124]

In August 1855, the Scheutz engine was taken from London to "l'Exposition Universelle" in Paris.[125] In the contract with Sparre, the Scheutzes had agreed to take the engine to this exhibition. Since both of

Entrée principale du Palais de l'Exposition.

Fig. 67 The main entrance of "l'Exposition Universelle de Paris" in 1855. Over 20.000 exhibitors took part in the event, of whom some 400 came from Sweden. Here the Scheutz engine was shown to a larger public than ever before. Photograph taken from Tresca, Visite à l'Exposition Universelle *(Paris 1855).*

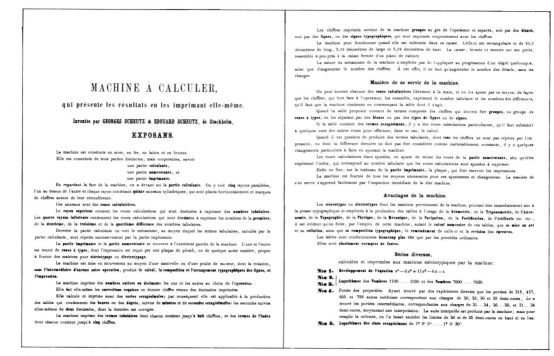

Fig. 68 These brochures in French, printed by a Stockholm printer, were available to the visitors to the Swedish section of the exhibition. Photograph by courtesy of the Stockholm University Library with the Royal Academy of Sciences, Stockholm.

them were in Stockholm, it was Sparre who had the responsibility of transferring the engine from London to Paris.[126] William Gravatt went along too.[127] The exhibition opened in the summer of 1855, with the aim of showing products from all the nations of the world.[128] The Scheutz engine was placed in the Swedish section for machines in the great annex, Over 20,000 exhibitors took part in the event, of which some 400 came from Sweden.[129] Gravatt had the task of demonstrating the engine at the exhibition, thus assuring the Scheutzes that a proper account of the machine was presented to French scientists who were interested in making a more detailed investigation of it.[130] Special brochures on the difference engine were available to visitors, see Fig. 68.

While the engine was on display to a greater public than ever before, Georg Scheutz devoted himself in Stockholm to translations and journalism. Nevertheless, the difference engine remained the focus of the attentions of both Scheutzs and this is reflected in their correspondence. In one letter, they mention it as "the invention for which, in the truest sense, we have risked everything."[131] It was with the greatest interest and expectations that they followed by letter the course of events at the world exhibition in Paris.[132] In the meantime, in England, Babbage was engaged on devising a method for distinguishing lighthouses and night signals at sea.[133]

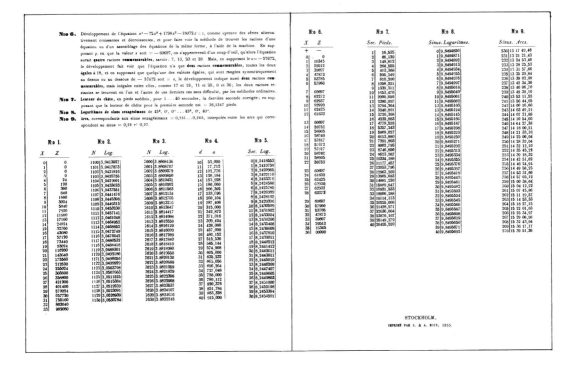

At the beginning of September, the Scheutzes received a letter from Babbage. Since the mechanical notation for the Scheutz engine was nearly ready, he had resolved to take it to Paris and show it to the Prize Committee, thus providing them with additional information on the mode of operation of the engine.[134] In September Henry Babbage demonstrated the notation for the engine, at a meeting of the British Association for the Advancement of Science in Glasgow.[135] Some time around the end of September 1855, Charles Babbage arrived in Paris.[136] On the 2nd of October Babbage made a contribution to publicizing the engine by writing a short paper on the notation and the engine. It was published in the *Comptes Rendus Hebdomaires de l'Academie des Sciences* after the meeting of the 8th of October 1855, when the notation for the Scheutz engine was presented for the French Academy of Sciences.[137] On the same day, Babbage wrote a letter to Georg and Edvard Scheutz. In it, Babbage said that he had not been admitted to the Exhibition buildings that morning when he had arrived there with the notation in the company of two workmen. He had been urged to protest about the matter, but had not done so − "I declined writing any note and under these circumstances, it is impossible for me to attend the jury tomorrow unless I receive an official application …"[138] The long hours expended on the notation were probably the cause of Babbage's anger about what had

195

happened. Eventually he managed to get an opportunity to demonstrate the notation of the engine for the jury.[139] The episode shows Babbage's interest in the matter. Probably, the actual demonstration of the engine before the exhibition jury was carried out by Gravatt and Sparre.[140] The response of the judges was positive. It was decided that Georg and Edvard Scheutz should be awarded a gold medal – the lesser of two gold medals awarded to Sweden at the exhibition.[141] (The other medal, intended for companies, was awarded to the Motala Engineering Works.[142]) It was the first concrete reward that they had received for the many years of work that they had devoted to the difference engine. A French newspaper also singled out the engine as something special – "We do not believe that the Universal Exposition supplies a single machine where inventive genius is more clearly and more completely revealed, than the calculating machine displayed by its inventors, M. M. George and Edouard Scheutz of Stockholm".[143] Both Babbage and Scheutz followed up this success, by publicizing the engine with further articles. These were published in London and Paris. It is clear from their correspondence that Babbage was concerned that the engine should receive the attention it deserved – "the sooner it [the article] gets in print in Paris & London, the better for the interest of the invention".[144] Towards the end of October, Babbage and Gravatt returned to London.[145]

At the beginning of November 1855, Georg and Edvard Scheutz were notified that Sparre had shown the papers registering the patents in Belgium and France, to the secretary of the Swedish legation in Paris.[146] The Universal Exhibition closed and the Scheutz engine was transferred to the Imperial Observatory of Paris, by order of the French Emperor, Napoleon III. There the engine was to be submitted to tests by Le Bureau des longitude, the publishers of *La Connaissance des temps*, as a first step towards a possible purchase by the French government.[147]

Unfortunately, exactly what happened at the observatory is unknown and I have not been able to consult the primary source material that presumably exists in France.[148] It is clear though that at some point purchase of the engine was not recommended. It was the Director of the Observatory, the successor of Arago, Urbain Jean Joseph Leverrier who decided the matter.[149]

Leverrier, who had studied at L'École Polytechnique and worked as an engineer and a chemist, had in the early 1830s turned his interest to astronomy and had soon become renowned for his investigations in celestial mechanics. In September 1846 Leverrier had discovered a new planet, namely Neptune.[150] He had found the planet by theoretical calculations. But the discovery had also its victim – the English mathematician John Couch Adams. The origin to the discovery had been the irregularities in the motions of Uranus (discovered by William Herschel). The astronomer George Biddell Airy had dismissed these irregularities as due to errors in the tables.[151] Adams had become interested in the matter and already in 1845 he had presented calculations, showing the existence of a new planet (Neptunus) to Airy. Airy's opinion had been that Adams had not solved the problem completely and he failed to see the importance of the results. This caused delays and eight months later, in June 1846, Leverrier's almost identical result (stating the theoretically found position of the new planet) had reached Airy. The latter had once again failed to act and the result of the whole affair was that Leverrier received the credit for discovering Neptune before the Englishman. After the discovery a dispute had started between Leverrier and the French scientists on one side and Airy together with John Herschel on the other. But because of Airy, Adams never got the honour he deserved.

Once at the Imperial Observatory, Leverrier examined the Scheutz engine. He discussed it with his colleagues and apparently had a printer study the printing part of the engine. Leverrier, the man in charge for the production of the *Connaissance des temps*, concluded − "that the invention was extremely ingenious, that it functioned reliably but that in practice, it provided no advantage to outweigh the considerable purchase price".[152] The price demanded was 50,000 francs, or 23,729 riksdaler, or approximately 1,998 pounds. More concretely, Leverrier could not see any practical usefulness in the engine and thought "that it only did by itself a fifth of the work necessary for calculating the tables, and this fifth, it did less quickly than an ordinary calculator".[153]

It is unclear what other French scientists thought of the matter. What is known is that somewhat later the mathematician Michel Chasles (without supplying any commentary of his own) presented a paper of Babbage on the engine to l'Academie des Sciences.[154] Charles Dupin intervened to stress that it was important that an inventor did not allow himself to become despondent over reversals but continued with the further development of his invention.[155]

Some years later, in an article in *Aftonbladet*, Georg and Edvard Scheutz provided an explanation of Leverrier's verdict. According to them, the observatory had carried out its investigation when Babbage and Gravatt who knew something about the engine, were no longer there. "The investigation on which Leverrier's judgement was based, was consequently carried out by persons who had little or no acquaintance with the engine and its method of operation".[156] It is possible that this statement was true but whether different circumstances would have altered Leverrier's views, is uncertain. Leverrier's verdict was final and the French government ceased to be interested in making a purchase.

On the 13th of February 1856, Georg Scheutz was elected a member of the Swedish Royal Academy of Sciences (Section of Practical Mechanics).[157] On the 12th of March Scheutz attended his first meeting at the Academy and was welcomed by the other members.[158] His election was in recognition of his invention of the difference engine. Neither Georg nor Edvard Scheutz was then aware how hard Charles Babbage had tried to make the engine better known. When they learned of his efforts, each of them wrote a letter in English to Babbage, expressing their gratitude. Georg wrote:

"Inventors are so seldom found that acknowledge the efforts of others for identical aims, that your liberality in this respect has, as we hear, made eclat in the french scientific world. Respecting me and my son we would not have been so much surprised, having had occasion before, during our stay in London, to learn at your house the true character of an English gentleman; although our admiration of it can only be surpassed by our deep sence of gratitude. We came as strangers; but you did not receive us as such: confirming to reality you received us as champions for a grand scientific idea. This rare disinterestedness offers so exhilarating an oasis in the deserts of humanity, that I wishes the whole world should know it as I do and feel its soothing effects as I do; it would be so much the better for the comfort and happiness of mankind."[159]

Edvard's letter was more sombre.

"Partly by letters from Paris and partly by returning visitors from the Universal Exhibition there, my father and I are informed of the excertions which you have been pleased to make in promoting a happy result of our labour for your grand idea in making use of machinery for calculating and printing Mathematical Tables: − an idea as important for humanity, in saving life and goods at sea, as for science. Your intervention in that respect has not only attracted the greatest attention of the scientific world, here and, as we are informed also in France, but moreover of the public in general. It has excited the more admiration, as inventors are usually seen to look with jealousy on them which strive in the same way. I ought not to conceal that it was prognosticated even to us, that we should meet an adversary in you; and we have found a protector!

Perchance that neither my father nor I may reap any fruit of our endeavours; but whatever may happen we shall find a consolation in the thought that we were at least comprehended by you. It would certainly be a sad destiny to see that hope vanish, which was our aim, the achieving of your object; but so unfortunate was the harvest of many other inventors, perhaps deserving a better lot, that I scarce know if we have a right to complain; how sad it would be if my old father and I should increase the long list of victims for great ideas. At all events I am fully convinced that this idea will break its own way in defiance of every obstacle which unfavorable times, and possibly even intrigues, might put up against it."[160]

The engine was still in France in April 1856. Babbage, who heard that it had been transferred to the Imperial Observatory of Paris, on the orders

198

of the Emperor, Napoleon III, was at first under the mistaken impression that it had in fact been bought.[161] On the 7th of April 1856, he sent an interesting letter to the Swedish King, Oscar I.

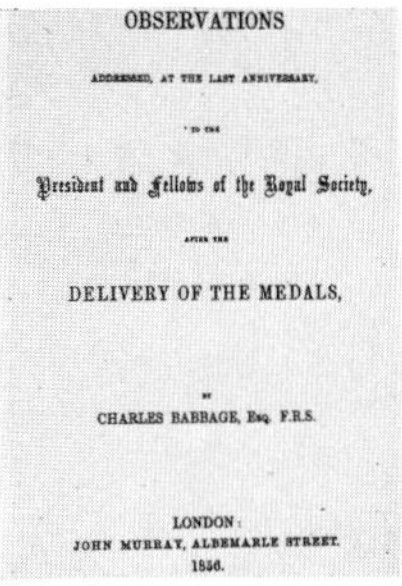
OBSERVATIONS

ADDRESSED, AT THE LAST ANNIVERSARY,

TO THE

President and Fellows of the Royal Society,

AFTER THE

DELIVERY OF THE MEDALS,

BY

CHARLES BABBAGE, Esq. F.R.S.

LONDON:
JOHN MURRAY, ALBEMARLE STREET.
1856.

Fig. 69 In 1856 Charles Babbage published this pamphlet, in which he criticized the Royal Society for not having honoured Georg and Edvard Scheutz with the award of one of their medals in 1855.

> "The science of mathematics is becoming too vast in its details to be completely mastered by human intellect and the time is approaching when the whole of its executive department will be transferred to the unerring power of Mechanism.
>
> Whenever that day shall arrive due honour must always be given to Sweden as the country which first produced mechanism to print the results of calculations regulated by a mathematical law."[162]

The words reveal much about the almost unlimited confidence Babbage, and many of his contemporaries, had in mechanical engineering. Interestingly enough, Babbage emphasized the printing capability of the engine over the fact that it could calculate, thus accentuating his own achievement. Along with the letter to the Swedish King, Babbage sent a recently printed pamphlet – *Observations addressed at the Last Anniversary, to the President and Fellows of the Royal Society, After the Delivery of the Medals.*[163] In it, he criticized the Royal Society for not having honoured the Scheutzes with one of their medals, in 1855. He stressed, just as he had done on other occasions, that the original idea was due to himself but that the Scheutzes had borrowed little apart from the basic principle. The aim of this pamphlet was to remind the Royal Society to keep Scheutz in mind when it came to the award of medals in 1856. In the pamphlet, which Babbage sent out to his friends and colleagues, to the fifteen guarantors who had supported Scheutz in 1852 and to a number of other interested parties, there is also an impressive tribute:[164]

> "Sweden has thus secured for herself the glory of having been the first nation practically to produce a machine for Calculating Mathematical Tables by Differences, and Printing the Results. Wealthier and more powerful nations will regret that the country of Berzelius should thus have anticipated them, in giving effect to an invention which requires for its perfection the tools of nations more highly advanced in mechanical science."[165]

On the 7th of April 1856, Georg Scheutz wrote an authorization to Edvard, giving him the right to sell the engine or the patent, to renew the patent or to take out new patents, as he (Edvard Scheutz) desired, see Fig. 70.[166] The document does not mention Sparre or the Scheutzes' agreement with him. It might be assumed that this agreement was still valid. As will be shown, however, Georg and Edvard Scheutz now feared that Sparre and Barck in some way would cheat them. This was the underlying reason for the authorization. The authorization marks an important turning point in the historical development, because thereafter Edvard became more and more the driving force in the venture.

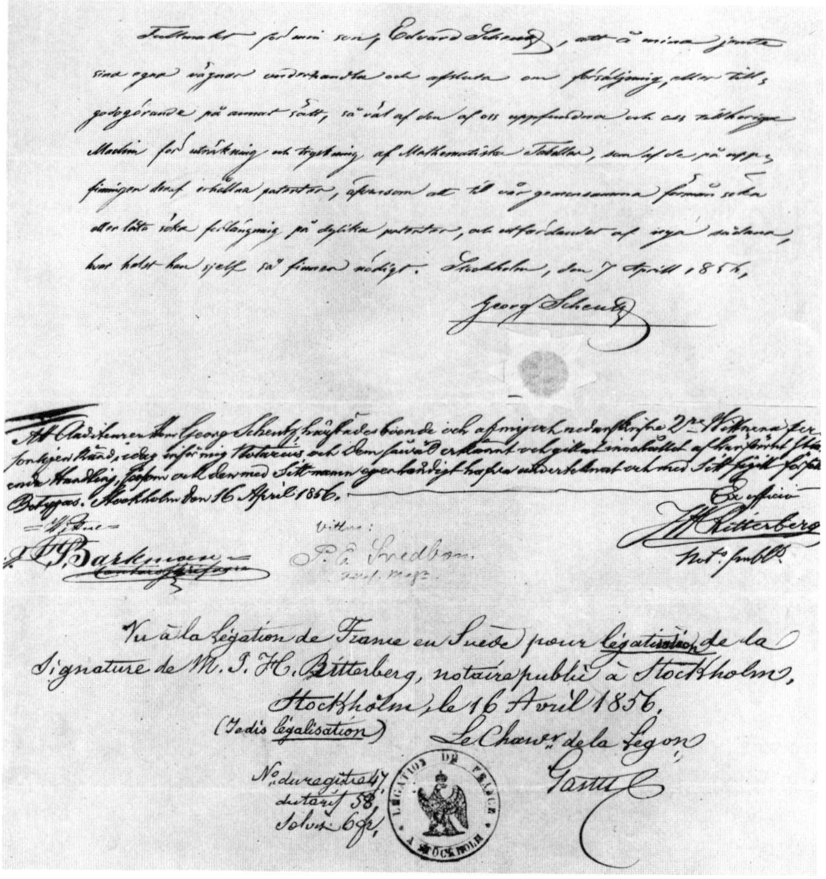

Fig. 70 Authorization by George Scheutz to Edvard Scheutz, giving him the right to sell the engine or the patent, to renew the patent or to take out new patents as Edvard desired. Dated Stockholm 7th of April 1856. Original kept in the Nordic Museum. Photograph by courtesy of the Nordic Museum, Stockholm.

On the 21st of April 1856, in a ceremony that took place in the Royal Palace at Stockholm, Crown Prince Carl handed out the awards that had been given to Swedes by the jury of the Paris Exhibition the year before.[167] Georg and Edvard Scheutz received their "Médaille d'Honneur", Fig. 71.[168] The same week, Edvard Scheutz set out for Paris, where the engine had meanwhile remained.[169] With him he had his father's authorization of the 7th of April 1856.

One evening at the end of April, 1856, Georg Scheutz was sitting at home, reading *Aftonbladet*. There was a report in it about those who had been made a member of the Swedish Order of Wasa and among their names he "was not a little surprised" to discover his own. No one had given him any hint of this forthcoming honour and if he had known (he wrote to Edvard), he would have certainly refused it. Next morning, he

*Fig. 71 At the Universal Exhibition in Paris in 1855 Georg and Edvard Scheutz were awar-
ded a gold medal − "Medaille d'Honneur" − for the invention of their difference engine. It
was one of the two medals that went to Sweden. The other one was given to Motala Engineering Works.*

rushed out to Fabian Wrede to enquire how one went about getting out
of the investiture itself. Wrede's reply was that the only method was to
leave Stockholm but that such an action would have the effect of "turning
goodwill into displeasure" and on hearing this, Scheutz' opposition
evaporated.[170] The episode reveals a lot about Georg Scheutz' character.
Quite unlike Babbage, he wanted neither glory nor honour, but was
satisfied by knowing that he had contributed in various ways to the
development of society. On the 28th of April 1856, he was officially
declared a Knight of the Order of Wasa, and on the 8th of May the
ceremony took place.[171] This distinction was intended to honour him for
his contributions to fostering industrial development and to the practical
applications of science, in his native land.[172]

It is clear that Georg and Edvard Scheutz feared the consequences of
the fact that Count Nils Barck, in collusion with Count Pehr Sparre, had
applied for a patent for the engine in his own name, in Belgium and
France, in May of 1855.[173] This was the main reason why Edvard had set
out for Brussels and Paris with such alacrity. It was high time to renew
these patents and the Scheutzes wished to forestall Barck and Sparre by
renewing the patent in Edvard's name. This was duly done, first in Brussels on the 7th of May 1856 and two days later in Paris.[174] "Only through
our own exertions [have the patents] been saved", wrote Georg
Scheutz.[175]

In Paris, Edvard made a point of meeting those scientists interested in
the difference engine.[176] Since, however, a French purchaser was not
forthcoming, he wrote on the 18th of May to his London agent Bryan
Donkin, asking about the possibilities of selling the machine in England.[177] Donkin, who was unable to give an opinion on the matter consulted Babbage, with whom he had had a five-hour discussion about the
engine. On the 25th of June 1856, Donkin replied to Scheutz' letter. He
asked Edvard about the lowest price he was willing to accept for the
engine without the patents and went on to say that Babbage had told him

that "there is a possibility of selling it for about 1,000, to go to a foreign country, if you were inclined to accept so small a sum for it".[178] The sum mentioned was only half of the price offered to the French.

Edvard Scheutz, who according to the contract with Sparre, see page 186, was to get two thirds of 3,200 pounds, i.e. 2,133 pounds, must have had little reason to hesitate. The remaining 1,067 pounds was to go to Georg. Accordingly, he wrote back to Donkin and said that he accepted the offer.[179]

But, who was this potential buyer? His name was Benjamin Apthorp Gould, an American astronomer who on the 28th of April had written to Babbage asking for detailed information about the capacity and the price of the Scheutz engine.[180] Gould was a member of the Scientific Council of the newly established Dudley Observatory at Albany, New York, and was an acquaintance of Babbage. In 1845, Babbage had shown him the unfinished difference engine. In 1855 at the Paris Exhibition, Gould had met Babbage and had seen the Scheutz engine.[181] Somewhat later Gould wrote − "it was with no small delight, that I heard of and saw the calculating engine of the Messrs. Scheutz; and I resolved anew, as often before, that, should it ever be within my power to contribute to the introduction of the system into actual use, no efforts should be want-ing".[182] But Benjamin Gould was apparently more eager to put the engine into use, than he was informed about the design and the useful-ness of the engine.[183] In his letter to Babbage, he asked a number of questions: − how much power was required to operate it; with what speed did it operate; did it print in matrices for stereotyping or on paper; was it the fourth or fifth difference that was assumed to be constant? He also asked whether the engine could solve equations. Furthermore, Gould suspected that the practical use of the difference engine was limited and wrote:

> "There are great many auxiliary tables which it would compute admir-ably but I fear that its application otherwise would be restricted to the computation of approximate ephemeris, for newly discovered planets & comets, − with such subsidiary tables as might be required from

time to time and which might be manually computed with not much greater trouble. If it were only an Analytical Engine!"[184]

Gould noted that he had not revealed his plans for a possible purchase of the Swedish engine for the Dudley Observatory. "Should further reflection lead in that direction, I should be inclined to use my best efforts to this end", he continued. Then he ended his letter to Babbage by saying that:

"It would be a source of legitimate & honourable pride to have first introduced this engine into practical usefulness. − But I fear much that its scope is not large enough to make its purchase a proper one to be strongly advocated at present. Will you please advice me?"[185]

Thus what had come from America was merely a set of questions about the engine and nothing else. No price was mentioned in Gould's letter and it must have been Babbage or perhaps Donkin who had named the sum of 1,000 pounds. Edvard was hopeful but the matter was far from being finalized.

In the middle of June, Edvard Scheutz travelled to London.[186] Apart from the fact that Donkin and Babbage were interested in talking with him about the possibility of the engine being purchased, there was another reason for his presence there.[187] Either Edvard Scheutz or William Gravatt had had the idea of printing a brochure about the second engine which would give an historical account of the machine and also examples of the tables.[188] The ultimate purpose was to find buyers for the invention and Edvard received two manuscripts from his father in Stockholm as a basis for this historical account.[189]

In June 1856, Edvard Scheutz was given a letter which had been addressed in February of the same year, to George Stokes, the chairman of the Royal Society Committee which in 1854 had inspected the engine in London.[190] The letter was from the superintendent of the American Nautical Almanac, Charles Henry Davis and it contained a request for further information, including the price, from the Scheutzes about their engine. It was the second time that an enquiry about the difference engine had come from America.

Edvard Scheutz returned to Paris to fetch the engine, since it was now agreed that the brochure should be printed.[191] In the French capital, he had an opportunity of showing the engine at work at the Imperial Observatory.[192] William Gravatt had prepared a special room in his London house for the engine, and it arrived there at the end of July 1856. Edvard, who had been ill in Paris, was also back in London and had now recovered.[193] The work on the brochure which received the title of *Specimens of Tables, Calculated, Stereomoulded, and Printed by Machinery*, was carried out by Edvard Scheutz, William Gravatt and Charles Babbage.[194] While Babbage busied himself with the revision of Georg Scheutz' historical account, Edvard Scheutz and William Gravatt turned out tables of logarithms from 1 to 10,000 and fourteen shorter tables which were designed to demonstrate in *Specimens* what the engine could do.[195] The historical account was continually revised during this work by Edvard Scheutz and Charles Babbage.[196]

Gravatt also contributed a mathematical description of the engine's mode of operation i.e. the method of differences. The aim of the brochure – as stated – was "to prove the practical usefulness of the invention".[197] Georg Scheutz had also another reason. In his view, journalists and commentators had often used the engine to draw attention to themselves rather than the engine and he was of the opinion that *Specimens* – "should be the most effective means of getting things going and silencing the objections of self-interest and ignorance."[198]

Despite the fact that Edvard Scheutz perceived the possibility of a purchaser eventually appearing, he had cause to be worried. The correspondence between Edvard and his father reveals that Edvard during his Continental visit was almost constantly plagued by illness. Moreover, he had economic problems to contend with, which stemmed from the fact that the engine was still unsold after a lapse of almost three years since its completion. Back in Stockholm, Georg managed with difficulty to arrange loans to pay for Edvard's stay abroad.[199] Both of them were also continously worried about how far their invention was really protected by the patents.[200] They were afraid that someone might take out a patent on the use of a difference engine, disregarding those patents they already held.[201] During Edvard's residence abroad, they kept each other informed of new developments by regular correspondence. Moreover, Georg Scheutz was able to get direct information from Bryan Donkin who paid a business trip to Stockholm in August 1856.[202] Sometime in September, they concluded a deal involving two patents.[203]

On the 18th of October, Gravatt conveyed some good news to Babbage – "I hesitate not a moment in sending you the first page (Proof! where there is no probability of error) for owning myself proud of even the humble part I am taking towards introducing the World 'Tables Calculated and Printed by Machinery'. I can understand what your feelings must be".[204]

It was probably not until August 1856 that Babbage answered Benjamin Gould's letter about the Scheutz engine. However, the many questions that Gould had raised, were not answered by Babbage himself. Instead he enclosed the report on the engine that Stokes and his colleagues had made in 1855. Babbage's comment about the report was that it was "cold and scarcely does justice to the machine". He continued to note that Leverrier had spoken against the engine to the French government, but that other scientists, such as Chasles and Dupin had been strongly in favour of it (cf. page 197). Babbage neglected however to say that Dupin had urged the Scheutzes to improve their machine, but he pointed out where Gould could read about what these two men had said about the engine. Babbage also informed Gould that, despite the fact that there were only four order of differences in the engine, one could actually calculate with eight. This, he said, was done by first letting the engine calculate Δ4 from Δ5, Δ6, Δ7, and Δ8, and then by putting in the (not constant) Δ4 manually at certain intervals. Finally, Babbage noted that the Swedish engine could be purchased at a price of 1,000 pounds.[205]

Beginning in the 1840s a series of observatories had been established in America. The Dudley Observatory in the State of New York was part of this "observatory movement".[206] Plans for a national university at Albany, had failed in 1852, to be replaced subsequently by the idea of founding an observatory. Members of a group of renowned American scientists, known as the "Lazzaroni" organized the observatory together with scientifically and culturally interested Albany citizens. Funds were supplied from private sources and the major sum came from Mrs Blandina Dudley of Albany, the widow of a senator. Members of the Lazzaroni formed the Scientific Council of the Dudley Observatory and a group a men of wealth and influence made up the Board of Trustees. The Dudley Observatory was intended to be in quite a different class from its American precedessors. It was to be an "American Greenwich".[207]

On the 4th of November 1856. Gould wrote back to Babbage, saying that he now had "the gratification of being empowered to purchase the engine for the use of the Dudley Observatory for the price named". The sum of 5,000 dollars, bequeathed to the Observatory by an Albany citizen – John F. Rathbone, was to be used for this purpose. Gould asked Babbage to inform Edvard Scheutz of the good news, and comforted Babbage by saying – "I feel confident that the trouble will be compensated to you by the pleasure of having brought about this first step towards that genial use which will ultimate in the construction *and use* of the Analytical Engine by some great public institution".[208]

In his letter Gould requested every conceivable detail about the operation and maintenance of the engine. He looked forward to receiving the technical drawings and "extended descriptions of all its parts". Eager to put the engine to work calculating ephemerides, perturbations and reduction tables, Gould asked for any formulae which he assumed that Babbage or Scheutz must already have developed for this purpose. Finally, he enquired about how soon the engine could be delivered.

Gould's letter was duly answered and on the 22nd of December 1856, he wrote to Edvard Scheutz and made arrangements for how the purchase money should be transferred. As soon as Bryan Donkin and Edvard Scheutz had certified that the engine was safely packed and had handed over the bill of lading to the firm of Georg Peabody and Company in London, this firm was then to pay the sum of 1,000 pounds sterling to Edvard Scheutz.[209] However, the engine could not be delivered immediately because the work on *Specimens* had not been completed.

The year 1857 promised to be a good one for the Scheutzes because at last the second engine would be sold. In Stockholm, Georg Scheutz was working as usual on the translation and editing of books. In addition, he had another responsibility which must have kept him busy. In April 1855, Sparre had won the hoped-for contract with the Swedish Post Office for the production of Sweden's first stamps.[210] In 1854-1855, he had bought all the necessary machinery in England and had organized a printing establishment for the purpose of stamp-production only.[211] There, Sweden's first stamps, including the famous shilling-banco series, had been produced at maximum rate of 500,000 specimens a month.[212] The production had started on the 1st of July 1855. But as Sparre frequently travelled abroad, he already in May 1856 (if not earlier) had asked Georg Scheutz to take care of the business now and then.[213] By the end of January 1857 Georg Scheutz began to deputize regularly for Sparre, and was thus increasingly occupied by the special demands that were involved in the printing of stamps as regards accuracy, colours, alignment etc.[214]

At the beginning of the year 1857, it seems that Edvard was ill in London.[215] Yet he was not abandoned to his own devices for there were several people there to take care of him. Among them, was his friend Charles Babbage, who on the 8th of January invited Edvard to come over "and take a share of my beefsteak".[216]

The purchase of the second difference engine was finalized, according to the agreement, in January 1857.[217] To Georg Scheutz who was then seventy-two years of age, it came as a great relief.

"Finally, after so many years of trials and tribulations, we are at last able to enjoy the fruit of our labours! I could scarcely believe my eyes when I opened, on Saturday, your letter of the 13th and discovered the two letters of credit worth together 500 pounds sterling."[218]

And he goes on to say that he could "thus begin what was undoubtedly the pleasantest trip in the course of my long life — namely that of going round and paying off our creditors".

The engine had been despatched to America and the purchase money had been paid out to Edvard. One question, however, remains. What happened to Sparre and his contract with the Scheutzes? According to the document in question, Sparre had committed himself to buying the engine and patent for 4,000 pounds sterling, (minus the amount payable to Virgin), should a buyer be found. The Scheutzes, for their part, were to exhibit the engine at the World Exhibition in Paris and to take out patents in certain countries. Apart from the fact that no patent had been sought or granted in Austria and Prussia (countries mentioned in the contract), the Scheutzes had otherwise kept their part of the agreement. But the engine had been sold at what was probably a much lower price (despite the fact that the patents had not been included in the purchase), than had been envisaged in 1854. It had turned out to be much harder than expected to make a sale. There are indications that Sparre did not pay out the much larger agreed sum. Thus Edvard Scheutz in the ensuing course of events, continued to be the driving force and always acted as the owner of the invention and the holder of its patents. Moreover, as will be shown, the Scheutzes were even in the future worried that Sparre and Barck might trick them in the matter of the patents. It seems very likely, therefore, that Sparre did not keep his promise and that the contract was somehow or other put aside.

Some more light can in fact be shed on this mystery, although the conclusive proofs are lost. It was sometime in the late 1850s that Sparre left Sweden to move to the Continent.[219] Two events coincide in time — Georg Scheutz' taking over Sparre's stamp-printing establishment, and the finalization of the purchase of Scheutz difference engine. Both happened in January 1857. Georg Scheutz actually continued to run the stamp business till 1870, when Edvard took over the responsibility till the end of 1871 when Sparre's contact with the Post Office expired.[220] There is a possibility that this was not a coincidence. I am inclined to believe that Sparre, unable to fulfil his commitment (perhaps because of financial reasons), handed over his probably lucrative contract with the Post Office to Scheutz — unofficially and as compensation.

Around April 1857 *Specimens* was ready.[221] The 50-page brochure was dedicated to Charles Babbage "by his sincere admirers George and Edward Scheutz", on Edvard's initiative. Both the book and its dedication received Georg Scheutz' approbation.[222]

Specimens was the core of the new marketing strategy, (to use modern terminology), that Scheutz together with Babbage and Gravatt had decided to adopt. Besides providing an account of the history of the technology and the mathematics of the engine, the book also included various examples of numerical tables. The most imposing was a logarithmic table, covering 29 pages, ranging from 1 to 10,000, and calculated to

PREFACE.

To those to whom this work is addressed it is unnecessary to point out the manifold advantages which have been derived in modern times from the various Numerical Tables now in the hands of the cultivators of science. The gigantic efforts that have led to the many important discoveries which have adorned the present century, would never have been made if these Tables had not existed. Astronomers, Navigators, Engineers, Actuaries, and indeed labourers in every department of science and the useful arts, could have made but little progress in their several vocations, had it not been for the resources supplied to them by those men of genius and of patience, who devoted their energies to this beneficial object: and when we contemplate the number and range of these Tables, and reflect upon the difficulties surmounted in their production, the time consumed, the labour employed, the capital expended, we cannot but regard with heartfelt gratitude and admiration those men who, without hesitation, and with an indomitable perseverance, devoted so many years of their lives to this irksome and herculean task; and that too, be it remembered, at a time when very few of their contemporaries could estimate the value of the work they were accomplishing. Such men may indeed be called the Martyrs of Science!

While acknowledging, however, the deep debt of gratitude which is due to the intellect, the industry, and the self-sacrifice of a Napier or a Briggs, we must still admit that, notwithstanding the pains taken to insure accuracy, much still remains to be done. There is scarcely any numerical table, or perhaps it may more truly be said that no one table has ever been published, which does not contain errors more or less numerous; and from a careful examination of a great number of existing tables, Mr. Babbage long ago arrived at the conviction that by

Fig. 73 Specimens of Tables *was completed in April 1857. It contained an account of the history of the Swedish difference engines, a description of the method of differences, and a number of specimen tables. In Georg Scheutz view* Specimens *"should be the most effective means of getting things going and silencing the objections of self-interest and ignorance." It was to be sent to many institutions and individuals all over the world.*

5 decimals.[223] In addition, fourteen examples of other type of tables were given. There were polynomials, one indicating that equations could be solved by the engine; trigonometrical and logarithmical functions calculated to 7 decimals; a military table, showing the ranges of shot with various charges; a statistical table – "Log. Value of Male Life in London"; and finally, there were four astronomical tables.[224] Thus, the book gave a clear picture of what the engine could do. It was the world's first collection of tables that had been produced by machinery.

The marketing strategy was to send out *Specimens* to potential buyers, and to people of influence. This is evident from a distribution list, made by Edvard Scheutz and Babbage, that has been preserved. This list which is given in full in the Appendix, contains about 400 names.[225] The whole summer of 1857 was spent by Edvard and Georg in distributing the book all over the world.[226] It was sent to 17 major observatories, as well as to several prominent astronomers in person. These addressees were, in my opinion, the most important in the campaign. Scientific societies, academies, universities, libraries, schools, banks, newspapers and journals, also received copies of *Specimens*. A large number of private individuals were also listed. These ranged from book printers, journalists, mathematicians, engineers, churchmen and military officers, to diplomats, presidents, emperors, kings, princes and queens. The mailing list, which was followed up rigorously, included all of the supporters of the Scheutz engine and the friends and colleagues of the Scheutzes. It is clear that Charles Babbage had helped Edvard to compose the list because it also included many of Babbage's personal friends and colleagues, and even people he admired.[227] Thus, the list had three other purposes beside the strictly commercial one. First, it contained the names of people who in one way or other, had helped the Scheutzes or Babbage. To them *Specimens* was given as a sign of gratitude. Secondly, there were the opponents and sceptics who had doubted the idea of producing tables by machinery and who formed a group of their own. To these men, the book was a lesson, proving that they had been wrong. Thirdly, *Specimens* was also distributed to spread knowledge about the inventors of the difference engine – in short, as a tribute to Babbage and Scheutz – for it is hard to believe that the inventors saw potential buyers in people like Charles Dickens, Jenny Lind and Pope Pius IX.

Already Georg Scheutz had voiced his hopes of producing a long series of his difference engines for a worldwide market:

"Such a matter of fact [*Specimens*] must catch on, if only from the financial point of view, and make the engine a necessity wherever there is an observatory, a university or a press dealing with mathematical works. Moreover, it will not take so many years for this to be the case."[228]

During the spring, Georg and Edvard Scheutz discussed the possibility of taking out a patent in several other European countries, among them Austria, Russia, Bohemia and Wurtemberg. This was done to ensure that no one would be able to build copies of their engine, now that – thanks to *Specimens* – it was better known than ever before.

In addition to these new problems, George and Edvard Scheutz were as usual worried that Sparre and Barck might steal the French and Belgian patents from them.[229] In April 1857, it was again time to renew the French and Belgian patents. Once more the Scheutzes succeeded in being one step ahead of the two Counts.[230] It was not until May 1857, that the inventors were finally able to relax, when the Bureau Général des Brevets d'Invention in Paris replied to Edvard's enquiry: according to French and Belgian law, they could never be dispossessed of any rights granted in these countries.[231]

In April 1857, the difference engine arrived at Albany only to be laid aside for over a year.[232] The reason for this, was that Benjamin Gould first moved to Albany from Cambridge, Massachusetts, when he was appointed the director of the Dudley Observatory in January 1858.[233] Gould, somewhat later, wrote down an account of his first experiences with the difference engine:

"Among the earliest steps after taking charge of the Observatory were the studying out [sic] of this engine and its preparation for practical work. No description of it has to my knowledge ever been published; and none accompanied it to this country. The only explanation afforded consisted in a single sheet of lithographic outline-drawings of the several parts, and a letter of Dr. Edward Scheutz, giving instructions for changing its adaption from the decimal to the sexagesimal system and the reverse, with the simple rules for setting it.

The dirt, which had accumulated on the passage, and thickened oil, impeded its action greatly, and after engaging the services [...] of a mechanical assistant, I went with him through the whole machine, until we had rendered ourselves familiar with all its parts, supplying such little improvements as native skill or suggestions might prompt; and after an extended series of experiments, to determine various points important in a practical and economical point of view, put the machine in action.

The strictly algebraical problems for feeding the machine made quite as heavy demands upon time, and thought, and perseverance, as did the problem of regulating its mechanical action; but all was soon in operation ..."[234]

Thus, despite the fact that Gould in his letter of the 4th of November 1856 had asked Edvard Scheutz to send all available information, he had in fact been given very little because of the Scheutzes' old fear that someone would steal their invention, whether in whole or in part. Indeed, they were not the only ones to be suspicious. Jean B. Bolinder, the Stockholm engineer and industrialist, had in the spring of 1856 warned the Scheutzes of this eventuality. Georg Scheutz took up the matter in a letter to Edvard:

"Bolinder at first had grave misgivings about releasing any information to the Americans, and immediately asked about patents. When I had enlightened him about this, he quietened down. Nevertheless, it seemed as though he believed that the yankees were set to take over the whole production of whatever Table-Engines might be needed."[235]

With respect to formulae and other necessary information to get the machine going, Gould had received nothing, although it is clear from a letter from Georg to Edvard that such material existed.[236]

Gould had also encountered some mechanical problems. These are specified in another document:

"It is now and then liable, in its computation, to the introduction of an error. This defect seems to be irremediable, and to be radically associated with the exquisite refinement of the construction; but, whenever an error may occur, it is readily traced to its origin, and the corresponding correction admits of easy application. There is also a small liability to error in the typographical portion of the instrument, but Dr.

Gould has here suggested a remedy which will probably be successful."[237]

This was in fact the first time that someone had observed any mechanical defects in Scheutz' engine.

Nonetheless, Gould managed to get the engine working, apparently around May 1858. Several astronomical tables were calculated and printed by the machine, such as "the True Anomaly of Mars", "the Eccentric Anomaly of Mars", and "the logarithm of its Radius-vector".[238] They must however be regarded as experiments and to the best of my knowledge, none of them were ever printed on paper.[239]

Merzbach has observed that these trials involved a commitment by Gould to produce ephemerides with the help of the engine, for the American Nautical Almanac Office. The Mars-tables were part of this trial. According to Merzbach, this was the first occasion on which the United States Government made a contractual commitment for machine produced printed computations.[240] But the trial was interrupted and abandoned and the engine was never "introduced into practical usefulness" again.[241] The reason was that Benjamin Gould was fired by the Board of Trustees of the Observatory. This happened on the 3rd of July, after Gould had been less than half a year in office.[242] The dismissal was the final phase in a long and extremely bitter controversy, between Gould and the Scientific Council on one side, and the Trustees on the other.[243] Since the difference engine in fact was involved in this remarkable controversy in the history of science, I shall examine these matters more fully in section 3.3.

Georg and Edvard Scheutz never learned what happened to their engine once it had left England. To them, the last memory of it was one of relief, satisfaction and confidence, reflected in a sentence from *Specimens*, which they often repeated − "the machine [...] now belongs to the Dudley Observatory, at Albany, being a gift to that Observatory from an enlightened and public-spirited merchant of that city, John Fr. Rathbone, Esq."[244]

2.5 The third engine

For Georg and Edvard Scheutz, the purchase of their engine by the Dudley Observatory was the proof that the scientific world had finally accepted the invention. Those who had raised critical voices, had been shown to be wrong. But father and son still had a greater ambition to realize. Their goal was to supply every observatory, press and institution which produced numerical tables, with a difference engine. Their dream was to free the world from tables studded with errors. A further step in this direction took place in the autumn of 1856, when discussions began about the preparation of a third engine.

One of the people with whom Edvard came in contact was William Farr, the Superintendent of the General Register Office, Britain's central statistical office, in London. This contact was to prove of considerable importance. At that time there were vast quantities of data that had arisen from the census of England and Wales that had taken place in 1841, and then again ten years later. In addition, there was material relating to the registration of births and deaths from the period 1838-1854.[1] This great amount of statistical material was to be summarized in tabular form.

Farr, the statistician, had perceived that the difference engine could be used to calculate some of the fundamental columns of this life-table.[2] On the basis of the accumulated data, Farr wanted to interpolate intermediate tabular values by using the difference engine and having them stereotyped. The ultimate aim behind such tables was their employment in the calculation of sums assured and life-insurance premia.

William Farr was an acquaintance of Charles Babbage and he had been interested in the Difference Engine No. 1 for a long time. In 1852, he had written a letter to Babbage, saying that he had calculated a large life table which he suggested, could be verified with Babbage's engine. He had also asked whether joint life tables could be produced with the machine.[3] Although I have not seen Babbage's answer, it must doubtlesss have been negative, considering the limited capacity of the unfinished engine.

Now a new complete and apparently powerful difference engine had been made and sold, and its inventor was in London. Edvard wrote to Georg in Stockholm keeping him abreast of what was happening. The news about new potential buyers appearing on the scene cheered up old Georg, who in the spring of 1857 wrote back to his son about some practical matters. His words revealed both his hopes and his fears:

"In fact the same sort of machinery [the engine] could be manufactured by Donkin's for various countries where it might be needed, and before the people there are in a position to produce it themselves. Can we not form a joint company with him for this purpose?"[4]

While matters remained undecided about the third engine, the second engine arrived at Albany in April of 1857, and at the same time *Specimens* was completed. After the latter had been carefully distributed, the Scheutzes received a number of letters from the recipients expressing their thanks. Edvard Scheutz, who during the spring of 1857, in accordance with paternal advice, had reached an agreement with Donkin about the latter's right to manufacture the engine, replied to these letters by offering directly to sell copies of the second engine. The sale price agreed by Donkin and Edvard Scheutz was 1,200 pounds. Engines with a larger capacity could be purchased if so desired, by paying an appropriately increased price.[5] Of the 1,200 pounds, 400 were to go to the Scheutzes, and the remainder to Donkin as soon as payment had been made.[6] The cost of materials was assessed at 200 pounds.[7] Georg Scheutz was clearly not altogether satisfied with the price but nevertheless declared it to be quite "businesslike".[8]

In July 1857, Edvard Scheutz was still in London, busily trying to sell further engines. *Specimens* and the host of articles that had appeared in the popular press in the course of the year, attested to the engine's satisfactory performance. In his sales efforts, Edvard made use of both of this material, and the fact that the engine which had won a medal at the International Exhibition in Paris in 1855, had now been sold to an observatory in the New World.

As usual, Charles Babbage devoted himself to helping Edvard Scheutz in marketing the engine. In this connection, Collier has discovered an interesting letter, from the engineer Isambard Kingdom Brunel to his friend Babbage.[9] In this letter, dated the 28th of July 1857, Brunel proposed to Babbage that they themselves should initiate a subscription for a new Scheutz engine. Brunel believed that by manufacturing a new engine, the demand for the Analytical Engine would be thereby stimulated. Babbage's response to this suggestion remains unknown but one thing is abundantly clear. The Analytical Engine was never completed, so that in this respect, Brunel's scheme failed to achieve its ultimate objective.[10]

William Farr, who in fact greatly admired the Scheutzes and their "beautiful machine" (as he described it), had perceived that it could be put to use at the General Register Office.[11] Encouraged by Farr's support, and after discussing the matter with the Registrar General, James George Graham, Edvard Scheutz was spurred to action. On the 3rd of July 1857, he sent off his tender for a difference engine to the British government.[12] The engine under consideration could operate with four differences and 15 digits like the second engine and was to cost 1,200 pounds. At Graham's suggestion, he stressed that such an engine would be "of great advantage in constructing Life Tables in the General Register Office as well as in some other Offices of the government...". Edvard added that the engine calculated and stereotyped a tabular value in one half, or one third, of the time taken by the compositor merely to arrange the types for it. Along with this bid, he enclosed a copy of *Specimens* by way of recommendation.[13]

The Chancellor of the Exchequer, Sir George Lewis, who received the letter, forwarded it to the Astronomer Royal, George Biddell Airy, with the request — "that he [Airy] will favour this."[14]

Already before Edvard had sent in his bid, Graham had contacted Lewis and pointed out, that in the light of the engine's high price, there could be no justification for purchasing it solely for the use of the General Register Office. Graham therefore revealed that it was conceivable that the engine could be used at the Royal Observatory in Greenwich, or at the Nautical Almanac Office.[15]

Meanwhile Edvard had gone to Paris to spread information about the

Fig. 74 The Astronomer Royal George Biddell Airy (1801–1892), the Director of the Royal Observatory at Greenwich. He once said that Babbage's difference engine was "worthless". In September 1857 he was consulted about his opinion to Edvard Scheutz' offer of a difference engine to the British government. Photograph taken from the Illustrated London News, 4th January 1868.

engine, with the ultimate goal of attracting other buyers. There he met the editors of the newspapers *Le Siecle* and *Revue des deux mondes*, who, according to Edvard were both warmly interested in the calculating engine and its success.[16] They tried to help him, and at least one article on the engine appears to have been published in the latter paper.[17] Edvard, having heard that newspapers in France had considerable influence, was pleased with this article. It is clear that he kept in touch with current affairs, from a letter in English he sent to Donkin.

"Reading an article in Galignani's Messenger yesterday concerning the sufferings of English men and women in India, I caught the idea that I too could perhaps do something to help them. I fear you smile a little when reading the above expression; but allow me to develop my scheme and I hope you will then find it possible. As you know are the stereotypes of the specimen tables still at Beaufort House. – The cost for the printing and binding of a thousand new copies [of *Specimens*] cannot be more than 40 but 1000 copies sold to 5 shillings each make a total of 250 whereof you find that at least 200 might be spared for the purpose I tend to. It is a pity the preface is not translated into French..."[18]

The event in India alluded to by Edvard, was the Mutiny. Donkin, however, was sceptical about a new edition of *Specimens* but agreed to talk to

214

Gravatt about it.[19] After some time, work on this French version started. Despite the fact that no suffering English man or woman ever received any help from this project, it is interesting to note the origins of the French version of the book.

It was only at the beginning of September 1857 that Airy replied, giving his opinion of Edvard's offer.[20] It is clear from the scope and contents of his letter that he was glad to have an opportunity to set forth his views. He raised two main points:

First of all, he made it plain that from a mechanical point of view, the engine was entirely satisfactory. He was well acquainted with it, and it had been demonstrated for him by Donkin. Airy (who was referring to the second engine), said that it was obviously incapable of carrying out its task incorrectly and moreover it had a long working life. Secondly, there was the question of the engine's practical utility. In Airy's view, Graham was quite right in suggesting the Royal Observatory, the Nautical Almanac Office and the General Register Office, as possible purchasers of the engine. Airy then proceeded to examine, point by point, the various possible areas of application, arising from the work of these institutions and to discuss the pros and cons of employing a difference engine. With regard to the first two institutions, Airy was of the opinion that the engine was impractical. In the case of the General Register Office, Farr had indicated a need for a difference engine, and this Airy was prepared to concede. His final recommendation was as follows: since the scientific world had for so long awaited the trial of a difference engine in the Government Service, it was right that such a trial should take place. The General Register Office was an excellent place to try it out. But Airy made it clear that he was basing his opinion entirely on Farr's statement about the need for a difference engine in the General Register Office.[21]

Airy's letter was received by the Secretary of the Treasury, Charles Edward Trevelyan, on the 9th of October 1857 and it was probably he who draughted a memorandum about it, in which it was stated that if there was no direct proof forthcoming from the General Register Office that the difference engine could save money, the government would not buy it.[22] The letter was forwarded to the Registrar General, Graham, for his view of the matter. The latter, who was very interested in the question, replied quite soon with a 15 page letter.[23] In it, he set forth the ways in which the difference engine would save money for the General Register Office. First of all, he dealt with Babbage's failure and the liability of 17,000 pounds incurred by the government. He then pointed out that the Scheutz engine, which was equipped in addition with a printing unit, only cost 1,200 pounds. Furthermore, one machine had already been sold to America. Next, Graham detailed the enormous amount of processing work entailed by the statistical material with which they had to deal. In order to cope with it, there were two solutions. One was to hire more staff i.e. human calculators. The second, which Farr recommended, was to buy the Scheutz engine. More staff would cost a great deal of money. On the other hand, by purchasing a difference engine, one would save money and at the same time acquire completely accurate stereotyped tables. This would mean a further saving of time and trouble. The engine would involve a yearly cost of 60 pounds only — "not half the yearly salary of a single clerk employed as a computer", Graham concluded.[24].

His statement reached Trevelyan on the 20th of October 1857.[25] Three months had passed since Edvard had made his offer to the government. There is every reason to suppose that he awaited the outcome with excitement. Donkin was clearly worried and it was perhaps in a mood of uncertainty that he wrote to Edvard in September.

"Under the circumstances you state, I think we should be disposed to name a less sum, than formerly fixed, but how much less I am not prepared to say, as I cannot find the copies of the papers, naming the price to the Government."[26]

The precise reason for this reaction on his part is unknown. The price, however, was never reduced.

On the 12th of November 1857, Trevelyan wrote a letter to Edvard Scheutz. The Lords of Treasury, after careful enquiry, had come to the conclusion that the probability that the engine could be of use to the General Register office was large enough to justify purchase. The government was therefore prepared to buy a difference engine from Edvard Scheutz for the sum of 1,200 pounds. The Treasury reserved the right to allow other government departments to make use of the engine.[27]

Edvard had been in Paris during the greater part of 1857 and it was there that he received the encouraging news about the order from the British government. He hurried to London to confer with Donkin, Graham and Farr. On the 7th of December 1857, he wrote a letter confirming the order to the Treasury. The engine would be delivered to the General Register Office by the Engineers Bryan Donkin and Co. within 18 months from the date on the Treasury's order.[28] In other words, the engine would be ready before 12th of May 1859.

A third Scheutz difference engine had been ordered. The purchaser was a country that had long awaited a difference engine. Now finally, such an engine was to be put to the test in the service of the government, in Britain's central statistical office. It was probably in Babbage's interest that the department was able to try out the engine in this way, but how far his influence in government circles had played a role in the matter, remains unclear. He was still the Scheutzes' friend and during the spring of 1858, he sent tickets to art exhibitions and the like to Edvard, who had remained in the capital.[29] Georg Scheutz received the news in Stockholm in November 1857 and despite his seventy-two years, he hurried to make a whole new set of alterations to the engine. Among other things, he recommended that the printing unit should be changed so that the tables

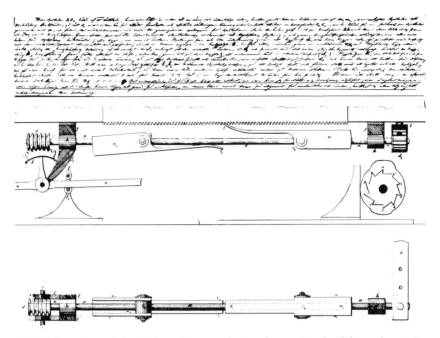

Fig. 75 Drawing and description of new mechanism for moving the slide on the printing table, made by Georg Scheutz at the age of 72. It was sent to Edvard in Paris in November 1857. The mechanism, in a somewhat different form, was incorporated in the third Scheutz engine.

could be printed where the argument decreased rather than increased.[30] This was in fact a matter that the Royal Society Committee had complained about in their report on the second engine in 1855.[31] Fig. 75 shows the drawing Georg made of this specific mechanism, and which he sent to Edvard in Paris.[32] Father and son devoted themselves to redesigning the engine by correspondence. Donkin set to work — exactly when is unknown — but in 1858 Edvard started to superintend the project.[33]

Edvard and Georg Scheutz were to receive 400 pounds from the project, but Edvard, who had been abroad for some time, without income flowing in, was in financial trouble. This forced him at the beginning of 1858 to approach the Registrar General, Graham, for an advance of 300 pounds.[34] Graham forwarded the question to the Treasury which agreed to meet the request. Bryan Donkin offered to provide security, by committing himself to repay the Treasury, if the engine should fail to be completed and duly delivered.[35] This assurance was given on the 24th of February. Apparently Edvard had great problems because already on the 8th of March, Donkin wrote to Graham stressing the importance of the advance for the Swedish inventor, who had "had heavy expenses in bringing forward his invention".[36] A fortnight later, the matter was decided by the Treasury.[37] Edvard duly got his advance, which was sent on to him in Paris by Donkin.[38] Edvard in turn forwarded some money to

Stockholm to settle various accumulated bills there.[39] Also the Belgian and French Patents had to be renewed – a matter which Georg was much concerned about – at a cost of some 25 pounds.[40] The 300 pounds were soon eaten up, and there was now only 100 pounds to collect when the engine was completed.

On the 28th of April 1858, a ceremony took place in the Swedish capital. Georg Scheutz was made a Knight of the North Star Order as a reward for his contributions to his native country.[41] It is not known, however, whether he was as opposed to the award of this honour as he had been to that of the Wasa Order. At home in Stockholm, he was, as usual, busily engaged on the printing of Swedish stamps and he corresponded with Edvard about the latter's idea that they should both try to reward Gravatt by having him made a member of the Royal Academy of Sciences.[42]

Given that Edvard's marketing campaign on behalf of the engine was as intense as ever, it seems plausible that he renewed the Belgian and French patents in the spring of 1858.[43] He had remained on the Continent of Europe and his father seems to have considered his residence there was in the best interests of their invention.[44] There are several indications that suggest that they were hoping to sell a machine to the French government. Edvard had now spent so much time in France that he spoke the language well enough to write the preface to the French edition of *Specimens* himself.[45] By the end of July, the *Spécimens de tables calculées stéréotypées et imprimées au moyen d'une machine* was ready to be distributed. Edvard took care of this task immediately and a new wave of information reached both French and English-speaking addressees.

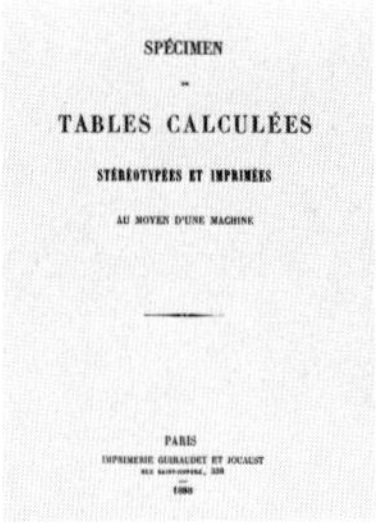
SPÉCIMEN

TABLES CALCULÉES

STÉRÉOTYPÉES ET IMPRIMÉES

AU MOYEN D'UNE MACHINE

PARIS

Fig. 76 The French version of Specimens *was published in 1858.*

Edvard Scheutz distributed the book to his French supporters and opponents in Paris. One copy was forwarded to Leverrier who, according to Edvard, had promised to send a positive report on it to the Minister of Education. However Leverrier used the opportunity (in Edvard's words) to "try to put down the idea again".[46] On the 12th of July, there was a meeting at the French Academy of Sciences, at which the engine was mentioned in connection with the presentation of a book by the Scheutzes to the Academy. Leverrier who was present at the meeting, once more maintained that the engine had a very limited practical utility. It was true that the price was now half that demanded for the engine offered before, but this did not affect his view of the matter.[47]

Leverrier's words were harsh. But Edvard Scheutz had his own group of supporters – the French newspapermen! The first article on the subject appeared on the 16th of July 1858. It was written by the chief editor of *Cosmos* – l'Abbé Moigno – a close friend of Augustus de Morgan, one of the supporters of Babbage and Scheutz. The article was cleverly written. To all appearances, it was a direct report on the meeting at the Academy of Sciences three days before. It began with the postive opinions of Jacques Babinet, and then went on to give Leverrier's arguments. The latter were then answered by counterarguments apparently due to the editor of *Cosmos*, in which a number of quotations from an old article of de Morgan were discreetly inserted. Moigno succeeded in making the article look like a report of the discussion, in which the supporters of the difference engine had the last word.[48] On the 11th of August, *Le Siecle* published a very similar article. It began with the words − "Never has mechanics been used to greater purpose in the service of intelligence than in the calculating engine of Messrs. Scheutz."[49] Not long afterwards, *La Propriété Industrielle*, told the story of the Scheutz engines and like the other papers, it noted that two other great countries had bought their copies of the machine:

> "*M.John Fr. Rahtbone* [sic] (yet another who deserves the honour of italics) offers the calculating machine to Dudley Observatory in Albany, in his native land, thus setting things in motion, England follows, the newspapers in France and abroad sound the trumpet of Fame and everything is said. What then of France? *nescio si....timeo ne...*
>
> MM. George and Edouard Scheutz have spent TWENTY FOUR years in making themselves known, and they have succeeded. But how many have succumbed during such struggles? What good will letters of patent, as they are now issued, do them?"[50]

Finally at the end of August 1858, *L'Illustration, Journal Universel* added its voice to those of the others.[51] But although the French papers no doubt had influence, they could not change the mind of the still more influential astronomer who was in charge of the Paris Observatory. No difference engine was ever sold to France.

On the 13th of October 1858, the efforts of Georg and Edvard in another direction, were to achieve success. It was on this day that William Gravatt was unanimously elected to the section of Practical Mechanics of the Swedish Academy of Sciences in Stockholm.[52] Four days before, Georg was given a still more prestigious honour. It is now time to turn to the somewhat mysterious story of how auditor Scheutz became a Knight of the Imperial Russian Order of St. Anne.

Shortly after his seventy-third birthday on the 23rd of September 1858, Georg had received a letter. It had been sent from St. Petersburg and was written in Swedish. Three copies of *Specimens* had been sent to the Russian capital. One was for the Emperor, Alexander II, one was for the Grand Duke Konstantin Nikolajevitch and one for the writer of the letter, an unidentified civil servant. In the letter, the Emperor and Grand Duke conveyed their thanks for the books.[53] A few days after this unremarkable event, another letter arrived. Its contents were considerably more interesting, and it ran as follows:

"Stockholm,26th September 1858
Most Esteemed Auditeur and Knight etc.,
The Russian Ambassador informed me in an official note yesterday that His Majesty, the Emperor of Russia, is pleased to appoint Herr

Auditeur Knight of the Imperial Russian Order of St. Anne, Third Class, as a reward for the copy of Herr Auditeur's calculating engine, which His Majesty has received [sic]. At the same time, may I also take the opportunity to say that His Royal Highness, the Crown Prince and Regent is pleased to allow Herr Auditeur to receive this new token of well deserved esteem which your valuable invention has everywhere occasioned. I congratulate you in this matter and I shall not fail to forward the decoration and the official letters of entitlement as soon as they arrive. I beg Herr Auditeur to receive the assurance of my most sincere respects and admiration.

Manderström"[54]

The letter states quite clearly that the Russian Emperor, Alexander II, had received a calculating engine from Georg Scheutz. A surprising piece of news indeed. First, let me make it clear that the Order of St. Anne was the 5th in rank among the Russian orders. The third class brought with it a personal enoblement in contrast to the first class which allowed the title to pass to one's heir. It was therefore in every sense a great honour, which had been bestowed on Georg Scheutz. Count Kristofer Rutger Ludvig Manderström had enjoyed a long and distinguished career as a diplomat and in the spring of 1858, he had become Sweden's Foreign Minister. It is however entirely possible that Edvard had met him earlier in Paris, because during 1856-1858 he had been Sweden and Norway's Ambassador in Paris and thus was the successor to Gustaf Löwenhielm, who had been well disposed to the Scheutz difference engine in the 1830's.

On the assumption that a Swedish difference engine had actually been given or sold to Russia, who could have built such a machine? First of all, there had to be drawings available or a machine to copy. "There is an overabundance of drawings here at home", Georg had written to Edvard, early in 1857.[55] So there was no problem in that respect. What of the builder? Wilhelm Bergström was certainly capable of building another engine at his workshop, where the jigs, fixtures and templates from the earlier project may have been preserved. Another possible candidate was Jean Bolinder, who not only had a large mechanical workshop but was also a very good friend of the Scheutzes. It is possible that the whole affair was hushed up, because of Edvard's agreement with Donkin, giving the latter the sole right to make all difference engines that were ordered. It is interesting to note that Russia often crops up in the correspondence between the Scheutzes. For example, when in the spring of 1857, they were curious about the possibility of patenting the engine in Russia, the following somewhat cryptic paragraph appeared in a letter from Georg to Edvard:

"As regards Russia, its patent laws are a closed book as far as I am concerned. But I shall not fail to speak with Baron Wrede about the

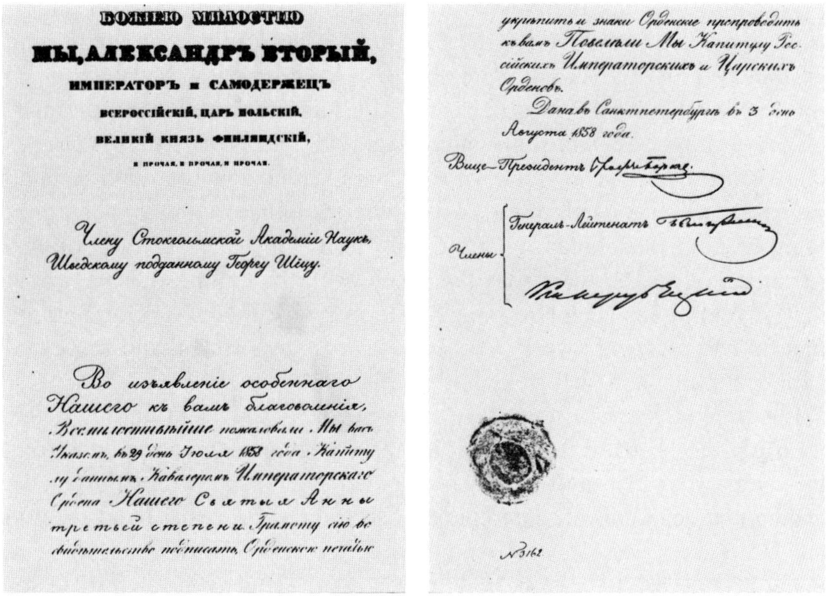

БОЖІЮ МИЛОСТІЮ
МЫ, АЛЕКСАНДРЪ ВТОРЫЙ,
ИМПЕРАТОРЪ И САМОДЕРЖЕЦЪ
ВСЕРОССІЙСКІЙ, ЦАРЬ ПОЛЬСКІЙ,
ВЕЛИКІЙ КНЯЗЬ ФИНЛЯНДСКІЙ,
и прочая, и прочая, и прочая.

Члену Стокгольмской Академіи Наукъ,
Шведскому подданному Георгу Шейцу.

Fig. 77 In the autumn of 1858 Auditor Pehr Georg Scheutz was appointed Knight of the Imperial Russian Order of St. Anne, third class, by Emperior Alexander II of Russia. The figure shows the letter of entitlement. This great honour was bestowed on Georg Scheutz for his invention – the difference engine. Original document in the Royal Library, Stockholm. Photograph by courtesy of the Royal Library, Stockholm.

engine's future in Russia, in the way you mentioned, as soon as the necessary copies of the book have arrived."[56]

It is quite possible that the whole affair was a result of a misunderstanding, where the Russians confused *Specimens* with the engine itself. Stranger things have happened.

On the 9th of October, Manderström wrote to Scheutz, saying that the Order and the letter of entitlement had arrived from Russia, and enclosing them with the letter, see Fig. 77.[57] It was a very informal event, Scheutz was asked by Manderström to send him a receipt for the order, which was to be passed to the Russian Minister in Stockholm. Thus Scheutz became a Knight of St. Anne.

One fact that speaks against the theory that the whole affair rested on some kind of mistake, is that an Order of this kind was not awarded without very good reasons. The letter of entitlement have been preserved. Georg Scheutz retained them until his death when they passed to Edvard.[58] However it is possible that if an error had been made, it might simply have been glossed over by treating the order as a reward to Georg Scheutz for his invention of the difference engine. In other words, the Order of St. Anne would have had basically the same motivation for its award, as the North Star Order and the Wasa Order.

Perhaps it was not the Russians, but Manderström who had misunderstood the Russian motive for the award. In order to find out whether an engine ever existed in St. Petersburg, I have examined a number of sources and have tried in other ways to obtain information on the matter.[59] But I have been unsuccessful in clearing up this mystery. As long as there is no conclusive evidence of a Russian Scheutz engine, I am inclined to believe that it was all due to a misunderstanding on the part of Count Manderström. Looking at the event from this perspective, one is reminded of all the fears that the inventors Scheutz entertained, about their invention being stolen. Imagine Georg's anxiety upon being notified that he had received a very great honour from a powerful and respected nation, for an engine which he had not made!

It is time to return to the study of the second engine. Around the New Year of 1859, Edvard Scheutz returned to Sweden. He had been abroad for over two and a half years, but it had not been wasted time. One engine had been delivered and another was under construction at Donkin and Co. Father and son were happily reunited and Edvard must have had much of interest to relate. In January 1859, they wrote an article for *Aftonbladet*, in which they corrected a number of errors that had appeared in an article in that paper, a couple of days before.[60] This allowed them to explain to the general public how the Swedish government grant towards the cost of the second engine had been used.

The Swedish press had in the course of the years reported the success of the Scheutz engine abroad. Edvard's return reawakened their interest. In *Illustrerad Tidning* of 29th January, Georg's old friend, the chief editor August Blanche, had an article, acclaiming Scheutz:

"Our ancient country, which nowadays, so they say, is reduced to practical insignificance and is one of the poorer as regards both population and money, has little left of those victories it won on the battlefield, save the memories of them, which people boast about on every conceivable occasion; and similarly the only persons to be praised and venerated, are those who according to the rules of the art have slaughtered people and laid waste cities. But Sweden has won other victories, which can be admired without a shudder and laurels which can be touched without getting stained with blood. There have been victories in art, science and engineering; there have been heroes in the infinite domain of spirit and intellect, who for their contemporaries and for posterity have made sacrifices which are a blessing for the earth, even although they have occasioned less clamour than the deeds of war. It is only destruction which makes a din and a roar. The good, the useful and the beneficial blossom peacefully and quietly like the lilies of the field."

Blanche then summarized the peaceful and silent achievements of his friend, at the same time expressing his confidence in the ultimate success of the engine:

"The machine which externally looks very like a street organ, is similarly set to work by means of a lever and one cranks forth the results with greater certainty than the best masters of arithmetic can attain. Banking institutions, engineering corps, statistics, astronomy and many more, must surely soon make use of the little lever, thus freeing the world from much cogitation and sparing the head many pains."[61].

Meanwhile the engineers at Donkin's workshop were engaged on the third engine. Edvard had promised that it would be ready before the 12th of May. But Donkin ran into problems, and at the end of May he wrote a letter to Georg Scheutz:

"I had hoped on this to have been able to report to you definitely and favourably of the New Calculating Machine, but regret to say it is not yet quite in working order. At the last, many things had to be done which we could scarcely foresee, nevertheless we have no great reason to be dissatisfied with the result so far, our experience however has taught us the defects, and we are now remedying them, and I have little doubt that in a fortnight's time, it will be in effective working condition."[62]

According to the letter, the engine was nearly ready. It is interesting to note the unforeseen difficulties that Donkin and Co. had encountered. Although the engine was not working perfectly, it was put on display at the Institution of Civil Engineers, on the 31st of May 1859. Babbage and Farr, who were invited "were much pleased with the machine".[63]

On the 3rd of June 1859, Edvard took out a patent in Stockholm for a new invention — a rotary steam engine.[64] This was not a completely new idea, but the particular design that Edvard adopted was new. Since he had no one to build the machine, he asked Donkin who replied that he was not able to help him. "I have but a very poor opinion of Rotary

Fig. 78 The third Scheutz engine, made by Bryan Donkin & Co. and finished on the 5th of July 1859, somewhat more than 19 months after the Treasury had ordered it. It was a copy of the second engine. Photograph by courtesy of the Trustees of the Science Museum, London.

Engines in general, and certainly should not think of taking such an invention in hand."[65] So Edvard had to look elsewhere for help.

On the 7th of July 1859, Georg and Edvard received a cheering letter from Donkin.[66] "I am happy at last to be able to say, that the Machine is finished; two days ago". In other words, it had been completed only three weeks after the original date agreed. The engine had been tested by Farr and the results had been satisfactory. The only thing that Donkin (and probably even more so, Farr) was not entirely pleased with, was the engraving of the type wheels in the printing unit, even although they would do for the moment. Donkin ended by congratulating the Scheutzes on the successful completion of their business.

The third engine was ready.[67] It had the same mathematical capacity as its predecessor and was in principle an exact copy of it, see Fig. 78. Certain weaker parts had been strengthened but the main difference between them at first sight was the colour. Donkin's engine was in this respect more akin to Babbage's machine and was made in a shining yellow copper alloy.[68]

By letting most of the surfaces of the parts of the engine remain untreated, the dominance of brass or bronze gave the engine a somewhat more massive appearance. A closer look at this engine reveals that the gearing system (connecting the handle with the two units) and the mangle wheel had been improved – in the latter case, to prevent malfunctioning. The most conspicuous differences between the second and third Scheutz engine were to be found in the printing unit. A new device allowed the operator, by rotating a crank, to obtain additional space between successive lines in a table, see Fig. 79. With another mechanism, the printing table sledge (upon which the matrix was fixed) could be made to go backwards. In addition, the numerator on this engine could also go backwards. These possibilities could be used when printing certain special tables, and they were improvements which had been made by old Georg in Stockholm. Curiously enough, he never saw either them or the completed engine itself. Finally, the printing unit was supplied with various arrangements of type wheel, with different type profiles allowing typographical variation. In the calculating unit, the new details were fewer. The parts were generally somewhat more strongly made but the improvements were minor.

The first tables which were made with the third engine, were Gravatt's *Mountain Barometer Tables* which were published in 1859.[69] This was a small booklet which could be used to determine altitude with the help of a barometer or thermometer. *Mountain Barometer Tables* consisted of only 8 table columns, which to Gravatt's delight were printed with old fashioned types – "in fact imitating the work of the pen".[70]

A month after Donkin had announced that the engine was ready and that the enterprise had been successfully brought to a close, Edvard Scheutz received a new letter from him.[71] The engine had been delivered to the General Register Office. Unfortunately, wrote Donkin, the print-

Fig. 79 Transfer mechanism and printing unit of the third Scheutz difference engine. The bell mechanism that can be seen to the left in the figure was added to the machine later, probably at the General Register Office. This mechanism can be set to ring after a certain number of addition cycles to notify the operator when new start values have to be inserted. Photograph by courtesy of the Trustees of the Science Museum, London.

ing unit was working badly and what was worse, the trouble had started when the government took receipt of the engine.[72] Another serious problem for Donkin was that he was not to be paid, until the Royal Society and the Astronomer Royal had tested and approved the machine for the government.

Donkin's letter contained a further piece of bad news. "The cost of the Machine to us has been £ 615 more than we shall get for it!!"[73] Doubtless Georg and Edvard Scheutz were pessimistic, once they had reflected on these harsh facts. What would happen when it became known that the engine was not error-free? Five days later, Donkin wrote again to Edvard Scheutz, expressing his disquiet over the fact that it would take up to two or three months before he would receive payment for the machine.[74] It turned out that his fears were justified.

On the 30th of August 1859, the machine had been inspected by both the Royal Society and the Astronomer Royal.[75] The Royal Society Committee consisted of the same scientists who had inspected the second engine in 1854. Stokes, Wheatstone and Willis participated in the actual inspection while Miller was only there to add his signature to the report. The committee was as generally positive in its judgement of the third engine as it had been in the case of the second machine. "Its execution is satisfactory in the highest degree, as might have been expected from the well-known skill of the constructor."[76]

The committee concluded its report by expressing the hope that the engine might sometimes be made available for scientific assignments other than those for which it had been expressly designed. The verdict of the Astronomer Royal was equally favourable and he was of the opinion that the general workmanship was better on this engine than on the second. Airy therefore assured the Registrar General, Graham, that Donkin "was fully entitled to immediate satisfaction of all claims."[77]

Donkin, however, was troubled by the fact that he had lost so much money on the project. He decided to do something about it. On the 3rd of September 1859, he wrote an official letter to Graham. In it, he said

225

that his loss amounted to a little more than 623 pounds. The reason why the construction of the engine had cost more than the price stipulated to the General Register Office (a price which he called an "estimate") was to be found in the many difficulties involved. First of all, the construction itself was "extremely intricate" with "a multitude and variety of minute fitting". Secondly, he had had nothing else to base his estimate on, except what Edvard Scheutz had told him "which necessarily was very imperfect." Thirdly, costly tools had been made specially for the job and lastly many alterations that had not originally been contemplated, had been introduced.[78] I am not disposed to attach much weight to any of these arguments used by Donkin, except perhaps the last one. As a leading manufacturer of machines like scientific instruments and printing presses, he must have known from the beginning, that the difference engine would be difficult to make. To shift the blame onto Edvard, was simply a tactical device. The last argument was perhaps the real reason for the increase in costs. It is not known who proposed these unforeseen alterations. They might well have been the result of defects in parts already made. Donkin ended his letter with a couple of arguments of a different kind:

"The importance attached by successive Governments to the principle of calculating and printing tables by Machinery, is well known, and appears in many reports and printed documents relating to the first Machine of this kind, ever attempted to be made.

By these reports and documents it will be seen, that the advantages to be derived, were considered sufficient to justify a very considerable expenditure of public money, and we therefore feel warranted in asking the unforeseen (comparatively trifling) extra expense, attending this Machine, should not fall upon us."[79]

The engine which Donkin alluded to, was Babbage's difference engine.[80] Yet despite the fact that Graham supported Donkin and contacted the Treasury, the outcome of Donkin's request was nonetheless negative.[81]

At any rate, the engine had been delivered to the General Register Office which had placed the order and the work of translating the statistical material into tabular form with the new mechanical helper could now go ahead under Farr's supervision.[82] A mood of optimism prevailed, especially now that Donkin had learned that he would soon receive payment for the engine.[83] In addition, Donkin was able to report to Edvard that interest had been shown in the machine by a number of potential customers abroad and he believed that Airy's favourable opinion might lead to another engine being ordered.[84] Then Donkin continued:

"I am not of opinion that the price will prevent some of these machines being ordered, and no doubt when a few shall have been made, they will cost less in their manufacture."[85]

About the beginning of October 1859, Donkin wrote a further letter to Edvard Scheutz. The tone of the letter was now harsh. The Lords of the Treasury had arranged matters so that Donkin's share of the money was to be paid to Edvard Scheutz. Donkin wrote: "Will you therefore be kind enough to send us <u>immediately</u> a legal document authorizing us to receive it—."[86] Edvard Scheutz who had already in advance received 300 of the 400 pounds he was entitled to, sent off the required authorization to Donkin. Edvard, however, pointed out that Donkin for his part, must ensure that the remaining 100 pounds was paid over to him.[87]

With these two letters, their mutual business was concluded. It had been a business that had in no way been a spectacular success for the parties involved, considering the financial and engineering difficulties that had arisen. In addition, it had taken more time than they had reckoned. Nonetheless they hoped that the future would be brighter, now that England finally had a difference engine at work; the rest of the world might now be induced to follow its example and place orders. It was with this in mind that Edvard Scheutz wrote to Donkin, asking him how much he would ask for building further machines. Donkin replied that for a single engine the price would be in the region of 1,500 pounds, to which would be added Edvard's profit. This was certainly a more realistic estimate than the previous figure. Donkin added that "several little matters have gone wrong, since it has been at work at Somerset house [General Register Office] and we have made some alterations..."[88] Donkin noted that any future engines would require to be improved mechanically, while still retaining the basic design. In this letter, he also mentioned that it was now clear that no additional payment would be forthcoming for the third engine.

The year 1859 drew to its close. In Sweden, the general public had been able to keep in touch with the difference engine's progress through various newspaper articles. *Aftonbladet* (perhaps Georg, himself) published translations of the statements made by the Royal Society and the astronomer Airy, and noted that the invention had thereby received official recognition abroad. "The State funds that had been made available by the Estates for the completion and publicizing of the invention, had borne fruit."[89] In the General Register Office in London, Farr and his associates worked away with the third engine, while the second engine was no longer in use after the dismissal of Gould in July 1858. It seems that even as late as October 1859, Georg and Edvard Scheutz were unaware of this latter fact.[90] Now that Donkin had indicated that he was prepared to build further difference engines, Edvard took steps to find new clients.[91] New offers were made and the price was raised to 2,000 pounds, thus allowing a profit of 500 pounds to the Scheutzes.[92]

During 1859, Edvard had attempted in Stockholm to find someone who would build the rotary steam engine. His friend Jean Bolinder agreed to fill the breach.[93] The engine was built at Bolinder's Engineering Workshop and was ready by September 1860. It was Edvard Scheutz' second great invention after the difference engine. The parallel between the two is striking, as the following quotation shows:

"It must surely seem somewhat bold when such engineers as Watt, Bramah, Donkin, Trevithick, William Congreve, Cochrane, Beale and Maudslay not to mention others, have failed in the construction of rotary steam engines, to take this question afresh and deal with it in such a way that as far as we can judge, it leaves little to be desired. Such a state of affairs, which does honour both to the inventor [Edvard Scheutz] and his native land, is a new proof that a problem is not insoluble because this or that great man has failed in his attempts along the same lines; rather it should serve to encourage those who consider themselves to possess the capacity and perseverance not to shrink back from the reverses and failures that have been the lot of their predecessors."[94]

The engine was offered for sale and produced in an unknown quantity.[95] It was used to drive lathes and other machinery in Bolinder's workshop, as well as being used on smaller sea-going vessels.[96] Scheutz' rotary steam engine was widely praised and when Bergsund's Engineering Workshop took over the production of the engine from Bolinder's, it was also offered for sale to interested parties abroad, see Fig. 80. In spite of this, it does not appear that the steam engine was a financial success as far as Edvard Scheutz was concerned.

In September 1860, Georg Scheutz celebrated his seventy-fifth birthday. Despite his age, his literary ambitions were undiminished and in the same year he published his book *Industriens Bok*.[97] It was in two volumes and presented, in historical perspective, the various techniques of industry. In 1861, an enlarged and revised edition came out. In the first volume of this new edition, Scheutz had added a chapter on "Calculating Engines".[98] It is amusing to note how in the introduction, the author admits the risk that he is not altogether impartial in his presentation of the material in this chapter and then to see how after a very short history of earlier calculating engines, he devotes the remainder of the chapter to the Scheutz difference engine.

On the 23rd of November 1860, King Carl XV signed a document of great importance for Georg Scheutz. The Estates and his Royal Highness had decided to reward him for his contributions towards scientific progress in his native country, by granting him an annual pension of 1,200 *riksdaler, riksmynt* (circa 67 pounds). The pension was to be paid to Scheutz for the remainder of his life.[99]

The initiative to this pension had been taken by Baron Rudolf Cederström who in November 1859 had introduced a motion in the Riksdag proposing its award. It will be recalled (see page 164) that it was Cederström who had supported Scheutz in the Riksdag of 1850-1851. The pension was in recognition of Scheutz' contribution as a writer and jour-

EDWARD SCHEUTZ'S
ROTATORY STEAM-ENGINE,
PATENTED IN GREAT BRITAIN, FRANCE, BELGIUM, SWEDEN, &c.

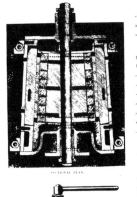

PRICES.

5 Horse-Power	- -	£167
10 „	- -	306
15 „	- -	445
20 „	- -	556
30 „	- -	800

For particulars, apply to Mr J H. JOHNSON 47, Lincoln's Inn Fields. W C.

Fig. 80 Small poster presenting Edvard Scheutz' rotary steam engine and offering it for sale to interested parties abroad. Photograph by courtesy of the National Museum of Science and Technology, Stockholm.

nalist but also because he "had devoted himself to one of the greatest triumphs of pure reason and had laid the fruits of his labours in the form of a magnificent invention before an amazed Europe, thus lending a new lustre to the Swedish name."[100] The Standing Committee supported the motion and when it came up for decision before the four Estates all but one gave it their unhesitating support.[101] As in the Riksdag of 1850-1851 the Estate of the Peasants proved the exception, on this occasion maintaining that a pension of 600 riksdaler was sufficient.[102] However the combined support of the other three Estates ensured that the motion was carried and that Georg Scheutz received his greatly needed pension.[103]

229

In 1861, a happy event took place in the life of the forty year old Edvard Scheutz. Up till then and during the long period of work on the engine, his personal life had centred round his father. Now he had met Carolina Wilhelmina Eleonora Lovisa Grafström and they were married on the 12th of February 1861.[104] On the 16th of July in the same year, their only son, Axel Georg Reinhold Scheutz was born.[105] Georg Scheutz was very proud of his young grandson.[106] These changes in Edvard's personal circumstances induced him to spend the greater part of the remainder of his life in Stockholm, perhaps finding peace and harmony in helping his wife in the little grocery which she owned.

In 1862, an International Exhibition was scheduled to take place in London. The seventy year old Charles Babbage who was still working on and off with his Analytical Engine, received an interesting suggestion from Gravatt.[107] Since 1842, the Difference Engine No. 1 had been on exhibition at the Museum of King's College, London. Babbage now, following Gravatt's advice began to think of the possibility of exhibiting this engine along with the latest Scheutz engine at the Exhibition. He had even begun to work out how he could modify his engine so that it and the Scheutz engine could be driven by a catgut belt connected to a prime mover, presumably a steam engine.[108] The great idea of tables calculated by steam was perhaps not dead after all. However, Babbage's plans came to nothing, because Farr refused to allow the Scheutz engine to be removed from the General Register Office.[109] The main reason he gave, was that the work in progress on the *English Life Table*, could not be discontinued and that the work could not be carried out in the exhibition premises suggested by Babbage. Babbage was so angered by the attitudes of both Farr and the Commissioners of the Exhibition, that he devoted a whole chapter of his autobiography to explaining how badly he had been treated.[110] Farr, however, provided a description of the third Scheutz engine which was handed out to curious visitors to the exhibition.[111] In addition, matrices, stereotype plates and examples of printed tables illustrating the work in progress at the General Register Office were put on display.[112] The Difference Engine No. 1 took part, according to plan, in the Exhibition of 1862.[113] Another exhibitor at this latter event was Edvard Scheutz, who put his rotary steam engine on display. Babbage's idea for a belt-driven difference engine and the occurrence of Edvard Scheutz' steam engine at the exhibition may be more than a mere coincidence.

Edvard Scheutz had received a grant from the Swedish Board of Commerce in Stockholm to build and display his machine at the London exhibition. In return, he was expected to study and take note of the various engineering innovations at the exhibition.[114] The rotary steam engine was demonstrated daily by Edvard himself. It was responsible for driving all the equipment and machinery in the Swedish engineering display. The impressive endurance of the engine and the minimal wear and tear that it involved, resulted in its being awarded an "Honourable mention" by the jury.[115] At Christmas 1862, Edvard Scheutz, for the first

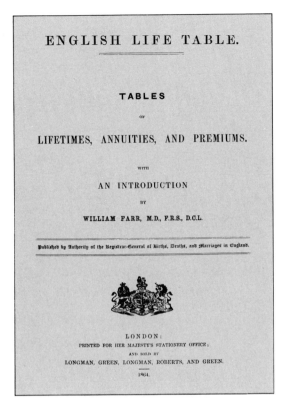

ENGLISH LIFE TABLE.

TABLES

OF

LIFETIMES, ANNUITIES, AND PREMIUMS.

WITH

AN INTRODUCTION

BY

WILLIAM FARR, M.D., F.R.S., D.C.L.

Published by Authority of the Registrar-General of Births, Deaths, and Marriages in England.

LONDON:
PRINTED FOR HER MAJESTY'S STATIONERY OFFICE;
AND SOLD BY
LONGMAN, GREEN, LONGMAN, ROBERTS, AND GREEN.
1864.

Fig. 81 The English Life Table *(London 1864) was the largest project in which a Scheutz engine was involved. However, only a quarter of the tables the book contained were calculated and printed by the machine.*

time for many years in good health, returned to his family in Stockholm.[116]

Prior to this, while Edvard was in London in June 1862, he had received a communication from Donkin. The difference engine was working badly and Farr wondered if Scheutz could rectify matters.[117] It would seem that something rather serious had gone wrong because Georg Scheutz speaks of "the disaster".[118] Edvard Scheutz, however, was able to put things right.[119] The work at the General Register Office proceeded, despite similar difficulties arising, as the following quotation of Farr makes clear:

"The Machine required incessant attention. The differences had to be inserted at the proper terms of the various series, checking was required, and when the mechanism got out of order it had to be set right. Of the first watch nothing is known, but the first steam-engine was indisputably imperfect; and here we had to do with the second Calculating Machine as it came from the designs of its constructors and from the workshop of the engineer. The idea had been as beautifully embodied in metal by Mr. Bryan Donkin as it had been conceived by the genius of its inventors; but it was untried. So its work had to be watched with anxiety, and its arithmetical music had to be elicited by

231

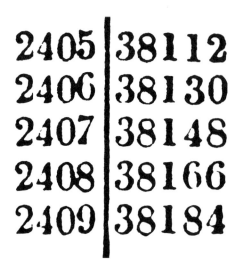

2405	38112
2406	38130
2407	38148
2408	38166
2409	38184

Fig. 82 Part of table printed by Scheutz' second engine. Taken from Specimens *(London 1857).*

frequent tuning and skilful handling, in the quiet most congenial to such productions."[120]

In 1864, the results of Farr's work at the General Register Office were published as the *English Life Table*, see Fig. 81. The book contained tables for single lives, and combinations of joint lives for male and female and ran to some 600 pages. The publishers were Longman, Brown, Green, Longmans, and Roberts who had also been responsible for *Specimens*. There had been an interval of seven years between the printing of these tables and they had been produced with two different engines. These engines hardly differed significantly in design but Fig. 82 and Fig. 83 show the clear deterioration in printing in the case of the Donkin engine. It is obvious that Farr had every reason to be displeased with the result. It turns out that only a quarter of the *English Life Table* was calculated and printed with the machine. Several tables, including some in smaller type, see Fig. 84, may have been calculated with the help of the engine, but are definitely type-set by hand.[121] This was because a certain typographic appearance was desired. It is also possible that the engine was employed simultaneously with ordinary calculators as a means of checking their results. In addition, some of the tables had to be calculated in the traditional manner, since more than four differences were involved in their computation.

With the printing of the *English Life Table*, a major statistical project came to an end. The work had involved a great many people and the difference engine of Georg and Edvard Scheutz had also played its part. But after the work was completed, the engine was stored away somewhere in the General Register Office, never to be used again.

At the beginning of 1864, a new director for the Dudley Observatory in Albany made a few last attempts to get the second engine into operation

70 | 3·3053854
71 | 3·2687188
72 | 3·2295172
73 | 3·1875675

Fig. 83 Fragment of table printed by the second Scheutz engine in Farr's English Life Table. *Donkin had had problems with the engraving of the steel type wheels and a clear deterioration in printing is seen in comparision with what the second engine could do, see Fig. 82.*

ENGLISH LIFE TABLE, No. 3.

JOINT LIVES :—MALE AND FEMALE LIFE.

Logarithms of the Series $D_{x,y}$ and $N_{x,y}$.

Age of Female (y)	Age of Male (x)	87 λ $D_{x,87}$	87 λ $N_{x,87}$	Age of Male (x)	88 λ $D_{x,88}$	88 λ $N_{x,88}$	Age of Male (x)	89 λ $D_{x,89}$	89 λ $N_{x,89}$
	55	3·5638879	4·1140787	55	3·4563225	3·9899981	55	3·3415447	3·8570011
	56	3·5466750	4·0952590	56	3·4391096	3·9703757	56	3·3243318	3·8383699
	57	3·5288870	4·0757028	57	3·4213216	3·9509244	57	3·3065438	3·8190192
	58	3·5104655	4·0553306	58	3·4029001	3·9306689	58	3·2881223	3·7988729
	59	3·4913419	4·0340567	59	3·3837765	3·9095207	59	3·2689987	3·7778457
	60	3·4714371	4·0117839	60	3·3638717	3·8873860	60	3·2490939	3·7558414
	61	3·4506618	3·9884073	61	3·3430964	3·8641385	61	3·2283186	3·7327563
	62	3·4289163	3·9638114	62	3·3213509	3·8397244	62	3·2065731	3·7084753
	63	3·4060906	3·9378728	63	3·2985252	3·8139991	63	3·1837474	3·6828767
	64	3·3820644	3·9104579	64	3·2744990	3·7867315	64	3·1597212	3·6558268
	65	3·3567070	3·8814252	65	3·2491416	3·7578983	65	3·1343638	3·6271855
	66	3·3298774	3·8506242	66	3·2223120	3·7273094	66	3·1075342	3·5968005
	67	3·3014243	3·8178965	67	3·1938589	3·6948052	67	3·0790811	3·5645122
	68	3·2711862	3·7830720	68	3·1636208	3·6601193	68	3·0488430	3·5301536
	69	3·2389909	3·7459760	69	3·1314255	3·6233724	69	3·0166477	3·4935457
	70	3·2046563	3·7064224	70	3·0970909	3·5840800	70	2·9823131	3·4545083
	71	3·1679897	3·6642169	71	3·0604243	3·5421479	71	2·9456465	3·4128396
	72	3·1287881	3·6191581	72	3·0212227	3·4973720	72	2·9064449	3·3683392
	73	3·0868384	3·5710353	73	2·9792730	3·4495424	73	2·8644952	3·3207941
	74	3·0419168	3·5196271	74	2·9343514	3·3984381	74	2·8195736	3·2699844
	75	2·9937895	3·4647068	75	2·8862241	3·3438297	75	2·7714463	3·2156798
	76	2·9422121	3·4060377	76	2·8346607	3·2854800	76	2·7198089	3·1576417
	77	2·8869302	3·3433735	77	2·7793048	3·2231428	77	2·6645870	3·0956930
	78	2·8270788	3·2764597	78	2·7201134	3·1565619	78	2·6053356	3·0293680
	79	2·7641827	3·2050335	79	2·6566173	3·0854733	79	2·5418395	2·9586107
	80	2·6961563	3·1288317	80	2·5885909	3·0096039	80	2·4738131	2·8830765
	81	2·6233037	3·0475431	81	2·5157383	2·9286708	81	2·4009605	2·8024830
	82	2·5453186	2·9609063	82	2·4377532	2·8423820	82	2·3229754	2·7163367
	83	2·4618847	2·8686110	83	2·3543193	2·7504367	83	2·2395415	2·6249356
	84	2·3726749	2·7703490	84	2·2651095	2·6525229	84	2·1503317	2·5273682
	85	2·2773521	2·6657995	85	2·1697867	2·5483231	85	2·0550089	2·4235113
	86	2·1755687	2·5546333	86	2·0680033	2·4375048	86	1·9532255	2·3130390
	87	2·0669669	2·4365125	87	1·9594015	2·3197288	87	1·8446237	2·1956061
	88	1·9511785	2·3110860	88	1·8430131	2·1946465	88	1·7288353	2·0708640
	89	1·8278251	2·1779966	89	1·7202597	2·0618960	89	1·6054819	1·9384522
	90	1·6965176	2·0368743	90	1·5889522	1·9211083	90	1·4741744	1·7979983
	91	1·5568571	1·8873326	91	1·4492917	1·7719041	91	1·3345139	1·6491316
	92	1·4084349	1·7289962	92	1·3008686	1·6138873	92	1·1860998	1·4914345
	93	1·2508285	1·5614556	93	1·1432631	1·4466583	93	1·0284853	1·3245232
	94	1·0836104	1·3842942	94	0·9760450	1·2698164	94	0·8612672	1·1479822
	95	0·9063393	1·1970903	95	0·7987739	1·0829181	95	0·6839961	0·9614021
	96	0·7185644	0·9994090	96	0·6109990	0·8855308	96	0·4962212	0·7643181
	97	0·5198245	0·7907846	97	0·4122591	0·6777053	97	0·2974813	0·5567784
	98	0·3096482	0·5707397	98	0·2020828	0·4574428	98	0·0873050	0·3368198
	99	0·0875508	0·3386526	99	9·9799884	0·2256969	99	9·8652106	1·1053739
	100	9·8530490	1·0937368	100	9·7454836	1·9810934	100	9·6307058	1·8613356
	101	9·6056315	1·8348656	101	9·4980661	1·7326339	101	9·3832883	1·6030361
	102	9·3447885	1·5594478	102	9·2372231	1·4477780	102	9·1224453	1·3287871
	103	9·0699969	1·2615008	103	8·9624315	1·1504494	103	8·8476537	1·0321157
	104	8·7807233	1·9232440	104	8·6731579	1·8135810	104	8·5583801	1·6963864
	105	8·4764239		105	8·3688585		105	8·2540807	
	106	8·1565447		106	8·0489793		106	7·9342015	
	107	7·8205213		107	7·7129559		107	7·5981781	
	108	7·4677790		108	7·3602136		108	7·2454358	
	109	7·0977327		109	6·9901673		109	6·8753895	

Fig. 84 English Life Table. The numbers in smaller type have been set by hand, while the numbers printed with larger type are printed and calculated by the difference engine. The smaller type numbers may however have been calculated, but not printed, by the engine for some reason.

again.[122] But it was used only sporadically and eventually it too was put away and forgotten.

1864 marked in practice the end of the story of Scheutz and the Swedish difference engines. More than thirty years had passed since Georg had with interest read about the remarkable English table machine. For more than twenty years, he had been involved with Edvard in developing, building and marketing his invention. The Scheutzes could look back with pride on the fact that they had been able with the simple means at their disposal to achieve what Babbage, despite his access to both money, mechanical engineering skills and machines, had failed to accomplish. They had built the world's first difference engine which could print its results and they had done this at a very low financial cost. Just as the British government had supported Charles Babbage so the Swedish government had finally agreed to give Scheutz financial support, albeit insufficient. It had been yet another honour for his native land to have built the first usable table machine, which then went forth into the wider world. Scientists, kings, engineers and journalists had all expressed their admiration for the engine both in Europe and America. At the great world's exhibition in Paris, both inventors had received a Medaille d'Honneur in gold. Georg, who cared little about fame, had received no fewer than three prestigious orders — two Swedish and one Russian. The engine had been sold to America, the new Promised Land of Progress and the new workshop of the world. Edvard had had a third engine built in London for the British government's account. Thereby the difference engine had been at last tested in practice in that country which had first displayed the greatest interest in the idea. In the meantime, thirty-six years had elapsed.

But there was as much failure as glory in the difference engine's apparent success throughout the world. From a financial point of view, as far as Scheutz was concerned, the whole project had been one long, fateful adventure. The expected profit had not materialized and there were now debts instead. These had arisen from the loans which the Scheutzes had taken out to allow them to build, protect and market their invention. The printing presses of the world's observatories and other table-producing institutions had not reacted as expected. The problem with errors in tables remained, despite the fact that the technical solution to the problem was available. Only two prominent institutions had each purchased a machine — but at a lower price than reckoned. Despite the meticulous distribution of *Specimens*, the news of the contracts that had been clinched and the reduced price of the engine, no new buyer emerged.

When the story of the difference engine was ended, life continued as before. Charles Babbage continued to develop the Analytical Engine until the 18th of October 1871 when he died, without having brought to fulfilment his grand vision of mechanical calculation.

Georg Scheutz continued to write and translate. Like his English friend, he was active to the very last. On the 22nd of May, 1873, he died at the age of eighty-seven.

As for Edvard, he had his wife and son to comfort him for the loss of his father. Georg had died as a virtual bankrupt and among the few possessions to pass in inheritance to Edvard was the Medaille d'Honneur of 1855, which properly speaking half belonged to him already.[123] After his return to Sweden in 1859, he had manufactured and sold his steam engine, worked with the printing of postage stamps and had made some minor inventions.[124] In two other ways, he followed in his father's footsteps. He translated books and wrote articles with a view to disseminating knowledge about foreign technology within Sweden.[125]

On the 30th of December 1879, Edvard Scheutz' wife died in his arms. For Edvard, with years of reverses and ill-health, it was — as he put it — "the last straw".[126] A year later on the 28th of January 1881, at an age of fifty-nine, Edvard passed away.[127] He too died a bankrupt leaving debts amounting to 3,500 riksdaler.[128] With the death of his son Axel, in February of 1883, at the age of twenty-one, this branch of the Scheutz family had come to an end.[129]

Silence lingered also over the difference engine. At the Science Museum in London, the Difference Engine No. 1 was placed on exhibition, perhaps smiling in its own mechanical way, at the daily visitors who stared at it. The Scheutz engines, for their part, slumbered away in three crates — one in Stockholm, one in Albany and one in London.

PART II
ANALYSIS

3. THE MACHINES, THE MEN, AND THE MARKET

3.1 The Machines — A comparison between Scheutz' and Babbage's engines

Since further relevant conclusions can be drawn from the engines that have been preserved, I intend to devote this section to their design and mode of operation. I will do this by way of a comparison, with the aim of providing useful information for the discussion in the two following sections. Were there perhaps underlying technical reasons for Charles Babbage's failure to complete his engine? Did such matters contribute to the commercial lack of success of Georg and Edvard Scheutz?

I shall start by briefly explaining some crucial mechanisms in the Difference Engine No. 1. Then Babbage's engine will be compared with Scheutz'. Some light will also be thrown on the development of the Scheutz engines. A reading suggestion might be made. To understand the basic ideas of this section, it is enough to read pages 242−246 where Johann Helfrich Müller's engine is discussed and the conclusions on pages 254−255. For the reader who is burning with a desire to build his own tabulating engine, some useful hints now follow.

Let me start by taking a closer look at Babbage's difference engine as shown in Fig. 13 and by considering, one by one, the mechanisms for addition and carrying and the "safety systems".

Addition is best explained by means of a sketch of the basic principle involved. Consider therefore Fig. 85. It shows a part of the mechanism of Babbage's machine, theoretically unfolded sideways in order to be more comprehensible. The figure thus does not give the correct geometry as regards the positioning of the axles in the actual machine, (cf. Fig. 88). The notation for the wheels and axles is Babbage's own. Three number wheels — the second and first differences and the result — are included in the diagram. They belong to the same power. The initial situation depicted in the figure is that the second difference wheel is set at 5 and is going to be added to the first difference which is 0. The operation takes place in three steps.

1. The bolting axis revolves so that the arm *a* presses on the slide *b* of the adding bolt and moves *b* to the right, see Fig. 85b.

2. Next the axle *c* in Fig. 85a revolves, causing the adding bolt which is fixed to the axle to rotate with it. All the wheels in the figure are free to move about their axles. The slide *b* is between two of the teeth on the underside of the adding wheel, see Fig. 85b, and thus moves the adding wheel 5/20 of a revolution, (corresponding to 5 units on the number wheel).

3. Thereafter the slide *b* is thrust back to its initial position by means of a cam *e*, see Fig. 86, which operates on the stud *f* on the slide *b*, see Fig. 85b. The axle *c* performs a half revolution and the slide *b* moves freely under the adding wheel without drawing it along.

Since the adding wheel engages the first difference's unbolting wheel and its number wheel, this number wheel has been rotated through five units and is now set at 5. The addition has been carried out. If the second difference's number wheel had initially been set at 0, the camtooth *e* in Fig. 85b would have prevented the slide *b*'s sideways movement in the first step.

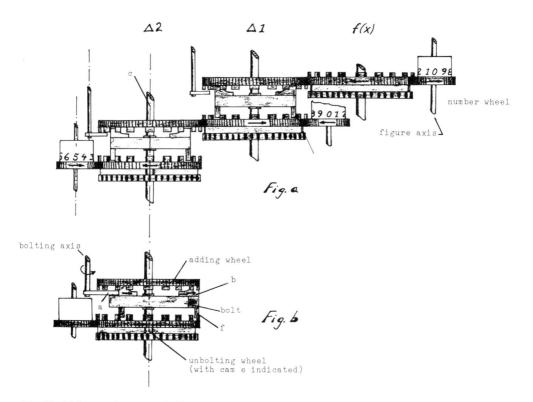

Fig. 85 Adding mechanism in Babbage's Difference Engine No. 1. The drawing does not give the correct geometry as regards the positioning of the axles in the actual machine. Here, the parts are theoretically unfolded sideways. Drawing by author.

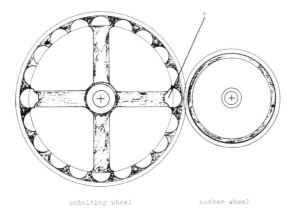

unbolting wheel   number wheel

Fig. 86 The unbolting wheel in the Difference Engine No. 1. Drawing by author.

Carrying was not involved in the previous example. Suppose that a similar addition is performed once more, i.e. a further 5 is added to the first difference. Now carrying has to take place. Prior to this addition, both the second difference number wheel and the number wheel in the first difference, are set at 5. The number wheel in the first difference representing the power of ten (not shown) is set at 0. In order to implement carrying, there is on the underside of the unbolting wheel a ratchet wheel which is fixed and belongs to the unbolting wheel, see Fig. 87. Resting against this wheel, there is a spring loaded claw i, see Fig. 87 and Fig. 89a. Carrying takes place in two steps:

1. First, the addition is performed so that the number wheel A in Fig. 87 increases from 5 to 9. When the addition is carried to completion, the wheel moves from 9 to 0. At the same moment that this takes place, the arm h is operated by the rotating number wheel A so that h's axle is made to revolve. In the upper end of this, there is a trigger j, see Fig. 89a. This is turned according to the arrow, so that the spring-loaded ratchet mechanism, with claw i, is moved one notch on (1/20 of a revolution) along the periphery of the ratchet wheel, in the direction of the arrow, see Fig. 89b. Preparation has been now made for the carrying operation.

2. Secondly, the figure axis, on which there is mounted a finger k, is turned, see Fig. 87 and Fig. 89b. The number wheels do not move because they are free to revolve around the figure axis. Consider Fig. 89c. The finger k during its rotation takes hold of the heel on the ratchet mechanism and pulls this (and thus also the claw i) and the ratchet wheel along 1/20 of a revolution in the arrow's direction. The ratchet mechanism is again caught by the trigger j as shown in Fig. 89a. Since the unbolting wheel C (in Fig. 87) is coupled to the number wheel B, which represents the power of ten, this has moved on one step from 0 to 1. Number wheel A is set at 0. Together they display 10 and carrying has been completed.

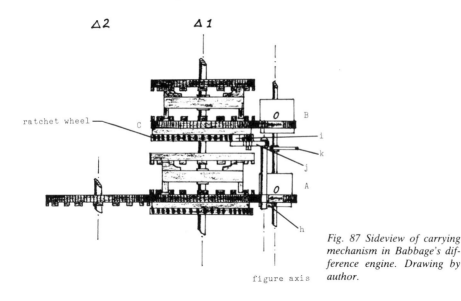

ratchet wheel

figure axis

Fig. 87 Sideview of carrying mechanism in Babbage's difference engine. Drawing by author.

In Babbage's engine, corresponding to each unbolting wheel, there were three smaller mechanical units which I have called *safety systems*.[1] Their task was to ensure that the unbolting wheels and thus the number wheels were reset and kept in the right position, irrespective of "any accidental disturbance".[2] In Lardner's article, the existence of these systems is explained as follows.

> "the purpose of which should be to obliterate all small errors or inequalities which might, even by remote possibility, arise either from defects in the original formation of the mechanism, from inequality of wear, from casual strain or derangement, − or in short, from any other cause whatever, Thus the movements of the first and principal parts of the mechanism [adding- and carry systems] were regarded by him [Babbage] merely as a first, though extremely nice approximation, upon which a system of small corrections was to be subsequently made by suitable and independent mechanism."[3]

From the quotation, it would appear that Lardner and also Babbage, primarily envisaged the safety systems taking care of errors arising from mechanical malfunctioning.

System 1 prevented the unbolting wheel and the corresponding number wheels from rotating backwards. This was a necessary precaution because of the design of the carrying mechanism. It consisted of the above mentioned ratchet wheel, the main purpose of which was carrying, see Fig. 89. The ratchet wheel had, therefore, a dual purpose.

System 2 prevented the unbolting wheel and corresponding number wheel from being set at anything other than the whole numbers. It immediately corrected minor improper settings. For example, if the number wheel was set at 1.2, it was turned to 1. It did not operate when the number wheel was positioned exactly halfway between two numbers e.g. 1.5. It consisted of a spring loaded roller which ran against the half-rounded teeth on the upper periphery of the unbolting wheel, see Fig. 90a. It transformed the whole numbers into stable positions on the number wheels and thereby kept the unbolting wheels in the right position for the bolts to carry out addition.

System 3 performed the same function as system 2, but operated with greater force and was therefore better able to correct incorrect settings. It consisted of a similar style of spring-loaded roller as in system 2, see Fig. 90b and Fig. 88. As the figure shows, it was, in addition, controlled completely by a rotating cam. It forced the unbolting wheel into the correct position in the event that the spring-loading of the two rollers was insufficient. The cam acted on the system after addition to the unbolting wheel. If one of the number wheels was positioned exactly midway between two whole numbers, the machine locked. This was a refinement which Lardner and many others identified as the system's main purpose.[4] "The consequence of this exquisite arrangement is, that the machine will either calculate rightly, or not at all."[5] This however was not the real reason for the inclusion of the system. Its main task was to keep the unbolting wheel still while addition took place *from* the unbolting wheel. System 3 thus had three functions. The use of a cam to steer system 3 had, as I see it, two major disadvantages. First of all the system could be easily destroyed by the operating lever being thrust forward too violently. Secondly, it would have worn out rather quickly. As far as the system's capability to lock the machine is concerned, it should be noted that even if the system had not been there, the engine would have been locked in any case by the bolt in the event that the number wheel had been incorrectly set.

The purpose of the safety systems in Babbage's difference engine was to increase its reliability. What kind of accidental disturbances were likely to arise? Lardner mentioned some possible causes in his article. "Defects in the original formation of the mechanism", could in my opinion, hardly be corrected by the systems. Furthermore, these could only deal with certain minor errors caused by "inequality of wear". Lardner also considered "casual strain or derangement, − or in short, any other cause whatever". But what could give rise to such disturbances? Could knocks or vibrations to which the machine was exposed, lead to internal dislocations? It seems unlikely. Knocks or vibrations could only have had a negligible effect on the heavy wheels and on the total mass of such a machine. Only extremely heavy blows would be able to throw the internal mechanisms off balance, and such blows would definitely damage the engine in other ways as well. It is therefore improbable that the engine needed the safety systems to guard against accidents of this type. On the other hand, whenever it was possible, the systems effectively corrected

Fig. 88 Portion of the Difference Engine No. 1 kept in the Science Museum, London. It was probably assembled around 1833 and is capable of showing the mechanisms for adding and carrying. A number wheel, an unbolting wheel an a cam-guided spring-loaded roller can be seen in the figure (the spring is not the original one). Photographed by author.

minor errors due to incorrect manual positioning, as well as faults arising from the operator neglecting to follow through the motion of the engine operating lever. The completed great engine would probably have been equipped with a crank or a wheel instead, making this latter capability of the safety systems less important. The adoption of the safety systems must thus be seen primarily as a way of combatting errors due to the human factor, or more specifically, as a means of correcting incorrect manual settings of the number wheels.

The fact that Charles Babbage incorporated these special mechanisms, to achieve optimum safety or security in the operation of the engine, brings me back to Johann Müller and his ideas. My conclusions in section 1.2 were that it is not certain if Babbage got his idea from Müller or not, although it is known that Babbage at some point learned about his German predecessor and that he was very interested in the matter. The latter statement is based on the fact that John Herschel translated all the details about Müller's engine in Klipstein's book published in 1786. When Herschel made his translation, he drew attention to the descriptions especially relating to Müller's difference engine, but also selected several points dealing with Müller's universal calculating machine. Herschel concentrated on matters of direct relevance to Babbage's difference engine. Furthermore, these facts − combined with the design of Babbage's engine, as described above − prove (as I will show below) that Babbage

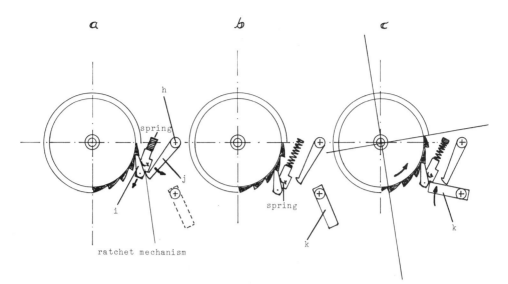

Fig. 89 Carrying in the Difference Engine No. 1. Ratchet wheel and ratchet mechanism seen in three different positions from above. Drawing by author.

must have taken design ideas from Müller. This, in consequence, means that he must have known about Müller at an early stage in the history of the Difference Engine No. 1. Babbage was thus not telling the whole truth, when he in *Passages* wrote that his difference engine was the "first" with which he was acquainted. He had read Klipstein, in Herschel's translation, long before 1864, when *Passages* was published.

My evidence for these assertions is the following. Herschel dealt with seven points in Klipstein. After the first four points, which were basically an introduction to Müller and his universal calculating machine and how to operate it, Herschel came to the fifth. Point five dealt with the "security of the engine".[6] This is the most interesting point because to the best of my knowledge, no inventor of a calculating machine prior to Müller had paid so much attention to this aspect of the matter. Nor, indeed, was this aspect much developed by inventors after Müller and Babbage. The first security device noted by Herschel was a bell in the machine, which rang when the number of digits exceeded the machine's capacity (15 digits). To the best of my knowledge, it was Johann Helfrich Müller who invented and first incorporated a bell in a calculating machine.[7] Babbage also used a bell in the part of Difference Engine No. 1 that was assembled. The second security device, was a mechanism having exactly the same function as Babbage's safety systems. It was described by Herschel as follows: *One does not have to put the number wheels in the exact position – Müller's "engine" does that by itself.* Herschel continued by saying that this was *not done solely by springs because they might sometimes fail to do the job!*[8] These words, I argue, prove that Babbage got his

245

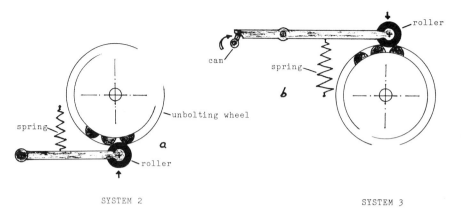

Fig. 90 The Difference Engine No. 1. Safety system 2 and 3. Drawing by author.

idea for his second safety system from Müller's remark that springs were used and that Babbage also took his cam-guided third safety system from Müller. From a mechanical point of view springs for this purpose can only be replaced by cam- or eccentric mechanisms. It would be too much of a coincidence if Babbage, who undoubtedly at some point knew about Müller's work, had designed mechanisms based on exactly the same principles invented by Müller, in order to perform a task which was unique in the history of computing, namely, the ability of the engine to correct an erroneous setting of the number wheels. The other parts of Herschel's translation are of less interest, except for the seventh point, which dealt with Müller's difference engine. As far as the security of the calculating machine was concerned, Müller concluded that the erroneous setting of the machine could only arise from human error.

It remains hard to say when exactly Babbage learned about Müller. My conjecture is that it was after the 9th of April 1822 when Babbage eagerly asked Herschel to investigate the ominous rumours about the French difference engine. Perhaps it was not the a Frenchman who was behind it after all.[9]

The archival material about Müller and Babbage, together with the parts of the engine in existence, show in my view that Babbage must have been aware of Müller's design, through Klipstein, at an early point in the history of the Difference Engine No. 1.[10]

Let me now turn to the comparison between Babbage's and Scheutz' difference engines. Since several machines were built, it is necessary to make a selection. I have chosen Babbage's Difference Engine No. 1 and Scheutz' third engine.[11] Babbage's engine will be considered both in the light of the small section that was assembled in 1833 and the projected complete machine. The reason for choosing the third Scheutz engine is that it was, like Babbage's, built entirely in metal and was intended to be used on a regular basis.

The engines of Scheutz and Babbage were based on the same mathematical principles. But in the matter of engineering detail, there were great differences between the two machines. Both had vertical axles in the calculating unit which formed a centre for the number wheels. In Babbage's engine, addition took place from left to right, while carrying took place from the bottom upwards. In the Scheutz engine, addition went from the bottom upwards and carrying from right to left. This difference was due to Lardner's description, which for explanatory purposes inverted the structure of Babbage's calculating unit. (As far as the engine's mode of functioning was concerned, this difference had no practical significance.) When completed, Babbage's engine would have been able to calculate with 18 digits and six differences. Scheutz' engine could deal with 15 digits and four differences. Most importantly, Babbage's engine lacked a printing unit.

Dimensions. Fully built, Babbage's engine − excluding the printing unit and result transfer mechanism − would have been roughly 2,600 mm high, 2,300 mm broad and 1,000 mm deep. The weight of the engine's calculating unit can be estimated to over 2,000 kilos. Scheutz' engine was 450 mm high, 1,600 mm broad and 520 mm deep. Its total weight was around 400 kilos. Fig. 91 illustrates the differences in dimensions between the two engines. Thus the calculating unit alone in Babbage's engine would have been considerably heavier than Scheutz' whole engine. In order to transfer the result from the calculating unit to the printing unit, Babbage would have been forced to design a number of additional large mechanisms.

Scale: The main reason for the greater size of Babbage's engine was that its parts were designed with very large dimensions. All of them were very strongly made. For example, the shelves carrying the number wheels in Babbage's engine were 8 mm thick, while in the Scheutz engine they were only 3 mm thick. Perhaps this does not seem particularly striking, but if it is taken into account that in terms of surface area, the shelves in the Babbage engine were 15 times greater than those in the Scheutz engine, the point at issue becomes clearer. A rough estimate of this difference in scale can be illustrated in another way. The parts needed to carry out addition in Babbage's engine (the bolt, the unbolting wheel, etc.) would fill an average size shoe box. The corresponding parts in the Scheutz engine (trap, trap wheel etc.) would take up an ordinary matchbox. The parts in Babbage's engine were thus much larger than those in Scheutz' engine.

I do not believe that − as has been suggested − this large scale was due to some sort of tradition in the mechanical industry or workshops of the 1830s. Neither do I accept the argument that the scale was a consequence of the purpose of the engine − to produce tables and to be strong enough to do this. If there is any reason at all behind it (and it is quite possible that they just started to build the first piece and it was large), then the only plausible one is that Babbage really intended to calculate tables *by*

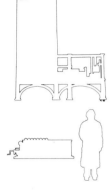

Fig. 91 Differences in size − the Scheutz engine and Babbage's complete difference engine. Drawing by author.

steam, and instinctively made the engine sturdy. The scale of the Difference Engine No. 1 was in fact closer to that of a steam engine, than to the scale of basically all other mechanical calculating machines — and definitely to that of all its predecessors.

Surface finish — Workmanship: Although the engines were made from the same material, namely steel, bronze and brass, the end results were quite different. Babbage's engine displays a better surface finish and finer tolerances than Scheutz'. Much greater care had in fact been taken by Clement and his men in achieving this finish. The parts of the Difference Engine No. 1, were made to an accuracy of 1-2 thousands of an inch, i.e. approximately 0,025-0,05 mm.[12] This was also the case with such parts as the short pillars which supported the shelves. Even the thickness of the shelves and decoration details on the columns were machined to this accuracy.[13] Donkin & Co. on the other hand, left surfaces that had been cast unfinished and which were rough and there were several rather badly made parts. The workmanship displayed on Babbage's engine was definitely superior to that on Scheutz' machine.

Addition: The system for addition in both the engines was basically the same. It consisted of a finger which fastened between a pair of teeth in a wheel above and pulled it with it. But there was one important point of difference. The Scheutzes relied entirely on gravity to bring about the required movements. The trap, stud and tongue were three elements in the addition mechanism which operated entirely by means of their weight. Babbage employed a completely different solution by making use of helical and plate springs to provide the forces required for the movements involved.

In the Scheutz engine the addition of two rows with 15 number wheels in each occurred simultaneously. Since this momentarily required extra force, addition led to an increased braking torque on the crank. However, since the parts that were involved were very small and light, the braking torque was correspondingly low and no special problems arose. In Babbage's engine, heavy wheels had to engage with others and pull them round during addition. He had not devised any special system to diminish the braking torque itself when this operation was being carried out.[14] Instead he distributed the braking torque which arose when the slide on the bolt was activated just before addition. This was accomplished by arranging things so that the bolts in each column carried out their work individually, one after the other, proceeding from the bottom upwards, see Fig. 92.

In the minor part of the Difference Engine No. 1 which was assembled, addition took place in one column containing six sets of wheels (figure wheel, adding wheel, unbolting wheel) at a time. The braking torque involved during addition was not, therefore, particularly large. But in the completed engine, with its 18 digits and six differences, addition would have involved a much greater braking torque. In it, no less than three columns with 18 sets of wheels, would have had to move simultaneously.

The braking torque during the addition operation in Babbage's large engine, would have been nine times larger than in the smaller model. Moreover the torque would probably have increased further just before addition, since three bolts (one for each column) would have been activated simultaneously.

Carrying: Babbage and Scheutz selected completely different mechanisms for carrying. One thing they had in common, was that when carrying was necessary, it occurred in two stages. There was a preparatory step (called "warning" by Babbage) when a mechanism was activated and a following step in which the wheel in the nearest higher power was turned forward one unit.[15] The major difference between the engines, as regards carrying, was that in Babbage's it took place very quickly, whereas in Scheutz' engine it went slowly. Another difference was that once again Scheutz made use of gravity while Babbage employed the more reliable plate springs.

Reliability: The most important quality required of a difference engine was that it should calculate and print table series correctly. This meant that they had to be reliable and free from weak points. How did Babbage's and Scheutz' engines measure up to this requirement?

As a way of ensuring increased reliability, Babbage had devised his three safety systems: the first to prevent the number wheels rotating backwards; the second to keep the number wheels set exactly at whole numbers; and the third to support the second and to lock the unbolting wheel during addition. None of these devices were to be found in the Scheutz engine. The first was superfluous since the carrying mechanism was based on a quite different design and the number wheels were therefore able to rotate freely in both directions when they were being set. The third system was also unnecessary in the Scheutz machine since there was no risk that the number wheel (which performed the same function as the unbolting wheel in Babbage's engine) would rotate during addition. The difference was that Babbage's unbolting wheel was subject to a tangential force (from the bolt when it was uncoupled), while the number wheel in the Scheutz engine was subject to an axial force (when the trap was to be put into action). However, it was a major defect that the second system was omitted on the Scheutz engine. There, the number wheels on account of their lightness were sensitive to knocks and vibrations. Due to the lack of the system, it was easy for the number wheels to be displaced by a blow or to be initially set wrongly (between two whole numbers) by the operator. The most common reason for them ending up in the wrong place, however, was due to their failing to stop immediately after addition. This could result in a trap fastening directly under a tooth on the number wheel above, so that the engine either locked or was damaged.

In fact the Scheutzes had considered this problem early on. In the patent application of 1854, a spring loaded ratchet mechanism is mentioned, which rests against the teeth of the number wheel and keeps it on whole numbers.[16] (See Fig. 51 where this ratchet mechanism can be seen.) For some reason or other, the mechanism was never fitted to any of the Scheutz engines. The problem must have become clear when Bergström had built the second machine. The lack of such a device caused problems at Albany and Gould's successors in fact proposed the introduction of something similar without probably being acquainted with the patent documents.[17] Farr undoubtedly had similar difficulties with the third engine. Thus in this respect, Scheutz' engine was less reliable than Babbage's.

Another threat to the reliability of the Scheutz engine was due to the fact that many parts in the addition and also in the carrying mechanism, were designed to be operated by gravity. If the parts had been heavier, everything would have been much better. Since, however, it was a question of parts which could be contained in a matchbox, they were unreliable when it came to performance. If one forgot to lubricate one of the traps, gravity was insufficient to operate it. The same was true of the stud on the trap. Babbage who had made use of springs had no such problems with his machine.

Another direct reason for the Scheutz engine being less reliable was that in places, as has been mentioned, it was carelessly made. Apart from aesthetic faults like the types on the type wheels which Donkin was dissatisfied with, there were more serious defects. Although not many in number, they formed weak links in the system. Several parts in the printing unit were badly made, and here and there, important lubricating points had been left out, although they were to be found on the second engine. In many respects the second machine was better made than the third. Airy's statement to the effect that the general workmanship on the third engine was superior to that on the second one, is consequently incorrect. Perhaps this erroneous conclusion arose from Airy's bad sight. He had "an eye affected with a peculiar malformation", which prevented him from carrying out a large number of astronomical observations.[18]

Some mechanisms (like the mangle wheel and the number wheels), had been redesigned for the better but Donkin's workmanship was still inferior to that of Bergström. I have not been able to compare the third engine with other machines made by Donkin and can therefore not draw any conclusion about Donkin's general ability as a machine builder.

Both Babbage's and Scheutz' engines suffered from the defect that they could get into a tangle through carelessness on the part of the operator, causing them to lock or even break down. This means that Babbage's idea of driving his own and Scheutz' engines by means of a steam engine via a catgut belt, at the Great Exhibition in London of 1862, could never have been carried out.

Durability: It is impossible to estimate how long the difference engines would have stood up to continuous use. All I can say, is that the cam mechanism in the third safety system of Babbage's engine was doomed to wear out relatively quickly, due to a design flaw. As a result there would have been too much play in the addition mechanisms and gradually the engine would have been unable to add, and would have locked. The Royal Society Committee Statement of 1829, regarding this point, was thus incorrect:

> "Of the adequacy of the machinery to work under all the friction and strain to which it can ever be fairly exposed, and of its durability, your Committee have not the least doubt. Great precautions are taken to prevent the wear of the parts by friction; and the strength, solidity, and equilibrium, in the whole apparatus, ensure it from all danger on the score of violence or constant wear."[19]

There was no comparable mechanism in Scheutz' engine exposed to this weakness.

Servicing: Scheutz' engine required especially careful and regular lubrication. This could be easily carried out, thanks to its open and spacious design. Babbage's engine also of course required to be lubricated, but this was more tricky on account of its extremely compact form. The repair and replacement of faulty or worn-out parts would have been necessary from time to time. In the Scheutz engine, this was easy. For example, only a few parts had to be taken out to change a trap wheel. In Babbage's machine, this would have entailed a lot of work. In order to change a wheel in the middle of the large engine, one would have been forced to strip down more or less the whole engine. On the other hand, due to the fact that the parts in Babbage's engine were large, strong and hardwearing, repairs would have been less frequent.

Speed: Apart from being reliable, it was important that the difference engine was fast. The change-down in gearing on the Scheutz engine was so considerable that it required 38 revolutions of the crank between printing one result and then the next. According to the Scheutzes, one could reckon on average with 120 results per hour, which means that one would have been forced to turn the crank at a rate of 1.27 r.p.s.[20] This was undoubtedly too physically demanding to be maintained for any length of time. A more realistic figure was probably 63 results per hour, which could be attained by cranking at a rate of 0.67 r.p.s. or 40 r.p.m.

The reason for the slowness of the Scheutz engine (as Collier has also noted) was that carrying took a great deal of time.[21] It involved 18 revolutions of the crank. Addition was the fastest operation with only 3 revolutions in all. Both carrying and printing could have been speeded up by increasing the gear ratio. However this would definitely have required the introduction of a safety system of Babbage's type 2. This was never carried out and I shall return to a discussion of this fact later.

Unfortunately, there is no information about the speed of Babbage's engine. It is clear, however, that the small version was much faster. Roughly speaking, one could reckon on being able to move the lever back and forth two times in four seconds, which corresponded to the time taken from moving from one result to the next. However, it is not possible to make a simple comparison between Babbage's machine and Scheutz', which not only had more differences and digits to contend with, but which also printed the results. It took at best 24 seconds for the Scheutz engine to go from one result to the next.[22] In connection with the speed of the Babbage engine, Collier remarks that "the provision of a printing apparatus might have slowed it down somewhat".[23] It is perhaps opportune to make an observation here. Collier says that the extension of the calculating unit in Babbage's engine to allow it to deal with 18 digits and six differences, would not have made it slower, due to its design.[24] However, in my opinion there would have been three axles involved simultaneously in addition in the larger model as against only one in the smaller machine; there would have been 18 wheels on each axle involved in the addition on the larger machine as against only six in the smaller machine; and three bolts would have been simultaneously activated as against only one on the smaller machine. Everything would have proceeded as fast as before, but it would have required a great deal more force. Earlier I have estimated that it would have needed at least nine times the force. If a printing unit had been added, it would have required considerable force for its operation (not least for moving the coordinate board) and Babbage's larger engine would have had to be geared down in relation to the part of the calculating unit from 1833. The exact amount is uncertain, but if, for example, Babbage wanted the large, fullsize engine to be as easily operated as the little one, he would have needed a gear-ratio of at least 10:1. This would have made Babbage's engine slower than Scheutz' machine.[25]

In the Scheutz' engine the low speed was due to the change down in gearing – owing to the lightness of the wheels, whereas, in Babbage's machine the low speed was due to change down in gearing – because of the heaviness of the wheels.

Design: While Babbage's engine was of superior quality throughout, Scheutz' machine had inherent construction defects which threatened its performance. On the other hand, the parts of the Scheutz engine were simpler, lighter, and consequently cheaper to make than those in Babbage's. Which machine was then best designed? The question has not only technical but also economic aspects. For the moment, it is enough to say that the Difference Engine No. 1 was not 17,000 pounds better designed than the Scheutz engine.

As far as the *development of Georg and Edvard Scheutz' difference engines*, is concerned the Scheutzes based their ideas upon Babbage's. In connection with this, it is amusing to point out how an inventor can become fixated on a particular solution of a technical problem because of earlier ways of tackling it. In Babbage's engine, the number wheels in two neigbouring columns were numbered respectively 0-9 and 9-0. In other words they were numbered in reverse order to one another, due to the fact that there were four cog wheels engaged from number wheel to number wheel. In the first Scheutz engine, the number wheels were numbered likewise although there was absolutely no reason for it. It only served to complicate matters and generate problems. My conclusion is that the Scheutzes had simply read in Lardner's article that the number wheels rotated in opposite directions in Babbage's engine and had adopted this idea without stopping to think. In the second and third engine, this piece of "unconscious adoption" was transformed into a necessity. When the Scheutzes discovered that the trap was in fact only activated in one direction, they were able in the later two engines to position the traps on the axles. The carriage mechanism employed on the first machine became unnecessary but the wheels *had* to rotate in different directions for otherwise they would have added all the time. In short, the example shows how the Scheutzes followed Lardner's words blindly on this point, and were consequently forced to make their engine unnecessarily complicated. The wheels rotated in different directions. Later on, they discovered how they could simplify the engine, but they were no longer able to rid themselves of the idea.

Georg and Edvard Scheutz made in the course of twenty years three engines – a prototype, a finished machine and a copy. The main development work thus took place during the making of the first and second engines but the number of improvements introduced in the second engine is actually very small. The basic change was in the adoption of the new carrying mechanism. In addition, there were some minor improvements which can be considered entirely natural in passing from prototype to a commercial product.

In the case of the third engine, their correspondence shows that the Scheutzes had new ideas and modifications in mind. One reason why they continued to work on the engine, was that they were probably not unaware of its weak points. "God grant only that the machine stands up to the work", wrote Georg Scheutz when it was given the task of printing *Specimens* in London.[26] In November 1857, Georg wrote a four page letter to Edvard, devoted to explaining refinements in the printing unit.[27] A couple of these were included on the third engine. Bryan Donkin also suggested ideas for minor improvements which were eventually incorporated.[28]

On the whole, however, there were few radical improvements to make the engine more reliable, nor are they even suggested in the surviving correspondence. I believe that the Scheutzes were forced to accept a certain amount of uncertainty in the machine's performance, as long as this could be kept at a low level and provided that the engine was properly looked after and operated. My opinion is based on the general tone in the correspondence between the Scheutzes, as well as on the following passage, written by Edvard in *Specimens*, which suggests that economic reasons were behind the fact that their second engine was not further developed:

> "The object of the Messrs. Scheutz in the present machine was not great speed; and if they had attempted to do more than they actually have done, the reader of the foregoing little history will readily see, they, from mere want of means, would probably have produced no *working* machine at all."[29]

A similar excuse is given in the same book for why they had not tried to improve the types on the type wheels.[30] Georg however did not approve of the fact that Edvard made these admissions.[31] Although this explanation relates to the second engine, I think it is valid also in the case of the third. It too was built on a tight budget and it is very probable that Donkin tried to save as much as possible. The engine's bad workmanship might be a sign of this. In this engine the mangle wheel and some other details were improved. However, while several refinements were introduced in the printing unit, nothing was done to make the number wheels more reliable in their operation.

Let me try to sum up the main points of this section. In Babbage's difference engine there were three systems for increasing its security in operation and avoiding errors due to the human factor. The existence of two of these systems proves that Babbage in fact must have learned about Müller's engine during the early stages of the history of the Difference Engine No. 1. In the comparison between Scheutz' third engine and Babbage's difference engine, it was found that the latter was of considerably larger dimensions. This was primarily caused by the number wheels and other parts in Babbage's engine being made in a large scale, in fact much larger than all other mechanical calculating machines. The workmanship displayed in Babbage's engine was definitely superior to that of Scheutz' machine. The former was in fact made consistently to very fine tolerances, while the latter even contained unpolished casting surfaces. Furthermore, when Airy had said that the workmanship on the third engine was superior to that of the second, he had been wrong. The system used for addition was similar in both engines but they employed different types of carrying mechanism. Babbage's engine was the more reliable of the two. The reason for this was the larger dimensions of the parts and the use of springs to supply forces, instead of light parts and the use of gravity in the Scheutz engine. Moreover, certain details of the third Scheutz engine were badly made. Both engines were liable to malfunction or even damage through careless operation. One mechanism in Babbage's engine would have worn out very fast because of a design flaw. In the Scheutz engine, there was no corresponding mechanism. Babbage's engine was harder to service and repair due to its compact construction. The Scheutz engine worked relatively slowly and optimally it could print a tabular value every 24 seconds. Babbage's partial engine of 1833 was able to calculate a tabular value every 4 seconds. However, the proposed large engine including the printing unit would have been much slower and would have had a speed comparable, or even inferior, to that of the Scheutz. With respect to the design, Babbage's engine was of superior quality; the Scheutz engine was simpler, lighter and less costly to make; but Babbage's was not 17,000 pounds better designed than Scheutz'. Finally, the development of the Swedish engines was discussed. Despite the fact that more than twenty years elapsed between the first prototype engine and the third engine, no noteworthy developments took place.

3.2 The Men − Babbage's failure analyzed

In the present study, the focus of attention has been on Johann Müller, Charles Babbage and Georg and Edvard Scheutz. Although united by a common interest in the difference engine, they differed from one another in several respects. One aim of this section is to see how their differing personalities were reflected in their interest in mechanical table calculation. First of all, I shall briefly summarize the motives which prompted their actions and note how far their aims were achieved. Thereafter the principal two part question of this section can be tackled: why did Babbage fail to complete his engine and why did Scheutz succeed?

A description has already been given in some detail of how the engineer Müller, the mathematician Babbage and the printer Scheutz first conceived the idea of building a difference engine. Müller wished to simplify the verification of previously computed tables and constructed an ordinary non-printing calculating machine. Babbage invented a printing table engine, having been irritated by the number of errors occurring in numerical tables and the time taken to compile such tables. Müller, while developing his universal machine, realized that a difference engine would be even better suited for the production of tables. Scheutz got his idea directly from Babbage.

But what were their reasons for continuing with their work? It is my contention that Müller was led to present his more or less fully fledged difference engine primarily from a delight in technical design. This inbuilt capacity of technology to fascinate and stimulate its practitioners to further invention, has often been neglected in considering the various sources of technological development. But Müller also entertained hopes of making some money by these efforts, apparently with the view of financing the further development of his ideas. If he had a practical purpose, it was to devise a machine that could calculate and print tables. At the same time he was too unsure about the demand for such a device, for this to have been a sufficient driving force in itself. He speculated instead about selling the machine to "a rich Englishman who sometimes has more use for useless things". In general, he seems (as far as I can judge) not to have considered the project as a way of attaining honour and fame.

The Englishman, Babbage, became involved with difference engines for quite other reasons. He was fascinated, at least initially, more by the mathematical and theoretical aspects of the thing than by the invention's practical possibilities. The economic motive was completely lacking in his case. His central practical aim was to design a machine which could calculate and print error-free tables. Most of all, however, I believe that Charles Babbage saw in the project a means of gaining social recognition. Because his career as a mathematician and scientist had not brought him the success which he sought, the difference engine offered a congenial way of gaining honour and the respect of others in the highly technologically oriented English society.

The primary force which drove Georg Scheutz, was a practical one: he was interested in making a machine which could calculate and print error-free tables. He had read about the problem of those errors which were difficult to eradicate, and wished to solve it. But he was also stimulated by the fact that he believed that the Englishmen were on the wrong track. Although in retrospect this seems quite correct, in actual fact Georg Scheutz was even further off course when he presented his 19 times smaller machine which was to operate with only *one* difference, calculate with 10 digits and print 20 in the result! However, it is plausible that his immediate reaction to Babbage's clumsy printing unit was significantly sounder and had a central role in spurring him on.

256

From an intellectual standpoint, the challenge presented, in particular by the printing unit, probably gave him the same kind of pleasure which Müller had experienced in his design work. Perhaps too, the difference engine also gave Georg a special feeling of satisfaction by allowing him to consider himself a genuine engineer who had been prevented by ill fortune from following that profession. There was also a national dimension to the challenge: Scheutz (and probably more so his friends and supporters) was stimulated by the thought that a Swedish difference engine might succeed where pioneering English efforts had failed. The financial aspect was also of importance to him and led him to attach great hopes to the project. From the very outset, he hoped to be able to open his own press for the printing of tables in Stockholm. On the other hand, I believe that he was indifferent to the thought that the difference engine might provide certain opportunities for social advancement, except in one respect: he saw the engine as a means of providing Edvard with a secure future as an engineer. As for Edvard, there are also his motives to consider. He had been given the task, as a young man at a school of applied technology, of grappling with the difference engine, and initially he must have been largely stimulated by the technical challenge involved. But as time passed, he began to see in the engine a possible source of income and also a way of distinguishing himself from other men.

Different factors had led these four men to become involved with the engine and different factors were similarly at work in leading them to continue with their development of the invention. Yet there was in addition a common denominator. All were keen to build a complete fully functioning machine as quickly as possible. However, various obstacles were to intervene in the achievement of this goal. Müller had such difficulties in selling his universal calculating machine that he never got round to the second step that he had proposed − the building of a difference engine. His ideas did not advance beyond the drawing board. The reasons for this may simply have been financial but he was perhaps never convinced of the utility of the table machine and was disappointed by the negative reaction to his publicity campaign in 1786. Babbage for his part, began modestly with a working model. He might have been satisfied with this but instead he wished to make a better printing machine. Unlike Müller, he was met by the opposite reaction. The utility of the engine was recognized and he received money to carry out the development work. Soon the modest model was left far behind and Babbage was dreaming of making the perfect engine. But this aim was never achieved. Instead, Babbage moved on to a new engine − the Analytical Engine, without ever succeeding in carrying his ideas into practice. Georg and Edvard built a prototype but their circumstances did not allow them immediately to build a fully functioning machine as they had wished. Eventually they had the possibility of building a better prototype, as they called it. They never lost sight of the idea of a practical machine and by means of various compromises, they at last achieved their goal, nearly seventy years after Müller.

At this point it would be pertinent to consider Charles Babbage's engine and the question of why he failed to complete it. Since I believe that there are misconceptions concerning the project, this matter will be dealt with rather thoroughly.

A very common view which is still repeated by several eminent scholars, is that Babbage "was ahead of his time". By this they presumably mean not only that the Analytical Engine is in retrospect the modern digital computer in mechanical form, but more generally that Babbage's ideas were too daring and speculative for his contemporaries. Yet even if this latter contention were true, it would not mean that it must inevitably lead to failure. A generalization of this kind says very little. Some, therefore, go one step further and try to make their view more precise by reference to the state of technology at that time.

> "His [Babbage's] ideas were eminently sound and it was only the backwardness of light-engineering and instrument-making techniques [. . .] which robbed him of the success he deserved."[1]

Dubbey puts it a little differently:

> "It was [. . .] a time in which precision in mechanical engineering was certainly not of a high enough order to make his own very elaborate engines a viable proposition."[2]

In a similar manner, Collier says that the Difference Engine "was pushing at the technical capabilities of the day, and thus became an expensive and protracted failure".[3] The economic historian Nathan Rosenberg, who has also taken an interest in Babbage, argues that:

> "Babbage's failure to complete his ingenious scheme was due to the inability of contemporary British metal-working to deliver the components which were indispensable to the machine's success. People like da Vinci and Babbage were, to use the popular phrase, 'far ahead of their time'."[4]

What exactly is meant by these statements, is rather unclear. Do they mean Babbage's work was held back because he had to improve existing workshop technology, before he was able to get on with the main project? Or do they mean that he failed to do just this, and thus as a result was prevented from bringing the project to completion? It should be noted that this kind of view is not simply a later interpretation. Babbage himself had the following to say:

> "When the first idea of contriving mechanical means for the calculation of all classes of astronomical and arithmetical tables occurred to

me, I contented myself with making simple drawings, and with forming a small model of a few parts. But when I understood it to be the wish of the Government that a larger engine should be constructed, a very serious question presented itself for consideration, namely: Is the present state of the art of making machinery sufficiently advanced to enable me to execute the multiplied and highly complicated movements required for the Difference Engine?

After examining all the resources of existing workshops, I came to the conclusion that, in order to succeed, it would become necessary to advance the art of construction itself."[5]

In order to evaluate such explanations which blame the backwardness of contemporary technology, it is useful to examine the facts of the matter. Let me present a few examples of complicated machines that had already seen the light of day. For example, consider what had been accomplished in clock-making, which was already highly developed by the beginning of the 1820's. Exceedingly complicated clocks had been built from the 18th century onwards, see Fig. 93. Other examples are the famous marine chronometers of the Englishman, John Harrison, invented for the purpose of precise navigation (the mechanical method), and the clocks of the Swiss craftsman, Ferdinand Berthoud.[7] Some of these clocks contained such technically sophisticated features as bimetallic devices to compensate for variations in temperature.[8] Many 18th century clocks had

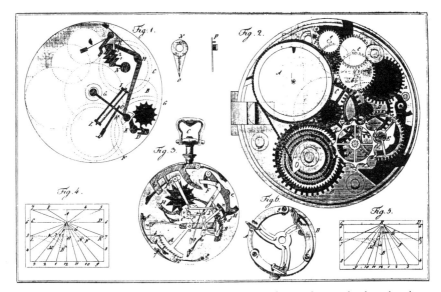

Fig. 93 Exceedingly complicated clocks, like these ones from a German book on horology, had been made from the 18th century onwards. Despite the scale factor, they involved the same technology and unconventional ideas that were necessary for the making of the Difference Engine No. 1. Drawing taken from Johann Henrich Poppe's Praktisches Handbuch für Uhrmacher (Leipzig 1810).

another simpler property that makes them of interest in connection with the difference engine, namely the fact that they contained parts with complicated shapes that had been designed to solve advanced technical problems. It might be objected that clocks were most often made in a much smaller format than the difference engine, but the technology and the unconventional ideas involved were common to both, despite the scale factor. Another example of a complicated shape on a larger scale is given by the ornamental lathes from the 17th and 18th centuries.

But it was not simply a question of complicated designs and unconventional ideas. Precision was also a feature of technology before 1820. From the middle of the 18th century onwards, instrument makers had managed to make theodolites, scales and many other instruments with high surface finish and fine tolerances, even although their tools were simple. For example, the Englishman James Short made several different telescopes, one of which, dating from 1764, is on display in the Science Museum, London. It has an extremely fine surface finish, especially when one recalls that probably this was achieved mainly by filing and polishing by hand. A larger telescope, the Shuckburgh Equatorial, of Jesse Ramsden, dating from the year 1791 is also exhibited in the same museum, and once again the quality of the workmanship is very high, see Fig. 94. Ramsden's circular dividing engine from 1763, is another example. Machine tools, like Henry Maudslay's bench lathe from 1810, which was produced in many examples, is also characterized by its high precision and surface finish. Rather than give additional examples of the available level of manufacturing technology, I suggest that the reader should pay a visit to any of the larger museums of science and technology in the world. Superbly made machines had been made before Babbage's time. It may be admitted that none of the examples I have quoted have quite the same quality of workmanship as the Difference Engine No. 1. Probably that level was never achieved before Babbage. But that is not the important point. What is important is that precision machines of very high quality, several of which contained complicated and ingenious ideas, had been made before the year 1820.

It follows that it will not do to speak blithely about some "backwardness of light-engineering and instrument-making techniques", or the "inability of contemporary British metal-working", as the crucial reason for Babbage's failure. Nor can one say that technology was not "of high enough order". On the other hand (and this is my point), what is true, is that contemporary engineering techniques were inadequate when it came to satisfying the demands that Babbage made.

Since it is thus impossible to blame contemporary technology and methods of production for Babbage's failure, the explanation must be sought elsewhere.

Is it, for instance, conceivable that Babbage failed because of shortage of time? The work on the Difference Engine No. 1 proceeded from the autumn of 1823 until the spring of 1833. For a period of approximately two years, it was abandoned. In other words, about eight years were spent on the development and design of the engine. Given that in addition to Babbage and Clement, many "first class" workmen were engaged on the project — in 1827 there were 8 workmen and an additional draughtsman involved — it will not do to put the blame on lack of time.[9] The latter, like the insufficency of the government's successive grants, was not in itself enough to explain Babbage's failure, which had another more profound cause.

Let me go right to the central issue. A major reason for Babbage's difficulties was that he was not an engineer. He lacked any such training when he first conceived the idea of the difference engine and it was only in the years that followed that he built up his knowledge of engineering matters. In section 1.2, his lack of experience of design was pointed out (30,000 types, rods instead of wheels etc.). Most scholars have ignored this fact and Hyman who without stopping to reflect upon his description, speaks of a "creative engineer of Babbage's calibre", is only the latest in a long line of authors to do so.[10] Babbage, however, maintained that he was not "a professional Engineer".[11] I believe that it was his uncertainty about the technical side of the project which made him nervous and ill when the thing began to get under way. From that moment onwards, he was dependent on trained mechanics and the skills of engineers.

In November 1871, an obituary of Charles Babbage appeared in the journal *Nature*. The author who otherwise extolled Babbage's versatile contributions, drew attention to two aspects of the deceased mathematician's character which had passed unnoticed:

"He was essentially one who began and did not complete.[12]

In saying this, the obituary author had in mind not simply the calculating machines but Babbage's writings as well. Several of Babbage's books were "generally incomplete sketches" — a description I am inclined to agree with.[13] According to the author, the reason for Babbage's many uncompleted endeavours, was that:

"His very failures arose from no want of industry or ability, but from excess of resolution that his aims should be at the very highest."[14]

I would interpret these assertions to mean that Charles Babbage was a man who embarked on a new scheme with the highest hopes and the greatest ambitions only to discover after some time that it did not live up to his expectations. Already eleven months before he had received the first grant towards the difference engine, he was writing to Herschel "I begin to be sick of the machine...".

The same day that Babbage met the Chancellor of the Exchequer and received word that the Government had decided to support the project, he wrote to Herschel:

"as I have liberal people to deal with I should not be annoyed about pence and the particular mode in which I may think it right to distribute them, and I shall, I hope, be able to bring the thing to perfection, or at least to a good practicable working state."[15]

It was his wish "to bring the thing to perfection" that was to become the project's motto.

The first scholar in modern times to have drawn attention to Babbage's perfectionism, is Collier.[16] Collier has also come to the conclusion that the errors in the tables only played a part in the initial stage of the difference engine's development, a matter which I have touched upon earlier.[17] Collier formulates his conclusion as follows:

"It is clear that Babbage does not fit this picture of the conventional technologist. Certainly he did not invent his calculating machines for profit, or to solve some practical problem; rather he found the process of inventing them to be its own reward, as a purely intellectual exercise. To be sure, it was the unsatisfactory character of manually calculating and checking mathematical tables that first directed his attention to the desirability of machines to do the job; but once he began considering them, their perfection became an end in itself, and the tables from which he had begun were no longer important. Of course, the Difference Engine was interesting only because it could actually calculate tables, but this was more a theoretical than a practical point."[18]

I find Collier's line of argument highly plausible.[19] However, I would like to develop it further. I shall do this in two ways, first by providing more evidence to substantiate the thesis that Babbage was indeed a perfectionist who attempted to apply scientific and theoretical methods to everything he encountered (for neither Collier nor anyone else has really provided such evidence), and second by developing and refining his line of argument.[20] The fundamental reason for the failure of the difference engine project was Babbage's perfectionism.

Let me begin with the machine itself. The Difference Engine No. 1 is the most convincing proof of this striving after perfection. It was compact, reliable and built with the utmost precision; in actual fact, it was too compact, too reliable and embodied too much precision! By going to extremes in these matters, the end result achieved was of quite unnecessarily high quality and as a consequence, there were major design and construction problems. The various components were packed together in the machine as tightly as possible. Such compactness was completely unnecessary and it was a waste of time to make special efforts to achieve it. The safety systems and the large scale chosen for the components provided unnecessarily high reliability when adequate reliability could have been obtained by means of fewer and simpler, smaller scale mechanisms. The approach chosen entailed further difficulties in design and construction.[21] Finally, consider the question of precision. The whole engine − including the purely decorative details on the columns − was made to an accuracy of 0.025 − 0.05 mm. There was no technical reason for building the entire machine with such accuracy.

Secondly, it was Babbage's mechanical notation, that theoretical tool to aid design which he had devised especially for the difference engine, which was the underlying cause of the difference engine's compactness and complexity. According to Babbage, the notation contributed to a better design solution by compressing the mechanical motions involved so that in practice a faster machine resulted, where the mechanisms in question had several functions. In my view, this resulted not in a better, but in a more complex and therefore more problematic and expensive solution. In addition the development of the notation took up valuable time that might instead have been devoted to the design work on the engine. I am of the opinion that the notation was one of Babbage's theoretical recreations and it is illuminating that this system of design for which he, on innumerable occasions, tried to win support, met with virtually no response from either scientists or engineers.[22] His wholehearted belief in theory is evident from the fact that he arranged for the notation for the Scheutz engine (which had been prepared by his son), to be exhibited at the Paris Exposition of 1855 in order to explain the operation of the engine, even although the engine itself was on display.[23]

A third illustration of Babbage's perfectionism is that he compiled a "perfect" table of logarithms, while at the same time at great cost to the government he proceeded to build the only solution to the negative effect of the human factor on table production.

Fourthly, his exaggerated experiment concerning the readability of numerical tables which involved tests with 150 different colours (including black ink on black paper) is an incontrovertible proof of perfectionism.

The fact that Babbage had initially only limited knowledge of engineering made him, as I have already observed, dependent upon the technical skills of others, or to be exact upon the skills of Joseph Clement. Both Babbage and Clement together must have been involved in developing the difference engine. Babbage must have come with various ideas perhaps sound in theory, which then had to be approved or dismissed as unworkable in practice by Clement. The construction of the large table engine presupposed this kind of close cooperation. The skilled men in the workshop must have had their part to play too; wars are not won by generals alone.

The way the design work appears to have been organized, reveals how both Clement and Babbage made their own particular contribution to the project. Babbage set out his proposals by means of sketches and his mechanical notation. Clement on the other hand employed his skill as a

Fig. 94 Superbly made machines had been made before Babbage's time. The photograph shows only one of them, the Shuckburgh Equatorial, made by Jesse Ramsden in 1791. Photograph by courtesy of the Trustees of the Science Museum, London.

draughtsman to prepare proper drawings and specifications. Such technical drawings were unusual. As in the case of the mechanical notation, the preparation and use of accurate technical drawings was rather rare and foreign to ordinary practice. The evolution from sketch via notation and drawing to the finished component, contrasted vividly with the traditional method of going from prototype to finished machine by trial and error. Today the use of technical drawings is standard practice. But at the time, it is not impossible that this novel and more theoretical approach in design, merely added to the difficulties to be surmounted.

The relations between Babbage and Clement have been the subject of some discussion. When difficulties arose about financing the project, Babbage turned against Clement. The latter was accused of profiteering and of trying to take possession of the tools which he had developed for the engine's construction. Both these charges proved to be unfounded: his bills had been scrutinized by experts and Clement had a legal right to all the machines which he had made.[24]

In the light of Babbage's failure and his attack on Clement, Clement has come in for a good deal of criticism, almost all of it devoid of any factual foundation.[25] Hyman, for example, speaks of "Clement's bloody-mindedness" and "extortionate profits".[26] This common complaint has contributed to the view that it was Clement who was to blame for Babbage's failure.

I should like to defend Clement by looking at the whole matter from a different perspective. Consider the following passage from Smiles:

264

"On one occasion Mr. Brunel of the Great Western Railway called upon him [Clement] to ask if he could supply him with a superior steam-whistle for his locomotives, the whistles which they were using giving forth very little sound. Clement examined the specimen brought by Brunel, and pronounced it to be 'mere tallow-chandler's work'. He undertook to supply a proper article, and after his usual fashion he proceeded to contrive a machine or tool for the express purpose of making steam-whistles. They were made and supplied, and when mounted on the locomotive the effect was indeed 'screaming'. They were heard miles off, and Brunel, delighted, ordered a hundred. But when the bill came in, it was found that the charge made for them was very high — as much as 40 l. [£] the set. The company demurred at the price, — Brunel declaring it to be six times more than the price they had before been paying. 'That may be'; rejoined Clement, 'but mine are more than six times better. You ordered a first-rate article and you must be content to pay for it'. The matter was referred to an arbitrator, who awarded the full sum claimed. Mr. Weld mentions a similar case of an order which Clement received from America to make a large screw of given dimensions 'in the best possible manner', and he accordingly proceeded to make one with the greatest mathematical accuracy. But his bill amounted to some houndreds of pounds, which completely staggered the American, who did not calculate on having to pay more than 20 l. [£] at the utmost for the screw. The matter was, however, referred to arbitrators, who gave their decision, as in the former case, in favour of the mechanic."[27]

Joseph Clement's speciality was a tough job requiring the greatest accuracy. It is quite obvious that the price he took for his precision work was not inconsiderable. Clement was not "bloody-minded". Babbage knew from the outset that the difference engine would involve "a very considerable expense" as he had noted in the letter to Sir Humphry Davy. Babbage certainly must have had the difference engine in mind when he added to the third edition of *Economy* the following passage:

"There are, however, many cases in which machines or tools must be made, where economical production is not the most important object. Whenever it is required to produce a few articles, — parts of machinery, for instance, which must be executed with the most rigid accuracy or be perfectly alike, — it becomes nearly impossible to fulfil this condition, even with the aid of the most skilful hands. In such circumstances it is necessary to make tools expressly for the purpose, although those tools should, as frequently happens, cost more in constructing than the things they are destined to make."[28]

Given that eight to ten skilled men were employed on the engine for a period of eight years and knowing that Clement could make some ten pounds a day from his planing machine alone, the sum of 17,000 pounds cannot be considered extortionate. Moreover, it is not known if all this money went only to Clement.[29] I also believe that it was just because Clement was famed for his precision work that Babbage chose him. Babbage must have ordered a "first-rate article".

But can one really know how far Babbage himself was the cause of the failure of the project? What about Clement's role? My thesis is that the mechanical notation, the multicoloured and ordinary logarithm tables are three independent examples of Babbage's perfectionism and his theoretical leanings. The compactness of the engine which was a direct consequence of the notation shows how these traits of character became embodied in the machine. On the other hand, the engine's reliability was the product of the design exertions of three men — Müller, Babbage and Clement. The precision, finally, was the hallmark of Clement's workmanship. Babbage was directly to blame for the failure of his project. At the same time, Babbage and Clement formed an unhappy combination where Babbage's perfectionism was reinforced by Clement's efforts in the same direction.

Before leaving Charles Babbage, I would like to develop some remarks made in section 2.2 (pp. 109–110) concerning his own view of the difference engine. In part, he looked upon it simply as a typical machine which mechanized difficult and monotonous manual work, but he also saw it in a more abstract and visionary way, which is reflected in Lardner's article and which must have puzzled and intrigued its readers. This latter almost metaphysical approach which provides further insight into Babbage's personality and his attitude to his engines, receives full expression in his book *The Ninth Bridgewater Treatise: A Fragment*.[30]

The Earl of Bridgewater bequeathed 8,000 pounds for the publication of a collection of books bearing his name, which dealt with arguments for natural religion.[31] Eight authors were chosen to carry out this assignment. Babbage was not among them but deciding to present the public with his views on religion and science, the mathematician published in 1837 at his own expense and initiative *The Ninth Bridgewater Treatise*.

Unlike several of his contemporaries, Babbage believed that scientific research and progress were important for man's understanding of religion. Science simply provided further proofs of God's existence and it was by studying God's work that such proofs were obtained. Babbage hoped that his book would provide the reader with greater insight into the Creator's power and omniscience.[32]

In his book, Babbage used the difference engine as a principal illustration in a number of different connections. In the first example, the reader was invited to consider a calculating machine which computed a sequence consisting of the integers 1,2,3 etc.[33] If anyone studied the wheels on a machine working in this fashion over a long period of time, he would inductively infer that the machine would always compute a sequence whose terms increased by one at a time. But suddenly, suggested Babbage, suppose that the machine began to calculate quite a different sequence. It would appear that the law which had up to that point regulated the process had been replaced by another. This new law could in a similar fashion be replaced by another at some point and so on. Yet the difference between the different laws (sequences) was only apparent. Each was the consequence of the previous one. Yet the observer would not be able to predict when the change from one law to the next, would take place.

Babbage now made a comparison between the difference and analytical engine. In the case of the difference engine, its inventor had to intervene to bring about the changes whereas in the case of the analytical engine these had been programmed into the machine from the start.[34] Babbage then asked the following question:

> "Which of these two engines would, in the reader's opinion, give the higher proof of skill in the contriver? He cannot for a moment hesitate in pronouncing that that on which, after its original adjustment, no superintendence was required, displayed far greater ingenuity than that which demanded, at every change in its law, the intervention of its contriver."[35]

Natural phenomena, according to Babbage, obey the same laws as his machines.[36] The laws are invariant for very long periods and then completely alter character:

> "In turning our views from these simple consequences of the juxtaposition of a few wheels, it is impossible not to perceive the parallel reasoning, as applied to the mighty and far more complex phenomena of nature."[37]

Since Babbage adopted a pre-Darwinian view of evolution, he was able to illustrate how new species suddenly emerged. He explained the great geological variations undergone by the earth in analogy with the workings of the calculating machine. From the very beginning, God had programmed all the changes which animals, plants and nature in general would experience in the course of the history of the earth.

> "Yet all [laws] submitted to some still higher condition, which has stamped the mark of unity on the series, and points to the conclusion that the minutest changes, as well as those transitions apparently the most abrupt, have throughout all time been the necessary, the inevitable consequences of some more comprehensive law impressed on matter at the dawn of its existence."[38]

The calculating engine was not simply a means of understanding the grandeur and foresight displayed in Creation; it also functioned as a link between God's work and that of Charles Babbage. In *The Ninth Bridge-*

water Treatise his engine became a working miniature of the universe, the product of the most remarkable inventor.

Once again making use of the example of a calculating machine, Babbage was also able to explain the occurrence of miracles.[39] If after computing a very long sequence of squares, the machine should suddenly compute a cube only to return immediately to computing squares as before, it would have thereby provided the observer with a mechanical counterpart to a miracle in nature. But both these types of deviation from the natural order of things had been programmed from the beginning.

Towards the end of the treatise, a special type of miracle is discussed, namely a dead man being brought back to life again.[40] In countering David Hume's argument against the occurrence of this and other miracles, Babbage once more resorted to his engine to illustrate his point. Man's belief that a dead man cannot be brought back to life, is based on personal experience and upon the assumed fact that no-one since the beginning of creation has come back to life again. Babbage then proceeded to quantify the argument and calculated that since the dawn of creation some 200,000,000,000 had been born and died. Babbage wrote:

"Such, then, according to Hume, are the odds against the truth of the miracle; that is to say, it is found from experience, that it is about two hundred thousand millions to one against a dead man having been restored to life."[41]

Babbage then asked the reader to consider the case where his calculating engine was set to reckon the integers 1, 2, 3, 4, 5 etc. Every integer could be taken to represent a member of mankind from creation onwards. In order to give weight to his argument, Babbage multiplied the foregoing number (two hundred thousand millions) by 100 million, thus giving a total of $20 \cdot 10^{19}$.[42] Now (said Babbage), imagine the calculating engine computing in the specified manner up to this figure and then suddenly producing the first and only exception to the previous pattern of performance.

"What would have been the chances against the appearance of the excepted case, immediately prior to its occurence? It would have had, according to Hume, the evidence of all experience against it, with a force myriads of times more strong than that against any miracle."[43]

Such was Babbage's counterargument to Hume's thesis. Only about one point, the mathematician thought, the reader might entertain a doubt: had such an engine really been conceived? The answer was "yes"...

Although Babbage's probabilistic argument is open to discussion, *The Ninth Bridgewater Treatise* provides an insight into his views both about God and Science and about the difference and analytical engines.

Babbage's metaphysical view of his difference engine was no mere passing fancy but a deeply held conviction which influenced him for the rest of his life. In *Passages* (1864), he devoted a whole chapter to the question of miracles and at the end of the book, he wrote:[44]

> "The explanation which I gave of the nature of miracles in "The Ninth Bridgewater Treatise", published in May, 1837, has now stood the test of more than a quarter of a century, during which it has been examined by some of the deepest thinkers in many countries. Its adoption by those writers who have referred to it has, as far as my information goes, been unanimous".[45]

I shall now turn by way of comparison, to the question why Georg and Edvard Scheutz managed to complete their engine. For them, the difference engine was essentially a tool, which was utterly reliable and incapable of making human errors. At the same time, at least initially, both Georg and Edvard as printers were also impressed by the fact that the machine could mechanize the typesetting of tables which it had itself computed.

But both Georg and Edvard Scheutz were thoroughly practical in outlook. It was on practical matters that their main interest concentrated and Georg openly despised "mere theories". As far as they were concerned, the difference engine was a purely practical exercise.

Whereas Babbage had become involved with the table engine without possessing an adequate background in technical design, at least Georg Scheutz had considerable experience of engineering and invention. Babbage on the other hand, grasped the necessary mathematical aspects of the matter fully while the Scheutzes were totally ignorant in this domain. But although ignorant in their respective ways, neither the Englishman nor the Swedes were able to stop being interested in the idea, once it had been conceived.

Because of external circumstances, the Scheutzes were compelled to build their first engine in the form of a simple but complete prototype. They were never interested in the idea of producing a perfect engine. If Edvard had been as meticulous as Babbage, his first difference engine would not have been scarred by rough file marks as indeed it was. The engine would never have seen the light of day, given the inferior tools they had at their disposal. If Georg Scheutz had been a perfectionist, he would not have permitted Edvard to build the engine at home; he would have commissioned a workshop to do it. Since he lacked the means for this, as a perfectionist, he would have waited until he possessed the money to pursue matters in this way. Instead they tailored their requirements to fit what was feasible. In developing their ideas, they advanced tentatively by trial and error. It is probable that in the case of the first engine the Scheutzes made use only of rough sketches. Since they built the engine with a wooden frame, it was easy for them to make alterations if they made an error. They made alterations, they tacked on new pieces and they moved bits about during the course of the work. The design and development work was closely integrated with the actual work of construction. Whereas Babbage tried "to advance the art of construction itself" and to set new standards for engineering drawing, the Scheutzes devoted themselves single-mindedly to developing the engine itself.

Another factor which contributed to the success of the Scheutzes, was the good working relationship between both men. Unlike Babbage and Clement, father and son worked as a compact and harmonious team, united by love and a common interest in completing the engine.

Furthermore, when young Edvard began to make the difference engine in association with his father, he was able to give his imagination and his delight in invention free rein. Edvard's detailed solutions to engineering problems were unorthodox, because he was not hide-bound by traditions and rules as Clement and his men had been. (It is true that the inexperienced designer Babbage was similarly unorthodox but, due to the demands he made and the expectations he entertained, these unorthodox ideas invariably led to great design problems.) An obvious illustration of this is provided by the addition elements and their traps. Another characteristic feature of his approach was the low level of abstraction involved in the design of certain parts in the first engine. His youthful imagination, which was still basically uninfluenced by outside ideas, was an important ingredient in the success of the Scheutzes in finally building a complete difference engine.

The step from the first to the second engine was comparatively straightforward and was largely a question of scale. The underlying principles were clear and had been worked out in practice. At the same time, the second engine marked the Scheutzes' definitive success compared with Babbage. They had reached the common goal first − the complete, fully functioning difference engine.

To sum up, the Scheutzes were in no way theoreticians. They were engineers, the elder an autodidact and the younger a trained engineer. They formed a close working partnership in which Edvard played the role of the innovative constructor. The most important reason of all why the Swedes succeeded, was that their ambitions were more modest and more feasible.

This section has dealt with several aspects of the characters of the men involved. It is an account of how men with different social backgrounds, education and professions sought, for different reasons and with different methods, to achieve the same goal and to solve the same problem with the help of technology. There is still a further conclusion to be drawn from my analysis. I have no doubt whatsoever that if Müller had tried, he would have built the best difference engine, at least as far as the calculating unit goes.[46] Babbage's engine, apart from the printing unit and its cost, comes in second place. The Scheutz engine, although the printing unit deserves special mention, must be ranked third, suffering as it did from certain imperfections. Yet despite that, neither Babbage nor Müller in the end completed their engines. Paradoxically, it was the difference engine of Georg and Edvard Scheutz which finally attained a complete and fully functioning form, and it was their engine which was offered for sale as a practical device.

3.3 The Market — Why was the Scheutz engine not a commercial success?

Georg and Edvard Scheutz succeeded in building a complete, full scale difference engine and also managed to sell two examples of it. In practical terms, however, the difference engine was not a commercial success. It proved extremely difficult to sell and when it finally came to be used in Albany and London, it was employed for only a short time. Despite continuous efforts to sell several engines, there were no prospective buyers. Georg Scheutz, who had been forced to borrow money to finance the marketing operation including his son's residence abroad, found himself heavily in debt because of the financial failure of the engine. What had gone wrong?

During the nineteenth century, several men built difference engines and Babbage and Scheutz were only the first of those to do so. Lardner's article was read by another printer, namely Alfred Deacon in London. He was also fascinated by the idea and began to build a difference engine, probably along the lines suggested by Babbage. But Deacon's engine was never completed. It was intended to calculate with twenty digits and three differences. According to *Specimens*, where the engine is mentioned in a note, Deacon was unable to build a printing unit because of the costs involved.[1] Babbage asserted that Deacon built his engine solely "for his own satisfaction".[2]

There was also another Swede, Martin Wiberg, who was captivated by the idea of calculating tables with the use of machinery. His interest had been aroused by the articles in the Swedish press about the Scheutz engines. Wiberg built at least two complete difference engines, the first around 1860. They had the same mathematical capacity as the later engines of Scheutz but were only a tenth of the size (25 kg.). This was due to Wiberg's adoption of a more compact approach to design.

Just as in the case of the Scheutz engine, the Royal Academy of Sciences took steps to inform King Carl about Wiberg and his machine. This took place in March 1860. The Academy proposed a reward of 3,000 riksdaler riksmynt to Wiberg for the development of his difference engine. The King proposed raising this sum to 5,000 riksdaler and the Estate of Burghers in turn introduced a motion to increase this still more to 8,000 riksdaler. Once again as in the case of the Scheutz engine, the Burghers' motion was introduced during a current session of the Riksdag.

On this occasion − apart from certain objections from the Nobles − the Estates voted to pay 8,000 riksdaler riksmynt to Martin Wiberg for his difference engine. It was during the same Riksdag that Georg Scheutz was awarded his life pension.

In contrast with the Scheutzes, Wiberg was primarily interested in selling the tables produced by his machine, not in selling the machine itself. In other words, something very similar to Scheutz' idea for a press specially for the printing of tables, in 1837. But despite the fact that a company was formed for the production of tables and that several tables of interest were made, the machine was not a success and Wiberg was faced with severe economic problems. Just like the Scheutzes, he had difficulties in getting his machine to print neatly and this was a contributing factor to his lack of success.[3]

Wiberg's difference engine, which Babbage himself was able to see directly after the Exhibition in London in 1862, after it had apparently arrived too late to appear on show, is highly interesting from another angle.[4] It is a striking counterexample to Babbage's claim that he required to "advance the art of construction itself" in order to build a difference engine. Wiberg's machine, complete with printing unit, could in fact have been built with the simplest manual methods a hundred years before Difference Engine No. 1.[5]

In the 1870s, in America, George Barnard Grant built a difference engine. According to his own account, he came upon the idea for such a machine when calculating tables, but it was first when he got to know of Babbage's and Scheutz' engines, that he got down to business.[6] Grant's large machine sharply contrasted with Wiberg's design and weighed over a ton − a striking example of how technical development does not always lead to better results, even although there can be indirect "spin-off" effects; Grant's work on the machine led to the founding of the Grant Gear Company.[7] But despite the fact that Grant was technically successful and obviously intended to make several engines, his machine also failed commercially.[8]

Although the history of these later developments, particularly that of Martin Wiberg and his machine, is interesting in its own right, I shall not discuss it in more detail since it does not alter my general thesis − that it was not only the Scheutzes who had difficulty in making a commercial success of the difference engine.

Writing in one of his magazines in 1833, Georg Scheutz had this to say of Babbage's engine: − "and even if the larger and more complete engine should later on remain the only example of its kind, it would suffice for the needs of the whole world".[9] This was to be his view of the engine for many years to come. One was enough. Babbage's engine was not a commercial product in the sense that it could or was intended to be sold in large numbers. On the other hand, the stereotypes which were produced, could be copied and sold all over the world. Yet somewhere along the line, Scheutz changed his opinion on this matter, perhaps at the same time that he was struck by the idea of making his machine small and portable. He suddenly began to see a potential large market for the difference engine and spoke of it as "a necessity wherever there is an observatory, a university or a press dealing with mathematical works."[10] When Bergström was almost finished with the second engine, it was time for the marketing to begin.

In the business of selling the machine, Edvard was the central figure. From November 1853, he devoted the next seven years almost exclusively to trying to find customers for the engine. He wrote letters, invitations and composed pamphlets. He travelled about with the machine and demonstrated its method of operation. He kept in contact with interested parties and was responsible for seeking and renewing the patents. But he was not alone. Gravatt, Donkin, Sparre and not least Babbage, made up a pressure and sales group of many talents. Because of his relatively youthful years and his lack of a scientific degree or hereditary title, Edvard Scheutz encountered various problems in reaching potential customers on a more personal level. In this respect, his friendship with Babbage and the others, was extremely useful.

I have used the word marketing about these men's attempts to sell the engine and there is no doubt that it was a marketing operation in today's sense of that term. There was a sales organization of five men, with Edvard at the head as decision-maker. Five sales strategies in various combinations were followed. The first consisted of personal contacts, with information about the engine by word of mouth. The second was goal-directed marketing with information in the form of a personal letter to potential customers. The third involved advertising in the form of articles in the daily press. The fourth made use of meticulously designed brochures in various languages, reaching its high point in *Specimens of Tables*. The fifth and last was the public exhibition of the difference engine at various strategically important places. All this was carried out in three different languages − Swedish, French and English. Strategy five was chosen in England and France, while the others were adopted internationally. As the distribution list for *Specimens* shows (see p. 379 in the appendix) great pains were taken to circulate the book and related information first and foremost to observatories and scientific institutions throughout the world.[11] In short, the marketing campaign for the difference engine was well thought out and well executed by the capable men involved. Bad marketing was not the reason for the failure of the Scheutzes.

In the final analysis, it was the demand for numerical tables which determined the market. Three types of table were primarily suited for machine production − the mathematical, the astronomical and the statistical. In contrast to the trade tables of various kinds, these more comprehensive tables involved numbers to several decimal places and required greater accuracy during calculation and printing. Moreover the two former types of table sold in large numbers of editions.

The potential purchasers of the difference engine were principally the institutions which produced tables rather than private individuals. Of the mathematical, astronomical and statistical tables, the latter catered for the smallest market. The reason for this was that social statistical publications like the *English Life Table* were at that time rather uncommon, compared to the large numbers of mathematical and astronomical tables that were produced.

Throughout the whole history of the difference engine, the mathematical tables were of central importance. "How easy it would be by this means to correct and still more to calculate the larger tables of logarithms", wrote Müller at an early stage. For Babbage, the exertions of Prony and others in producing mathematical tables all provided convincing examples of how the difference engine could have made a superior contribution. Since Georg Scheutz, like the majority of those who had to carry out calculations in the course of their work, was best acquainted with logarithmic tables, he believed that these would constitute the primary field of application of the difference engine as regards mathematical computations. However, the market for machine-computed and typeset mathematical tables was in reality not at all as great as Georg and Edvard Scheutz supposed.

Early on, sceptical voices had been heard about the difference engine. In 1822, Wollaston had remarked caustically:

"All this is very pretty but I do not see how it can be rendered productive."

Babbage's comment on this remark was that with such encouragement, it was not to be wondered at, if one began to have doubts oneself. The following year, John Croker, Secretary of the Admiralty, expressed his view on the matter:

"At present indeed it is more a matter of curiosity than use, and I believe some good judges doubt whether it ever can be of any."

Shortly afterwards, Babbage's friend, Francis Baily noted in a letter to him that:

"A celebrated mathematician, who has seen your machine, says that it would take as much time to make calculations [as] with the pen!!! You see how difficult it is to lead the public."[12]

Who this mathematician was, is unknown. Airy, the Astronomer Royal, did not entertain a high opinion of Babbage's difference engine. In 1837, he is said to have declared that the machine was "humbug" and five years later he described it as "worthless". Sir Robert Peel was also unconvinced of its value. Peel had a sound knowledge of mathematics and thus was in a position to make an informed judgement of Babbage's work.

The following underlying facts about the numerical tables, although occasionally noted during the 19th century itself, have been entirely ignored by the scholars who have written about the difference engines. *First* of all, the most important mathematical tables were the standard ones for logarithms and the trigonometric functions. *Secondly*, the trigonometrical tables of Rheticus (1596), Pitiscus (1613) and Vlacq (1633) were computed to between ten and fifteen decimal places and remained standard for the natural values of the trigonometrical functions throughout the three subsequent centuries. They were not surpassed in accuracy until 1915.[13] *Thirdly*, Vlacq's table of logarithms (1628) reckoned to an accuracy of ten decimal places, was to become similarly the authority in its respective area for an equally long period.[14] *Fourthly*, and perhaps not least important, after all the colossal calculation work of these pioneers, trigonometric and logarithmic tables were no longer computed afresh — *they were merely copied*. For example Michael Taylor did not calculate his comprehensive collection of tables (1792) from scratch. Instead, he made use of Vlacq's *Trigonometria Artificialis* (1633) which were calculated to ten decimal places, to interpolate and to round off to seven decimal places.[15] This was the *standard procedure*. The authors of books of tables invariably mentioned in the introduction that they had checked the values in their tables with such-and-such authoritative works. This was certainly a way to keep the number of errors down, but it was often no more than a polite excuse for the fact that their tables were a modified version of some previous compilation.[16] If the foreword to Babbage's own logarithm table (1827) is read carefully, it is clear that he did the same. His starting points were the tables of Callet (1814) and von Vega (1794) which he in fact copied and rounded off to seven decimals.[17]

To some extent, there was nothing wrong with this method. It was obviously completely unnecessary to calculate a table of logarithms from scratch, when this had been done long before; it would have been tantamount to writing out a new manuscript when a new edition of a book was to be published. Indeed one of the reasons why new sets of tables were published, was precisely because an earlier edition had sold out. Another reason for the publication of tables was a desire to win scientific merit on the part of their authors. Naturally not all the tables were copied. This was impossible when, for example, a new function was to be computed. But as soon as this had been accomplished, with sufficient accuracy, it too could be copied. Let me conclude with a remark of Glaisher:

> "It is thus seen that, with the exception of the TABLES DU CADASTRE, and the second half of Mr. SANG'S table, every one of the hundreds of the [logarithmic] tables that have appeared has been copied from BRIGGS or VLACQ".[19]

It is indeed interesting that Babbage's main example — *Les Tables de Cadastres* was an exception.[20]

In 1844, the astronomer Nils Haqvin Selander wrote that "Logarithmic, trigonometric and other tables, which are purely mathematical in character, and which do not rely on information from experimental results or observation, have already been computed with such accuracy that they leave little to desire".

Ten years later, the scientists Stokes, Willis, Wheatstone and Miller inspected the Scheutz engine and presented their views in a report. They observed that the machine could be mainly used for producing mathematical tables, but noted at the same time that standard tables for logarithms and trigonometric functions had long been available. However, according to the report the engine could be employed in part to calculate and print other tables and in part to produce new editions of already existing tables, since it was both rapid and correct in its operation.[21]

Could all these men be wrong? Wollaston, Croker, Peel and Airy with their scepticism and decided views about the utility of the engine; Glaisher, De Morgan, Fletcher and Comrie, among the foremost experts on numerical tables and their history; Selander, Stokes, Willis, Wheatstone and Miller, the respective representatives of Swedish and British science?[22]

My answer is no. All the major important mathematical tables had already been computed once and for all, a couple of hundred years before Babbage sent his letter to Sir Humphry Davy. Moreover since errors in these standard works had been noted down and collected and had become generally known through errata lists, reviews etc., more reliable tabular values were available than ever before.[23] Taking accuracy as one's watchword, it was possible to compile an error-free table based on previous tables and indeed Charles Babbage himself had demonstrated this. Fletcher and his coauthors support this with a more general conclusion: − "It is true that by the middle of the last century [19th] the slow and laborious process of continual re-editing had enabled the ordinary seven-decimal table of common logarithms of five-figure numbers to be cleared of error, but this was a case in which special efforts had been made."[24] Thus the tables, which Georg and Edvard Scheutz believed were to form one of the main tasks of the difference engine, had already been provided.

When Georg and Edvard Scheutz and their first commercial engine arrived in London in 1854, they were undoubtedly full of pride and hope. It must therefore have been something of a disappointment for them to read in Stokes' report that the most important mathematical tables had long since been computed. If, in addition, they were aware that Selander had had the same opinion, they must have begun to wonder. Stokes suggested in his report that the engine could be employed to produce new editions of already existing tables, or to put it in the words of the committee, that it "would be very useful even for the mere reprinting of old tables."[25] In other words, the focus of attention shifted to the printing unit of the engine.

The Scheutz engine could print at most eight digits including decimals. There could be no question of surpassing the ten decimal tables from the 16th and 17th centuries. Apart from the fact that the common five to seven place tables (like those of Babbage) in everyday use were more or less error-free, there was also another new factor to be taken into account. This was stereotyping, which by 1854 had long been a natural component of the printer's trade. Stereotyping meant that once a table had been set correctly, then it would thereafter remain free from error. Babbage had stereotyped his tables. The stereotypes were preserved, could be copied easily by casting and could be used for subsequent editions. Stereotypes were used to print the German and Hungarian editions of Babbage's table which illustrates the not unimportant fact that numerical tables were international products. Only the foreword required to be translated and the idea that one difference engine could in principle suffice to supply the whole world's demand for such tables, is of course based on just this circumstance.[26]

But the Scheutz engine, nevertheless, had a rather large mathematical capacity. Since it was able to cope with eight digits, it could be used for example to reprint Babbage's table of logarithms. Stokes, Willis, Wheatstone and Miller had considered that the main advantage of the engine, was to be found in the fact that it "could calculate and print more quickly than a good compositor could set the types, and that without risk of error."[27] Unfortunately this was not quite true.

In *Specimens* it is stated that the five figure table of logarithms (from 1 to 10,000) which forms the kernel of the book, had been calculated in 75 hours. The speed of operation during this calculation was stated to be 120 results per hour. Preparing the machine was estimated to take two hours and a similar time was allocated to the calculation of the start values. In all, according to the authors, "seventy-nine or say eighty hours" were required.[28] If one wished to have more than five digits in the result, this was technically possible, but the calculations themselves were affected by this. As mentioned in section 1.3, the higher the order of difference that is available, the greater is the number of correct digits in the answer. If it is desired to have more correct digits in the answer, a shorter interval of interpolation has to be chosen. If a large number of correct digits is required, but the machine lacks higher order differences, this can still be accomplished by inserting new start values more often. The Scheutz engine lacked high-order differences. Its four differences entailed not only more manual work in the form of calculation and setting and resetting the machine, but it naturally also affected the speed of the engine.

It was claimed in *Specimens* that the engine calculated 120 results in an hour. However, as was shown in section 3.1, it was humanly impossible to crank the engine continuously at this rate. In my view, 63 results per hour is a more realistic figure. This would mean that it would take — or indeed took — at least 142 hours simply to crank forth the five digit table, leaving aside calculation of start values and setting up the machine. If an eight place table was required, one was forced − in order to avoid computational errors − to compile the table in shorter intervals. The five digit table was computed with an interval of 400 logarithms per setting, in order to ensure its correctness.[29] A similar eight digit tablewould require, assuming the same safety margin, that only 74 values were calculated per setting.[30] This entailed that instead of the 23 settings needed in the case of the five figure table, 122 settings were necessary in making an eight figure table.[31] Still more serious was the fact that this meant an increase in the amount of manual calculation involved by a factor of at least five.[32] As I set out to show in section 1.3, it was the calculation of the start values that was the really time-consuming and laborious process. It cannot possibly be true that two hours sufficed for the logarithm table in *Specimens*, bearing in mind that 15 figure numbers were involved in the manual calculations. To reprint an eight figure table with the help of the Scheutz engine, would have required in total at least 243 hours of continuous work.[33] It is difficult to say how long it would have taken to set the logarithm table as it appears in *Specimens,* but with eight figures instead. It suffices to remark that in the case of a normal table the engine could not "calculate and print more quickly than a good compositor could set the types."[34]

In other words, there was little to be gained by reprinting an old standard table with the machine.[35] The table was already computed; the errors in large measure had been eliminated and the text had been preserved for future editions on stereotypes. If one decided to reprint a table making use of the engine, it would have meant a considerable amount of work in computing the start values needed before the subsequent machine computation could get under way. Given that the table was already in existence, this work seems quite unnecessary. If one allowed a printer to reset the table, there was time left over for careful proofreading, before and after, and in addition the result, from the standpoint of lay-out, was quite independent of the limitations of the engine.[36]

Stokes and his colleagues judged the design of the engine to be good, noting that it worked with "the greatest freedom and smoothness" and they thought it unlikely to malfunction provided proper care was taken.[37] The second factor (in addition to the speed of operation) which the committee drew attention to, was that the engine calculated and printed "without the risk of error". As has already been made clear, the Scheutz engines were by no means error-free. Unfortunately they sometimes made mistakes in their computations. But Stokes and the others apparently did not know this.

Mathematically the Scheutz engine was limited. Georg and Edvard did not have the requisite knowledge to realise this. It was at least fortunate that Georg did not arrive in London with an engine operating with only one difference, as he had originally planned. Babbage's Difference Engine No. 1 with its six order of differences and 18 figures would have provided a possibility of superseding the great mathematical tables in accuracy. With its large number of differences and by making do with fewer start values, the work could have been carried out in a shorter time. In the beginning, however, even Babbage had believed that four differences were enough.

As far as the potential market for the engine was concerned, there was another fallacy in Scheutz' reasoning. There were in fact no institutions, whether universities or presses, which produced and printed mathematical tables. Scheutz seems to have realized early on that this was the case in Sweden. There were no conceivable purchasers quite simply because tables, whether mathematical or otherwise, were not regularly produced within the country. He knew little about the situation abroad, but he believed that there was a possible market there. If one looks at the history of numerical tables and examines the efforts of the Babylonians, Ptolemy, Maginus, Pitiscus, Napier, Briggs, Gunter, Kepler, Vlacq, Sherwin, Gardiner, Dodson, Schulze, Taylor, von Vega, Callet and Babbage, it is evident that nearly all the tables were produced by individuals. There were exceptions. The *Alphonsine Tables*, *Opus Palatinum* and *Les Tables de Cadastres* were among those best known. In these cases, it is possible to speak of a temporary institutionalization of the work and of state involvement in the production of tables of the kind which Babbage hoped to create with his difference engine. A more highly developed Scheutz engine would have fitted into such a scheme of things. The problem was, however, that such grand projects were extremely rare. A period of approximately 350 years separated the *Alphonsine Tables* and *Opus Palatinum*; and from the publication of the latter to *Les Tables de Cadastres* took another 190 years. Babbage's idea, however, was conceived only 35 years after Prony's work. Nearly all numerical tables had been produced by individuals, a circumstance which did not enhance the commercial possibilities of the engine. In fact, both Georg Scheutz and Martin Wiberg toyed with the − at first glance − sounder idea of retaining their respective engines and letting others print whatever mathematical tables they wanted, with the engines. But Wiberg's machine, which had the same low capacity as the Scheutz engine, demonstrated that this idea was not commercially well founded either.

According to Stokes' report, there was still another possibility, namely tht various other tables could be constructed by the Scheutz engine. In fact, it was to be the Dudley Observatory and the General Register Office, producers respectively of astronomical and statistical tables, that were to purchase the engine. It was just such institutions which Scheutz had really been aiming at.

On the subject of astronomical tables, Selander had maintained that "the improvement of astronomical, physical and similar tables depends primarily on access to more exact observational data".[38] Another astronomer who had raised doubts, was George Biddell Airy, the Director of the Greenwich Observatory. It has been said that Airy's harsh words about Babbage's engine were rooted in personal antagonism and lacked factual support.[39] I shall, however, show that Airy was opposed to difference engines in general. First of all, it should be noted that Airy was well aware how mathematical tables were normally constructed, since he had produced at least one himself. Glaisher said of it − "The table is improperly described as having been *computed* under the direction' &c: it is, of course, only a simple rearrangement."[40] In order to find out a little more about Airy's views on the table engine, let me return to September 1857.

When Edvard invited the British government to purchase the third engine, the authorities were placed in a position of having to obtain the approval of the scientific establishment. Lewis wrote to Airy for his opinion, requesting at the same time that "he [Airy] will favour this". Graham had suggested that as well as being employed at the General Register Office, the engine could also be of use at the Royal Observatory and the Nautical Almanac Office, since tables were compiled there. In his reply to Trevelyan, the Secretary of the Treasury, Airy expressed the view that these institutions were well suited to employing the difference engine.[41] But then he proceeded to discuss the pros and cons for the employment of the engine at each of the three institutions mentioned. He began with the Royal Observatory:

"The Machine would be entirely useless."[42]

His argument was that the engine required that the start values had to be computed "with the pen". Airy also had another reason which was linked to the fact that the engine was limited to computations employing at most four differences:

"During the twenty-two years in which I have been connected with the Royal Observatory, not a single instance has occurred in which there was a need for such calculations."[43]

Turning to the Nautical Almanac Office, Airy once more took up the point that in using the difference engine to calculate tables, a great amount of preparatory work "with the pen" was necessary to obtain the start values, which were to be fed into the machine. Despite the mechanization of addition, this preparatory work remained. He, therefore, was of the opinion that the engine would have no fruitful role at the named institution. However to check this, he had asked the Superintendent of the Nautical Almanac for his view of the matter. It was "clear and unhesitating":

"no advantage would be gained by the use of the Machine, and that he [the superintendent] would prefer the pen-computation of human computers, in the way in which it has hitherto been employed."[44]

280

A further reason why the engine would have no useful function at the Nautical Almanac Office, was that a simple labour-saving method was employed there. It consisted in a number of auxiliary tables and had been in use at the Nautical Almanac Office since 1832. It simplified the method of difference greatly, so that one needed to compute with only a single decimal place more than was needed in the result. To support his case, Airy sent Trevelyan a copy of the book describing the method.[45]

Lastly, Airy took up the proposal to use the Scheutz engine at the General Register Office. He accepted the advantages which Farr believed would benefit the institution, from having the use of the machine. According to Farr, it would save money, it could be used in recalculating older tables which was a common occurrence at the Office and it was also fast. Moreover Farr said that he had more confidence in tables which had been compiled by machine than in those done with the pen. Most of all, the machine would economize on manpower. It was on this basis that Airy supported the purchase of the engine. But he had reservations and vigorously continued to maintain that "pen and paper" calculations were both cheaper and more convenient in connection with proof-read stereotypes, than the use of a difference engine.

In Airy's opinion, the difference engine had no useful role to play at the three prominent institutions which had been proposed. These were not institutions that had been picked at random; they represented some of the most important areas of potential application for the engine − astronomy, navigation and statistics. In these institutions, tables had to be produced over a long length of time by manual methods and various refinements in these procedures had been introduced. Airy's counter-argument was threefold. *First* the machine only replaced part of the manual work and a great deal still remained; *second*, it was cheaper and more convenient to use the traditional methods and stereotype the proof-read manuscript than to employ a machine; *third*, he suggested that the Scheutz engine with only four differences, lacked the mathematical capacity to make it interesting to institutions other than perhaps the General Register Office. When the engine was set to work at Albany, this deficiency was also noted:

> "Our past experience has lead us to believe that such a machine would be greatly enhanced in value, by the addition of one or two more orders of differences; since in that case, a much longer series of numbers could be computed from one set of constants."[46]

It may be noted lastly that Airy, despite possible conservatism on his part, showed his impartiality by supporting the purchase and thereby allowing a difference engine to be tried out at a British government office. He was prepared to support such an experiment, because like Farr, he placed complete reliance on the engine's design. But as has been shown earlier in this book, it did, in fact, suffer from serious faults.

Airy's opinions had the support of other competent authorities in the field. Already in 1823, the Board of Longtitude had "doubted that the invention was likely to be practically useful to a degree to justify a grant of this nature" in commenting on the financing of Babbage's engine.[47] In France at the Imperial Observatory, Airy's colleague Urbain Jean Joseph Leverrier had rejected the engine for almost precisely the same reasons as Airy. Although, on one occasion in disagreement about the discovery of the planet Uranus, they were now, most probably quite independently of one another, agreed about the limited use of the difference engine. For these prominent astronomers, as well as for Selander, the engine's utility was nil.

But if this was the case, how did it come about that the Dudley Observatory in Albany purchased the engine? My answer is very different from the one given by Merzbach in her monograph on Scheutz where Benjamin Gould and the Dudley Observatory are seen as representing American progressiveness and receptiveness to new ideas, in contrast to Europe's conservative and uncomprehending reaction to the difference engine.[48]

In actual fact the only thing that Benjamin Gould knew about the difference engine, when he wrote for the first time to Babbage for more information, was its appearance.[49] The sole thing he was clear about, was his fear that the engine's practical utility was seriously limited compared to manual methods. − "If it were only an Analytical Engine!" It seems as if Gould attached more importance to the honour of buying and trying to use the engine than he did to its actual utility:

> "It would be a source of legitimate and honourable pride to have been first to introduce this engine into practical usefulness − But I fear much that its scope is not large enough to make its purchase a proper one to be strongly advocated at present. Will you please advise me?"

When Babbage answered Gould's enquiry, he enclosed a copy of Stokes' report. There, Gould could have had his fears confirmed if he had wished. But Babbage had described the report as "cold" and said that it scarcely did "justice to the machine" − expressions which Gould in his enthusiasm to buy the engine, no doubt paid some attention to. Thus Gould bought the engine and was to discover for himself that the "strictly algebraical problem for feeding the machine made quite as heavy demand upon time, and thought, and perseverance, as did the regulating of its mechanical action."[50] Gould used the engine to produce some astronomical tables but only for a period of *two months*, where upon he was dismissed. He had begun to cooperate with the American Nautical Almanac Office in order to compile ephemerides with the engine, and the conclusions of that institution were as follows:

> "The object has been to ascertain, by a trial that would involve a very small expense, whether this extraordinary instrument could be

employed with advantage on the work of preparing the Nautical Almanac [...] the result thus far has not been such as to demonstrate to my satisfaction that any considerable portion of the Almanac can be computed more economically by this machine than by ordinary methods, or that it would be expedient to continue, at present, the trial further than the completion of the tables already begun."[51]

Thus the American career of the second engine was both short and unsuccessful. Merzbach concludes:

"Leverrier's position vis-à-vis machine calculation provides a classical example of the essential conservatism of one responsible for a successfully established scientific enterprise – especially an enterprise that must produce periodic results. The Dudley Observatory's Scientific Council, on the other hand, demonstrates the willingness of reputable scientists engaged in forming new institutions to take greater risks, including some scientifically not motivated."[52]

Merzbach has not perceived the engine's technical limitations and therefore accuses Leverrier of conservatism. But what were the risks taken by the Scientific Council? Dudley Observatory was not even in existence when these scientists set about instituting an American Greenwich. There were no routine procedures and standard practices to disturb or build upon. The only people to take any risks, were the Trustees of the Dudley Observatory, whose capital was entirely in the hands of the Scientific Council. Furthermore, it is clear that the purchase of the difference engine was not scientifically motivated. Benjamin Gould was a very difficult person to get on with. This is clear both from contemporary sources and from Mary Ann James' exhaustive dissertation *The Dudley Observatory Controversy* (1980) where this fact is spelled out. Gould was a constant source of problems. He was very hostile, with an "arrogance of demeanour towards his equals and an overbearing conduct towards his assistants."[53] As James puts it: – "Gould's personality was one which, in a sense, doomed him to disaster in Albany from the day of his arrival."[54] He was a major contributing factor to the Dudley Observatory Controversy.[55] In a series of incidents, Gould refused to move to Albany from Cambridge, he refused to set up the telescopes and get work going at the Observatory and he refused to take responsibility for any expenses incurred during his period as director.[56] A number of large expenditures had been made in 1855, when Gould was sent to Europe to buy instruments for the Observatory. On this trip, he saw the Scheutz engine. At the end of October 1856, according to the Trustees, Gould had "urged" them to buy the engine.[57] I shall let the Trustees of the Dudley Observatory relate in their own words what happened:

"Neither Transit, Meridian Circle, Chronographs, Clocks or Dials, in all of which large investments had been already made, were received, and nothing was in working order. Great as was their respect for science, and entire as was their confidence in their scientific advisers, they could not always repress the regret and disappointment they felt, that, as yet, so little that was visible or practical, had been accomplished. Still, they retained their confidence in Dr. Gould, and gave their consent that he should purchase "the calculating machine," although the funds of the observatory scarcely justified the expense."[58]

But soon the Trustees became aware that something was wrong:

"The 'machine' had been exhibited and held for sale, both in Paris and in London, without finding a purchaser. Its utility had yet to be demonstrated. Not another Observatory in the world had ventured to invest the amount required, in such an experiment. It was left for the Trustees of the Dudley Observatory, led on by a blind confidence in Dr. Gould, to expend their money in this novel adventure. The *machine* was purchased in December, at a cost of five thousand dollars. It arrived in April, 1857, but was laid aside for more than twelve months, when it brought forth a column of printed figures, and the Trustees were charged two hundred dollars for 'bringing it into use'."[59]

It should be added that one of the co-authors of this attack on the Scientific Council and on Gould in particular, was the "enlightened and public-spirited" John F. Rathbone − the man who had paid for the purchase.

Let me turn to another part of the story of the engines, also concerning America. At the end of the 1860's, the inventor Martin Wiberg, full of hopes, wrote for advice to the famous and established inventor, his fellow countryman, John Ericsson in America. Ericsson replied and began very flatteringly:

"If the tables that were sent, were calculated and printed by the same machine, then I consider this machine to be the greatest triumph of human understanding over matter."[60]

But this pleasing prospect of glory was then dashed, by what Ericsson had to say next, which conjured up the more probable prospect of failure:

"As far as America is concerned [...] I can assure you that such an invention would not induce the capitalists to take the least risks. A new rat-trap or a new method of making shoe nails would arouse more interest than your admirable calculating machine. My advice therefore is that you dismiss America from your mind."[61]

The astronomical observatories formed at least theoretically the principal market for the Scheutz engine. There were many such potential customers throughout the world and Edvard sent *Specimens* to not less than 17 different observatories (see p. 379 ff). Yet apart from the fact, that mathematically and technically speaking, the engine was inadequate, which was sufficient to dissuade anyone from buying it, there was another reason which the Scheutzes were unaware of. The astronomical tables were also copied. There were only three observatories which made independent new calculations of ephemerides — Greenwich Observatory, the Imperial Observatory in Paris and the Observatory at Bologna.[62] What Lorenzo Respighi, the director of the Bologna Observatory thought about the engine, is not known.[63] He did not buy a machine and as far as the directors of the other two institutions are concerned, their opinions need not be repeated.

At the General Register Office, the second purchaser of the Scheutz engine, William Farr was to learn bitterly of its deficiencies in calculating and printing. In the *English Life Table* he recounts that the engine was not reliable:

"But it is a delicate instrument, and requires considerable skill in the manipulation. It consists of a multitude of pieces, and some of these occasionally get deranged, so as to print errors, which can, however, by a due system of checks, be almost invariably detected and rectified. It approached infallibility in certain respects, but it is not infallible, except in very skilful hands."[64]

Even the hope of saving manpower with the help of the engine, proved, in practice, to be vain.[65] Among the documents in the Public Record Office, there are some of Donkin & Co.'s bills which had been sent to the General Register Office. They concerned a certain Mr. White, one of Donkin's engineers, who had been regularly at the General Register Office "attending the Calculating Machine".[66] The bills which cover maintenance, repairs and cost of material, amounted to 12 guineas per month, i.e. 144 guineas per annum. Using Graham's method of comparison, this was more than the yearly salary for a single clerk employed as computer.[67]

An additional proof that the third engine failed to live up to expectations, is to be found in Graham's final remarks to the Secretary of the Royal Society, after the engine's delivery. The printing unit had already revealed its defects. Graham noted in his letter that if it had not been for the supporting opinion of the Royal Society Committee of scientists, he would have had difficulty in assuming the responsibility of reporting to the Lords of the Treasury that the work which had been entrusted to Mr. Donkin by the government, had been carried out in a very satisfactory manner.[68] To sum up, it is obvious that the need for and the utility of the difference engine had been exaggerated. There was really no market for these machines, no matter how remarkable they were. The comparatively high price had only a superficial effect on matters.

When it became known that Farr was not satisfied with the engine, and it can be assumed that potential customers contacted him first, a further Donkin machine was no longer of any interest. Clearly there were errors in the tables. There still are. But the problem did not have the importance that was attached to it. One solution was to mechanize the method of differences and the printing of the tables. Another, older but not necessarily inferior solution was to use "paper and pen". The mere fact that mechanization was possible, mesmerized both the inventors and their supporters, some of whom had influence and audacity enough to ensure that the engines received financial support. Articles were written on the difference engines in which they were described as the "curious", "remarkable" and "beautiful" invention and it was claimed that their significance could not be overestimated. Georg Scheutz read some of them and was unable to resist the temptation. Babbage, however, must have known more than he admitted about the true facts of the situation. He had one of England's largest collections of tables, including almost everything mentioned in this book. Both de Morgan and Glaisher based a considerable part of their articles on the tables in Babbage's collection and in that of the Royal Society to which Babbage of course had access. But when the Scheutzes came to London, he did not enlighten them about the fact that tables were copied and that their engine was inadequate etc. I believe that the reason is that Babbage, despite his failure, had achieved the position he wanted: he was the inventor of the Difference Engine No. 1. He was the authority who did not wish to risk anything. But he was also something more. Charles Babbage was the man behind all the information about the great problem of errors in tables. All articles on this subject can be traced back to him or his close friends.[69] He was the foremost commentator on the problem and its solution. He was also the chief promoter of the invention. But all this the Scheutzes failed to perceive.

By January 1861, the long story of Georg and Edvard Scheutz and the difference engine, was over. Looking back, Edvard at last began to see what had been wrong. By then it was too late. In a letter to Charles Babbage, he wrote:

"Nearly three years are gone since we met together, nevertheless I remember the moment as if it were yesterday. How dreary the future had been looking. I have still borne in mind your kind words when I parted and my desire of being worthy of the friendship by which you honoured me has many times aroused me to new exertions. The past has indeed been a real time of trial to me. Only he who has seen his most cherished hopes disappear, the one after the other, can comprehend such a situation. By the opposition of Mr. Leverrier I failed completely in my efforts of obtaining an order of a calculating engine in France and the yet lingering hope of getting orders from other countries has long since vanished in view of the high price Mr. Donkin is obliged to ask for covering his loss by the manufacture of the engine at Register Office. Happily I did understand a short time after my return home, that no certain income could be expected by a thing which, even during more favourable circumstances, would have rather few purchasers ....."[70]

Epilogue

The history of the difference engine − that glorious invention − is the tale of an unsuccessful technology in which the chief participants emerge less as heroes than as ordinary men enthralled by too grandiose an idea.

Sir Humphry Davy helped Charles Babbage to draught the letter to himself. Babbage and John Herschel were cofounders of the Astronomical Society. Herschel made sure that Babbage got the Astronomical Society's gold medal for his invention − the first that was ever awarded. The medal paved the way for the government's support of the project. Babbage was to become his own greatest supporter and was behind all the articles which promoted his invention. At the same time, the project took a toll on his health and he wished that he could "give up the machine at once and smile at the world". But what did he really know about technology? On the Royal Society Committees, Herschel gave his friend Babbage his full support. In 1829, he spoke of "Mr. Babbage's determination to admit of nothing but the very best and most finished work in every part; a contrary course would have been false economy, and might have led to the loss of the whole capital expended on it".[1] Babbage put the blame on Clement for the failure of the project, but at the same time he was given workshops in his own garden, where he was able to continue lavishing his enormous private wealth on his hobby. In Sweden, Georg Scheutz misunderstood Babbage's design and believed that he could simplify the engine by taking away a mass of unnecessary differences. But what did he really know about mathematics? The learned men at the Royal Academy of Sciences believed that they were in a position to confirm that such an engine "must possess a great value for practical calculation". Georg Scheutz offered to build an engine for the French that was both simple and cheap − without being in a position to do so. Jöns Jacob Berzelius and the others inspected the engine and failed to note that it made errors in its calculations. Scheutz was reluctant to seek state funds from a king to whom he was politically opposed. When, however, this monarch's more benevolent son came to the throne, it was time to speak about King Alphonso's renowned tables. Fabian Wrede, to help the cause of the difference engine, kept the King and the Riksdag in the dark. Backdoor tactics helped to get the matter debated by the Four Estates, thus providing some of the representatives with a certain amount of political capital. But what did they really know about technology and mathematics? Georg and Edvard Scheutz were given money for a prototype, but made use of the opportunity to build a working engine that could be sold. Pehr Sparre thought that he had made the best investment of his life and the Scheutzes believed that they had arranged a rather good deal. But was there a chance that Sparre or someone else might steal the patent or the idea from them? How would Babbage react when they met him in London? Despite everything, it was his invention. Or was it? George Stokes and his colleagues noted that the engine had only a limited use. Leverrier said much the same thing, but in his case it may well have been simply a consequence of the fact that the engine had not been demonstrated for him by skilled operators. William Gravatt carefully embellished the engine's performance in *Specimens* and Babbage helped Scheutz with the marketing of his old idea. However, he carefully concealed the difficulties. In Paris, Babbage showed the engine to an American with an empty observatory to fill, a gentleman who really wanted the Analytical Engine. George Biddell Airy, probably fed up with the whole affair, at last gave, with certain misgivings, his blessing to William Farr and the British government took a bite at the sour apple. If Stokes and his committee had not approved Bryan Donkin's work, the buyer James George Graham would not have done so. As for Farr, the apple tasted more sour than expected and Gould got in the end what he wanted − the honour "to first have introduced this engine into practical usefulness". Thanks to Jean Bolinder's advice to Scheutz, however, he had to work out for himself how this was to be done. John F. Rathbone was somewhat less pleased to be associated with the engine. His money at least went to another worthy cause, namely to paying Georg and Edvard Scheutz' debts in Stockholm.

The history of the difference engines is still open to new analyses and there are several subsidiary themes which are merely touched upon here, which might be fruitfully studied in greater detail. In the not too distant future, this piece of history will certainly be viewed in quite another way and other explanations will be suggested. More than a century ago, parts of the history I have related, could be analyzed in accordance with the methods of that age:

> "I was in perfect ignorance of this character [Charles Babbage] having constructed a calculating machine; but the chief qualifications of this [phrenological] examination point out immediately how & why such invention has been made by this person."[2]

The difference engine of the American George Barnard Grant marked the end of the history of the machine.[3] Private individuals ceased to invent them either for money or glory. At some institutions, such as the Nautical Almanac Office and the General Register Office, there were attempts, at the beginning of the present century, to produce tables by means of commercial adding- and accounting machines.[4] It was however only with the advent of the electronic digital computer that the problem of errors in tables could begin to be finally solved. While calculating machines of brass and steel − and in our own time of silicon and gold − have diminished the need for tables for the simple operations as a computing aid, the production of numerical tables has not ceased. During the 1500s 9 tables were produced, in the 1600s 70, in the 1700s 84, in the 1800s 985 and in the first part of our own century, more than 2,300 tables were produced.[5] The first seventy years of the century has witnessed a manifold increase in the number of tables produced in the previous centuries. The traditional standard tables are a thing of the past. They have played an important role in the history of the industrialized countries but since the beginning of the 20th century, they have been replaced more and more by new tables of special functions. In the cheap scientific electronic pocket calculator of the late 1960s, despite its small size, all the standard tables − trigonometrical, logarithmic, powers and roots and even indeed Herwart ab Hohenburg's 999 page multiplication table in folio − are built in.

Around 1820, the Frenchman, Thomas Xavier de Colmar, invented a universal calculating machine, based on Leibniz's stepped reckoners. It became a success and at the turn of the century it was mass produced in thousands of examples. It was the first commercial calculating machine. In the 1880s, the Odhner type calculating machine was invented and soon became popular since it was reliable, simple and fast. Unluckily Edvard Scheutz became involved in two prestige projects − the difference engine and the rotary steam engine − and unlike others, succeeded technically. If he and his father had been more attuned to market forces, and had concentrated on building an ordinary calculating machine − then their fortune would have been assured.

Someone has said that the electronic digital computer was a solution looking for a problem. The same was, in a way, true of the difference engine. For reasons which lie beyond the scope of this book, we know that the computer was very successful in finding its problems. The world's first electronic digital computer Eniac, finished in 1946, was built to produce numerical tables − firing and bombing tables for the American armed forces.[6] Since then, we are all aware of the incredibly fast development and ever widening use of the computer − the difference engine of the twentieth century − in all areas of society. Its full implications are still hard to see. Its potential applications are boundless. But might it not be the case that some of the problems which the computer has found, could be solved in a more appropriate fashion "with the pen"?

Notes

Commentary on the notes in this book

I have chosen to set out the full title of the source, in the original spelling, when it is mentioned for the first time. In my view, this makes it easier for the reader who wishes to locate it than if a modernized and perhaps abbreviated version is used instead. If further reference is made to the same source, I have abbreviated the title.

Note to introduction

[1] In the present work, *invention* means the idea to a solution of a problem embodied on paper, in a model or in a drawing etc. It denotes the first stage in a general and simple way.

Development consists in giving concrete form to the idea by embodying in it those characteristics it must have in order to be used in practical applications. Thus development involves the consideration of the choice of materials, details of design, cost, service and maintenance etc. During the development stage, invention takes place repeatedly.

Innovation begins the moment the completed object is ready to be delivered to the user.

As employed in this book, *inventor* does not mean *professional inventor*, i.e. someone like Thomas Alva Edison, who earned his living from his inventions. Here, *inventor* is the person who makes the invention. Thus Müller was the inventor of a difference engine; Babbage was the inventor of the Difference Engine No. 1; and the Scheutzes were the inventors of the first difference engine with a printing unit.

I am indebted to Thomas Parke Hughes for interesting discussions on these matters. See also: Thomas Parke Hughes, *Networks of Power: Electrification in Western Society 1880-1930* (Baltimore 1983).

Notes to section 1.1

[1] Charles Hutton, *Mathematical Tables: Containing the common, hyperbolic, and logistic logarithms, also sines, tangents, secants and versed sines, both natural and logarithmic. Together with several other tables useful in mathematical calculations.*

Also the complete description and use of these tables. Fourth edition (London 1804).

Hutton has a large introduction dealing with the history of numerical tables on pp 1-124. The first edition appeared in 1785. The sixth edition was printed 1822. Editions after and including 1830 omit the important historical account. They are edited by Olinthus Gregory.

Augustus de Morgan, "Table", Charles Knight (ed.), *The English Cyclopaedia: a Dictionary of Universal Knowledge* 7 (Arts and Sciences), (London 1861), pp 976-1015. An earlier version of this article was published in *The Penny Cyclopaedia* in 1842.

James Whitbread Lee Glaisher (Secretary of the Committee), "Report of the Committee on Mathematical Tables", *Report of the Forty-Third Meeting of the British Association for the Advancement of Science, held at Bradford in September 1873* (London 1874).

See also the journal *Mathematical Tables and other Aids to Computation* Nos. 1-68, 1943-1959, which contains a number of interesting articles.

[2] All good general and mathematical dictionaries contain definitions of the word table. I have studied several of them, and have found the one used here to be the clearest and most comprehensive. *Webster's New International Dictionary of the English Language* (Springfield, MA 1949).

[3] Otto Neugebauer, "Ancient Mathematics and Astronomy", Charles Singer, E. J. Holmyard and A. R. Hall (eds.), *A History of Technology* 1 (London 1954), pp 786-787.

[4] Otto Neugebauer, *A History of Ancient Mathematical Astronomy* 2 (Berlin 1975), p 969 ff.

[5] Charles Hutton, *A Mathematical and Philosophical Dictionary* 1, new edition (London 1815), pp 105-106.

[6] *Ibidem*, vol. 2, p 479.

[7] A detailed picture of the situation is given in Neugebauer (1975).

[8] Other editions were printed in 1492, 1521, 1545 etc.. Hutton *Dictionary* vol. 1, pp 105-106.

[9] Kurt Vogel (ed.), *Das Bamberger Blockbuch, Ein xylographisches Rechenbuch aus dem 15. Jahrhundert* (Munich 1980). Facsmile edition of the original in the Public Library, Bamberg.

[10] Glaisher, p 26.

[11] *Ibidem*, pp 43-44.
De Morgan, pp 988-990.

[12] Glaisher, pp 44, 158.
De Morgan, p 989.

[13] *Ibidem*, pp 44-45.
A. Fletcher, J. C. P. Miller, L. Rosenhead and L. J. Comrie, *An Index of Mathematical Tables* 2 (Edinburgh 1962), p 895.

[14] De Morgan, p 979.
Glaisher, p 16.

[15] E. W. Hobson, *John Napier and the Invention of Logarithms, 1614* (Cambridge 1914). See also Hutton who has an historical account of the logarithms in his *Mathematical Tables*, p 20 ff.

[16] Glaisher, p 55.

[17] *Ibidem*.

[18] John Napier (Authore ac Inventore), *Mirifici Logarithmorum Canonis Descriptio* (Edinburgh 1614), p 58 ff.
Glaisher, p 65.

[19] Glaisher, p 141.

[20] The argument is the value x which is looked up in the table in order to find the designated function value f(x). If for example sin 30° is sought then 30° is the argument.

[21] Adian Vlacq, *Trigonometria Artificialis: sive Magnus Canon Triangulorum Logarithmicus, Ad Radium 100000,00000, & ad dena Scrupula Secunda* (Gouda 1633), 270 pp.

[22] Its title was *Chilias Logarithmorum ad Tiodem Numeros ...*, and it was published in Marburg. A supplement was also published in 1625. Hutton, *Mathematical Tables*, p 31; Hutton, *Dictionary*, vol. 1, p 702. De Morgan, p 994.

[23] Hutton, *Mathematical Tables*, p 33.

[24] See e.g. *ibidem*, pp 36-41.

[25] Dionysius Lardner, "Babbage's Calculating Engine", (Excerpt from the *Edinburgh Review*, July 1834, No. CXX), reprinted in Henry Prevost Babbage (ed.), *Babbage's Calculating Engines, being a Collection of Papers Relating to them; their History, and Construction* (London 1889), p 54.

[26] Glaisher, p 95.

[27] *Ibidem*, pp 102-103, 126-127, 129-131, 138-141.
Henry Sherwin, *Sherwin's Mathematical Tables* (London 1741), third edition.
William Gardiner, *Tables de Logarithmes* (Avignon 1742), new edition.
Carl Johan Schulze, *Neue und erweiterte Sammlung Logarithmischer, trigonometrischer und anderer zum gebrauch der Mathematik unentbehrlicher Tafeln* (Berlin 1778), 2 vols., combined German and French edition.
Georg von Vega, *Thesaurus Logarithmorum completus* (Leipzig 1794), also with German text.

[28] Charles H. Cotter, *A History of Nautical Astronomy* (London 1968), p 183.

[29] *Ibidem*, p 309.

[30] *Ibidem*, p 310.

[31] *Ibidem*, pp 127, 181.

[32] *Ibidem*, pp 51-52.

[33] Cotter, p 309 ff., has a chapter (VIII) on the history of navigation tables.

[34] See e.g. Commissioners of Longitude, *Tables Requisite to be used with the Astronomical and Nautical Ephemeris* (London 1766).

[35] Glaisher, p 45.

[36] Cotter, pp 48, 313.
For the early history of the *Nautical Almanac* and more about Maskelyne, see: Eric G. Forbes, *Greenwich Observatory: The Royal Observatory at Greenwich and Herstmonceux 1675-1975* vol. 1: "Origins and Early History" (1675-1835) (London 1975), *passim*.

[37] Owen Gingerich and Barbara Welther, *Planetary, Lunar, and Solar Positions - New and Full Moons, 1650-1805* (Philadelphia 1983), reprint from the *Memoirs series of the American Philosophical Society*, vol. 59S.
This article deals with the accuracy in ephemerides and astronomical almanacs during the 17th and 18th centuries. It also contains an historical account, which gives information about how the various ephemerides were connected to each other in sequences. For instance, what can be considered as an unbroken sequence from Kepler's *Ephemerides Novae Motuum Coelestium*, published in Linz in 1617, to the present day, in the form of the *Connaissance des temps*, p. xi, Fig. 1 on p xii.

[38] Michael Taylor, *Tables of Logarithms of all Numbers, from 1 to 101 000; and of the Sines and Tangents to Every Second of the Quadrant* (London 1792).
Glaisher, pp 135-136.

[39] Glaisher, pp 134-135.

[40] *Ibidem*, p 56.
Charles Babbage, *On the Economy of Machinery and Manufactures* (London 1832), first edition, pp 153-158.

[41] *Glaisher*, pp 56-57.

[42] Charles Babbage, *Table of Logarithms of the Natural Numbers, from 1 to 108 000* (London 1831), pp v-xii.

[43] John Radford Young, *Mathematical Tables: Comprehending the Logarithms of all Numbers fom 1 to 36.000; also the Natural and Logarithmic Sines and Tangents […] with Several other Tables* (London 1834), p. v.

[44] Lardner, H. P. Babbage, p 58.

[45] Charles Babbage, *Logarithmen der natürlichen Zahlen 1 bis 108 000* (London 1834).
Charles Babbage, *Logarithmai 1 töl 108 000 ig* (London 1834). Both translated by Karl Nagy.
The English editions were published in 1827, 1829, 1831, 1844, 1872, 1889 and 1915.

[46] Glaisher, p 135.

[47] In the sequel the process of making this impression in the matrix, will be called *printing*. This is the same term as in direct printing, with printer's ink on paper, which is the subsequent and final printing process. This usage conforms with the terminology used in the case of the difference engines by Charles Babbage and others.

Notes to section 1.2

Unless stated to the contrary, this section is based on:

Harry Wilmot Buxton, "The Life and Labours of the late Charles Babbage, Esq., F.R.S.". Microfiche copy of the original undated manuscript Buxton vol. 16-17, kept in the Oxford Museum of the History of Science. This 19th century manuscript was never published.

Charles Babbage, *Passages from the Life of a Philosopher* (London 1864).

Research for this section has been carried out as follows: I have studied the works of Collier, Bell, Hyman, Dubbey and Moseley (see bibliography), as well as the 19th century material. A large number of more modern secondary works have been consulted, but not found useful. These are not listed in the bibliography. The primary sources for information about Babbage's life and works, are his letters and other papers, of which the major part has survived. These are kept in three collections − his manuscripts in the British Library, his correspondence with John Herschel in the Royal Society Library, and other papers in the Buxton collection (which Buxton used for writing the biography) in the Oxford Museum of the History of Science.

With the exception of the Buxton collection, I have studied the British Library and Royal Society source material personally. Neither Collier nor Bell, has consulted the Royal Society collection. The manuscripts in the British Library amount to some 20,000 items, which have been only partly used by scholars. Among these papers one can still find information that can shed new light on the story of Babbage (and also on Scheutz) and the difference engines. The Herschel-Babbage correspondence in the Royal Society has provided new material about Babbage and his engine and it is far from exhausted.

Finally, the discussion of Müller's contributions, at the end of this section, is based mainly on primary sources previously unnoticed, or not discussed in relation to the difference engines.

[1] Taken from an article by the English astronomer, Babbage's friend, Francis Baily, entitled: "On Mr. Babbage's new Machine for Calculating and Printing Mathematical and Astronomical Tables", H. P. Babbage, p 225. The article was originally printed in Schumacher's *Astronomische Nachrichten*, No. 46. It was reprinted in *Philosophical Magazine*, May 1824.

[2] Various sources disagree about when and where Babbage was born. However Hyman, pp 10-11, has managed to resolve these questions.

[3] Buxton, p 70.

[4] *Ibidem*.

[5] J. A. Venn (ed.), *Alumni Cantabrigenses. A Biographical List of all known Students, Graduates and Holders of Office at the University of Cambridge, from the earliest Times to 1900*, 1, part two, (Cambridge 1940), p 106.

[6] Buxton, pp 76-78.

[7] RS, HS.2.29, Letter from Charles Babbage to John Herschel, Chudleigh, Devon, 10th August 1814.

[8] [anon], "Herschel, Sir William", Leslie Stephen and Sidney Lee (eds.), *Dictionary of National Biography* 26 (London 1891), p 268 ff.

[9] [anon], "Herschel, Sir John Frederick William", *ibidem*, p 263.

[10] John Herschel was born on the 7th of March 1792.

[11] Dubbey, p 18.

[12] Philip C. Enros, "Cambridge University and the Adoption of Analytics in Early Nineteenth-Century England", Herbert Mehrtens, Henk Bos and Ivo Schneider (eds.), *Social History of Nineteenth Century Mathematics* (Boston 1981), p 138 ff.

[13] This is evident from many letters in: RS, HS. 2.1 ff., Letters between Charles Babbage and John Herschel from 20th June 1812.

[14] Venn, vol. 1, p 106.

[15] RS, HS.2.25, Letter from Charles Babbage to John Herschel, Chudleigh, 1st August 1814.
RS, HS.2.29.

[16] *Ibidem*.

[17] *Ibidem*.

[18] RS, HS.2.25.

[19] RS, HS.2.27, Letter from Charles Babbage to John Herschel, written shortly after 10th August 1814.

[20] RS, HS.2.31, Letter from John Herschel to Charles Babbage, Trinity, 25th October 1814.

[21] The universal language is mentioned in *Passages*, p 26. For details about their interests, see RS, HS.2. *passim*.

[22] RS, HS.2.35, Letter from Charles Babbage to John Herschel, London, 11th February 1815.
RS, HS.2.36, Letter from John Herschel to Charles Babbage, Trinity, 16th February 1815.

[23] RS, HS.2.22.

[24] RS, HS.2.34, Letter from Charles Babbage to John Herschel, London?, 12th December 1814.

[25] RS, HS.2.27.

[26] Hyman, pp 34-35.

[27] *Passages*, pp 473-474.
BL, Add.Ms 37182, 64, Letter from James Ivory to professor John Playfair, Royal Majesty's College, 26th March 1816.

[28] RS, HS.2.58, Letter from Charles Babbage to John Herschel, London, 9th March 1816.

[29] Buxton, p 148. For detailed account of activities in the Analytical Society, see: Bell, pp 2-67; Dubbey, pp 31-50.

[30] Bell, pp 2-24.
Dubbey, pp 10-28.
Cf. Enros, pp 135-148 and Walter W. Rouse Ball, *A History of the Study of Mathematics at Cambridge* (Cambridge 1889), pp 118-120.

[31] By notation is meant the chosen system of symbols. Newton denoted the derivative of x by a dot, $\dot{x}$ while Leibniz wrote dx. For simple cases there was no great advantage, but in the case of several variables, Leibniz' system was preferable. Modern research has shown that Newton had priority in discovering the calculus and that Leibniz developed it independently. The differential and integral calculus used today is based on these ideas but has been further developed by the successors of Newton and Leibniz. Both the dot and d-notation are still used.

[32] Silvestre Francois Lacroix, *An Elementary Treatise on the Differential and Integral Calculus* (London 1816), translation and addition by Charles Babbage, John Herschel and George Peacock. The book consists of 720 pages of which Babbage translated the first 170.

[33] *Passages*, p 40.

[34] Dubbey, p 20.

[35] *Passages*, p 47.

[36] BL, Add.Ms. 37182, 149-158, Printed letter of recommendation for Charles Babbage, including a list of publications (9 articles). Venn, vol. 1, p 106.

[37] *Passages*, p 474.

[38] The "list of Mr. Babbage's Printed Papers" that Babbage included in *Passages*, pp 493-496 contains 17 titles published by 1820. The list has however been shown to contain errors. A more accurate annotated list has recently been published: Alfred W. van Sinderen, "The Printed Papers of Charles Babbage", *Annals of the History of Computing* 2, No. 2, April 1980, pp 169-185, esp. pp 172-173.
Dubbey, pp 220-221.

[39] *Passages*, p 474.
Bell, pp 79-80.
Hyman, pp 45-46.
Moseley, p 55.

[40] RS, HS.2.67, Letter from Charles Babbage to John Herschel, London, 27th September 1816.
RS, HS.2.29.

[41] Agnes M. Clerke, *The Herschels and Modern Astronomy* (New York 1895), p 146 ff, *passim*.
RS, HS.2.68, Letter from John Herschel to Charles Babbage, Slough, 10th October 1816.

[42] RS, HS.2.28, Letter from John Herschel to Charles Babbage, Shaw, 7th August 1814.

[43] RS, HS.2.34.

[44] Neither Bell, Collier, Dubbey, Hyman nor Babbage himself (*Passages*) gives any indication about this. In 1818, he had gone down in a diving bell which had drawn his attention to the problems of submarine navigation and later (exactly when, is unknown) he constructed an open submarine vessel (*Passages*, pp 208-212). This he described in an article in 1826 and it can thus date from later on. Another case occurred around 1819 when Babbage was designing means for accurately dividing astronomical instruments (*Passages*, p 42). I have read all the letters (112) between Charles Babbage and John Herschel in the Royal Society (HS.2), up to 1819, without coming across any mention of engineering or technical matters in them, apart from the invention of the lock.

[45] Quoted by Collier, p 13.

[46] Collier, pp 15-18. As Collier correctly has noted the account given by the 72-year old Babbage in *Passages*, p 42, where he says that the idea first arose in 1812-1813, is not supported by any primary source. It is based on a friend's information to Babbage.

[47] RS, HS.2.169, Letter from Charles Babbage to John Herschel, 20th December 1821. Due to lack of time, I have only been able to check carefully the correspondence for the period prior to March 1819.

[48] Quoted by Collier, pp 15-16. From a manuscript in the Buxton collection, vol. 7. (Apart from volume 16 and 17 of this collection, which are available on microfiche, I have not been able to study the other Buxton volumes in Oxford.)

[49] The account alluded to, was also written by Babbage, but in September 1834. See Collier, pp 16-17.

[50] *The Compact Edition of the Oxford English Dictionary* (Complete Text Reproduced Micrographically) 1, (New York 1975), pp 886-887, see esp. points 7-8. See also *ibidem*, 2, p 3035 under "Steam-engine".

[51] *Ibidem*, p 887, point 7.

[52] The others examples are beer engine, fire engine, garden engine and water engine. (The section "*E-everybody*" in the *Oxford English Dictionary* was ready for publication in July 1891, *ibidem*, p x).

[53] *Ibidem*, "*Calculating*", p 317. I have not been able to find the word calculating engine used in any other case than when talking about difference engines.

[54] Based on an example by Babbage, *Passages*, pp 49-50.

[55] W. de Beauclair and H. Hauck, *Rechnen mit Maschinen* (Braunschweig 1968), p 12, pp 18-19.

[56] It was rediscovered and made known in 1957. *Ibidem*, p 12 ff.

[57] *Ibidem*, p 12 ff.

[58] H. W. Dickinson, *Sir Samuel Morland: Diplomat and Inventor, 1625-1696* (Cambridge 1970), p 28 ff.

[59] These designations are due to the present author.

[60] Charles Babbage, "A Letter to Sir Humphry Davy, Bart., President of the Royal Society, &c. &c., on the Application of Machinery to the Purpose of Calculating and Printing Mathematical Tables", H. P. Babbage, p 212.

[61] *Passages*, p 44.

[62] "A Letter to Sir Humphry Davy", H. P. Babbage, p 212.

[63] RS. HS.2.173, Letter from Charles Babbage to John Herschel, London, 10th June 1822.

[64] This somewhat unclear point is discussed by Collier, pp 31-32. There he gives the following very plausible explanation. Six to eight figures probably meant that the machine had three number wheels in the result column, two in the first difference column, and one for the second difference. With this arrangement it could calculate the first 30 numbers of the equation x^2+x+41, which Babbage said that the machine had done (see: "A letter to Sir Humphry Davy", H. P. Babbage, p 213).

[65] RS, HS.2.173.
"A Letter to Sir Humphry Davy", H. P. Babbage, p 213.

[66] RS, HS.2.92, Letter from John Herschel to Charles Babbage, 26th April 1818.

[67] David S. Landes, *The Unbound Prometheus: Technological Change and Industrial Deveopment in Western Europe from 1750 to the Present* (Westford, MA 1979), p 104.

[68] Lord Byron, *Don Juan*, Canto X, ii (1818-1824).

[69] James Moran, *Printing Presses: History and Development from the Fifteenth Century to Modern Times* (London 1973), pp 107-108.

[70] Lacroix, *Treatise*, pp 464-579. See especially pp 551-579.

[71] See e.g.: Thomas Manning, "New method of computing logarithms", *Philosophical Transactions of the Royal Society* 1806 (London 1806), pp 327-341.

Thomas Knight, "On the construction of logarithmic tables", *Philosophical Transactions* 1817 (London 1817), pp 217-233.

Thomas Knight, "Two general propositions in the method of differences", *ibidem*, pp 234-244.

I have examined all the articles in the *Transactions* up to the early 1820s.

[72] M. R. Williams, "The Scientific Library of Charles Babbage", *Annals of the History of Computing* 3, No. 3, July 1981, p 239. Several of the tables used in section 1.1 are to be found in the large Royal Society collection of tables.

[73] Charles Babbage "Note on the Application of Machinery to the Computation of Astronomical and Mathematical Tables", reprinted in H. P. Babbage, p 211.

[74] "A Letter to Sir Humphry Davy", H. P. Babbage, p 213.

[75] *Ibidem*, pp 214-215.

When the idea for a difference engine was conceived, Babbage had already visited Paris on several occasions. It was there that he saw Prony's *Les Tables de Cadastres* with his own eyes. Later, he would often refer to the work, based on the division of labour, and use it as an example of how the difference engine worked. It is clear from the foreword to his table of logarithms (p vii, 1827, first edition) that around 1825 he had had an opportunity to compare his table with Prony's work. It has been suggested that it was the knowledge about how the work involved in producing *Les Tables de Cadastres* was organized, that provided the idea of a difference engine; see e.g. Hyman, pp 43-44, 50, who, without giving any reference, says that Prony's work had the greatest effect on Babbage's own work. This, however, is not certain. The hypothesis is quite reasonable because the step from the rationalization achieved by Prony in table calculation to full mechanization seems an easy one in retrospect. However, I have not found any evidence for this theory.

[76] RS, HS.2.176, Letter from Charles Babbage to John Herschel, Teignmouth, 3rd August 1822.

[77] "A Letter to Sir Humphry Davy", H. P. Babbage, p 215. The philosophers of Laputa were the scientists in Jonathan Swift's *Gulliver's Travels*, who neglected usefulness and were devoted to visionary projects.

[78] RS, HS.2.176. This point has not been noticed before.
"A Letter to Sir Humphry Davy", H. P. Babbage, p 211.

[79] Collier, pp 276-277.
Bell, p 187.

[80] For more about these activities see e.g. Bell, *passim*.

[81] Venn, 3, p 342.
Leslie and Lee, 26, p 263.
Venn, 5, pp 56-57.
[anon], "Obituary Notices of Fellows deceased": George Peacock, *Proceedings of the Royal Society of London* 9 (London 1859), p 537. This source will in the sequel be abbreviated *Proceedings*.

[82] RS, HS.2.29.
RS, HS.2.25.
RS, HS.2.28.

[83] Evidence to support this statement will be given later.

[84] RS, HS.2.176.

[85] *Passages*, pp 44-45.
"A Letter to Sir Humphry Davy", H. P. Babbage, pp 212-213.

[86] Ibidem, pp 212-213.

[87] According to Collier, p 28, Babbage inspected a variety of printing presses. Some of the devices that he might have come across and incorporated in his engine, will be discussed in section 2.3.

[88] Charles Babbage, "On the Theoretical Principles of the Machinery for Calculating Tables", H. P. Babbage, pp 216-219. The letter, upon which the article in *Brewster's Journal* is based, is dated 6th November 1822.
For the title of the article read at the Astronomical Society, on December 13th, see note 73.

[89] [anon], "On Machinery for Calculating and Printing Mathematical Tables", *The Edinburgh Philosophical Journal* 7, (Edinburgh 1822), pp 274-281.

[90] H. P. Babbage, pp 218-219.

[91] *Passages*, 42.
Cf Hyman, p 51.

[92] RS, HS.2.173.

[93] *Ibidem*.

[94] BL, Add.Ms. 37182, 425, Letter from Olinithus Gregory to Charles Babbage, 16th July 1822, First quoted by Collier, p 34.

[95] *Ibidem*, 431-432, Letter from Edward Ffrench Bromhead to Charles Babbage, 20th August 1822. First quoted by Collier, pp 34-35.

[96] BL, Add.Ms. 37182, 433-434, Letter from Edward Ffrench Bromhead to Charles Babbage, undated, but with the inscription 20 August 1822. It is clear from the content that the letter belongs to a later date, between the time of Bromhead's election to the Royal Society and the end of April 1823.

[97] [anon], "Obituary Notices of fellows deceased": Davies Gilbert, *Proceedings* 4 (London 1843), p 251.

[98] Louis J. Jennings (ed.), *The Croker Papers: The Correspondence and Diaries of the Late Right Honourable John Wilson Croker, LL.D., F.R.S., Secretary to the Admirality from 1809 to 1830* 1 (London 1884), pp 113-114.

[99] *Ibidem*, pp 262-263.
The enclosure that Peel mentions may have included the "Note on the Applica-

tion of Machinery", i.e. Babbage's letter to the Astronomical Society, dated 2nd June 1822, in which the formula in question is mentioned.

[100] Virgil, *Aeneid*, II: 46-48.
Compare Hyman, p 52, who has not observed Peel's change in the quotation.

[101] Jennings, pp 263-264.

[102] Parliamentary Paper, No. 370, printed 22nd May 1823, "Statement relative to the Difference Engine, drawn up by the late Sir H. Nicholas from the Author's Papers", *Passages*, p 69.

[103] The members of the Committee were "Sir H. Davy, Mr. Brande, Mr. Combe, Mr. Baily, Mr. (now Sir Mark Isambard) Brunel, Major (now General) Colby, Mr. Davies Gilbert, Mr. (now Sir John) Herschel, Captain Kater, Mr. Pond (Astronomer-Royal), Dr. Wollaston, and Dr. Young". Information taken from Charles Richard Weld, *The Eleventh Chapter of the History of the Royal Society* vol. 2, chapter XI (London 1848), pp 371-372.

[104] *Ibidem*, p 372, note 5. (Dr. Young).

[105] Henry Thomas Colebrooke, "Address [...] On Presenting the Gold Medal to Charles Babbage, Esq., F.R.S.", H. P. Babbage, p 223.
Passages, p 144.

[106] RS, HS.2.184, Letter from Charles Babbage to John Herschel, London, 27th June 1823.

[107] Compare Collier, pp 41-42, who says that there is no evidence that the award had any effect on the government's decision.

[108] RS, HS.2.184.

[109] *Ibidem*.
"Statement relative to the Difference Engine", *Passages*, p 70.

[110] Weld, p 373.

[111] RS, HS.2.184.

[112] "Statement", *Passages*, p 71.
Weld, pp 372-373.
"Statement" and Weld give more or less detailed and similar accounts of Babbage's problems concerning government support.

[113] Augustus de Morgan, "Mr. Babbage's Calculating Machine", *The Athenae um*, 14th October 1848, p 2. Review of Weld's *The Eleventh Chapter*, reprinted as an appendix in Weld. Cf. Weld, p 373 and "Statement", *Passages*, p 71.

[114] De Morgan, "Mr. Babbage's Calculating Machine", *The Athenaeum*, 1848, p 2, esp. note 1.

[115] "Statement", *Passages*, p 71.

[116] Samuel Smiles, *Industrial Biography, Iron Workers and Tool Makers* (London 1863), p 244. Chapter XII is about Clement. It is, to my knowledge, the only existing biography of Joseph Clement.

[117] *Ibidem*, p 236 ff.

[118] *Ibidem*, p 245.

[119] *Ibidem*, p 236 ff.

[120] "Statement", *Passages*, p 71.

[121] Smiles, p 244, note *. I have inspected the printed drawings mentioned by Smiles, and they are in fact very well made.

[122] *Transactions of the Society for the Encouragement of Arts, Manufacture, and Commerce* XXXVI (London 1818), pp 133-177. For what it could do, see also the plates of the instrument drawn by Clement. Smiles, pp 244-245.

[123] Smiles, p 245.
A *slide rest* is a device that guides the cutting tool very accurately. It is operated by a handle, or acts by itself (by means of a rotating screw), and produces a better surface with a higher degree of precision than the alternative hand held cutting tool.
Both Bramah and Maudslay had made important contributions to the development of the lathe before Clement ceased working for them. It can be concluded, from Clement's inventive character, that his lathe was of equal quality, if not superior to their machines. It is clear (Smiles, p 245) that his lathe had a cross feed mechanism, which means that the cutting tool could be moved in two orthogonal directions. For information about Maudslay's and Bramah's lathes see Robert S. Woodbury, "History of the Lathe to 1850", *Studies in the History of Machine Tools* (Cambridge, MA 1972), pp 100-108, and also: K. R. Gilbert, *The Machine Tool Collection. Science Museum Catalogue of Exhibits with Historical Introduction* (London 1966), pp 37-38, 55.

[124] Smiles, p 249.
A planing machine has the ability to make metal surfaces absolutely flat. To do this work by hand, especially on larger surfaces, was a laborious process. According to Smiles, Clement had his planing machine in operation prior to the year 1820. This important machine tool was invented and put into use independently by several British engineers during the second decade of the 19th century. See L. T. C. Rolt, *Tools for the Job* (London 1968), pp 100-101.

[125] RS, HS.2.218, Letter form John Herschel to Charles Babbage, 22nd Decem ber 1827. The letter mentions Clement making suggestions about some technical details.

[126] "A Letter to Sir Humphry Davy", H. P. Babbage, p 213. Here, Babbage states that "the computed table is presented to the eye at two opposite sides of the (model) machine". This implies a different mechanical approach from that adopted in the Difference Engine No. 1, in which the table could be read from one side only.

[127] Many drawings were made for the construction of the difference engine. By February 1829 they covered a surface of 400 square feet or approximately 37

square meters (H. P. Babbage, p 233). Many of these have survived, and are kept at the Science Museum Library, London. See also Collier, pp 294-296.

[128] During his work on his calculating engines, Babbage made notes, sketches etc. in what he called "Scribbling Books". These are also kept at the Science Museum Library, but they are of little help regarding the early development of the difference engine, since the first apparently starts around the year 1827.

[129] RS, HS.2.218.

[130] "Statement", *Passages*, p 71.

[131] *Transactions of the Society* [...] *of Arts, Manufacture, and Commerce* XLIII (London 1825), pp 138-142.
BL, Add.Ms. 37196, 264-265, Letter from Joseph Williamson to Charles Babbage, 6th July 1855.

[132] BL, Add.Ms. 37196, 264.

[133] Gilbert, p 40.

[134] BL, Add.Ms. 37196, 265.

[135] *Passages*, chapter IX, pp 142-146 contains a description of the mechanical notation.
The notation was first described by Babbage at a Royal Society meeting on the 16th of March 1826, see: "On a Method of Expressing by Signs the Action of Machinery". Originally printed in *Philosophical Transactions of the Royal Society* (1826), p 250 ff. Reprinted in H. P. Babbage, pp 236-241.

[136] *Passages*, p 142.
The notation of a machine showed three things: *1st*, Shape and position of the pieces in the machine. *2nd*, Time and duration of every motion. *3rd*, How all movable pieces are connected with every other part on which they act (*Ibidem*, pp 142-143).

[137] *Ibidem*, p 142.

[138] Bell, p xii.
Hyman, p 65.
Mosely, p 83.
Hyman, p 65, note 11, says that Georgiana died in August or September. It is clear from the following reference that it was September.
RS, HS.2, 216, Letter from Betsy Plumleigh Babbage to John Herschel, 15th September 1827.

[139] Hyman, p 62.

[140] Hyman, pp 63-64.

[141] RS, HS.2, 215, Letter from Betsy Plumleigh Babbage to John Herschel, 8th September 1827.
RS, HS.2, 216.
RS, HS.2, 217, Letter from Charles Babbage to John Herschel, Aachen, 17th November 1827.

[142] Collier, p 47.

[143] By October 1827 3,475 pounds had been used, including the 1,500 pounds furnished by the Treasury ("Statement", *Passages*, p 72).

[144] Weld, p 374 ff.
"Statement", *Passages*, p 72 ff.
Collier, p 47 ff.
Bell, p 221 ff.

[145] *Ibidem*.

[146] John Herschel, (Chairman of the committee) "Report of the Committee appo inted by the Council of the Royal Society to consider the subject referred to in Mr. Stewart's Letter relative to Mr. Babbage's Calculating Engine, and to report thereon - Feb. 1929", H. P. Babbage, pp 233-235.
This report was also reprinted in March 1831 in *Journal of the Franklin Institute* vol. vii new series (Boston, MA 1831), pp 210-213.

[147] *Ibidem*, H. P. Babbage, p 233. Cf. note 127 above.

[148] *Ibidem*, p 233-234..

[149] *Ibidem*, p 233.

[150] *Ibidem*, p 235.

[151] Weld, p 376.

[152] *Ibidem*, p 377.

[153] *Ibidem*, pp 377-378.

[154] *Ibidem*, p 379.
Collier, p 53 ff, provides a detailed account of these matters.

[155] Weld, p 379.
Collier, pp 58-59.

[156] RS, HS.2.239, Letter from Charles Babbage to John Herschel, London, 6th May 1829.

[157] *Ibidem*.

[158] Collier, p 57.

[159] *Ibidem*, pp 53-60, 71-72.
Weld, pp 378-382.

[160] BPL, Ms.E.210.19.v.2.(42), Letter from Charles Babbage to Nathaniel Bowditch, London, 20th March 1830.

[161] BL, Add. Ms. 37185, 98-99.
In the preface (p v), Babbage states that the book had nothing to do with the difference engine.

[162] Bell, pp 68-126, *esp*. 100-126.
Hyman, pp 75-102, *esp*. 88-102.

[163] Bell, pp 126-168.
Jack Morell and Arnold Thackray, *Gentlemen of Science. Early Years of the British Association for the Advancement of Science* (Oxford 1981), *passim*.

[164] BL, Add.Ms.37182-37201, *passim*.
Passages, *passim*.
Hyman, *passim*.

[165] *Passages*, pp 29-34.

[166] *Ibidem*, p 34 n.

[167] Weld, pp 379-380.
See also Collier, pp 72-73.

[168] Weld, p 380.
RS, HS.2.239. This letter states that Charles Babbage had just bought Wollaston's house at Dorset Street No. 1. It is dated 6th May 1829.

[169] Hyman, p 126.

[170] Weld, p 380.

[171] "Statement", *Passages*, p 80.

[172] *Ibidem*, pp 80-83.
Weld, pp 380-383.
Hyman, pp 126-127. In these two pages Hyman gives a description of the buildings erected. See also the drawing of the building on page 128 in Hyman's book.

[173] Weld, pp 380-381.

[174] Field had replaced Maudslay as inspector of the accounts when Maudslay died.
Ibidem, p 382.
"Statement", H. P. Babbage, p 81.

[175] Collier, pp 77-78.

[176] Smiles, p 256.

[177] Weld, p 383.
Collier, p 78.
Hyman, p 130.

[178] Smiles, p 255.
This will be further discussed in section 3.2.

[179] Collier, p 80.

[180] *Ibidem*.
Bell, pp 236-237.

[181] Collier, p 80.

[182] *Ibidem*, p 104.

[183] *Ibidem*.

[184] Such a machine, see Fig. 88, or part of a machine is to be found in the Science Museum, London. Another has recently been discovered in New Zeeland by Gary J. Tee of the University of Auckland, New Zealand.
See: Gary J. Tee, "The Heritage of Charles Babbage in Australasia", *Annals of the History of Computing*, 5, No. 1, January 1983, pp 45-59, esp., pp 53, 59.

[185] Babbage states this sum himself in a letter to the Earl of Derby, written in June 1852, and reprinted in *Passages*, see esp. p 103.
Different sources give somewhat different figures. Lardner, H. P. Babbage, p 81, e.g. says that the sum was 15,000 pounds. Weld, p 383, published in 1848, agrees with the amount stated by Babbage above.
No scholar has, however, tried to find support for this figure in the documents that may have survived from the Treasury.

[186] "Statement", *Passages*, pp 70-71. See also Collier, pp 48-49.

[187] *Passages*, p 103.

[188] John H. White Jr., *The John Bull: 150 Years a Locomotive* (Washington, DC 1981), p 22.

[189] "Statement", *Passages*, p 87.

[190] Collier, p 104.

[191] Williams, p 239. In another classification, given in Robert Tucker *The Mathematical and Scientific Library of the late Charles Babbage* [...] *To be sold by Private Contract* (London 1872), the number of tables is 265.

[192] *Ibidem*.
De Morgan, "Table", p 993 used Babbage's "large and rare collection" as one of his sources for his exhaustive article. Glaisher also had the opportunity to consult Babbage's tables for his work, see Glaisher, "Report of the Committee on Mathematical Tables", p 52.

[193] Williams, p 240.

[194] Williams p 240 says that there was a very sudden decrease in acquisitions during the early 1830's, in some cases dropping to less than half a dozen items per year. He notes that this coincides with the period when Babbage was putting his greatest efforts into the design and construction of the engine.

[195] A brief list of the most important tables in Babbage's Library illustrates the point: *Alphonsine Tables* (1492), Rheticus *Opus Palatinum* (1596) and *Magnus Canon Doctrinae Triangulorum* (1607), Pitiscus *Canonum Triangulorum* (1608) and *Theasurus Mathematicus* (1613), Briggs (1617, 1624, 1631 etc.), Kepler *Chili as Logarithmorum ad Tiodem Numeros* ... (1624), Vlacq (1628), Dodson (1747) and *The Antilogarithmic Canon* ... (1742), Maskelyne *Tables Requisite* (1766, 1781, 1802), Gardiner (1770), Schulze (1778), Taylor *A Sexagesimal Table*

(1780) and *Table of Logarithms* (1792), Vega (1794) and (1797), Callet (1795 tirage 1814 stereotyped), Hutton (1804). In addition to these examples the collection also contains 29 anonymous items. (Tucker, pp 134-137). Information taken from Tucker, *passim*. Williams mentions only some of the most famous tables in the Babbage collection.

[196] *Passages*, pp 474-477.
Hyman, pp 58-59.

[197] Charles Babbage, *A Comparative View of the Various Institutions for the Assurance of Lives* (London 1826).

[198] The title of this multicoloured table, which I have not examined, was: Charles Babbage, *Specimen of Logarithmic Tables, printed with different coloured inks and on variously-coloured papers, in twenty-one volumes 8vo* (London 1831). The colours of inks were: light blue, dark blue, light green, dark green, olive, yellow, light red, dark red, purple, and black (*Passages*, p 494, no. 43). These volumes are now together with the rest of Babbage's library in the Crawford Collection, in the library of the Royal Observatory in Edinburgh. See Williams, pp 235-236.

[199] *Passages*, p 495.

[200] Williams, p 239.

[201] Babbage, *Table of Logarithms*, p xi. I have also come across specimens of this table with black ink on light green paper, as well as ordinary white paper.

[202] BL, Add.Ms. 37183, 354, Letter from Francis Baily to Charles Babbage, 8th November 1826.

[203] Collier, p 40 states that Babbage in May 1823 was advised by a friend to aquire knowledge about the matter for this purpose.

[204] BL, Add.Ms. 37182, 430, Copy of a letter from the Earl of Stanhope to Stephen Lee, Carlsruhe, 29th July 1822. This letter, in Babbage's possession, indicates his early interest in Lord Stanhope's famous calculating machines. The writer, the son of Lord Stanhope, says that he has his father's machines in his possession, but that he does not quite understand their mode of operation. He adds that their value is little, and more of curiosity, than the very ingenious machine Lee mentions (probably Babbage's). The writer intimates that he will bring the machines for demonstration upon his return to England.
It is also clear, from another letter, that Babbage was particularly concerned about the question of interference. See:
BL, Add.Ms. 37182, 435, Letter from Stephen Lee to Charles Babbage, 22nd August 1822.

[205] Williams, p 238.

[206] *Ibidem*, pp 238-239.
Beauclair and Hauck, pp 12, 23.

[207] BL, Add.Ms. 37183, 72-77, "Machine for multiplying any number of digits by any number", Versailles, 10th July 1789, Technical description of a machine invented by an Englishman. This was received by Babbage in September 1823 and therefore it provides evidence for his early interest in machines calculation. See note 204 about Babbage inspecting machines himself.

[208] [anon], *Catalogue of the Special Loan Collection of the Scientific Apparatus at the South Kensington Museum* (London 1876), pp 5, 21-22.
H. W. Dickinson, p 31.
Passages, pp 154-155.

[209] Charles Babbage, *On the Economy of Machinery and Manufactures* (London 1832), p iii.
In the sequel I shall refer to this book as *Economy*.

[210] Hyman has a chapter on Babbage's *Economy*; chapter 8, pp 102-122.

[211] *Economy*, pp iii-iv.

[212] Hyman, esp. pp 121-122.

[213] *Passages*, p 495, no. 44.

[214] Allan G. Bromley, "Charles Babbage's Analytical Engine, 1838", *Annals of the History of Computing*, vol. 4, No. 3, July 1982, pp 196-217.

[215] See e.g.:
M. V. Wilkes, "How Babbage's dream came true", *Nature*, vol. 257, October 16, 1975, pp 541-544.
Idem, "Babbage as a computer pioneer", *Historica Mathematica*, 4, 1977, pp 415-440.
A. K. Petrenko and O. L. Petrenko, "The Babbage machine and the origins of programming", *Istoriko-matematicheskie Issledovaniia*, 24, 1979, pp 340-360. (Article in Russian).
N. Metropolis and J. Worlton, "A Trilogy on Errors in the History of Computing", *Annals of the History of Computing*, vol. 2, No. 1, January 1980, pp 49-59.

[216] Only one modern article about Müller has been published before, namely: Otto Weber, "Ein 'Computer' des 18. Jahrhunderts", *Photorin: Mitteilungen der Lichtenberg-Gesellschaft* 3, (1980), pp 13-23. It does not, however consider the fact that Müller invented the first difference engine, nor does Weber discuss this in relation to Babbage or other difference engines.
The fact that Müller preceded Babbage has been given no attention by historians, although it has been noted in some sources, e.g.: Louis Jacob, *Le calcul mécanique* (Paris 1911), pp 46, 55, 114-115. See also: Brian Randell, *The origins of Digital Computers: Selected Papers* (Heidelberg 1973), pp 3, 200, 447.

[217] The main source for the following information about Müller is his autobiographical article of 21 pages, written sometime after the year 1820. It was edited by Wilhelm Diehl, and published under the title "Lebensbeschreibung des Obristen und Oberbaudirektors, auch Direktors des Oberbaukollegs Johann Helfrich von Müller", and published in *Hessische Cronik* 1-2 (1930), pp 1-21. It was not used by Weber. Unless stated to the contrary, Müller's autobiography has been the prime source to the following passages. I will refer to it as: Diehl.

[218] Diehl, p 13.

[219] *Ibidem*, p 5.
See also: Weber, p 17 ff.

[220] Weber, p 17.

Letter from Johann Helfrich Müller to Georg Christoph Lichtenberg, Darmstadt, 22nd May 1783, Ulrich Joost and Albrecht Schöne, *Lichtenberg Briefwechschel* 2 (München 1985), pp 615-619 esp. 615.

[221] *Ibidem*. Hahn probably got his idea from reading about Leibniz' calculating machine. See Weber, p 15.

[222] Diehl, p 5.
Weber, p 18.

[223] Joost and Schöne, p 617.

[224] Rudolf Krause, "Geschichte und heutige Bestände des Physikalischen Kabinetts in Hessischen Landesmuseum Darmstadt", *Naturwissenschaftlicher Verein Darmstadt e.V., Bericht 1963/64* (Darmstadt 1965), p 41.

[225] Diehl, p 1.

[226] Joost and Schöne, pp 615-619.

[227] See e.g. Weber, p 14. For some more information about Müller's wish to show his machine to the members of the Academy in Göttingen, see Joost and Schöne, Vol. 12, pp 863, 866-870.

[228] Letter from Johann Müller to Georg Christoph Lichtenberg, Giessen, 9th September 1783, Joost, vol. 2, pp 902-905, esp. 903.
Weber, p 14.

[229] Joost and Schöne, p 904.

[230] Diehl, p 6.
Despite attempts, I have not been able to locate a copy of this book.

[231] Joost and Schöne, p 905. This postscript was first noted by Weber, pp 19-20.

[232] Letter from Johann Müller to Georg Christoph Lichtenberg, Giessen, 5th October 1784, Joost and Schöne, vol. 2, p 921.

In this letter he indirectly asks Lichtenberg about the usefulness of the machine, as he mentions that he has written to another professor (Albrecht Ludwig Friedrich Meister) about the matter, saying that he is very eager to get an answer to this question.

I have not been able to locate any of the answers given to these questions.

[233] The book was edited by Philipp Engel Klipstein.

[234] Klipstein, pp 48-50.

[235] *Ibidem*, pp 48-49.

[236] *Ibidem*.

[237] *Passages*, p 47.

[238] BL, Add.Ms. 37198, 189-191. Annotated translation (five pages) of Klipstein,

1786 by John Herschel for Charles Babbage. Undated, but placed among the manuscripts from around April 1861 in this collection. The document has a comment written on its reverse side by Babbage's son Henry Prevost Babbage that he has seen the German original among his father's papers but has forgotten where. (He dates this comment 10th of May 1903.) No kind of scientific test has been carried out to determine the date of the translation.

[239] Collier, p 24.

[240] *Ibidem*, pp 25, 69.

[241] RS, HS.2.363, Letter from John Herschel to Charles Babbage, undated.

[242] RS, HS.2.171, Letter from Charles Babbage to John Herschel, 9th April 1822.

[243] I have examined all *Comptes Rendus* from 1800 to 1860.

[244] Randell, p 3.

[245] Klipstein, p 48.

[246] Weber, p 22.

Notes to section 1.3

[1] Despite many attempts, I have only been able to locate one source which gives any substantial information on the history of the method of differences, namely Charles Hutton's *A Mathematical and Philosophical Dictionary* 1, pp 416-417. Hutton was Professor of Mathematics at the Royal Military Academy, Woolwich. Briggs presented the method in his *Arithmetica Logarithmica* (chapters 8-13) in 1624. Hutton says that Briggs was the originator of the method. I believe that Briggs perhaps was the first to write about the method, but that it must have been known and used long before the 17th century.

Hutton uses the term *differential method*, which appears to have been common when he wrote his first edition of the book in 1795. In the beginning of the 19th century the term "method of differences" was adopted, presumably to make a distinction from the differential and integral calculus.

See also Hutton, *Tracts on Mathematical and Philosophical Subjects; comprising, among Numerous Important Articles, The Theory of Bridges, with several Plans for recent improvement. Also the Results of Numerous experiments on the Force of Gunpowder, with Applications to the Modern Practice of Artillery* 1 (London 1812), pp 377-387, and *idem: Mathematical Tables*, pp 71-73.

[2] Hutton. Dictionary, pp 416-417.

Isaac Newton, *Philosophiae Naturalis Principia Mathematica* (London 1687), pp 481-483.

[3] Hutton, *Dictionary*, pp 416-417. Information about Stirling is taken from this source. I have not been able to examine the books of Jones and Stirling. The information is obtained from the *Catalogue of the Library of Congress*, which also states that a second edition in English was published in 1749 of Stirling's book.

See also [anon], "Jones, William", Sidney Lee (ed.), *Dictionary of National Biography* 30 (London 1892), pp 173-174.

[4] One practical illustration of the method is given by William Gravatt in [Charles Babbage, Georg and Edvard Scheutz, William Gravatt], *Specimens of Tables, Calculated, Stereomoulded and Printed by Machinery* (London 1857), pp 4-5. Gravatt founded his version on the fifth lemma of the third book of Newton's *Principia*. Gravatt's formulae are not always clear and in the example he gives on page 8 there are a number of errors.

[5] In the general case, the fourth degree polynomial for the interval $[x, x+4y]$ can be calculated from the following scheme:

$f(x)$	$\Delta 1 - \Delta 3$	$\Delta 4$
$f(x) = k + ax + bx^2 + cx^3 + dx^4$		
$f(x+y) \ldots$		
$f(x+2y) \ldots$		
$f(x+3y) \ldots$		$24dy^4$
$f(x+4y) \ldots$		

[6] Lardner, H. P. Babbage, p 51.

Notes to section 1.4

This section is mainly based upon my inspection of Babbage's engine at the Science Museum, South Kensington, London, during November-December 1981.

[1] *Passages*, p 67.
   A somewhat different version of this story is given in Hyman, p 129. There it is a lady who asked the question.

[2] The basis for this description is taken from Babbage himself in *Passages*, pp 63-66.

[3] The engine could be reset so that these three wheels could be used to expand the second difference to six digits if so desired.

[4] Baily, H. P. Babbage, p 225.

[5] John Herschel, "Report of the Committee", H. P. Babbage, p 233.

[6] *Passages*, p 65.

[7] This drawing was first published in Hyman, p 259. A large collection of drawings and notations relating to Babbage's calculating engines is to be found in the Science Museum Library, South Kensington, London. This material is in the process of being closely studied by Allan G. Bromley.

[8] Lardner, in his article (H. P. Babbage, p 71), gives larger slightly exaggerated dimensions.

[9] Lardner, H. P. Babbage, p 70, erroneously states (referring to this design in particular), that there should be only ten punches. Eleven punches (0-9, including one for the decimal point), can be seen in the drawing (Fig. 14).

Notes to section 2.1

Unless stated to the contrary, this section is based on the following sources:

Carl Fredrik Bergstedt, "Georg Scheutz: Auditör, skriftställare och mekanisk uppfinnare", *Lefnadsteckningar öfver Kongl. Svenska Vetenskapsakademiens efter år 1854 aflidna ledamöter* 2 (Stockholm 1878-1885), pp 155-179.

Harald Wieselgren, "Georg Scheutz", *Ny Illustrerad Tidning* 25, 21st June 1873, pp 1-2. This article is reprinted in *idem*, "Georg Scheutz: 1873", *Ur vår samtid: Femtio porträtt med nekrologer* (Stockholm 1880), pp 94-101.

Most of the articles in the *Biografiskt Lexicon* are anonymous, but were usually autobiographical. Georg Scheutz is identified as the author of this article in Harald Wieselgren, "Georg Scheutz", p 60, *Ny Illustrerad Tidning* 25, 21st June 1873, p 2.

[Georg Scheutz], "Scheutz, Georg", *Biografiskt Lexicon öfver namnkunnige Svenska män* 14 (Uppsala 1847), pp 54-66.
This important autobiography by Georg Scheutz has not been noted by Merzbach, p 60. It gives a detailed account, with interesting personal comments, of Scheutz' life and the first difference engine, up to some time between December 1844 to 1847. In the sequel, I shall refer to this article as [Scheutz], 1847.

Research for chapter 2 has been carried out as follows: I have studied the book by Uta C. Merzbach on Georg Scheutz and his engines, a work based primarily on printed sources in Sweden and in the USA, and on letters by Scheutz, Babbage and others in Babbage's manuscript collection in the British Library. Like Merzbach, I have used Archibald's biography and bibliography on Scheutz and the difference engine (published in 1947). Before writing this chapter, I have examined, with a few exceptions, the sources used by Merzbach. In addition, I have read all letters and other manuscript documents that I have been able to find, written by Georg and Edvard Scheutz, or in any other way relating to them and to the engines. This hitherto unobserved treasure of primary source material is to be found spread out in various Swedish archives (KTHB, KVA, NM, RA, SF, SSA and TM). I have also used unknown material in foreign archives (e.g. PRO). In the sequel I will not (except in certain important cases) draw special attention to when one of these new sources has been used. I hope to show the reader that this reexamination of Merzbach's work and her sources, combined with the analysis of the hitherto unused, but important, primary source material, will result in quite different conclusions than those that have been drawn before.

[1] Georg Scheutz, previously Schieutz, changed the spelling of his surname around 1805. Wieselgren 1873, p 1.

[2] Sigurd Schartau, "Eldsvådorna 1785 och 1790: Staden i början av 1800-talet", Ernst L. Hartman, C. O. von Porat, Algot Friberg och Robert Johansson (eds.), *Jönköpings historia* 4 (Jönköping 1921), p 100.

[3] Ludvig Borgström, "Borgström, Ludvig: Sjelfbiographie", *Biografiskt Lexicon öfver namnkunnige Svenska män* 2 (Uppsala 1836), p 391.

[4] Barbro Edlund (ed.), *Lunds universitets matrikel 1732-1830* (Lund 1979), p 163.

[5] [Scheutz], 1847, p 59.

[6] *Ibidem*.
Merzbach, p 3, mentions that Scheutz attended the University of Uppsala briefly, and suggests that it appears as though he did not complete the bergsexam.

As shown above, it was just a short visit and he never matriculated at the University in Uppsala. See also: Otto Brenner and Gösta Thimon, *Uppsala Universitets matrikel 1595-1817: Register*, Acta universitatis Upsalienses 20 (Uppsala 1971).

[7] Rolf Torstendahl, *Teknologins nytta: Motiveringar för det svenska tekniska utbildningsväsendets framväxt framförda av riksdagsmän och utbildningsadminist-ratörer 1810-1870* (Uppsala 1975), p 18, p 22 ff.

[8] *Ibidem* pp 19-20.

[9] RA, Eriksbergsarkivets autografsamling, 184, Letter from Georg Scheutz to Magnus Jacob Crusenstolpe, Jönköping, 26th March 1812.

[10] KB, Brevskrivararkivet, Ep.V.4:18, Letter from Georg Scheutz to Per Adam Wallmark, Jönköping, undated, 1812.

[11] KB, Brevskrivararkivet, Ep,V,4:18, Letter from Georg Scheutz to Per Adam Wallmark, Jönköping, 30th May 1812.

[12] KB, Brevskrivararkivet, Ep,V,4:18, Letter from Georg Scheutz to Per Adam Wallmark, Jönköping, undated, 1812.

[13] Sten Lindroth, *Kungl. Svenska Vetenskapsakademiens historia 1739-1818* 2 parts in 3 vols. (Uppsala 1967).

[14] [Georg Scheutz], *Journal för Manufakturer och Hushållning*, May 1825 - December 1826, January 1833 - December 1834, *passim*. In the sequel, it will be abbreviated *JFMH*.

[15] Arthur Montgomery, *Industrialismens genombrott i Sverige* (Stockholm 1947). See chapter 5: "Hantverk och fabrikssystem", p 121 ff, esp. pp 129-130.

[16] Eli F. Heckscher, *Svenskt arbete och liv: Från medeltiden till nutiden* (Stockholm 1980), p 253, *passim*.

[17] RA, Kommerskollegie Huvudarkiv, Kammarkontorets årsberättelser, Fabriker serie 1, 1811, städer, p 298.
It has been repeatedly noted by Swedish economic historians that this source is somewhat inaccurate. This is also immediately evident when the material itself is studied, especially with regard to later years. (Factories listed one year, might be omitted next year, only to return again in the statistics a year later etc.) The question of what conclusions can be drawn from this material (especially for the period 1830-1896) is discussed by Torsten Gårdlund, *Industrialismens samhälle* (Stockholm 1942), pp 451-452, note 33. He argues that the information given about the number of factories, their number of employees and the amounts produced, is relatively accurate, but that the numbers given should always be regarded as minimum values. I agree with this and I also believe that this is applicable to the earlier period which is discussed here. (I have used the manuscript statistics. From 1830 these statistics were published.)

[18] RA, Kommerskollegie Huvudarkiv, Kammarkontorets årsberättelser, Fabriker serie 1, 1811, städer, pp 272-275.

[19] Gertrud Bergman, "Charles Apelquist", *Daedalus* 1952, pp 129-146.

[20] Fredrik Schütz, "Samuel Owen", *Daedalus* 1975, pp 93-140.

[21] KB, Brevskrivarearkivet, Ep,V,4:18; 12 Letters from Georg Scheutz to Per Adam Wallmark, from 1812 to 1837.

[22] Heckscher, pp 163-164, says that the mortality in cities abroad was normally as high as 4%. It was not until the 1870s Stockholm achieved such low figures on a regular basis. The normal figure was 5%, sometimes going up to 6%.

[23] Among those belonging to the circles in which Scheutz had moved since his student days, was his best friend, the radical author and lawyer, Magnus Jacob Crusenstolpe. See RA, Ericsbergsarkivets autografsamling, vol. 184; 19 letters from Georg Scheutz to Magnus Jacob Crusenstolpe, from 21st March 1811 to 18th December 1860.

[24] Wieselgren, 1873, p 2.

[25] *Ibidem.*

[26] Cederborgh and Scheutz had a contract about *Anmärkaren.* According to this, if the newspaper was confiscated, Scheutz was to replace it with *Anmärkarne.* The first issue was published in January 1820. But Cederborgh suddenly severed his connections with Scheutz and asked to be allowed to publish *Anmärkaren* again which Scheutz granted "as a special favour", (Wieselgren, 1873, p 2). It is clear that Cederborgh had acted in breach of the contract. *Anmärkaren* appeared again in February, this time with Cederborgh as the sole publisher. See KB, I. s. 10, "Contract" between Georg Scheutz and Fredrik Cederborgh regarding the publication of *Anmärkaren* and *Anmärkarne*, Stockholm, 21st October 1819. There is further detailed information about these two newspapers in Bernhard Lundstedt, *Sveriges periodiska litteratur 1645-1899: Bibliografi* 2 (Stockholm 1896), pp 4-5, 13-14.

[27] Wieselgren, 1873, p 2.

[28] *Argus* was published jointly by Scheutz and Johan Johansson, who eventually became sole publisher and writer. ([Scheutz], 1847, p 61, note 11). See also Lundstedt, vol. 2, pp 14-16.

[29] Wieselgren, 1873, p 2.

[30] See *JFMH* and also Lundstedt, vol. 2, p 29.

[31] *JFMH*, 1825-1826, 1833-1834, *passim.* Scheutz only occasionally mentioned where he had obtained his information.

[32] [Georg Scheutz], "Till Läsaren" ("To the Reader"), *JFMH*, December 1834, the 2 last pages. See also Lundstedts vol. 2, p 56.

[33] *Svenska Industriföreningens Tidskrift*, January 1836, pp 22-23.

[34] [Georg Scheutz], "Till Läsaren", *JFMH*, December 1834, at the end.

[35] "Utdrag ur Svenska Industriföreningens Minnesböcker: 1, Föreningens Stadgar antagna den 23 oktober 1832: Första kapitlet: Föreningens syftemål, §1", *Svenska Industriföreningens Tidskrift*, December 1834 (first issue), p 7. In future this will be abbreviated *SIT*.

[36] *Ibidem*, pp 15-20. Here there is a list of the society's members giving their name, title and place of business. Many call themselves merely manufacturers, company directors, mill owners and the like. At the very least some 34% of them were textile manufacturers.

[37] [Georg Scheutz], "Slöjdexpositionen i Stockholm 1834", *JFMH*, June 1834, p 214.

[38] *Ibidem*, pp 213-214. Together with note.

[39] *Ibidem*, pp 206 ff.

[40] *Ibidem*, p 212.

[41] *Ibidem*, pp 209-212.

[42] *Ibidem*, p 210.
It is interesting to note that at this point Georg Scheutz refers his readers to what Charles Babbage says in *Economy* for further information about this ability to market goods.

[43] Pontus Henriques, *Skildringar ur Kungl. Tekniska Högskolans historia* 1 (Stockholm 1917), p 118.

[44] The fate of the Swedish Industrial Association is unknown. I have not been able to find out anything more about it, although it seems as if it continued to be active at least for a time after this event.

[45] [Georg Scheutz], *Tidning för Näringarne*, No. 1, 2, 7th November 1840, p 1. See also Lundstedt, vol. 2, p 67.

[46] KB, Rare book, [Georg Scheutz], *Handbok för så wäl enklare som mera konstig Blekning Winter- och Sommartiden, af Lin, Blånor och Lingarn, Drell, Hollandslärft, Bomullsgarn och Bomullstyger, Papper, Wax och Halm, gamla Böcker och Kopparstick, mm, i sammandrag...* (Stockholm 1817). For information about this series, see Lundstedt, vol. 2, pp 46-47.

[47] [Olry] Terquem, *Handbok i algebra*, Bibliothek för konst, slöjd och tillämpad vetenskap (Stockholm 1832). Unsigned translation by Magnus Luttrop, edited and adapted by Georg Scheutz, see Lundstedt vol. 2, p 47. List of titles intended to be published in the series, see *Handbok i algebra*, p 401.

[48] See e.g. [Georg Scheutz] *Handbok för bleckarbeten*, Bibliothek för konst, slöjd och tillämpad vetenskap (Stockholm 1849), an original work by Georg Scheutz containing a great wealth of information about all aspects of sheet metal working including a complete glossary of technical terms. (This is the second, enlarged edition, printed at the Eckstein press. Earlier the same year, it had been published by Brudin's press.)

[49] Inga Britta Sandqvist, "Tekniska tidskrifter före Teknisk Tidskrift", Nicolai Herlofsson, Svante Lindqvist, Erik Tholander (eds.), *Vilja och kunnande: Teknikhistoriska uppsatser tillägnade Torsten Althin på hans åttioårsdag den 11 July 1977 av vänner* (Uppsala 1977), p 115.
Heckscher, p 249, assigns the technical journals a specially important role in fostering internationalism in Sweden's historical development. According to

Heckscher, the technical journals had a more prominent part in the introduction of new ideas from abroad, which increased dramatically from the beginning of the nineteenth century, than immigrant mechanics, engineers etc. See pp 247, 249. This further emphasizes the significance of the technical journalism and popularisation of Scheutz and his colleagues.

[50] Sandqvist, p 114.

[51] *Ibidem*, p 120.

[52] *Ibidem*, pp 121-122.
Henrik Björck, "På de tillfälliga uppfinningarnas oroliga haf", *Polhem: Tidskrift för teknikhistoria*, No. 2, 1986, pp 57-126, esp. p 63 f.

[53] [Scheutz], 1847, p 61.

[54] RA, Skrivelser till Kungl. Maj:t, Georg Scheutz, "Commerce Collegium angående Auditeuren G. Scheutz ansökning rörande privilegium exclusivum å åtskillige vid boktryckerier användbare Mechaniska Machiner", (Nr 1040), 21st June 1820.
Some sources indicate that Scheutz made this application already in 1817. There is no evidence, either in RA, Kommerskollegie Huvudarkiv or at KVA, that this was the case.

[55] I maintain that Scheutz' interest in the difference engine owes as much to his role as an inventor as it does to his career in technical journalism and scientific popularization. This is why I have examined in some detail his practical and technical achievements.
The first law in Sweden offering the inventor protection for his invention dates from April 1819. The term *privilegium exclusivum* continued to be used until December 1834, when it was replaced by the word *patent* which was standard abroad.

[56] Georg Scheutz, *Register öfwer Stockholms tidningar* (Stockholm 1819), p 3.

[57] Samuel E. Bring and Ernst Rikard Kulling, *Svenska Boktryckereföreningen 50 år: Kort historik över Boktryckeri-Societeten och Svenska Boktryckereföreningen utgiven med anledning av föreningens femtioårs jubileum: 1893-1943* (Göteborg 1943), pp 113-114.

[58] This application does not seem to be among the papers preserved in the relevant archive (RA, Kommerskollegie Huvudarkiv). However, it is clear that such an application was made in that year. See the reference mentioned in note 61 and also the following:
KVA, "Scheutz's ansökning", KVA protokoll 1823, p 107.
Bengt Bengtsson, Emil Malmborg, Ture Nerman, *Typografiska Föreningen i Stockholm ett hundra år: Minneskrift 1846-1946* 1 (Stockholm 1946), p 152.)

[59] Bring and Kulling, p 114.

[60] *Ibidem.*

[61] KVA, "Scheutz's ansökning", KVA protokoll 1827, p 3, Scheutz requested a decision from the Kommerskollegium regarding his application for a privilegium exclusivum in 1823. (Cf. the reference given in note 58). See also KVA, Bilagor

KVA protokoll 1827, p 31; Letter from Georg Scheutz to KVA, Stockholm, 6th January 1827.

[62] KVA, "Scheutz's ansökning", KVA protokoll 1827, p 3. One of the members of the Academy of Sciences (Gustaf Magnus Schwartz) was unwilling to take upon himself the task of demanding a decision from the Kommerskollegium. The matter was entrusted to someone else.

[63] RA, Kommerskollegie Huvudarkiv, Acta Privatorum, EXVII d:2, vol. 403, Georg Scheutz privilegieansökan, No 45, Stockholm, 13th January 1831.

[64] *Ibidem*, as well as KVA, Bilagor KVA protokoll 1827, p 1, where Scheutz enclosed a copy of *The Times* to illustrate this fact.

[65] RA, Kommerskollegie Huvudarkiv, D II d:2, Register över patent 1820-1853, "*Förteckning å de af Kongl. Commerce Collegium beviljade Privilegia Exclusiva och Patenter från och med år 1820 till och med år 1842*", p 3. The patent was granted on the 31st October 1831.

[66] [Scheutz], 1847, p 61, note 13.

[67] On one occasion, Scheutz maintained that the press could produce 1,200 sheets per hour. However during a trial run, before a potential customer (Lars Johan Hierta), he tramped away at his press "so that his forehead was lathered in sweat" without achieving a rate of more than 250 sheets per hour − a performance comparable to that of the normal press of the time. See Bengtsson et al. *Typografiska Föreningen i Stockholm*, pp 153-154.

[68] *Ibidem*, pp 144-145.

[69] *Ibidem*, p 151.

[70] Gustaf Edvard Klemming and Johan Gabriel Nordin, *Svensk boktryckeri-historia 1483-1883: Med inledande allmän öfversigt* (Stockholm 1883), p 429.
This invention is nowhere mentioned in the relevant archive (RA, Kommerskollegiums arkiv) from which I infer that no patent was sought for it.

[71] [Scheutz], 1847, pp 61-62, note 16.
Klemming and Nordin, p 430, maintain, contrary to what Scheutz himself asserts, that the etching instrument was unusable. One interpretation of this might be that it was not sufficiently good to be produced, and adopted by other printers. There is no evidence that a patent was sought for this invention.

[72] [Georg Scheutz], "Säkerhetsventil för ångpannor, som fritt medgifver minskning, men icke förökning, af den en gång för alla bestämda ångtryckningen", *SIT*, September 1835, pp 270-272, Fig. (1) on p 296 recto. The machine was employed at the clothes factory in Stockholm belonging to the Chairman of the Industrial Association, J. E. Öberg, *Ibidem*, p 270. There is no indication that a patent was sought for this invention.

[73] RA, Kommerskollegie Huvudarkiv, patentansökningar, EXVII e:1, vol. 7, Georg Scheutz, "*Uppfinning, att medelst ånga, blandad med luft, åstadkomma en rotatorisk rörelse*", No. 964, Stockholm, 26th May 1840.

[74] RA, Skrivelser till Kongl. Maj:t, Georg Scheutz, "Commerce Collegium

angående ett af auditeur Scheutz sökt privilegium exclusivum på ett Hydrauliskt Instrument", (No. 1250), Stockholm, 6th October 1825.

KVA, Bilagor KVA protokoll 1825, pp 78-79. Utlåtande angående Scheutz privilegie ansökan för ett Hydrauliskt Instrument, Stockholm, 23rd September 1825.

[75] RA, Kommerskollegie Huvudarkiv, Acta Privatorum, EXVII d:2, vol. 411, Georg Scheutz, *"Alun, hvars kristallform är kubisk"*, (No. 1931), Stockholm, 28th November 1832.

[76] RA, Kommerskollegie Huvudarkiv, patentansökningar, EXVII e:1, vol. 8, Georg Scheutz, *"Portfeuille Iconografique, eller Afbildningsbok"*, (No. 1702), Stockholm, 21st September 1841.

[77] *Ibidem*, vol. 9, Georg Scheutz, *"Sinus-delare"*, (No. 888), Stockholm, 14th May 1842. Vol. 17, and; Georg Scheutz, *"Method att bränna Tak- och Murtegel"*, (No. 1795), Stockholm, 25th November 1850.

[78] RA, Kommerskollegie Huvudarkiv, D II d:2, Register över patent 1820-1853, *"Förteckning [...] 1842"*:
Rotatorisk rörelse, 4th June 1840, eight years, p 50.
Hydrauliskt Instrument, 14th November 1825, p 5.
Kubiskt alun, 31st July 1833, ten years, p 3.
Portfeuille Iconografique, 5th Oktober 1841, eight years, p 49.
Sinus-delare, 23rd May 1842, p 51.
The date is that when the patent was granted.
RA, *Ibidem*, "Förteckning å de af Kongl. Commerce Collegium beviljade Patenter Åren 1843-1850":
Tak- och Murtegel, 29th November 1850, five years. No page numbers, see: *Tegel*.

[79] [Georg Scheutz], "Flygande Skottkärror", *JFMH*, fourth issue 1825, pp 102-104, and; fifth issue 1825, p 160, "Tillägg" (Addition). It is Carl Sahlin who in the article "Svenska linbanekonstruktioner", *Daedalus* 1931, pp 56-57, first drew attention to this case.

[80] [Georg Scheutz], *JFMH*, fourth issue 1825, p 102.

[81] *Ibidem*, pp 102-103, fifth issue, p 160.

[82] *Ibidem*, pp 103-104.

[83] Carl Sahlin, p 57, does not, however, give any substantial evidence that it is from Scheutz that these later applied improvements have been derived, although they might very well have been observed and used by Scheutz' readers. Nor is it actually known to what extent these improvements or additions were new from a national and international point of view. My point is that Scheutz did make improvement inventions and probably many more than is mentioned here.

[84] Silvestre Francois Lacroix, *Handbok i landtmäteriet: Innehållande första grunderna för jordsträckors mätning och kartläggning, äfvensom för afvägningar och rymdmätningar. Till tjänst för Landtmän och dem som icke förut känna Geometrien*, Bibliothek för konst, slöjd och tillämpad vetenskap (Stockholm 1832), An unsigned translation probably by Magnus Luttrop, See Lundstedt, vol. 2, p 47. Arranged with an addition by Georg Scheutz, also unsigned.

[85] *Ibidem*, pp 82-85.

[86] I am indebted to the article by Nils Hanson, "Reflektioner kring en fotografisk metod från år 1832 för bestämning av en orts meridian", *Värld och Vetande: Populärvetenskaplig tidskrift* 3 1960, pp 73-76, for drawing my attention to this event. Scheutz reveals that he was the author to the addition about the method in: [Georg Scheutz], "Ljusmålning", *SIT*, April 1839, p 117, note. The article "Ljusmålning", *Ibidem*, pp 115-119, is a reprint of the addition made by Scheutz in Lacroix's book.

In the second edition of *Handbok i landtmäteriet*, which was published in 1849, the addition in question has been bound separately at the end of the book: "Tillägg G. Till Nr. 58, sidan 57", pp 136-140. The fact that it is named "Addition G", and there are additions *A* to *G* in the book, indicates that Scheutz may have done much more than is mentioned here.

[87] One of Georg Scheutz early private works in this genre has been preserved: KB, I. s. 10, Georg Scheutz, *"Chiffonier* innehållande *uselhet*, men förvaras ändå till minne af mina pojkår". Small bound manuscript containing poetry and prose poems etc. Dated 1806, but continues to 1813.

[88] In his autobiographical article ([Scheutz], 1847, p 61) he says that his literary production also included "a great number of pieces in verse and prose, contributed to other newspapers and journals, larger and shorter essays in belles-lettres, physics, technology and politics, art criticism and reviews as well as editorial articles on issues of the day".

[89] An example of this is his short story "Trollkammaren" which appeared anonymously in *Aftonbladet* in 1841, nos. 195, 197, 199-201, and his book review in the same newspaper the year before. (This review was described by one contemporary as masterly). The book was Bernhard von Beskow's *Har Sverige publicitet och publicister?* (Uppsala 1820), which dealt with political journalism and the freedom of the press. The comprehensive review displays Georg's thorough knowledge of history and politics. It was serialized in five parts in *Aftonbladet* in 1840; nos. 145, 149, 155, 182 and 185.

The reference to this anonymous review as well as the opinions expressed about it, are taken from Carl Wilhelm Liljecrona, *Bakom Riksdagens kulisser: C.W. Liljecronas dagbok under Riksdagen 1840-41: Med inledning, noter och personregister af Gustaf A. Aldén* (Stockholm 1917), p 178.

As already mentioned, Georg Scheutz published many of his books anonymously. A further example of this is *Vägen till naturens riken: En elementarbok i naturhistorien: För lägre läroverk och sjelfundervisning*, which was published in 1843. It was printed at Hierta's press in Stockholm and in the preface, it is noted "that the author [Scheutz] placed his name on the title page only upon the express request of the publisher [Hierta]".

[90] The first scholar to give Scheutz' literary production any serious consideration was Uta C. Merzbach, see p 59. In her book, pp 68-72, she gives a comprehensive bibliography of his works with the newspaper and journal articles excluded. Furthermore, she encourages the reader (in 1977) to further study of Scheutz' publications and his role in Swedish literary history. So far, no one has dealt with this interesting matter in depth.

It might be noted that Merzbach has not had the opportunity to check more than a few of Scheutz' publications, and she also adds that the bibliography is preliminary (Merzbach, p 59). I have found that Scheutz' correspondence and other manuscripts in the Swedish archives contain information of value for further study of this matter. Also other Swedish sources (see, for example, the previous note) are of importance.

[91] According to Bergstedt, p 175, the book's Swedish title was, *Brasilien enligt de nyaste och säkraste underrättelser skildrat av hofrådet von Zimmermann* (Jönköping 1809).

[92] [Scheutz], 1847, p 60, note 6.

[93] I have not inspected all of these publications. The titles are taken from Bergstedt, pp 175-176. Cf. Merzbach, pp 68-72.

[94] Bergstedt, p 178.
[Scheutz], 1847, p 60, note 5.

[95] *Passages, passim,* e.g.: pp 144-145.
Doris Langley Moore, *Ada: Countess of Lovelace: Byron's Legitimate Daughter* (Southampton 1977), p 164.

[96] [Georg Scheutz], "Kranpumpar: Georg Scheutz's Patent, af den 14 November 1825", *JFMH*, eighth issue 1825, pp 225-236, and ninth issue, Fig. "Tab 8", p 288 recto.

[97] [Georg Scheutz], "Om Sug- och Presspumpars bruk, i åtskilliga slöjder", *Ibidem*, pp 237-240.

[98] See for example: [Georg Scheutz], "Säkerhetsventil...", *SIT*, September 1835.

[99] KVA, Letter from Georg Scheutz to Carl Palmstedt, Stockholm, 6th July 1838.

Notes to section 2.2

[1] [Georg Scheutz], "Om Babbages Räknemachin", *JFMH*, November 1833, pp 363-372.

[2] *Ibidem*, pp 363-364, here translated from the Swedish original to English. Merzbach p 6, says that Scheutz selected several chapters from the third edition of Babbage's *Economy* (London 1833) as the basis for the translations and paraphrases that he published in *JFMH*. In fact, Scheutz only made use of one chapter, namely V, which dealt with the invention of tools and machines, in an article in *JFMH* in June 1834, pp 185-194. On the other hand, Scheutz used Babbage's book for two articles in *SIT*. One was entitled "Strödda uppsatser uti industriella ämnen" (Diverse essays on industrial subjects), November 1835, pp 350-360. The other was called "Om sättet att bese större fabriker eller manufakturanläggningar" (Concerning the study of larger factories or manufactories), which appeared in March 1836, pp 74-79. Merzbach further maintains that Babbage's chapter XX, about Prony's tables, was to have a central role in Scheutz' involvement in the history of calculation. I show in this section that this was not the case.

[3] *JFMH*, first number May 1825, foreword.

[4] [anon], "Mr. Babbage's Calculating Machinery", *Mechanics Magazine*, 488, 1832, p 173.

[5] [Georg Scheutz], "Om Babbages Räknemaskin", pp 371-372, note *.

[6] *Economy*, chapter XX, pp 191-202.

[7] [Georg Scheutz], "Om konsten att uppfinna redskap och machiner: En vink för uppfinnare och användare", *JFMH*, June 1834, pp 187-188, note *. Based on chapter XXVII in *Economy*, third edition (London 1833).

[8] [Georg Scheutz], "Strödda uppsatser uti industriella ämnen", *SIT*, November 1835, p 351.

[9] *Ibidem*.

[10] *Ibidem*.

[11] *Economy*, third edition, (London 1833), pp 198-199, note *.

[12] A copy of this rare work is to be found in KB.

[13] Georg Scheutz, *Portatif räknemachin i form af en liten bok: En tillämpning af John Nepers, Baron af Marchiston, Räknestafwar* (Stockholm 1834), p 8.
It is Scheutz himself who uses the word calculating machine ("räknemachin"). This work by Scheutz also includes a short section on Napier and Briggs and their work on the logarithms, (see pp 7-8). Scheutz says that he has read Napier's book "*Rabdologiae, seu numerationis per virgulas, libri duo: cum appendice de expeditissimo multiplicationis promptuario...*", the edition published in Leyden 1626 (p 8, note).

[14] Although Merzbach includes *Portatif räknemachin* in her Scheutz bibliography (pp 70-71) she does not mention it in the text.

[15] *Typografiska Föreningen 1*, p 55.

[16] *Handbok i Algebra*, the title page and pp 361-399.

[17] "Statistisk Tabell öfver Ekers Socken uti ÖREBRO Härad och NERIKES LÄN, 1822", *Argus- den tredje: Politisk, Litterär och Commersiell Tidning*, no. 76, 24 September 1823, p 324.

[18] See e.g.: Åke Claesson Rålamb, *En liten och kort Hand-Bok utaf Adelig öfning, att bruka wid många tillfällen. Till stor hjelpreda i Daglig Handel* (Örebro 1824, 1827), or C. W. Thuring, *Intresse-uträkning på Större och Mindre Capital efter 5 och 6 procent ifrån en dag till och med Ett År* (Örebro 1804, 1810, 1817, 1824), 69 pages.

[19] KB, Brevskrivarearkivet, Ep. L. 19:6, Letter from Georg Scheutz to Nils Magnus Lindh, Jönköping, 13th July 1813. Together with a further 6 letters, 1813-1853.

[20] Hans Jacob Seseman, *Multiplications- och Divisions-Taflas Intresse-Räkning à 6 Pro Cent om Året, som utwisar Intresset icke allenast för År, Månader och Dagar, utan för alla 360 Dagarna i Året, efter Större och Mindre Capitaler, så wäl*

uti Koppar och Silfwer, samt Specie-Mynt med sina Fördelningar (Stockholm 1811), last page.

[21] This information is based upon my investigation of the tables in the collection of KB, March 1984.

[22] Dionysius Lardner, "Babbage's Calculating Engine", *Edinburgh Review*, No. CXX, July 1834, reprinted in H. P. Babbage, pp 51-82. The quotation from pp 52-53.

[23] Buxton, p 1602, says that the article was written under the immediate supervision of Babbage, and in the latter's house. The article was also based on seven papers (six of them by Babbage) regarding the difference engine, see Fig. 20.
   See also Collier, p 85 ff., who says something more about the origins of Lardner's article.

[24] Lardner, H. P. Babbage, p 52.

[25] Bergstedt, p 162.
   [Scheutz], 1847, p 62.

[26] [anon], "Lardner, Dionysius (1793-1859)", *Dictionary of National Biography* XI (Oxford 1917), p 586.

[27] Lardner, H. P. Babbage, p 58.

[28] *Ibidem*, p 59.

[29] *Ibidem*, pp 65-66.

[30] *Ibidem*, pp 66-69.

[31] *Ibidem*, p 68.

[32] *Ibidem*.

[33] *Ibidem*.

[34] *Ibidem*, p 73, note *.

[35] This is evident when one reads Babbage's *The Ninth Bridgewater Treatise: A Fragment* (London 1837), which is discussed in section 3.2.

[36] Lardner, H. P. Babbage, p 74.

[37] *Ibidem*.

[38] *Portatif räknemachin*, p 8. Scheutz suggests that two or more *Portatif räknemachin* are used, and put side by side on a table.

[39] Lardner, H. P. Babbage, pp 70-72.

[40] *Ibidem*, p 71.

[41] *Ibidem*, p 81.

[42] [Scheutz], 1847, p 62.

Notes to section 2.3

Unless stated to the contrary, the section is based on the following sources:

KB, X279, [Georg Scheutz], "Historique de la machine calculer & imprimer les tables de mathematique, inventée par Mrs. George et Eduard Scheutz, père et fils", (8 pp fol.). This manuscript is endorsed "Escrit par la maine de G. Scheutz". The handwriting is also identical to that of Georg Scheutz. It is undated, but judging from its contents, written sometime after the end of April 1856.

KB, X279, [Georg Scheutz], "Historical Sketch", (8 pp, 4o). Unsigned manuscript, but written in the handwriting of Georg Scheutz. It is also stated in an handwritten inventory to the X279-collection in the Royal Library, Stockholm, entitled: "Bref och handlingar rörande Georg och Edvard Scheutz' Räknemaskin", 1884, p 1, that the "Historical Sketch" was written by Georg Scheutz. It is undated, but can (from its contents) be assigned to sometime after 15th August 1854.

The "Historical Sketch" and the "Historique" are not identical. They both give an account of the history and origin of the Scheutz' engines, but differ in many details. Together they form an accurate source of information, which is used here for the first time.

[1] "Historical Sketch", p 1.

[2] KB, Edvard Scheutz, *Vackra flickor finnas äfven i Sibirien: Lustspel i två akter* (Stockholm 1836). (Together with a separate note by Edvard, to the effect that he himself had been responsible for the printing.)

[3] SSA, Allmänna BB:s födelsebok.
Herman Hofberg, "Scheutz, Edvard", *Svenskt biografiskt handlexikon* 1 (Stockholm 1876), p 243, upon which all other scholars have relied, erroneously states that he was born on the 3rd of September.

[4] *Ibidem.* (She also wrote her name Sjoman).

[5] SSA, BOU 1823-II-141, Anna Margaretha Schaumann's inventory, Stockholm, 23rd July 1823, pp 142-143.
SSA, Klara likbok 1811-1828.

[6] SSA, Allmänna BB:s födelsebok. It was Anna Schaumann's second child.

[7] SSA, BOU 1823-II-141, p 142.

[8] Since 1876 known as the Royal Institute of Technology.
RA, KTH arkiv, D 1 a, Nr. 932: Edvard Georg Scheutz, "Matriklar över ordinarie elever", vol. 3. He matriculated on the 6th of November.

[9] Henriques, p 283.

[10] *Ibidem*, p 95. (Statutes date 8th June 1826).

[11] *Ibidem*, p 96.

[12] *Ibidem*, p 125.

[13] *Ibidem*, p 125 ff.

Torstendahl, *passim*.

The interesting question of how far the practically oriented Georg Scheutz lent his support to Gustav Magnus Schwartz must remain unanswered on the basis of the known source material.

[14] Henriques, pp 257-258.

[15] *Ibidem*, p 177.

[16] RA, KTH arkiv, F II baa, "Examenshandlingar för 1828-1839 (T. I.)", vol. 1. Unnumbered collection of manuscripts.

[17] In *JFMH* Georg Scheutz published a notice about the Royal Technological Institute, noting that it had recently opened and mentioning the subjects that were offered. This is evidence of his interest in the Institute from its start. See [Georg Scheutz], "Strödda underrättelser", *JFMH*, ninth issue 1826, p 287.

[18] KVA, Letters from Georg Scheutz to Carl Palmstedt, 12 items, from 26th August 1837 to 12th October 1842.

Scheutz also published the Chalmerska Slöjdskolans Årsberättelser (Chalmers Craftschool's Annual Reports), written by Palmstedt, in *SIT*. These were long detailed descriptions of the courses and the practical work (also a standard feature there) of the school. Scheutz viewed this kind of information as providing interesting documents about the progress in technical and industrial education in Sweden. (*SIT*, June 1834, p 170). See "Insända Meddelanden och Uppsatser", *SIT*: June 1834, pp 171-185, August 1835, pp 233-257, July 1836, pp 186-209, June 1837, pp 161-178.

[19] Henriques, p 112.

[20] *Ibidem*, p 113, esp. p 177.

[21] RA, KTH arkiv, D 1 a, Nr. 932, "Matrikel över ordinarie elever", vol. 3.

[22] RA, KTH arkiv, F II baa, "Examenshandlingar". This piece of information and those that follow, about the courses taken by Edvard Scheutz at the Royal Technological Institute, are to be found *passim* in this source.

[23] Henriques, p 157. A plan of the lower floor of the building from the beginning of the 1840s is shown on this page. There is every reason to believe that the situation was very much the same during the somewhat earlier period discussed here.

[24] *Ibidem*, pp 257-258.

[25] See e.g., Jonas Samuel Bagge, *Elementarkurs i Fysiken* (Stockholm 1835) or Joachim Åkerman, *Elementarkurs i Kemien* (Stockholm 1836).

[26] See note 22.

[27] See note 22.

[28] RA, "G. Scheutz, [...] anhållan om understöd af allmänna medel för fullbordandet af en utaf honom upfunnen Räknemachin", undated, but handed in per-

sonally by Georg Scheutz to the Royal Palace, 31st August 1844, Ecklesiastik-Departementet, ingående skrivelser, augusti - december 1844, No. 599.

In Merzbach p 8, it is asserted twice that Georg had built *one* (rough) model of the difference engine. This is incorrect, inasmuch as no such complete model was ever built before Edvard's engine. It was rather a matter of various very simple models of components of the engine, such as addition elements or parts of the printing unit.

[29] KVA, "Scheutz anhållan om granskning af förslag till en machin för beräkning och stereotypering af Mathematiska Tabeller", Bilagor KVA protokoll 1837, p 269 ff. Dated, Stockholm, 3rd October 1837.

[30] "Historical Sketch", p 2.

[31] *Ibidem*. Merzbach, p 8, says that Edvard had produced a metal engine at this point. There is no evidence to support this statement.

[32] KVA, "Scheutz anhållan", Bilagor KVA protokoll 1837, p 269 ff. The pages of this document are unnumbered. For the purposes of reference I have labelled them (1-11), pp 8-10.

[33] *Ibidem*, p 10. This is the first time this proposal has been noted. Merzbach, p 8, says that Georg Scheutz requested that the Academy should support a grant application to the Swedish government for a full-scale difference engine. As mentioned above, Scheutz did not request this.

[34] *Ibidem*, p 8.
The first logarithmic table published in Sweden was Petrus Elvius' sixteen page *Tabula compendiosa logarithmorum sinum ad quadrantis gradus, eorumq; partes decimas, nec non numerorum absolutorum ab unitate ad 1000* (Uppsala 1698).

[35] KVA, "Scheutz anhållan", p 2.

[36] *Ibidem*, p 4.

[37] *Ibidem*, p 8.

[38] *Ibidem*, p 9.

[39] *Ibidem*, p 10.

[40] *Ibidem*, p 11.

[41] KVA, Protokoll 1837, p 66.
The four men were Gustav Erik Pasch, Jöns Svanberg, Fabian Wrede and Nils Haqvin Selander. Pasch was a chemist and technologist and was a professor at the Royal Academy of Sciences. Svanberg was an astronomer at the same institution, as well as being a theologian. These two men seem to have had a secondary role in the subsequent chain of events. The existing source material says nothing about their views and there is nothing to suggest that they were later involved. Wrede and Selander, on the other hand, were to play an important part in the story of the Scheutzes and their machine.

[42] KVA, Utlåtande angående Scheutz räknemaskin, Bilagor KVA protokoll 1838, p 79. Dated, Stockholm 14th February 1838.

[43] In addition there is an ambiguity in the report, p 79, which makes it unclear if Scheutz refused to make a statement about his own engine or about Babbage's.

[44] *Ibidem.*

[45] *Ibidem.*

[46] *Ibidem*, p 80. Merzbach, p 8, suggests that the Academy perhaps did not support Scheutz' request (cf. note 33), because it was influenced by the ominous stories of Babbage's machine. As shown here, the case was quite the contrary. The cost was furthermore considered as being "relatively cheap".

[47] RA, "G. Scheutz, [...] anhållan", 31st August 1844. The information is taken from the penultimate page.

[48] *Ibidem.*

[49] [Scheutz], 1847, pp 62-63. This is also based on my examination of the engine.

[50] This statement is based on the rediscovered engine itself and is further discussed below.

[51] RA, KTH arkiv, F II baa, "Examenshandlingar för 1840-1847, (T. I)", vol. 2. Unnumbered collection of manuscripts.

[52] [Scheutz], 1847, p 65-66.

[53] *Ibidem*, p 65.

[54] *Comptes Rendus Hebdomaires de la Academie des Sciences: Paris* 7 (1838), pp 1031, 1056.

[55] Despite having written on two occasions to l'Academie des Sciences I have received no pertinent information; No archivist has been able to locate any material whatsoever that can shed further light on this offer. I am indebted to Claudine Pouret for taking the trouble to look into this matter in May 1984.
In Sweden several of sources have been checked, including the following ones, but with no success:
RA, Utrikes Departementet, Beskickningens i Paris arkiv:
Inkomna skrivelser, vol. 83, 1838.
Utgående diarium, vol. 95, 1837-1847.
Registratur, vols. 54-55, 1837-1839.
Koncept, vols. 30-31, 1838-1839.
(Every letter to and from Löwenhielm has been specially checked). According to Merzbach, p 8, Georg Scheutz sent out feelers to other institutions of learning, including the one to l'Academie des Sciences. There is, however, no evidence that any similar action was taken by Georg Scheutz regarding any other country at the time. This is also stated in Bergstedt, p 165, which Merzbach has used. Furthermore, the contact that Georg Scheutz took with the French, was not at all a cautious proposal or suggestion in order to test their reactions, but rather a very serious offer of a fully complete operating difference engine ([Scheutz], 1847, pp 65-66).

[56] [Scheutz], 1847, pp 65-66. It is unknown when the French asked about this.

[57] *Ibidem*, p 66.

[58] Hyman, pp 41-42.

[59] RA, "G. Scheutz, ... anhållan". Third page from the beginning.

[60] The Scheutz correspondence, preserved in Swedish and British archives is concentrated around the period 1855 to 1860. Virtually no letters from the time of the work on the first Scheutz engine have survived.

[61] "Historical Sketch", p 2.

[62] *Ibidem*, p 3.

[63] "Historique", p 3.

[64] It is evident from the artefact (the machine itself) that its basic design was conceived at an early stage. Probably the Scheutzes made sketches of the wooden frame and the units that were to be mounted in it. The frame also appears to have been built early on, since it bears marks of having been altered on several occasions. If this is true, it follows that the space in the frame for the printing unit, as well as the shape of the unit itself, must also have been decided at an early stage of the work.

[65] KVA, Protokoll 1842, p 66. The men were once more Fabian Wrede and Nils Haqvin Selander.
KVA, Georg Scheutz, "Praktisk Differensräkning för Geometriska Serier", Bilagor KVA protokoll 1842, pp 537-539, (all pages not numbered). Dated, Stockholm, 12th October 1842.

[66] KVA, Protokoll 1842, p 66.

[67] *Ibidem*, p 84.

[68] *Ibidem*.

[69] KVA, "Praktisk Differensräkning", p 539.

[70] [Georg Scheutz], *Journal för Manufakturer och Hushållning* (Stockholm 1825-1826, 1833-1834), *passim*. [Magnus Luttrop], *Handbok i Svarfkosten, innehållande fullständiga underrättelser om denna konsts alla delar* (Stockholm 1839). Published and revised by Georg Scheutz.

[71] TM, 966r, Joachim Åkerman, "Inventarium å befintliga Redskap och Verktyg m.m. vid inventeringen af Kungl. Teknologiska Institutets Werkstäder den 20 Januari 1846". An inventory was also made in the year 1848, and it shows only minor changes in the numbers of tools and machine tools on the premises.

[72] *Ibidem*, pp 1-3.

[73] *Ibidem*, pp 12-19.

[74] I have not been able to locate any inventory of the workshops at the Institute of earlier date. It might be assumed that the above mentioned has survived merely by accident. Nevertheless, the models that were made by the students indicate

the existence of a well equipped and also frequently used machine tool workshop, see note 76.

[75] The purpose of the Mechanical Alphabet was pedagogical. Playing with these models, made the pupils acquainted with the foundations of mechanics, and trained their abilities in assembling more complex machinery.

There is really no good description of the Alphabet available, but for some information, see: William A. Johnson (ed.), *Christopher Polhem: The Father of Swedish Technology* (Hartford, Connecticut 1963), esp. p 35, 157 and illustration on p 158.

Some of the original models of the Mechanical Alphabet are exhibited at the National Museum of Science and Technology, Stockholm.

[76] A large collection of these models, made at the Technological Institute from the 1820's to the 1850's by the students, is preserved at the National Museum of Science and Technology, Stockholm.

[77] RA, "G. Scheutz, [...] anhållan", third page from the beginning.

[78] According to [Georg Scheutz], 1847, pp 64-65, the inspectors also issued a certificate in French, in which three additional properties of the engine, were mentioned. *First*, it could solve equations (of degree 3) although, as is made plain, this was not its primary purpose. *Secondly*, the printing of a tabular value together with the argument, in the matrix material, took 1/4 second to perform. Commenting on this, the inspectors added that "it [the time required] has not been checked", which would suggest that Berzelius, Selender and Lilliehöök themselves had not measured it, but that this had been done at an earlier occasion. *Thirdly*, a later refinement (construction unknown) is mentioned, which allowed one to treat constant differences which end in periodic decimals as though they were rational numbers.

Perhaps these additions reflect questions that had been put to Scheutz by the French when he made his offer in 1838. There is also a remote possibility that the French version of the certificate was intended for the Swedish King Carl XIV Johan, who only spoke French, (see p 131).

[79] KB, X279, Statement concerning the difference engine of Georg and Edvard Scheutz, Stockholm, 18th September 1843. In the sequel, I shall refer to this document as the *Berzelius statement*. The original is given in facsimile in the appendix. This statement has not been used by other scholars who have written about Scheutz. It has been partly published in, e.g. *Specimens of Tables* (London 1857), p x, where however, the beginning and the end are omitted.

[80].The Scheutzes always refer to this machine as the "model engine" (modell-machinen). However, to avoid misunderstanding that might arise from the word "model", I shall refer to it as the first engine or the prototype engine.

[81] See, e.g. *Specimens*, p x, Collier, p 228 and Merzbach, p 9.

[82] Neither the Minutes of the Academy (KVA Protokoll) nor the supplements to the Minutes for 1837-1844 give the slightest indication that the committee was appointed by the Academy. In addition, all the correspondence in the Academy's archive between Berzelius, Selander, Lilliehöök and Scheutz has been checked without revealing anything which counters this. Furthermore Scheutz, 1847, p 63, speaks about scientists only and not about any official committee.

83 KVA, Protokoll 1837, p 66. At this meeting, on the 11th of October, Berzelius as was customary, led the discussion. He also signed the Academy statement of 14th February 1838 and was naturally also present at the meeting itself which took place the same day. See KVA, Bilagor KVA Protokoll 1838, p 78 ff, and KVA Protokoll 1838, p 20.

84 [Scheutz], 1847, p 55.

85 Henrik Gustaf Söderbaum, *Jacob Berzelius: Själfbiografiska anteckningar* (Stockholm 1901), p 24.

86 Borgström, p 390.

87 Jan Trofast, (ed.), *Brevväxlingen mellan Jöns Jacob Berzelius och Carl Palmstedt* 3 vols. (Lund 1979, 1981, 1983), *passim*.

88 RA, Kommerskollegie Huvudarkiv, Acta Privatorum, EXVII d:2, vol. 411.

89 Söderbaum, pp 106-107.
Trofast, vol. 3, p 421.
Crusenstolpe was sentenced for an article in which he had accused King Carl XIV Johan of breaking the sabbath because he had authorized a military promotion on a Sunday. The Court Chamberlain had intervened and Crusenstolpe was given (on the 19th of June 1838) a three year prison sentence. The newspapers devoted a great deal of attention to the case and a riot broke out when the verdict was announced. Crusenstolpe became a martyr to the cause of the freedom of the press and a hero of the opposition. It was perhaps due to this and his great popularity, that his spell in prison was relatively speaking a pleasant one.

90 RS, HS 2.235, Letter from Betty Plumleigh Babbage to John Herschel, London, 6th October 1828.
The event took place on the 9th of September 1828. See Trofast, vol. 1, pp 276-277.

91 Söderbaum, pp 55-64, esp. pp 55, 60.

92 *Ibidem*, pp 72-77, The information about Löwenhielm's friendship with Berzelius is taken from this source. It is supported by: Sven Klemming (ed.), *Jöns Jacob Berzelius och Gustaf Carl Fredrik Löwenhielm: En brevväxling 1818-1847* (Västerås 1968), *passim*.
According to Trofast, *passim*, both Berzelius and Palmstedt were on good terms with Löwenhielm, Arago and Olivier. In KVA there are a number of unpublished letters which further underline their good relations.

93 Merzbach, pp 1, 42.

94 This assertion is based on the fact that no earlier calculating machine is mentioned in any historical or technical work or article. In further investigating this matter, the following documents in the National Archives, Stockholm: RA, Kommerskollegie Huvudarkiv, were checked:
D II d:1, Register över patent, "Förteckningar och register över privilegia exclusiva och patent samt tillståndsbevis 1740-1865".
D II d:2, Register över patent 1820-1853: "*Förteckning* [...] 1820 [...] 1842": "Förteckning [...] 1843-1850",: "Patenter År 1851, 1852, 1853"..
From this, it can be concluded that no calculating machine of any kind is filed

among the patent applications for the period 1740-1853. The search was based on the words: *calculating, -machine, -apparatus, -instrument, table, calculator* and *calculus* (with c and k), *difference* and *mathematics* (but of course their Swedish equivalents). Given this, it is reasonable to suppose that no Swedish calculating machine had been constructed before Scheutz'. In an article in *Daedalus* 1932, pp 105-109, Tore Andersson asked if the Scheutz machine was the first Swedish calculating machine. The answer is therefore yes.

[95] Harald Wieselgren, "Nils Haqvin Selander 1870", *Ur vår samtid*, pp 25-29.

[96] Lindroth, vol. 1:2, p 844.

[97] *Ibidem*, pp 858-860.

[98] KVA, Protokoll 1837, p 66.
KVA, Bilagor KVA protokoll 1838, p 78 ff.

[99] KVA, Protokoll 1842, pp 66, 84.

[100] See e.g. [Georg Scheutz], *Spegeln*, No. 14, 5th April 1838.

[101] August Giron, "Lillehöök, Carl Bertil", Torsten Dahl (ed.), *Svenska män och kvinnor* 4 (Stockholm 1948), p 591.

[102] PRO, T. 1. 4893/25814, Various notes on envelopes concerning Scheutz' offer of a large difference engine to the British government. It is stated on one envelope that Georg Scheutz' letter in this matter was dated 31st October 1843. The reference to this material was found in PRO, "Home Department", vol. 183, 1843, p 97.

[103] RA, "G. Scheutz, [...] anhållan", third and fourth page from the beginning.

[104] While investigating Scheutz' offer to the British government at PRO in 1981, I was very pleased to find a file (T.1.4893/25814) dealing with the matter. I was less happy when I got the box in question and discovered that it only contained a couple of envelopes. (These contained some dates, used in note 102 above). It turned out that the file in question had been weeded and destroyed by the staff of the PRO many years ago. The information is thus unfortunately lost. I am indebted to Alice Prochaska at the PRO, for her helping me in trying to locate the file and for finding out why its contents have disappeared. She has also checked the PRO, Home Office-files, 1843 HO 46/1A and 1B, which turned out to contain nothing on the Scheutz engine.
In Sweden the following sources have also been checked in an attempt to find more information about this offer. Nothing of interest has however been found.
RA, Utrikes Departementet, Beskickningens i London arkiv:
Inkomna skrivelser, vol. 93, 1843-1846.
Ingående diarium, vol. 137, 1836-1846.
Utgående diarium, vol. 136, 1836-1846.
Koncept, vol. 23, 1843-1844.
RA, Utrikes Departementet, Generalkonsultatets i London arkiv:
Inkomna skrivelser, vol. 687, 1843.
Utgående skrivelser, vol. 692, 1844.

[105] [Scheutz], 1847, p 65.

[106] RA, "G. Scheutz, [...] anhållan", fourth page. This original English version has been lost.

[107] *Ibidem.*
[Scheutz], 1847, p 65. On the assumption that this unknown professor might have been Babbage, a search was made of his correspondence (BL, Add. Ms. 37192-37193). Nothing was found to support this.

[108] RA, "G. Scheutz, [...] anhållan", fourth page.
[Scheutz], 1847, p 65.

[109] Trofast, vol. 3, pp 127 ff, 237 ff.
Palmstedt visited Björnstjerna in London at the end of August 1843, *ibidem*, pp 237 ff., 240.

[110] KVA, Protokoll 1838, p 20.

[111] [Scheutz], 1847, p 65.
Despite the help of the personnel of the British Library, in going through the printed Government publications relating to Treasury matters, nothing has been found which can throw more light on this matter.
I have examined Peel's correspondence with Sir James Graham for the period 28th August 1843−9th April 1844, which is to be found in the British Library and which contains some 400 letters. No mention, however, is made of the Scheutz offer in this correspondence, BL.Add.Ms. 40449, vol. CCLXIX.

[112] Babbage's work on the Analytical Engine has been described by various authors, including Babbage himself. See e.g.:
Passages, pp 112-141.
Hyman, pp 164-210.
Collier, pp 106-207.
Bell, pp 279-336.
H. P. Babbage, pp 5-50. (Lists of drawings and notations of the engine are collected on pp 271-294.)
For a good description of the design and mode of operation of the Analytical Engine, see:
Allan G. Bromley, "Charles Babbage's Analytical Engine, 1838", *Annals of the History of Computing* 4, No. 3, July 1982, pp 196-217.

[113] *Passages*, pp 113-115.

[114] For further details about the various issues involved, see e.g. "Statement", *Passages*, pp 83-96.
Weld, pp 384-391.
Collier, pp 89-105.

[115] Lardner, (H. P. Babbage, pp 80-82), was one of those who, in the end of this article, asked Babbage frankly about the suspension of the project, and urged him to act in the matter.
De Morgan's article "Mr. Babbage's Calculating Machine", published in *The Athenaeum* 1848, was in fact of the same character.

[116] This is evident from the sources listed in note 114. See especially: "Statement", *Passages*, pp 83 ff.
Collier, pp 90-94.

117 "Statement", *Passages*, pp 85-86.

118 *Ibidem*, pp 93-94.

119 BL, Add. Ms. 37192, 189-194, "Recollections of an interview with Sir Robert Peel on Friday November 11 - 1842 at 11 am", written by Babbage, probably shortly after the event.

120 *Ibidem*, pp 192-193.

121 *Ibidem*, p 194.

122 "Statement", *Passages*, p 94, note *.

123 PRO, "Home Department", vol. 183, 1843, p 97.

124 [Scheutz], 1847, p 65.

125 [anon], "Obituary Notices of Fellows deceased": George Biddell Airy, *Proceedings* 51 (London 1892), pp i-xxi.

126 It should be noted that this information is based on a second hand source, the famous English actor William Charles Macready, see: William Toynbee (ed.), *The Diaries of William Charles Macready 1833-1851* 1 (New York 1912), p 410.
This source and statement, was first noted by Moseley, p 83.

127 Wilfred Airy (ed.), *Autobiography of Sir George Biddell Airy*, (Cambridge 1896), p 152.
This source was first quoted by Collier, p 101.

128 RA, "G. Scheutz, [...] anhållan", fourth page. The figure 30,000 pounds was an exaggeration.

129 *Ibidem*. Carries the inscription that Scheutz handed it in, in person, to the Palace. Regarding what is said here (and later) about Scheutz and government finance, cf. Merzbach p 9, right hand column.

130 [Georg Scheutz], *Spegeln*. All numbers, from no. 1, 12th January 1837 to no. 52, 29th December 1838, have been examined. *Spegeln* was a continuation of the confiscated *Svenska Bondens Tidning* (established May 1835). See Lundstedt, vol. 2, pp 57, 60.

131 Published in Stockholm.

132 The information that he had set out his name in some copies of the book, is recorded in a copy of this book in KB.

133 *Slägtvälde*, p 94.

134 *Ibidem*, p 89, *passim*.

135 *Ibidem*, pp 101, 110 ff., 120 ff.

136 *Ibidem*, pp 100 ff.

[137] RA, "G. Scheutz, [...] anhållan", fourth page.

[138] *Ibidem*, fifth page. Merzbach, p 9, says that Scheutz requested money for a full-scale model. This was not the case.

[139] *Ibidem*, fifth and sixth page.

[140] *Ibidem*, sixth page.

[141] KVA, Protokoll 1844, p 58.
At the same meeting, note was taken of an essay of Georg Scheutz on his "Sinus-delare" (Sine-divider). This essay has vanished and nothing more is known about the matter. (*Ibidem*, p 60).

[142] [anon], "Wrede, Fabian (V) Jacob Fabiansson", *Biografiskt lexicon öfver namnkunnige Svenska män* 22 (Örebro 1855), pp 312-316.
Svante Arrhenius, "Fabian Jacob Wrede", *Lefnadsteckningar över Kungl. Svenska Vetenskapsakademiens ledamöter* 5 (Uppsala 1920), pp 480-534.

[143] KVA, Protokoll 1844, pp 74-75.

[144] KVA, "Selander, utlåtande angående Scheutz ansökan", Bilagor KVA Protokoll 1844, p 395 ff.

[145] *Ibidem*, and: RA, Anders Retzius, "Wetenskaps Academien ang. Auditeuren G. Scheutz und. anhållan om understöd af allm. medel för fullbordande af en utaf honom upfunnen Räknemachin", Ecklesiastik-Departmentet, ingående skrivelser, augusti-december 1844, No. 599, second page.
Selander's and Wrede's draft in the former source is word-for-word identical with the final report which the Academy's president Retzius presented to the Crown.

[146] RA, Retzius, second and third page.

[147] *Ibidem*, third page.

[148] KVA, "Selander", Bilagor KVA Protokoll, p 395 ff. (Pages are not properly numbered.) What Merzbach, p 9, says about the Academy's opinion, is thus incorrect.

[149] *Ibidem*. Wrede's draft is added to Selander's. Both are signed.

[150] RA, Georg Scheutz ansökan om statligt stöd, "Protocoll öfver Ecclesiastik-Ärender, hållet inför Hans Majt. Konungen i Statsrådet på Stockholms Slott den 3 December 1844", Ecklesiastik-Departementet, Statsråds-Protokoll 1844, augusti-december, no. 20.

[151] [Scheutz], 1847, p 65.

[152] The reason why Selander was no longer concerned with the Swedish table engine is unknown.

[153] [Scheutz], 1847, p 66.

[154] All numbers of *Aftonbladet* from 1837 to 1850 have been checked. The newspaper was published daily.

[155] See the sources in RA, listed in note 94 in this section.

[156] Bennet Woodcroft (ed.), *Alphabetical Index of Patentees of Inventions: From March 2, 1617 to October 1, 1852* (London 1854).

[157] *Tidning för Näringarne*, October 1836, pp 275-288.

[158] *Ibidem*, pp 275-276.

[159] RA, KTH arkiv, D 1 a, Nr. 932, "Matrikel över ordinarie elever", vol. 3.

[160] The title "Civilingenjör" (abbrev. Civ.ing.) has no exact equivalent in the English-speaking world and certainly must not be confused with the English term "Civil Engineer" (in Swedish, "väg- och vatteningenjör"). It is given to students who have successfully completed the theoretical and technical courses at those higher institutions of learning devoted to engineering and applied science. ("Tekniska högskolor"). It is similar in character to the designation "Diplom Ingenieur" in Germany.
The title was at first applied to graduates of the Artillery School at Marieberg, probably in 1842, when it opened its doors to civilian applicants. Later – though not before 1850 – it was introduced at the Technological Institute. Edvard Scheutz adopted it first in 1861, in *Stockholms Adresskalender*, (Stockholm 1861), (the Stockholm Directory for 1861). Before that, he called himself "engineer" ("ingenjör"). For more information about the history of the title, see Torsten Althin.

[161] RA, KTH arkiv, D 1 a, Nr. 932, "Matrikel", vol. 3.

[162] *Ibidem*.

[163] Klemming and Nordin, p 430.

[164] *Ibidem*. According to this source, the press was sold to Rudolf Wall's mother, and was transferred to Wall when he reached maturity. In 1864 Wall founded the newspaper *Dagens Nyheter*, which is today Sweden's largest daily newspaper. Wall ran the Scheutz press until 1890, when it was closed down. See Gudmar Hasselberg, *Rudolf Wall: Dagens Nyheters skapare* (Stockholm 1945), p 33.

[165] KB, I. s. 10, Contract between Georg Scheutz and Lars Johan Hierta regarding Scheutz' employment at *Aftonbladet*. Stockholm, 29th December 1842.
Leif Kihlberg, *Lars Hierta i helfigur* (Stockholm 1968), p 133.

[166] KB, I. s. 10, Contract regarding *Aftonbladet*.

[167] Harald Wieselgren, *Lars Johan Hierta* (Stockholm 1880), p 14 ff.

[168] Lars Johan Hierta, *Biografiska anteckningar* (Örebro 1863), pp 15-16.
Kihlberg, pp 26-27.

[169] For more information about *Aftonbladet's* history, see Kihlberg, pp 39-60 and Gunnar Fredriksson, Dieter Strand, Stig Hadenius and Karl Erik Gustafsson *Aftonbladet - en svensk historia* (Stockholm 1980). See also: Lundstedt, vol. 2, pp 40-46.

[170] Wieselgren, *Lars Johan Hierta*, p 53.

[171] Bengtsson, Malmborg and Nerman, vol. 1, pp 153-154.
This is the event mentioned in section 2.1, note 67.

[172] Hierta, p 16.

[173] Charles Babbage, *Observations Addressed, at the Last Anniversary, to the President and Fellows of the Royal Society, After the Delivery of the Medals* (London 1856).
This pamphlet is reprinted in H. P. Babbage, pp 260-261. Quotation from p 260.

[174] Merzbach, p 10, says that Scheutz' book *Nytt och enkelt sätt att lösa nummereqvationer* was based on the writings of John Mortimer Agardh, Carl A. Agardh's nephew. This is incorrect. It was C. A. Agardh himself who was the originator of the method used by Scheutz. See Scheutz, p 72.

[175] *Nytt och enkelt sätt att lösa nummereqvationer*, p 74. That this book contains information about the first engine has not been noted before.

[176] It is known that Babbage calculated tables with both his model engine and the part of the Difference Engine No. 1. But they were of course never printed.

[177] Bergstedt, p 165.

[178] For an account about the rediscovery and the restoration of the engine, see Appendix.

[179] This section is based on experience gained during the restoration work, undertaken during the period January-March 1980 at the Nordic Museum, Stockholm. This section is not intended to be an exhaustive technical description of the Scheutz Engine. Emphasis has been put on pointing out the most important details in the design. Readers who by now have been gripped by an irresistible desire to construct a difference engine, ought to wait until they have read the second part of the book, in which several useful hints are given.

[180] This mode of division differs from that employed in Berzelius' statement. However, this break-down seems more natural and has certain pedagogical advantages.

[181] Compare hodometers in cars, or counting mechanisms in tape recorders.

[182] KB, X279, Berzelius' statement.

[183] Alan H. Lloyd, "Mechanical Time-keepers", Charles Singer, E. J. Holmyard, A. R. Hall and Trevor I. Williams (eds.), *A History of Technology* 3 (New York 1957), pp 668-669.

[184] *Observations*, pp 4-5.
It should be noted that Babbage's opinions were based on his inspection of the second Scheutz' engine. Since the latter was in essence identical with the first engine, his view applies to both. The carrying mechanism was, however, different in the two Scheutz' engines. But it was also different from that in the Difference Engine No. 1.

[185] [anon], *A Brief Account of Bryan Donkin F. R. S. and of the Company he founded 150 Years ago* (Chesterfield 1953), p 23.

[186] James Moran, *Printing Presses* (London 1973), p 73, pp 234-235. It may be pointed out that Bramah's note-numbering press was in fact a "numerator" with type wheels.

[187] Bengtsson, Malmborg and Nerman, vol. 1, p 62.

[188] In turning with a fixed support, the cutting tool is guided with the thumbnail resting on the support, which had the form of a horizontal ruler. This method was used for turning metal in Sweden right up to the early decades of our century.

[189] When Georg Scheutz in "Historical Sketch", p 3, says that the engine (on the 19th of April 1840) could calculate with *one difference*, he is actually saying that the shelf $\Delta 3$, with its addition elements, had been completed. But, to say that the machine could *calculate* with one difference was probably not true, because it is clear from the machine, that the uppermost shelf f(x), was not ready until later. This statement is based on the fact that Edvard's skill increased as the work proceeded.

[190] RA, Kommerskollegie Huvudarkiv, Kammarkontorets årsberättelser Fabriker serie 2 1837 städer, pp 496-528.

[191] RA, Kommerskollegie Huvudarkiv, Kammarkontorets årsberättelser Fabriker serie 1 1811 städer, pp 268-298.

Notes to section 2.4

I am very much indebted to Göran B. Nilsson for illuminating the politics surrounding Scheutz' application to the Swedish government in 1850-1851, presented here for the first time. Cf. Merzbach, pp 10-11.

[1] "Historique", p 5.
There is no information whatsoever, whether in KVA Protokoll or in Bilagor KVA protokoll for 1850, about this committee. However, it is mentioned in KVA protokoll 1851, p 8. The event here alluded to, has not been noted before.

[2] This is shown by the fact that the construction of the (now rediscovered) first engine tallies with the description given in Berzelius' statement from 1843.

[3] RA, Georg Scheutz' application to the King, undated, but received 28th January 1851, Ecklesiastik-Departementet, Konseljakter, 29th April 1851, no. 28.
In the application Scheutz uses the word "model" and not "prototype". I have chosen to translate it as prototype, to avoid the risk of confusion with model in the sense of a small scale, (conceivably non-functioning), machine. It was what we now call a prototype that he was referring to.

[4] *Ibidem*.

[5] Several sources including Bergstedt, p 166, and *Observations*, p 261, give the amount of money that was sought as 5,000 riksdaler. However according to the original documents, there is no doubt that 3,333 riksdaler and 16 skilling banco was the correct amount. The erroneous sum originated in Bergstedt. By the time he wrote his biography, a new type of riksdaler had been introduced - the riksdaler *riksgälds*. One riksdaler riksgälds was equal to 1.5 riksdaler banco.

[6] KVA, Protokoll 1851, p 8. Abstracts of a meeting held on the 12th of February 1851, regarding the statement of the Academy on Scheutz' application to the King.

RA, Statement of the Royal Academy of Sciences, to the King, regarding Scheutz' application to the King, Stockholm, 12th February 1851, Ecklesiastik-Departementet, Konseljakter, 19th April 1851, no. 28.

[7] *Ibidem.*

[8] *Ibidem*, pp 82, 84.

[9] Dahl, p 591.

[10] RA, "Auditeuren Georg Scheutz i underdånighet gjorda ansökning angÄåenÅde understöd för tillverkande af en modell till räknemaskin", Ecklesiastik-Departementet, Statsråds-Protocoll, 29th April 1851, no. 28.

RA, Copy of the King's rescript to the Royal Academy of Sciences, signed on behalf of the King by Paulus Genberg, the Minister of Ecclesiasticial Affairs and Public Instruction, Stockholm Castle, 29th April 1851, no. 87, Ecklesiastik-Departementet, Registratur 1851.

See also: KVA, Protokoll 1851, pp 59-60, Abstract of a meeting held on the 18th of June 1851.

[11] Göran B. Nilsson, *Banker i brytningstid: A O Wallenberg i svensk bankpolitik 1850-1856* (Stockholm 1981), *passim.*

[12] KVA, Letter from Georg Scheutz to Peter Fredrik Wahlberg, Stockholm, 4th June 1851. In this letter, it is stated that Georg Scheutz got the message about the government's decision directly from Wahlberg, on the 4th of June.

[13] *Ibidem.*

[14] KVA, Protokoll 1851, p 60.

[15] This was laid down by Paragraph 56 of the Riksdag's Rules of Procedure:
"No motion may be shelved without the express consent of the Estate. Nor, with the exception of constitutional questions, may new matters be raised by members of the Riksdag, after a month has elapsed from the beginning of the Riksdag according to Paragraph 27, inasmuch as such questions are not the direct outcome of decisions, which have already been taken, or of matters which have already been raised or of events which have occurred during the Riksdag."
Swensk Författnings-Samling 1851 No. 50, Kongl. Maj:ts och Riksens Ständers fastställda Riksdags-Ordning, Dat. Stockholm den 10 Februari 1810; Med de derefter, och sist wid Riksdagen i Stockholm åren 1850 och 1851, af Konungen och Riksens Ständer antagna förändringar. (Stockholm 1851), p 33.

[16] *Hedervärda Borgar-Ståndets Protokoller vid Lagtima Riksdagen i Stockholm Åren 1850 och 1851* 6 (Stockholm 1851), pp 155-157.

Hans Björklund, "Partigrupperingar i borgarståndet vid 1853/54 års riksdag", *Partiliv i ståndsriksdagen: Adel och borgare 1850-1865*, Acta Universitatis Stockholmiensis 23, (Stockholm 1977), p 20 note 1, p 42.

[17] *Borgar-Ståndets Protocoller 1850/51* 6, p 155.

[18] *Ibidem*, p 156.

[19] *Ibidem*, p 157.

[20] *Ibidem*.

[21] "Stats-Utskottets utlåtande, N:o 294", Stockholm, 31st July 1851, *Bihang till Samtliga Riks-Ståndens Protokoll vid Lagtima Riksdagen i Stockholm Åren 1850 och 1851*, fjerde samlingen, andra bandet, första afdelningen (Stockholm 1851), pp 14-17, esp. p 16.

[22] *Ibidem*, p 16.

[23] *Ibidem*, p 17.

[24] *Protocoll hållna hos höglofliga Riddareskapet och Adeln vid lagtima riksdagen i Stockholm, åren 1850 och 1851* 9 (Stockholm 1851). (Plenary meeting 15th August 1851), pp 247-248, esp. p 247.

[25] *Ibidem*, p 247.

[26] *Ibidem*, pp 247-248.

[27] *Ibidem*, p 248.

[28] *Ibidem*.

[29] *Protocoll hållna hos vällofliga Borgare-Ståndet vid lagtima riksdagen i Stockholm åren 1850 och 1851* 4 (Stockholm 1851), (Plenary meeting 15th August 1851), p 834.

[30] *Högvördiga Preste-Ståndets protokoll vid Lagtima riksdagen i Stockholm år 1851* 10 (Stockholm 1852), (Plenary meeting 14th August 1851), p 411.

[31] *Hedervärda Bonde-Ståndets Protokoller vid Lagtima Riksdagen i Stockholm åren 1850 och 1851* 6 (Stockholm 1851), (Plenary meeting 15th August 1851), pp 185-186, esp. p 185.

[32] "Stats-Utskottets memorial, N:o 328", Stockholm, 18th August 1854, *Bihang till Samtliga Riks-Ståndens Protokoll 1850/51* fjerde samlingen, andra bandet, första afdelningen (Stockholm 1851).
Bonde-Ståndets Protocoller 1850/51 6, (Plenary meeting 21st August 1851), pp 269-270.

[33] "Expeditions-Utskottets Förslag till und. Skrifvelse N:o 189, Stockholm den 20 augusti 1851", *Bihang till Samtlige Riks-Ståndens Protokoll vid Lagtima Riksdagen i Stockholm Åren 1850 och 1851*, tionde samlingen, första bandet, första afdelningen (Stockholm 1851), pp 514-515.

[34] *Ibidem*, p 515. Original in Swedish: "hafva Rikets Ständer icke betviflat nyttan af ifrågavarande machin, dock som Rikets Ständer icke kunnat så tillförlitligt bedöma värdet af denna uppfinning".

[35] Statement by King Oscar I regarding Georg Scheutz' application to have the grant paid out in advance, Stockholm Castle, 24th October 1851, KVA, Bilagor KVA protokoll 1853, pp 1105-1107.

³⁶ *Ibidem.* This statement did not arrive at the Academy of Sciences until 15th November 1851. Furthermore, it was not before the 10th of December that the Academy had a meeting and discussed the matter, see next note.

³⁷ KVA, Protokoll 1851, pp 92-94. Abstracts of a meeting regarding how the payments of the Government grant were to be regulated, held on 10th December 1851.

Such were the economic circumstances under which Georg Scheutz was forced to work, namely advances of small sums of money against securities. However, Merzbach, p 12, says that "To initiate its construction, some individual or group had to be willing to supply the capital and to run the risk of loss if the project proved unsuccessful". From the above, nonetheless, it is clear that the individuals (who came forward) did not actually supply the capital but rather underwrote the loan. The Academy of Sciences, which had responsibility for the money, was also in charge of the payments.

³⁸ *Specimens*, p xii.

³⁹ Rune G:son Kjellander, "J. W. Bergström, mekanikus och daguerrotypist", *Daedalus* 1953, pp 100-107.

⁴⁰ [Georg Scheutz], Short comment on J. W. Bergström's production of glass, *SIT*, January 1837, pp 16-17.

Idem, Short comment on J. W. Bergström's production of glass, *SIT*, January 1838, pp 17-18.

⁴¹ G:son Kjellander, p 101.

⁴² Bo Sahlholm, *Mekaniska verkstadsbyggnader under 1800-talet: Den moderna verkstadsplaneringens ursprung*, Stockholm Papers in History and Philosophy of Technology 2002, (Stockholm 1978), *passim*.

⁴³ *Specimens*, p xii.

⁴⁴ The information about the identity of the 15 guarantors is to be found in *Specimens*, p xii. Only the surnames are given there, some of them with initials. In one case (Berg) the initial given in *Specimens* has proved to be wrong. These names have been compared, and corrected, with the mailing list on p xx in Appendix. The information about the guarantors presented below, has been taken from various wellknown Swedish biographical sources and encyclopaedias, unless stated to the contrary. See also next note.

⁴⁵ I am indebted to Sigrid Högberg for finding this information, as well as much more, regarding the guarantors, in the archives of SSA.

⁴⁶ KVA, Protokoll 1853, pp 96-98, and Bilagor KVA Protokoll 1853, pp 1117-1125, deals with the practical organization of the payments to Georg Scheutz, as well as copies of the standardized receipt that he had to sign. None of the signed receipts nor the bail bonds seems to have survived.

⁴⁷ KB, Ep. L. 20:13, Letter from Georg Scheutz to the firm of Nils Magnus Lindh, Stockholm, 1st October 1852.

⁴⁸ SF, "Bolinders huvudbok år 1853", under the heading: Bergström, J. W. It is difficult to say what the plate was for. The price, 11 riksdaler 12 skilling banco,

however, is quite high in comparison with those quoted in other entries in the ledger, so that it may well have been intended for the large base to the engine. Bergström's perhaps were unable to make it, on account of its size.

[49] "Historique", p 6.

[50] Bergstedt, p 166.

[51] KVA, Protokoll 1853, p 96.

[52] Statement regarding the finished second engine, by Fabian Wrede and Lars Wallmark, to the Academy of Sciences Stockholm, 9th November 1853, KVA, Bilagor KVA protokoll 1853, p 1111.

[53] *Ibidem*, p 1112.

[54] Draught of the final report to the King based on Wrede's and Wallmark's report, Stockholm, 9th November 1853, *ibidem*, pp 1115-1116.

[55] "Kongl. Maj:ts Nådiga Proposition, N:o 51, Stockholm den 13 januari 1854", *Bihang till samtlige Riks-Ståndens protokoll vid Lagtima riksdagen i Stockholm åren 1853-1854*, första samlingen, andra afdelningen, första bandet (Stockholm 1854).

[56] *Ibidem*. The decision was made somewhat earlier, on the 2nd December 1853. See RA, Ecklesiastik-Departementet, Statsråds-Protokoll 1851, no. 15.
No other motive is given in the available archival material.

[57] "Stats-Utskottets Utlåtande, N:o 136, Stockholm den 29 maj 1854", *Bihang till samtliga Riks-Ståndens protokoll vid Lagtima riksdagen i Stockholm åren 1853-1854*, fjärde samlingen, första afdelningen, andra bandet (Stockholm 1854).

[58] *Hedervärda Bonde-Ståndets Protokoller vid Lagtima Riksdagen i Stockholm Åren 1853 och 1854* 5 (Stockholm 1854), (Plenary meeting 14th June 1854), p 303.

[59] *Protocoll hållna hos högloflige Ridderskapet och Adeln vid Lagtima Riksdagen i Stockholm Åren 1853-1854* 8 (Stockholm 1854), (Plenary meeting 14th June 1854), p 155.
Högvördiga Preste-Ståndets Protokoll vid Lagtima Riksdagen i Stockholm År 1854 5 (Stockholm 1854), (Plenary meeting 14th June 1854), pp 222-223.
Protocoll hållna hos vällofliga Borgare-Ståndet vid Lagtima riksdagen i Stockholm åren 1853 och 1854 4 (Stockholm 1854), (Plenary meeeting 14th June 1854), p 80.
"Expeditions-Utskottets förslag till underd. Skrifvelse. N:o 64, Stockholm den 1 juli 1854", *Bihang till samtlige Riks-Ståndens protokoll vid Lagtima riksdagen i Stockholm åren 1853-1854*, tionde samlingen, första afdelningen, första bandet (Stockholm 1854), pp 97-98.

[60] "Riksdagsbeslut, §20, Nr 34, Stockholm den 1 juli 1854", *Bihang till samtliga Riks-Ståndens protokoll vid Lagtima riksdagen i Stockholm åren 1853-54*, tionde samlingen, första afdelningen, andra bandet (Stockholm 1854), p 33.

[61] *Specimens*, p xiii.

[62] *Sveriges Riksbank 1668-1924* (Stockholm 1931), 5, pp 150-152.

[63] KVA, copy of contract between Georg and Edvard Scheutz regarding their second difference engine, Stockholm, 1st November 1853.

[64] Unless otherwise stated, the work of this section is based upon the following sources:

My investigations of the second difference engine, carried out at the Smithsonian Institution, Washington, June 1980.

KB, X279, "Machin för beräkning och tryckning af matematiska tabeller. Af Georg and Edvard Scheutz", undated manuscript of Edvard Scheutz.

[anon], *Letters Patent, Specification of Georg Scheutz and Edvard Scheutz, Calculating Machines, A.D. 1854, No. 2216* (London 1855).

[65] Bergstedt, p 166.

[66] The lower and longer part of the tooth z_1 was designed to operate upon the sexagesimal number wheels. These had longer teeth than the decimal wheels.

[67] The shelves and several small parts in the calculating unit have a very gold shine to them. It is possible that it is gold, but it is also possible that this effect could have been produced chemically.

[68] I have not, however, been able to locate any example of a mangle with this mechanism. I imagine that it would have been particularly useful and productive in the textile industry, perhaps on mangles driven by steam or water power.

[69] "Historique", p 7. According to Merzbach, pp 17-18, the engine was taken to England "under the auspices of Bryan Donkin and Company". However, it is not stated where this information comes from and I have been unable to find any document supporting this statement.

[70] KB, X279, "Contract angående Räknemachinen". Contract between Georg and Edvard Scheutz and Pehr Ambjörn Sparre relating to the latter's right, under certain conditions, to purchase the second engine and all patent rights, London, 17th October 1854.

[71] Information about Sparre is taken from the following sources. (The dates given vary somewhat from source to source, and should not be taken as entirely exact.)

Ernst Grape, *Enhetsportot och frimärket* (Stockholm 1955), p 105 ff.

Hugo Olsson, "Något om Greve P. A. Sparres tryckmaterial samt redskap och maskiner för tillverkningen av skilling banco-frimärkena", *Postryttaren* 1954, p 40 ff.

Paul Gerhard Heurgren, "Greve Pehr Ambjörn Sparre; Ritade, graverade och tryckte de första svenska frimärkena", *Frimärkets dags årsbok* 1945. This source does not however seem to be very reliable, see esp. p 18.

Erik Castegren, *Riksbankens pappersbruk Tumba; Minnesskrift till dess tvåhundraårsjubileum 1955* (Stockholm 1955), p 126 ff.

Torgny Lindgren, *Riksbankens sedelhistoria 1668-1968* (Stockholm 1968), esp. p 145.

[72] Grape, p 105.

[73] *Letters Patent*.

[74] KB, X279, "Contract angående Räknemachinen".

[75] *Ibidem*, p 3.

[76] *Ibidem*, p 4.

[77] "Historique", p 7.

[78] [anon], "Obituary Notices": Bryan Donkin, *Proceedings* 7, (London 1856), pp 586-589.
[anon], *A Brief Account of Bryan Donkin F.R.S. and of the Company he founded 150 Years ago* (Chesterfield 1953).

[79] [anon], "Obituary Notices": William Gravatt, *Proceedings* 16 (London 1868), pp xvi-xvii.

[80] L.T.C. Rolt, *Isambard Kingdom Brunel; Engineer, visionary and magnetic personality, he transformed the face of England* (Reading 1982), p 114.

[81] "Historique", p 7.
Proceedings 6, (London 1854), p 166.

[82] "Historique', p 7.

[83] *Ibidem*.

[84] *Ibidem*.
NM Letter from Charles Babbage to Georg Scheutz, London, 7th April 1856.

[85] There is no evidence that Babbage and the Scheutzes corresponded with each other before this meeting. (All the archives used for this book have been checked up to November 30th 1854). However, as mentioned on p xx there is little doubt that Babbage heard about the Swedish engine long before this.

[86] Buxton, p 74. Williams, p xx.

[87] [Georg Scheutz], "Industrialismen", *Tidning för Näringarne*, No. 5, 1840.

[88] *Ibidem*. (The article continues in No. 6.)

[89] *Passages*, p 392.

[90] BL, Add. Ms. 37196, 372, Draft or note by Charles Babbage. Undated, but placed between letters dated 10th December 1855 and 5th January 1856.

[91] Hyman, pp 75-87.
Passages, pp 258-275, see also pp 276-291.

[92] First edition printed in London 1833. I have used the 1856-edition.

[93] BL, Add. Ms., 37196, 418-420, Letter from Edvard Scheutz to Charles Babbage, Stockholm 22nd February 1856, together with a letter from Georg Scheutz to Charles Babbage, Stockholm, 22nd February 1856.

[94] "Historique", p 7.

[95] KB, L 10:12, Letter from Georg and Edvard Scheutz to Per Erik Svedbom, Stockholm, 31st August 1855.

[96] *Specimens*, p xiii.

[97] George G. Stokes, William H. Miller, Charles Wheatstone and Robert Willis, "Report of a Committee Appointed by the Council to Examine the Calculating Machine of M. Scheutz", (from the *Proceedings of the Royal Society*, January 21st 1855), reprinted in H. P. Babbage, pp 264-268, quotation from p 265.

[98] *Ibidem*, p 268.

[99] *Letters Patent*, p 11.

[100] *Ibidem*, p 1.
Merzbach, p 19, says that the issue of the patent caused a certain amount of publicity, and that the *London Daily News* first published an account of the machine (on 25th April 1855), while "a number of journals" devoted to mechanical topics presented articles on the machine with reviews of the patent, during the following weeks. I have been unable to find a newspaper with this name, (see also Merzbach's bibliography, p 66, where the *London Daily News* is listed only as a source for information about the Paris exhibition in 1855). Merzbach pp 66-67, only lists two articles dealing with the Scheutz engine, one of them stated to be based upon the patent, both published in the *Practical Mechanic's Journal* in 1855. I have not been able to check these articles.

[101] *The Illustrated London News*, 30th June 1855.

[102] *Ibidem*.

[103] [anon], "Den Scheutziska Räknemaskinen", *Illustrerad Tidning*, No. 28, 21st July 1855, pp 1-2. It is very possible that this article was written by Georg or Edvard, because it is written in a style quite similar to that of an article written in 1859. That article was written by them, and it also had the same title "Den Scheutziska räknemaskinen", *Aftonbladet* 17, 1859.
The model shown in Fig. 66 has not been rediscovered.

[104] *Ibidem*, p 2.

[105] *Ibidem*, note on p 2.

[106] Technically, it was definitely possible, since the machine required little power.

[107] KB, Brevskrivarearkivet, L10:12, Letter from Georg and Edvard Scheutz to Per Erik Swedbom, Stockholm, 31st August 1855.

[108] I have found no comments in BL. I have not, however, been able to check RS or Greenwich Observatory with respect to this specific question.

[109] KB, X279, Letter from Count Nils Barck to Georg and Edvard Scheutz, Paris, 15th May 1855.

[110] *Svenska Män och Kvinnor, Biografisk uppslagsbok* 1 (Stockholm 1942).

[111] Collier, pp 233-234.

[112] BL, Add. Ms., 37196, 253, Draft of a letter from Charles Babbage to George Stokes, London, 24th June 1855.

For information about Babbage's work on the Analytical Engine, see Collier, pp 106-206, 242-270, and Bromley.

According to Collier Babbage worked on the Analytical Engine from 1834 to 1846, from 1857-1859, and from 1863 to his death in 1871.

[113] Collier, pp 207-220.

It might be noted though, that there is at least a couple of drawings in the Babbage collection in the Science Museum that show parts specifically intended for difference engines, designed in 1836 and 1842. Thus, perhaps this reawakened interest did not manifest itself so suddenly after all. See e.g., SML, BAB. [A] 39. The mechanism is stated to have been designed between 31st of October and 12th of November 1836. See also SM, BAB [A] 118, showing "Sketch of a proposed Anticipating Carriage for Difference & Analytical Engines, 24 November 1842".

For additional information about the Difference Engine No. 2, see *Passages*, pp 97-111.

[114] Collier, p 209.

[115] *Ibidem*, p 211.
Passages, p 105.

[116] Among the several drawings and notations that have been preserved in the Babbage collection in SML, these figures vary somewhat. The drawings and notations are in the process of being organized by Dr. Alan G. Bromley. When I studied them they were not marked properly, but see: SML, MSR 10 (drawing of Difference Engine No. 2); One piece of notation with comments, probably by Babbage, dated 21st August 1848.

[117] *Ibidem*.
SML, BAB. [A] 146, "Sketches of the Printing and Stereotyping Apparatus of the Analytical and of the Difference Engine. December 1846".

[118] *Ibidem*.

[119] *Passages*, pp 100-107.

[120] *Ibidem*, p 98.

[121] *Ibidem*, pp 105-106.

[122] *Ibidem*, p 107.

[123] *Collier*, p 216.

[124] *Passages*, p 107.
BL, Add.Ms., 37195, 118, Copy of letter from Talbot, Secretary of the Earl of Derby, to Earl of Rosse, 16th August 1852.

[125] BL, Add.Ms., 37196, 302-303, Letter from William Gravatt to Charles Babbage, Paris, 29th August 1855.

[126] KB, L10:12.

[127] Edvard and Georg Scheutz, "Den Scheutziska räknemaskinen: Till Redaktionen för Aftonbladet", an article for the editoral committee of *Aftonbladet*, dated 21st January 1859, in *Aftonbladet* 17, 1859.

[128] John Allwood, *The Great Exhibitions* (London 1977), p 33 ff.

[129] M. Tresca, (ed.), *Visite l'Exposition Universelle de Paris, en 1855* (Paris 1855), pp 6-7.

[130] KB, L10:12.

[131] *Ibidem.*

[132] *Ibidem.*

[133] NM, Letter from Charles Babbage to Georg or Edvard Scheutz, London, 31th August 1855.

[134] NM, Letter from Charles Babbage to Georg or Edvard Scheutz, London, 4th(?) September 1855.

[135] Collier, p 234.
H. P. Babbage, "On Mechanical Notation, as Exemplified on the Swedish Calculating Machine of Messrs. Scheutz", H. P. Babbage, pp 246-247.

[136] NM, Letter from Charles Babbage to Georg or Edvard Scheutz, London, 4th September 1855.
BL, Add.Ms. 37196, 314-316, Draft of a letter from Charles Babbage to the Secretary of the French Academy of Sciences, Paris, 1st October 1855.

[137] BM, Add.Ms. 37196, 318-324, Draft by Charles Babbage of an article for *Comptes Rendus*: "Notice relative to the Swedish Calculating Machine of the Messrs Scheutz", Paris, 2nd October 1855.
BM, Add.Ms. 37196, 326-336, Translation of Babbage's draft for the article for *Comptes Rendus*: "Note sur la Machine Suédoise ...", Paris, 2nd October 1855.
Charles Babbage, "Note sur la machine suédoise de MM. Schutz [misspelling by Babbage] pour calculer les Tables mathématiques par la méthode des différences ...", *Comptes Rendus Hebdomaires des Séances de l'Academie de Sciences* 41 (Paris 1855), pp 557-560.

[138] NM, Letter from Charles Babbage to Georg or Edvard Scheutz, Paris, 8th October 1855.

[139] Georg and Edvard Scheutz, "Den Scheutziska räknemaskinen", *Aftonbladet* 17, 1859.

[140] *Ibidem.*

[141] *Ibidem.*
[anon], *Exposition universelle de 1855, Rapports du jury mixte international* (Paris 1856), p 405.

[142] *Aftonbladet* 17, 1859.

[143] [anon] "Exposition universelle de 1855: L'exposition Suédoise au Palais de l'industrie", *Extrait du bulletin de la Revue des deux mondes* (reprint), original article printed on the 15th October 1855, pp 5-6.

[144] NM, Letter from Charles Babbage to Scheutz, Paris, 28th October 1855.

NM, Letter from Charles Babbage to Scheutz, Paris, 21st October 1855.;
The articles are only mentioned in these two letters. I have not been able to locate the actual articles, although the *Galignanis Messenger* is mentioned.

[145] *Aftonbladet* 17, 1859.

[146] KB, X279, Letter from the legation secretary, G. Adelswärd (the Swedish and Norwegian legation in Paris) to Georg or Edvard Scheutz, Paris, 31st October 1855.

[147] *Aftonbladet* 17, 1859.
BL, Add.Ms., 37196, 421-422, Letter from ? Guerry to Charles Babbage, Paris, 22nd February 1856.

[148] Cf. Merzbach, pp 20-22.

[149] [Moigno], "Academie des Sciences: Séance du Lundi 12 juillet", *Cosmos* 13, 16th July 1858, pp 78-84.
This report is translated from French in its entirety, by Merzbach, pp 56-58.
Aftonbladet 17, 1859.
Bergstedt, p 169.

[150] For the following story see e.g.: Colin A. Ronan, *Astronomers Royal* (New York 1969), pp 102-120.

[151] *Ibidem*, pp 106-107.

[152] [Moigno], p 81.

[153] *Ibidem*.

[154] *Comptes Rendus Hebdomaires de la Academie des Sciences* 42, vol. 1 1856, (Paris 1856), pp 798-799.

[155] *Ibidem*, p 800.
Cf., [anon], "Académie des Sciences: Séance du 20 Avril 1856", *Cosmos* 8, p 476.
Merzbach p 22, states that the mathematician Augustin Louis Cauchy supported Leverrier's position. I have not been able to find the source from which this statement is taken.

[156] *Aftonbladet* 17, 1859.

[157] KVA, KVA protokoll 1856, pp 14-15.

[158] *Ibidem*, pp 45-46.
On the 8th of October, Georg Scheutz was fittingly elected a member of the publishing committee of the Academy. *Ibidem*, pp 101-102.

[159] BL, Add.Ms. 37196, 418, Letter from Georg Scheutz to Charles Babbage, Stockholm, 22nd February 1856.

[160] BL, Add.Ms., 37196, 419-420, Letter from Edvard Scheutz to Charles Babbage, Stockholm, 22nd February 1856.

[161] BL, Add.Ms., 37196, 456-457, Draft of a letter of Charles Babbage to the Principal Secretary of the Emperor of France, London, 5th April 1856.

Collier, p 235, remarks that it was due to this misunderstanding that Babbage proposed that Georg Scheutz should be made a member of the Legion of Honour.

[162] BL, Add.Ms., 37196, 460, 461-463, Draft of a letter of Charles Babbage to the King of Sweden, undated, but posted in London, 7th April 1856.

[163] The pamphlet had been presented to the Royal Society on the 30th of November, 1855, H. P. Babbage, p 260. It is reprinted in H. P. Babbage, pp 260-261.

[164] NM, Letter from Charles Babbage to Georg Scheutz, London, 7th April 1856.

[165] *Observations*, p 8.

[166] NM, Authorization by Georg Scheutz to Edvard Scheutz, giving Edvard the right to sell the engine and patent, in accordance with his own wishes. Signed and witnessed at the French Legation in Stockholm, 7th April 1856.

[167] *Specimens*, p xiii.

[168] Medals of this type had clearly a symbolical value. But they also had a concrete monetary value, and it was quite common for the prize-winner to melt down the medal and exchange it for ready money. The symbolic, sentimental value was the one prized by Georg Scheutz, for it was the first reward he had received for all his efforts on the engine. Despite all his financial difficulties, he did not have the medal melted down during his lifetime. This information is based on the fact that in Georg Scheutz' inventory (SSA, BOU 1873-IV-307), the medal is included.

[169] NM, Letter from Georg Scheutz to Edvard Scheutz, Stockholm, 23rd May 1856.

[170] *Ibidem*.

[171] KB, I. s. 10., "Wasa Orden". Letter of entitlement to Georg Scheutz, written and signed by King Oscar I, Stockholm Castle, 28th April 1856.

[172] "Historique", p 8.

[173] NM, Letter from Georg Scheutz to Edvard Scheutz, Stockholm, 23rd May 1856.
NM, Letters from Georg Scheutz to Edvard Scheutz, Stockholm, 21st March - 7th April 1857.
It appears from the correspondence that Barck and Sparre were working together.

[174] NM, Letters from Georg Scheutz to Edvard Scheutz, Stockholm, 21st March - 7th April 1857.

[175] NM, Letter from Georg Scheutz to Edvard Scheutz, Stockholm, 23rd May 1856.

[176] KB, X279, Letter of introduction from the Swedish Minister in Paris, Kristofer Rutger Ludvig Manderström to Edvard Scheutz, Paris, 22nd May 1856.

[177] BL, Add.Ms., 37197, 38-39, Letter from Bryan Donkin to Charles Babbage, London, 28th May 1856.

[178] KB, X279, Letter from Bryan Donkin to Edvard Scheutz, London 5th June 1856.

[179] BL, Add.Ms., 37197, 41, Letter from Bryan Donkin to Charles Babbage, Bermondsey, 9th June 1856.

[180] BL, Add.Ms., 37196, 483-486, Letter from Benjamin Apthorp Gould to Charles Babbage, 28th April 1856. The major part of this letter was first quoted by Merzbach, pp 24-25.

[181] Benjamin Apthorp Gould, *Reply to the "Statement of the Trustees" of the Dudley Observatory* (Albany, N. Y. 1859), p 140.

[182] *Ibidem.*

[183] Merzbach has, in great detail, told how, when and why the second engine was bought by the Americans, see Merzbach pp 22-28. I believe that in her book, however, she has passed over some important facts regarding Gould and his purchase of the engine which I will draw attention to in the following pages and which will throw light on the American purchase from a somewhat different angle.

[184] BL, Add.Ms., 37196, 484.

[185] *Ibidem*, 485.

[186] NM, Letter from Georg Scheutz to Edvard Scheutz, Stockholm, 11th July 1856.

[187] KB, X279, Letter from Bryan Donkin to Edvard Scheutz, London, 5th June 1856.

[188] NM, Letter from Georg Scheutz to Edvard Scheutz, Stockholm, 11th of July 1856.
Specimens, p xiv.

[189] NM, Letter from Georg Scheutz to Edvard Scheutz, Stockholm, 11th July 1856.
The manuscripts (which have been used as sources to this book), were: "Historique" and "Historical Sketch", both by G. Scheutz. Cf Merzbach, p 26.

[190] BL, Add.Ms., 37197, 53, Note by Charles Babbage that a letter from Charles Henry Davis, Office of the American Astronomical Ephemeris, dated 26th February 1856, had been sent to George Stokes, and had been forwarded to Edvard Scheutz on 15th June 1856.

[191] *Specimens*, p xiv.

[192] *Ibidem.*

[193] *Ibidem.* BL, Add.Ms., 37197, 77, Letter from William Gravatt to Charles Babbage, London, 28th July 1856.

[194] NM, Letter from Georg Scheutz to Edvard Scheutz, Stockholm, 11th July 1856.

[195] *Ibidem*. In the sequel, I shall use the abbreviation *Specimens* for both this English version and a French edition published in 1858.

[196] *Ibidem*.

It is obvious that this historical introduction, which like *Specimens* in its entirety (except for Gravatt's chapter on the method of differences), was written anonymously, was originally written by Georg Scheutz. See note 189 above. The revisions most probably due to Babbage, are occasionally incorrect (especially dates), and differ in some details from what Georg Scheutz wrote in "Historical Sketch" and "Historique".

[197] *Specimens*, p xv.

[198] NM, Letter from Georg Scheutz to Edvard Scheutz, Stockholm, 11th July 1856.

[199] *Ibidem*.

[200] NM, Letter from Georg Scheutz to Edvard Scheutz, Stockholm, 3rd September 1856.

[201] *Ibidem*.

[202] NM, Letter from Georg Scheutz to Edvard Scheutz, Stockholm, 29th August 1856.

[203] RA, Kommerskollegie Huvudarkiv, "Namnregister till patent, meddel. av Kongl. Komm. Kollegium, åren 1835-85". See under heading "Georg Scheutz". Two patents are listed, dated 10th and 11th of September 1859, carrying the numbers 50-51. This also gives a reference to the heading "Donkin, B", under which the two patents (one for some kind of method involving paper, one for the making of gas for light), are mentioned. It is also noted that the patents have been transferred. It is evident, from the letter cited in the previous note, that Georg Scheutz took out the patents in his name, for some practical reason, and then transferred them to Donkin, who probably was the original inventor.

[204] BL, Add.Ms., 37197, 108, Letter from William Gravatt to Charles Babbage, London, 18th October 1856.

[205] BL, Add.Ms., 37197, 336. Draft of Charles Babbage's answer to Benjamin Gould's letter (of the 28th of April 1856) regarding the possible purchase of the Scheutz engine. This draft is erroneously dated August 1858. Judging from its contents, August 1856 seems to be the correct date.

[206] Mary Ann James, *Commitment to Basic Research in Astronomy in Nineteenth Century Albany: A Paper submitted to the Second History Conference of Hudson Valley Colleges & Universities*, Bard College, 22nd October 1983, p 2.

[207] *Ibidem*, pp 4-13.

[208] KB, X279, Transcript of letter from Benjamin Gould to Charles Babbage, Cambridge, MA, 4th November 1856.

[209] NM, Letter from Benjamin Gould to Edvard Scheutz, Cambridge, MA, 22nd December 1856. Among Babbage's correspondence there is a copy of this letter: BL, Add.Ms., 37196, 136-137.

[210] Grape, pp 105-106.

[211] Olsson, p 41 ff.

[212] Nils Westberg, "Sveriges första frimärken", *Postryttaren* 1954, pp 46-66.
Grape, p 106.

[213] NM, Letter from Georg Scheutz to Edvard Scheutz Stockholm, 23rd May 1856.

[214] NM, Two letters from Georg Scheutz to Edvard Scheutz, Stockholm, 30th January 1857.
NM, Letter from Georg Scheutz to Edvard Scheutz, Stockholm, 21st & 26th June 1857.
Cf. Grape, p 107.
Westberg, pp 47-48 says that Georg took over the establishment (for the first time) at the beginning of 1857. It is evident from the Scheutz' correspondence that this happened already in 1856. Westberg also says that "the lack of experience in the field" of printing (stamps?) of Georg Scheutz is evident in some of the editions that were printed during 1857. Since Scheutz evidently started to do the job long before, I do not agree with that statement.

[215] NM, Letter from Georg Scheutz to Edvard Scheutz, Stockholm, 30th January 1857.

[216] NM, Letter from Charles Babbage to Edvard Scheutz, London, 8th January 1857.

[217] NM, Letter from Georg Scheutz to Edvard Scheutz, Stockholm, 24th February 1857.

[218] *Ibidem*. The sum of 500, was more than the amount Georg, according to his agreement with Edvard, was entitled to (1/3). Probably Edvard enclosed money to pay off his debts, or perhaps he let his father have half of the total sum.

[219] Åkerstedt, p 2, says that Sparre first left in 1856, only to come back occasionally as a director of the printing establishment in 1858 and 1861. (This is supported by the contents in Scheutz correspondence at NM.)

[220] *Ibidem*.

[221] BL, Add.Ms., 37197, 200. Letter from Edvard Scheutz to Charles Babbage, London, 30th May 1857.

[222] NM, Letters from Georg Scheutz to Edvard Scheutz, Stockholm, 21st March - 7th April 1857.

[223] *Specimens*, pp 13-42.

[224] *Ibidem*, pp 45-50.

[225] See p 379.

[226] This is evident from the Scheutz correspondence in NM, as well as from the many (always dated) copies of *Specimens* that I have examined in various archives and libraries (BL, BPL, KB, KVA, NM, RS, SML, TM, etc.).

[227] The majority of the people included in the list, are to be found as correspondents in Babbage's correspondence in BL.

[228] NM, Letters from Georg Scheutz to Edvard Scheutz, Stockholm, 21st March - 7th April 1857. The English phrase "matter of fact" is Scheutz' own.

[229] *Ibidem.*

[230] *Ibidem.*
Also see the following documents which deal with the French and Belgian patents:
KB, X279, Letter from de Fontainemoreau, Bureau Général des Brevets d'Inventions, to Edvard Scheutz, Paris, 18th May 1857.
KB, X279, Letter from de Fontainemoreau to Edvard Scheutz, London, 5th May 1857.
KB, X279, Letter from de Fontainemoreau to Edvard Scheutz, London, 27th May 1857.

[231] KB, X279, Letter from de Fontainemoreau to Edvard Scheutz, Paris, 18th May 1857.

[232] Thomas Olcott, John F. Rathbone et. al., *The Dudley Observatory and the Scientific Council. Statement of the Trustees* (Albany 1858), p 31.
Gould, 1859, pp 221-222.

[233] Mary Ann James, *The Dudley Observatory Controversy*; unpublished doctoral thesis, Rice University, Texas, 1980, p 163.

[234] Gould, 1859, p 141.

[235] NM, Letter from Georg Scheutz to Edvard Scheutz, Stockholm, 11th July 1856.

[236] NM, Letter from Georg Scheutz to Edvard Scheutz, 23rd May 1856.

[237] Joseph Henry, Alexander Dallas Bache, Benjamin Pierce, *Defence of Mr. Gould by the Scientific Council of the Dudley Observatory* (Albany 1858), pp 75-76. (The preface is dated July 1858.)

[238] Gould, 1859, p 142.

[239] Merzbach, p 28, mentions that there were plans to print some of them.

[240] *Ibidem*, pp 27-28.

[241] For the further history of the second engine, which is now exhibited at the National Museum of American History, Smithsonian Institution, Washington D.C., see Merzbach, pp 40-41.

[242] James, 1980, pp 253-254.

[243] James, 1980, gives the whole history, with an exhaustive account of the many ups and downs in the Dudley Observatory controversy, in which Benjamin Gould played the leading part.

[244] *Specimens*, p xv.

Notes to section 2.5

[1] William Farr (ed.) *English Life Table. Table of Lifetimes, Annuities, and Premiums* (London 1864), p CXLi.

[2] F.J. Williams, "The Swedish Calculating Machine at the General Register Office, Somerset House", *Companion to the Almanac for 1866* (London 1865), pp 7-8.

[3] BL, Add. Ms., 37195, 135-136, Letter from William Farr to Charles Babbage, London, 2nd September 1852.

[4] NM, Letter from Georg Scheutz to Edvard Scheutz, Stockholm, 21st March - 7th April 1857.　　　　　　　　　　　　　ƒ

[5] KB, X279, Draft of a letter by Edvard Scheutz, containing a quotation for engines, probably intended for the Emperor Napoleon III of France, 1857. (The letter is undated but its date is clear from the contents).
　　KB. X279, Letter from Edvard Scheutz to Silvain van de Weyer (a Belgian civil servant) containing a quotation for engines, intended for the Belgian government, London, 12th July 1857.

[6] KB, X279, Letter from Edvard Scheutz to Bryan Donkin, Paris, 12th September 1857.

[7] NM, Letter from Bryan Donkin to Edvard Scheutz, Bermondsey, 19th September 1857.

[8] NM, Letter from Georg Scheutz to Edvard Scheutz, Stockholm, 21st June–24th July, 1857.

[9] Collier, p 239. BL, Add. Ms. 37197, 230-231, Letter from Isambard Kingdom Brunel to Charles Babbage, 28th July 1857. Collier hints that this iniative on the part of Brunel in July 1857, marks the starting point for proposals about a third engine. However, the Scheutz correspondence reveal that these had already been discussed in the autumn of the previous year, if not earlier.

[10] Collier, p 242.

[11] NM, Letter from William Farr to Edvard Scheutz, London, 16th May 1857.

[12] PRO, T.1.6098B/19264. Letter from Edvard Scheutz to the Chancellor of the Exchequer, Sir George Lewis, London, 3rd July 1857.

[13] *Ibidem.*

[14] *Ibidem.*

[15] PRO, T.1.6098B/19264. Letter from the Registrar General, James George Graham to the Chancellor of the Exchequer, Sir George Lewis, London, 7th June 1857.

[16] KB, X279, Letter from Edvard Scheutz to Bryan Donkin, Paris, 12th September 1857.

[17] *Ibidem.*

[18] *Ibidem.*

[19] KB, X279, Letter form Bryan Donkin to Edvard Scheutz, Bermondsey, 19th September 1857.

[20] PRO, T.1.6098B/19264. Letter from the Astronomer Royal, George B. Airy to the Secretary of the Treasury, C.E. Trevelyan, Greenwich, 30th September 1857.

[21] *Ibidem*, p 14.

[22] *Ibidem.*

[23] PRO, T.1.6098B/19264. Letter from the Registrar General, James George Graham to the Secretary of the Treasury, Charles Edward Trevelyan, London 19th October 1857.

[24] *Ibidem*, p 14.

[25] *Ibidem*, Note on the envelope.

[26] KB, X279, Letter from Bryan Donkin to Edvard Scheutz, Bermondsey, September, 1857.

[27] PRO, T.1.6098B/19264. Draft of a letter from the Secretary of the Treasury, C.E. Trevelyan to Edvard Scheutz, London, 12th November 1857.

[28] PRO, T.1.6098B/19264. Letter from Edvard Scheutz to the Treasury, London, 7th December 1857.

[29] KB, X279, Letter from Charles Babbage to Edvard Scheutz, London, 25th March 1858.
NM, Letter from Charles Babbage to Edvard Scheutz, London, 31st March 1858.

[30] NM, Letter from Georg Scheutz to Edvard Scheutz, Stockholm, 27th November 1857.

[31] Stokes et.al., H. P. Babbage, p 268.

[32] I have found this drawing in the Royal Library (KB, X279), and have discovered that the letter (kept in NM) mentioned in note xx in this section, actually includes the description of the drawing.

[33] I have not had the chance to investigate the possibility that records relating to the Engineers Bryan Donkin & Co. are preserved somewhere in England.

[34] PRO, T.2.6118/005153. Note, by someone at the Treasury, saying that Mr Graham forwards an application for an advancement by Mr Scheutz, dated 13th February 1858. It is also noted that the Treasury agrees to Scheutz' request, dated 16th February 1858.

[35] PRO, T.1.6118/005153. Letter from Bryan Donkin to James George Graham, Bermondsey, 24th February 1858.

[36] PRO, T.1.6118/005153. Letter from Bryan Donkin to James George Graham, Bermondsey, 8thMarch 1858.

[37] PRO, T.1.6118/005153. Minister of the Lords of the Treasury regarding the decision about the payment of an advance to Edvard Scheutz, 22nd March 1858.

[38] See note 42.

[39] NM, Letter from Georg Scheutz to Edvard Scheutz, Stockholm, 28th April 1858.

[40] *Ibidem.*

[41] KB, I.s. 10, "Nordstjerne-Orden". Letter of entitlement to Georg Scheutz, written and signed by Prince Carl, the Castle of Stockholm, 28th April 1858.

[42] NM, Letter from Georg Scheutz to Edvard Scheutz, Stockholm, 28th April 1858.

[43] I have not been able to ascertain whether this actually was done.

[44] BL, Add. Ms. 37197, 323, Copy of letter from Edvard Scheutz to William Gravatt, Paris, 21st July 1858.

[45] *Ibidem.*

[46] *Ibidem.*

[47] [Moigno], p 81.

[48] *Ibidem.* Merzbach, pp 56-58 has obviously failed to note this, because she calls this article "Discussion at the Academy of Sciences, Paris", without any further comments. My interpretation of Moigno's article, as being a very partisan version of a minor reference to the engine at the French Academy, and not a discussion in the true sense of the word, is supported by the fact that it is not mentioned in *Compte Rendus Hebdomaires de la Academie des Sciences* for the year 1858. In the letter quoted in note 44 Edvard mentions delightedly Moigno's support for him in an article against Leverrier. What the supporters of the engine actually said in Moigno's article will be discussed in section 3.3.

[49] [anon.], "Mécanique appliquée à la solution de problèmes mathématiques et autres", *Le Siècle*, 11th August 1858.

[50] [anon.], *La Proprieté Industrielle: Journal Judicaire de L'Industrie*, 19th August 1858, p 3.

[51] A. Rivere, "Machine à calculer", *L'Illustration, Journal Universel*, 28th August 1858.

[52] KVA, Protokoll 1858, p 82.

[53] NM, Letter from (signature illegible) to Georg Scheutz, St:Petersburg, 10th - 22nd September 1858.

[54] KB, I. s. 10, Letter from Kristofer Rutger Ludvig Manderström to Georg Scheutz, Stockholm, 26th September 1858.

[55] NM, Letter from Georg Scheutz to Edvard Scheutz, Stockholm the 21 st March - 7th April 1857.

[56] *Ibidem.*

[57] KB, I. s. 10, Letter from Kristofer Rutger Ludvig Manderström to Georg Scheutz, Stockholm, 9th October 1858.

[58] They are now in KB, I. s. 10.

[59] Since 1980 I have written a number of letters to several institutions of history and science in the Soviet Union. I have also been helped by a Soviet Technical Attaché in Stockholm. Despite these attempts, I have not been able to contact anyone possessing knowledge of the history of the Observatory at St:Petersburg, the place where a possible machine might have gone to. Furthermore, I have made an equally unsuccessful investigation of all the pertinent material belonging to the Swedish Legation in St:Petersburg:
RA, Utrikes Departementet, Beskickningens i Petersburg arkiv:
Registratur, 1856-1859.
Mottagna skrivelser, vols. 292-294, 1857-1959.
I am indebted to Jan Garnert for skilful help in translating and interpreting documents in Russian.

[60] Anonymous article on Scheutz' engine in *Aftonbladet* 14, 1859.
Aftonbladet 17, 1859.

[61] [August Blanche], "Georg Scheutz", *Illustrerad Tidning*, 29th January 1859, front page.'

[62] KB, X279, Letter from Bryan Donkin to Georg Scheutz, London, 6th June 1859.

[63] *Ibidem.*

[64] RA, Kommerskollegie Huvudarkiv, "Namnregister till patent". See under "Edvard Scheutz". I have not examined the patent documents.

[65] KB, X279, Letter from Bryan Donkin to Georg Scheutz, London, 6th June 1859.

[66] KB, X279, Letter from Bryan Donkin to Edvard Scheutz, London, 2nd July 1859.

[67] What will be said about the design and mode of operation of the Donkin engine is based on my examination of the engine, carried out in the Science Museum, London June 1979, and: KB, X279, "Machin för beräkning och tryckning af matematiska tabeller. Af Georg och Edvard Scheutz." Undated manuscript of Edvard Scheutz.

[68] Bronze and/or brass.

[69] William Gravatt, *Companion to the Barometer, Mountain Barometer Tables; Calculated and Stereotyped by Messrs. Scheutz's Calculating Machine No. 2 and Printed by Machinery* (London 1859).

[70] *Ibidem*, p 4.

[71] KB, X279, Letter from Bryan Donkin to Edvard Scheutz, London, 24th August 1859.

[72] *Ibidem*.
The malfunction was caused by friction between the type wheels and between the type wheels and their axle, which prevented the stepped tooth cams from falling on the snails as they should have done. This led to the wrong digits being printed. The error could be rectified according to Donkin by using a thinner oil.

[73] *Ibidem*.

[74] KB, X279, Letter from Bryan Donkin to Edvard Scheutz, London, 29th August 1859.

[75] NM, Copy of letter from the Astronomer Royal, George B. Airy to the Registrar General, James George Graham, Greenwich, 31st August 1859. (A printed version is also to be found in NM.)

[76] NM, *Report on the Calculating Machine recently constructed by Mr. Donkin*, printed copy of a report by G. G. Stokes, C. Wheatstone, R. Willis and W. H. Miller to the Registrar General, I. Graham, undated. (Handwritten copy also in PRO, T.1.6396/005153).

[77] NM, Letter from the Astronomer Royal, George B. Airy to the Registrar General, James George Graham, Greenwich, 31st August 1859.

[78] PRO, T.1.6396/005153, copy of letter from Bryan Donkin to James Graham, Bermondsey, 3rd September 1858.

[79] *Ibidem*.

[80] PRO, T.1.6396/005153, copy of another letter from Bryan Donkin to James Graham, Bermondsey, 3rd September 1858.

[81] *Ibidem*, Various drafts and copies of letters (some partly illegible) by James George Graham and George Lewis, September 1858. NM, letter from Bryan Donkin to Edvard Scheutz, London, 16th November 1859.

[82] NM, Letter from William Farr to Edvard Scheutz, London, 14th September 1859.

[83] KB, X279, letter from Bryan Donkin to Edvard Scheutz, London, 29th September 1859.

[84] *Ibidem*.

[85] *Ibidem*.

[86] NM, Letter from Bryan Donkin to Edvard Scheutz, London. Undated, but stamped Hamburg 3rd of October 1859, and received by Edvard Scheutz on the 6th of October 1859.

[87] NM, Authorization by Edvard Scheutz to Bryan Donkin, concerning the right to receive payment for the third difference engine. Undated. Probably a copy of the original document.

[88] NM, Letter form Bryan Donkin to Edvard Scheutz, London, 16th November 1859.

[89] *Aftonbladet*, 253, 1859.

[90] KB, Ep.A.4:24, Letter from Georg Scheutz to Johan A. Ahlstrand, Librarian at the Royal Library, Stockholm, 13th of October 1859.

[91] The correspondence in the Royal Library shows that Edvard kept in touch with interested parties abroad but no letters mentioning details about tenders for the engine, are preserved.

[92] Heinrich Meidinger, "Die Scheutz'sche Rechenmachine", *Dinglers Polytechnisches Journal*, 156, nr 4, 1860, p 335.

[93] "Edvard Scheutz roterande ångmaskin", *Illustrerad Tidning*, 16th February 1861.

[94] "Roterande Ångmaskin af Edvard Scheutz" *Tidskrift för Byggnadskonst och Ingenjörsvetenskap*, 1863, p 146.

[95] *Ibidem*, p 148.
"Roterande ångmaskin af Edvard Scheutz", *Tidskrift för Byggnadskonst och Ingenjörsvetenskap*, 1861, p 12.
NM, "Ångmaskinen", a collection of documents (copies of certificates) concerning Edvard Scheutz' rotary steam engine, 1860-1863.
From the above sources, it appears that at least three steam engines were made and put to use in 1861.

[96] NM, "Ångmaskinen".

[97] Georg Scheutz, *Industriens Bok*, 1-2 (Stockholm 1860).

[98] Georg Scheutz, *Industriens Bok. Uppfinningarne och slöjderna. Skildrade från historisk och teknisk ståndpunkt*. 1-2 (Stockholm 1861). The chapter on "Calculating Engines" is to be found on pp 509-526

[99] KB, I. s. 10, "Resolution på pension för Auditeuren G. Scheutz", signed by King Carl, the Castle of Stockholm, 23rd November 1860.

[100] *Protocoll, hållna hos högloflige Ridderskapet och Adeln, vid Lagtima Riksdagen i Stockholm år 1859-1860* 1 (Stockholm 1859), (Plenary meeting 30th November 1859), pp 570-572, esp. p 571.

[101] "Stats-Utskottets Utlåtande N:o 152", *Bihang till samtlige Riks-Ståndens Protokoll vid Lagtima Riksdagen i Stockholm åren 1859 och 1860*, fjerde samligen, första afdelingen, första bandet (Stockholm 1860), pp 64-64.

Protocoll, hållna hos högloflige Ridderskapet och Adeln, vid Lagtima Riksdagen i Stockholm år 1859-1860 9 (Stockholm 1861), (Plenary meeting 29th August 1860), p 343.

Högvördiga Preste-Ståndets Protocoll vid Lagtima Riksdagen i Stockholm åren 1859 & 1860 7 (Stockholm 1861), (Plenary meeting 25th August 1860), p 540.

Protocoll, hållna hos vällofliga Borgare-Ståndet, vid Lagtima Riksdagen i Stockholm åren 1859 och 1860 5 (Stockholm 1861), (Plenary meeting 29th August 1860), p 976.

[102] *Hedervärda Bonde-Ståndets Protokoller vid Lagtima Riksdagen i Stockholm åren 1859-60* 7 (Stockholm 1860), (Plenary meeting 25th August 1860), pp 566-567.

The Estate of Peasants wished to reduce the size of Scheutz' pension because he had already received financial support for his second machine and because his fellow countryman Martin Wiberg during the same Riksdag had been awarded 8,000 riksdaler for his difference machine. (The latter machine will be discussed in section 3.3). *Ibidem.*

[103] "Expeditions-Utskottets Förslag till underd. Skrifvelse N:o 205", *Bihang till Rikets Ständers Protokoll vid Lagtima Riksdagen Åren 1859 och 1869*, tionde samlingen, första avdelningen, andra bandet (Stockholm 1860), pp 312-313, (325).

[104] SSA, Storkyrkoförsamlingens lysnings- och vigselbok.

[105] SSA, Storkyrkoförsamlingens dopbok.
SSA, BOK 1881-III-111, Edvard Scheutz' inventory, Stockholm, 24th February 1881.

[106] NM, Letter from Georg Scheutz to Edvard Scheutz, Stockholm, 25th November, 1862.

[107] *Passages*, pp 150-151.

[108] *Ibidem*, p 152.

[109] Farr. p cxxxix.

[110] *Passages*. See Chapter X: "The Exhibition of 1862", pp 147-167.

[111] Farr, p cxxxix.

[112] *Ibidem.*

[113] *Passages*, p 153.

[114] KTHB, MS3, Nr 53, Travel Report by Edvard Scheutz to the "Kommerskollegium", Stockholm, 19th June 1863.

[115] *Ibidem*, p 4.

[116] *Ibidem*, p 2.
NM, Letter from Georg Scheutz to Edvard Scheutz, Stockholm, 25th November, 1862.

[117] NM, Letter from Bryan Donkin to Edvard Scheutz, London, 2nd June 1862.

[118] NM, Letter from Georg Scheutz to Edvard Scheutz, Stockholm 25th November 1862.

[119] *Ibidem.*

[120] Farr, p cxi.

[121] NM, Letter from Georg Scheutz to Edvard Scheutz, Stockholm 25th November 1862.

[122] [George Washington Hough], *Report of the Astronomer in change of the Dudley Observatory. For the Year 1863* (Albany 1864), pp 37-42.
[Lewis Boss], *Dudley Observatory. Annual Report of the Astronomer for 1877* (Albany 1878), p 8.

[123] SSA, BOU 1873-IV-307, Georg Scheutz' inventory, Stockholm, 31st July 1873.

[124] RA, Kommerskollegie Huvudarkiv, "Namnregister till patent". See under "Edvard Scheutz": "Bokstafslek för barn", 2nd November 1872. "Läs- och räknelåda", 12th March 1879. "Ritvinkel och delningslinjal", 30th May 1879. The dates are when the patent was granted.
During the years 1870 and 1871 Edvard Scheutz was in charge of the stamp-printing establishment. See: Sven Åkerstedt, "Frimärksleverantörerna", Sven Åkerstedt (ed.), *Handbok över Sveriges frankstecken* 1855-1963 (Karlshamn 1964), p 2.

[125] Bergstedt, pp 177-178, says that Edvard Scheutz translated volumes 2 and 3 of W. Wägner, *Rom. Dess tillkomst, utvecklings, verldsvälde och förfall. En skildring för den klassiska fornålderns vänner* (Stockholm 1869-1872). Volume 1 was translated by Georg Scheutz.
With respect to Edvard's articles, which e.g. dealt with the introduction of the "American System of Manufactures", for rifle production to Sweden see: esp: BL, Add. Ms., 37198, 142 ff. Letter from Edvard Scheutz to Charles Babbage, Stockholm, 25th January 1861.
BL, Add. Ms., 37197, 296, Letter from Edvard Scheutz to Charles Babbage, London, 30th March 1858.

[126] KB, Autografsamlingen, Letter to "broder Sydow" (unidentified) from Edvard Scheutz, Stockholm, 30th December 1879.

[127] SSA, Adolf Fredriks, död- och begravningsbok.

[128] SSA, BOU 1881-III-111.

[129] SSA, Storkyrkoförsamlingens dödbok. Axel Scheutz died on 17th February 1883.

Notes to section 3.1

The section is mainly based on the author's investigations of the engines in question:

Babbage's difference engine, London, November-December 1981.
Scheutz' first engine, Stockholm, January-March 1980.
Scheutz' second engine, Washington, June, 1980.
Scheutz' third engine, London, June 1979 and November-December 1981.

It is the first time that a detailed comparison between the engines has been made. Cf. Collier, pp 229-232, and Hyman's one-sentence comparison and conclusion - "Compared with Babbage's compact and elegant engineering, the Scheutz engine is like a piece of Meccano" (A mechanical construction set for children, by which simple machines can be built). Hyman, p 239.

[1] The name "safety system" is perhaps not the best, given that in certain situations, they had another purpose. However it will suffice, since the important thing is not the name, but what the system did. According to a very recently published report, Babbage called these mechanisms "lockings", see: Allan G. Bromley *Babbage General: The evolution of Charles Babbage's calculating engines*, Technical Report 272, November 1985, Basser Department of Computer Science; the University of Sydney (Sydney 1985), p 7.

[2] Lardner, H. P. Babbage, p 69.

[3] *Ibidem*.

[4] *Ibidem*.

When Babbage began to work on the large engine, voices were often heard praising the engine's amazing capacity "to correct its own errors". Among other things, this led Georg Scheutz early on to believe that this was in fact the case, see section 2.2, p 99.

Typical remarks about the engine's self-correction capability are to be found in RS, DM.4,130. "Mr. BABBAGE'S INVENTION. Copies of the correspondence of the Lord Commissioners of His Majesty's Treasury and the President and Council of the Royal Society, relative to an Invention of Mr. Babbage. Whitehall 21 May 1823, No. 1", p 3.

Other authors since then have also erroneously given this as the main purpose of the system. See for example, M. R. Williams, "The difference engines", *The Computer Journal*, 1976, vol. 19, 1, pp 82-89.

[5] Lardner, H. P. Babbage, p 69.

[6] BL, Add. Ms., 37198, 189-191, John Herschel's translation of Klipstein (1786) for Charles Babbage, undated.

Cf. Klipstein, pp 27-35, under the heading "Von der Sicherheit der Maschine", (about the security of the machine).

[7] Klipstein, p 7.

Letter from Johann Helfrich Müller to Georg Christoph Lichtenberg, Darmstadt, 22nd May 1783, Joost and Schöne, p 615.

[8] Mechanically, springs for this purpose can *only* be replaced by cam- or eccentric mechanisms.

[9] See p 69.

[10] It should also be noted that there were frequent contacts between the Herschels and their relatives and various scientists in Göttingen. See e.g. RS, HS. 2, *passim*; Clerke, and the biographies of father and son Herschel in *Dictionary of National Biography* (London 1891).

Part of George Peacock's correspondence with Airy, Herschel and Babbage is to found at the University of Texas, Austin, Texas. This has been examined but it contains no information about Müller. I am grateful to the people at the University of Texas who helped me with this matter.

All the correspondence between Airy, Babbage and Herschel in the Royal Society Library (comprising approximately 300 items in addition to those in HS.1 and HS.2) has been examined but nothing throwing further light on this matter was found.

[11] Since Babbage's Difference Engine No. 2 was never built, it will not be considered.

[12] Bromley, p 204. (Bromley has carried out these measurements together with Michael Wright at the Science Museum, London.)

[13] I am indebted to Allan G. Bromley for providing me with this additional information by correspondence.

[14] Ball bearings and similar devices were very rare, and really not invented in their modern shape until the end of the 19th century.

[15] [Benjamin Herschel Babbage], *Babbage's Calculating Machine, or Difference Engine, A description of a portion of this machine put together in 1833 and now exhibited, by permission of the board of works, in the educational division of the South Kensington Museum, Science and Art Department*, (London 1872), p 7.

[16] *Letters Patent*, p 7.

[17] When Gould complained about the engine sometimes making errors, i.e. malfunctioning (see p xx), he was probably referring to this.

Later, Gould's successors, while attempting to put the engine into operation added a mechanism to eliminate this defect. At each one of the number wheels a small piece of "leather or rubber, pressed against its circumference, by means of a spring", was attached. They even suggested the addition of a ratchet mechanism. See [Hough], p 42.

[anon], *Annals of the Dudley Observatory* 1 (Albany 1866), p 125.

[18] A. J. Meadows, *Greenwich Observatory: The Royal Observatory at Greenwich and Herstmonceux 1675-1975* vol. 2: "Recent History (1836-1975)", p 3.

[19] John Herschel, "Report of the Committee", H. P. Babbage, p 234.

[20] *Specimens*, p xvi.

[21] Collier, pp 230-231.

[22] SML, "Babbage's Scribbling Book", vol. IX, December 1864 - November 1866. Microfiche D10, fiche 1/9, p 4, 13 January 1865. In this Babbage gives the normal speed of the Scheutz engine as 2.5 calculations per minute, or 24 seconds for each result.

[23] Collier, p 231.

[24] *Ibidem*, p 284.

[25] Collier p 231, who says that the Scheutz engine "was tremendously much slower" than Babbages, has not considered these facts.

[26] NM, Letter from Georg Scheutz to Edvard Scheutz, Stockholm, 11th July 1856.

[27] NM, Letter from Georg Scheutz to Edvard Scheutz, Stockholm, 27th November 1857.

[28] KB X279, Letter from Bryan Donkin to Edvard Scheutz, London, 24th August 1859.

[29] *Specimens*, p 7, note.

[30] *Ibidem*, p xvii.

[31] NM, Letter from Georg Scheutz to Edvard Scheutz, Stockholm 21st June 1857.

Notes to section 3.2

[1] *The Science Museum, The First Hundred Years*, (London 1957), p 48.

[2] Dubbey, p 173.

[3] Collier, p 273.

[4] Nathan Rosenberg, *Perspectives on Technology* (Binghamton, N. Y. 1976), p 200. (An almost identical statement appears on p 276).
   In the case of Leonardo da Vinci, the popular phrase is more fitting since certain of his ideas eg. his aircraft required technology and material which did not exist at that time (eg. combustion engines and light metals).

[5] Charles Babbage, *The Exposition of 1851; or Views of the Industry, the Science and the Government of England* (London 1851), p 175.

[6] [anon], *L'Art de l'Horlogerie, enseigné en trente lecions ou manuel complet de l'horloger et de l'amateur, d'aprés Berthoud et les travaux de Wuillamy, premier horloger du Roi d'Angleterre, Georges IV*, (Paris 1827).

[7] Maurice Daumas, "Precision Mechanics", Charles Singer, E. J. Holmyard, A. R. Hall and Trevor I. Williams, *A History of Technology, Vol. IV, the Industrial Revolution c. 1750 to c. 1850*, (London 1958), pp 409 ff.

[8] *Ibidem*, p 413.

[9] Weld, p 375, notes that by the end of 1828 many workmen were occupied daily in building the engine. Smiles, p 257, says that the workman were all first class.

[10] Hyman, p 55.

[11] "Statement", *Passages*, p 92. This, Babbage said as late as 1836.

[12] [anon], "Charles Babbage: Died the 20th of October", *Nature*, No. 106, 9th November 1871, p 28. This article was first noted by Collier.

[13] *Ibidem.*

[14] *Ibidem*, p 29.

[15] RS, HS.2.184.

[16] Collier, pp 274, 277.

[17] It is of course Collier who has inspired me to think in these terms.

[18] Collier, pp 276-277.

[19] They are summarized in his fifth chapter "Conclusion", Collier, pp 272-280.

[20] Collier has concluded that Babbage "throughout his life, advocated the application of scientific methods to practical problems", see Collier, p 9.

[21] I am of the opinion that, for example, safety system 3 was unnecessary, i.e. the one which Müller had put forward. If the scale had been smaller, the work could have been simplified considerably and large expensive machine tools would not have been needed.

[22] Lardner, H. P. Babbage, pp 77-78.

[23] The notation to the Scheutz machine was in the form of a very large descriptive schema on a sheet of paper measuring 5 square meters. It is kept in the Babbage Collection, SML.

[24] Weld, p 384, note 16.

[25] Some scholars have based their views of Joseph Clement on the letters of a certain C. G. Jarvis to Babbage. Jarvis was a draughtsman employed by Clement and he worked on the difference engine. In all his letters, Jarvis describes Clement in very unflattering terms. However, I would maintain that Jarvis is not a reliable witness in this matter, since it is not inconceivable that he hoped to gain from his accusations. See Collier, pp 75, 82-84; Hyman, pp 131-132.

[26] Hyman, pp 126, 131.
Hyman's way of describing Clement is very unfortunate.

[27] Smiles, pp 256-257.
Weld's example is taken from Weld, p 374, who states that the arbiters were Brunel, Donkin and Field. The latter two being the ones that also were chosen to look into the matter of Clement's bills relating to the engine.

[28] *Economy* (1833), p 215.

[29] Smiles, p 251.
A realistic figure is also obtained by assuming an average income of a pound per worker per day, not counting the cost of material.

[30] A comparison has also been made with the Swedish translation of the second English edition (1838). See Gustaf Thomée: *Nionde Bridgewater-afhandlingen. Aphorismer, Bibliotek för Populär Naturkunnighet, Andra afdelningen 9* (Stockholm 1846).

Cf. Hyman, pp 136-142, who has a chapter on this book.

[31] *The Ninth Bridgewater Treatise*, p v ff.

[32] *Ibidem*, p ix.

[33] *Ibidem*, p 33 ff.

[34] The word 'programming' is much more recent and was not used by Babbage.

[35] *Ibidem*, pp 40-41.

[36] *Ibidem*, p 43 ff.

[37] *Ibidem*, p 44.

[38] *Ibidem*, pp 48-49.

[39] *Ibidem*, p 94 ff.

[40] *Ibidem*, p 138 ff.

[41] *Ibidem*, p 139.

[42] $20 \cdot 10^{19} = 200,000,000,000,000,000,000$

[43] *Ninth Bridgewater Treatise*, pp 140-141.

[44] *Passages*, pp 387-391.

[45] *Ibidem*, p 440.

[46] This assertion is based on the fact that Müller was without doubt the most talented machine designer of the four men. His universal calculating machine provides a concrete proof of this fact, as well as what he says in Klipstein (1786).

Notes to section 3.3

[1] *Specimens*, p ix, note *.

The Scheutz correspondence, *passim*, reveals that Alfred Deacon became their friend and supporter.

See also: Brian Randell, "A Mysterious Advertisement", *Annals of the History of Computing*, vol. 5, No. 1, January 1983, pp 60-63.

[2] *Passages*, p 48.

[3] "Kongl. Maj:ts Nåd. Proposition N:o 108", Stockholm, 30th March 1860, *Bihang till samtlige Riks-Ständers Protokoll vid Lagtima Riksdagen i Stockholm*

Åren 1859 och 1860, första samlingen, första avdelningen, första bandet (Stockholm 1860), pp 20-21.

Protocoll, hållna hos vällofliga Borgare-Ståndet, vid Lagtima Riksdagen i Stockholm åren 1859 och 1860 5 (Stockholm 1861), (Plenary meeting 25 th July 1860), pp 370-371.

"Stats-Utskottets Utlåtande N:o 169", Stockholm, 24th August 1860, *Bihang till samtlige Riks-Ständers Protokoll vid Lagtima Riksdagen i Stockholm Åren 1859 och 1860*, fjerde samlingen, första afdelningen, tredje bandet (Stockholm 1860, pp 3-5.

Protocoll, hållna vid högloflige Ridderskapet och Adeln, vid Lagtima Riksdagen i Stockholm år 1859-1860 10 (Stockholm 1861), (Plenary meeting 5th September 1860), pp 58-59.

Högvördiga Preste-Ståndets Protocoll vid Lagtima Riksdagen i Stockholm åren 1859 & 1860 8 (Stockholm 1861), (Plenary meeting 1st September 1860), p 104.

Protocoll hållna hos vällofliga Borgare-Ståndet, vid Lagtima Riksdagen i Stockholm åren 1859 och 1860 6 (Stockholm 1861), (Plenary meeting 5th September 1860), p 152.

Hedervärda Bonde-Ståndets Protokoller vid Lagtima Riksdagen i Stockholm åren 1859-60 8 (Stockholm 1860), (Plenary meeting 1st September 1860), p 51.

"Expeditions-Utskottets Förslag till underd. Skrifvelse N:o 129", Stockholm, 18th September 1860, *Bihang till Samtlige Riks-Ståndens Protokoll vid Lagtima Riksdagen i Stockholm Åren 1859 och 1860*, tionde samlingen, första afdelningen, första bandet (Stockholm 1860), pp 396-397.

For information about Wiberg, see e.g.:

Helgo Wiberg, "Några av Martin Wibergs uppfinningar", *Daedalus* (1955), pp 111-118.

Tore Andersson, "Wibergs räknemaskin", *Daedalus* (1933), pp 98-99.

Helgo Wiberg, "Martin Wiberg, En svensk uppfinnare inom grafiska branschen", *Grafiskt forum*, No. 9, 1954, pp 271-273.

Helgo Wiberg, "Svensk gjorde första användbara sättmaskinen", *Stockholms-tidningen*, 1st December 1954.

Martin Wiberg, *Med maskin uträknade och stereotyperade räntetabeller jemte en dagräkningstabell*, (Stockholm 1860).

[4] TM, 26.467, 132, Letter of introduction by Charles Babbage for Martin Wiberg, addressed to "Monsieur Guerry de la Institut de France", London, 15th November 1862.

TM, 26.467, 132 b, Copy of a letter of introduction by Charles Babbage for Martin Wiberg, addressed to "Monsieur M. Mathieu Membre de l'Institut de France & c & c", London, 16th November 1862. According to these two letters, Wiberg was en route to Paris. He hoped to try to recoup his investment in the machine, by having it calculate and print logarithm tables there, which he planned to sell.

[5] This assertion is based on my examination of Wiberg's machine, kept in the National Museum of Science and Technology, Stockholm, in October 1981.

[6] Merzbach, pp 33-37 has a detailed account on Grant and his engine.

[7] M. R. Williams, "The Difference Engines", *The Computer Journal* 19, 1976, p 87.

[8] Merzbach, p 35.

[9] Part of quotation on p 98.

¹⁰ Part of quotation on p 209.

¹¹ In order to estimate how far the fourth strategy of specially sending out copies of *Specimens* was implemented, I have carried out the following investigation. I wrote (in February 1984) to 14 of the observatories and other institutions which appear in the distribution list on p xxx in appendix. 13 replies were received. In only four cases had *Specimens* been preserved — in Brussels, Göttingen, Leyden and Berne. There was no follow-up letters which would have shown that a combination of strategies 4 and 2 had been used although there may be room for a more exhaustive search here, than was possible on this occasion, given the time at my disposal. Taking into account the effects of bombing, weeding, of documents being misplaced and of the time that has elapsed, I consider this result highly satisfying. I am indebted to all the persons who have kindly helped me with this investigation.

¹² Quoted by Collier, p 40.

¹³ Fletcher et. al., vol. 2, pp 895, 784.
    Glaisher, p 45.

¹⁴ Fletcher et. al., vol. 2, p 925.
    Glaisher, p 45.

¹⁵ Glaisher, p 135.
    Taylor, preface, second page.

¹⁶ I have arrived at this conclusion after studying most of the tables mentioned in section 1.1 and by taking note of what is said in Glaisher and de Morgan (1861), *passim*.

¹⁷ Glaisher, p 144, also bears this out.

¹⁸ De Morgan, "Table", pp 1000, 1002.

¹⁹ *Ibidem*, p 53.
    Vlacq calculated his 1628-tables independently from Brigg's. See, de Morgan, "Table", p 995. In the 1633-version, twenty thousand of Brigg's logarithms were added, *ibidem*, p 996.

²⁰ Comment: Mr. Sang's table was published the year Babbage died.

²¹ See p 45 and p 100.

²² The British mathematician, Leslie John Comrie, was one of the foremost authorities on numerical tables. He was a co-author of Fletcher, see Fletcher et. al.,

²³ The rewards could be in the form of money; e.g. von Vega (1794) offered a ducat for every error detected by the reader. A German printer of tables in the 1850's, on the other hand, offered books.
    See, Glaisher, p 139. (About Vega).
    Ludvig Schrön, *Sjuställiga vanliga logaritmer för alla hela tal från 1 till 108,000 och för sinus, cosinus, tangenter och cotangenter för alla vinklar i qvadranten från 10 till 10 sekunder* (Stockholm 1868). Translation from German original by F. W. Hultman. See the printer's words in the preface. First edition apparently printed in Brunswick 1859.

[24] Fletcher et. al., p 1.

[25] See quotation on p 190.

[26] Schrön's table mentioned in note 23 above, is another example of how stereotyped tables could easily be distributed internationally. In 1859, it was printed in Brunswick with a German foreword. In 1865, the stereotypes reached London and the same year a new edition was published with an English foreword. A Swedish edition was made in Stockholm in 1868 from the same stereotypes. (Glaisher, p 126).

[27] See quotation on p 190.

[28] *Specimens*, p 7.

[29] It is claimed that this corresponded to ten forward and ten backward calculations. This was not properly speaking true. There were at least 23 and not 20 settings required (because 9,000 tabular values/400 = 22,5). *Ibidem*, p 7.

[30] *Ibidem*, see the discussion about errors on p 4; I have calculated that $n = 148/2 = 74$, where 2 is the safety marginal used in the five digit table.

[31] The figure of 122 settings implies that "only" $122/2 = 61$ calculations of start values must be carried out. This was because for every set of start values, one could calculate in two directions simply by altering the sign of the odd differences.

[32] Because $122/23 = 5.30$.

[33] My estimated figures are as follows: 142 hours for turning the handle; one hour per calculation of each set of start values, i.e. 61 hours (see note 31); twenty minutes per setting of the number wheels; and the same time for putting new matrices in the printing unit now and then, which is approximately 40 hours, since it has to be done 122 times.

[34] [Moigno], pp 83-84. Here Moigno has added Alfred Deacon's words (the inventor of a difference engine and a friend of the Scheutzes), to defend the Scheutz engine against Leverrier's criticism. Deacon states that it would have taken at least some 180 hours to set the logarithmic table in *Specimens*. This means six hours per page. This seems very high, even though proof reading should be included. It should also be noted that what Deacon says about the speed of the engine is a slight exaggeration (no more than 64 hours in all). Bearing in mind that Deacon was trying to defend the Scheutzes, I conclude that his opinion agrees with my conclusion about the speed of the Scheutz engine versus a compositor.

[35] It is interesting to note that this is *precisely* what Georg and Edvard Scheutz, together with Gravatt and Sparre, did even in the case of the five figure logarithm table in *Specimens*. To assert, as Gravatt does, that the logarithms which are necessary before one produces the start values, have to be *calculated* (see *Specimens* p 7) is pure nonsense. It is clear that what they did, was to look them up in some authoritative seven place table. Since other tables formed the basis of those reckoned by the engine, this shows vividly that Brigg's and Vlacq's work could not be surpassed by the machine made by Scheutz.

[36] See pp 232.

[37] See quotation on p 190.

[38] See quotation on p 133.

[39] See e.g. Bell, p 264 f.

[40] Glaisher, p 66. The 48-page table was logarithmic-trigonometric, and was published in 1838.

[41] PRO, T.1.6098B/19264, Letter from George Biddell Airy, to Charles Edward Trevelyan, Greenwhich, 30th September 1857.

[42] *Ibidem*.

[43] *Ibidem*.

[44] *Ibidem*.

[45] *Interpolation Tables, used at the Nautical Almanac Office*, (London 1857).

[46] *Annals of the Dudley Observatory*, p 126.

[47] Taken from quotation on p 51.

[48] Merzbach, p 22.
For what I say about Gould and the Observatory, c.f. Merzbach, pp 22-28.
Curiously enough Merzbach mentions most of these assertions, but does not comment upon what the assertions of Gould and the others in fact mean.,

[49] See p 202 ff.

[50] Quotation from p 210.

[51] [anon], *Report of the Secretary of the Navy 1858* (Washington D.C. 1858), p 441.

[52] Merzbach, p 42.

[53] James, 1980, p 180.

[54] *Ibidem*.

[55] *Ibidem*, p ii, *passim*.

[56] *Ibidem*.

[57] [Olcott, Rathbone et. al.], pp 29-30.

[58] *Ibidem*, p 30.

[59] *Ibidem*, pp 30-31.

[60] TM, 26.247, Letter from John Ericsson to Martin Wiberg, New York, 18th December 1868.

[61] *Ibidem.*

[62] I am very much indebted to Owen Gingerich, at the Smithsonian Astrophysical Observatory, Cambridge, MA, with his great experience of the history of astronomy, for helping me to corroborate this theory. Nothing has been written about how ephemerides were copied and there is in general very little written about their history. I have already referred to the work of Owen Gingerich and Barbara L Welther (1983), but this deals only with the 17th and 18th centuries (for some information see p 14).

[63] I am equally indebted to A. Braccesi, at the Department of Astronomy, at the University of Bologna, for trying to help me to find more information about this matter.

[64] Farr, p cxlii.

[65] See p 216.

[66] PRO, T.1.6257/005153, Copy of bills from Bryan Donkin to the Registrar General, James George Graham, Bermondsey from 23rd August 1859 to 3rd August 1861.

[67] See p 216.

[68] RS, MC.6.33. Letter from George Graham to the Secretary of the Royal Society, London, 5th September 1859.

[69] I have looked in vain for literature before the 1820s dealing with the problem of errors in tables, in England, USA and Sweden. The first exhaustive article on the subject is Babbage's letter to Sir Humphry Davy (1822). There then followed a whole series of articles, among them, those in *Brewster's Journal* and *The Edinburgh Philosophical Journal*, both published in 1822. Babbage's friend Francis Baily contributed an enthusiastic article in Schumacher's *Astronomische Nachrichten*, on tables and errors, which was reprinted and (although it is not stated that this was the case) probably used by Lardner. Lardner's very detailed article in the *Edinburgh Review* (1834) was the culmination of Babbage's efforts to spread printed information about his idea.

[70] BL, Add.Ms.37198, 142, Letter from Edvard Scheutz to Charles Babbage, Stockholm, 25th January 1861.

Notes to Epilogue

[1] John Herschel, "Report of the Committee", H.P.Babbage, p 234.

[2] BL, Add. Ms., 37195, 95-96, Report from a phrenological examination of Charles Babbage, 17th June 1852: - "Phrenological Examination, made by the aid of Dr. T. Leger's modification of Mr. Rutter's Magnetocope".

[3] A German manufacturer of commercial calculators, Hamann in Berlin, made a difference engine in 1909 for two scientists who wished to produce an eight figure logarithm table. Since the engine had only two differences, it must have involved

a great deal of laborious work. It could print its results. See: M. R. Williams, "The Difference Engines", *The Computer Journal* 19, 1, 1976, p 87.

[4] Williams, "The Difference Engines", pp 87-88.
L. H. Dudley Buxton, "Charles Babbage and his Difference Engines", *Transactions of the Newcomen Society*, 14, 1935, pp 58-62.

[5] Harold T. Davis and Vera Fisher, *A Bibliography of Mathematical Tables* (Evanston, Illinois 1949), p ii.

[6] Herman H. Goldstine, *The Computer: From Pascal to von Neumann* (Princeton, N.J. 1980), pp 129, 135-138.

Appendix 1

Rediscovery and restoration

When the work on this book began, the first Scheutz engine, built between 1837 and 1843 had vanished. Apart from what Berzelius' statement had to say about the machine, nothing was known. The whole construction of the engine took place in silence. No drawings or sketches of the engine are preserved and it is by no means certain that any were made. In consequence, the information available was meagre and many questions arose. What became of the engine and most of all, what did it look like?

REDISCOVERY:

This lack of material induced me to look for new sources of information and on 4th December 1979, a visit was paid to Stockholm's City Archives.

In the inventory of Edvard Scheutz' estate, made in 1881 by a deputy of Stockholm's municipal court, it was stated that his son Axel Georg Reinhold Scheutz aged 19 years, was the sole beneficiary. The estate was placed in the trusteeship of Carl Dahlgren and Carl J. Grafström. Under the heading "miscellaneous" in the inventory, the following entry appeared:

"In the keeping of Arthur Hazelius at the Nordic Museum, the model of a calculating engine, valued at .... 500:—".

In the hope of finding the missing machine I therefore paid a visit to the Nordic Museum (Nordiska Museet), which had been founded in 1873 by the same Arthur Hazelius.

The engine — the first Scheutz difference engine — was discovered the same day, listed in the register of holdings of the Nordic Museum. In the main index, was the following encouraging entry:

"39204 *Model of a calculating machine*
Of the calculating engine of Messrs. Georg and Edvard Scheutz. Together with papers and books concerning the engine. Acquired from

Fig. 95 Arthur Hazelius (1833–1901), founder of the Nordic Museum in 1873 in Stockholm. It was in the collections of the Nordic Museum that Edvard Scheutz hoped that the first Scheutz engine from 1843 should be "preserved for the benefit of posterity". Photograph by courtesy of the Nordic Museum, Stockholm.

the trustee, Karl J. Grafström, Stockholm, appointed to administer the estate of Edvard Scheutz, bankrupt – 50 crowns. 18/7 1881."

It turned out that the machine was still in existence, stored away among the collections. There is a certain obscurity about the exact course of events that led to the engine passing into the ownership of the Nordic Museum. The main index entry says that it had been acquired from the estate of Edvard Scheutz, who had died an undischarged bankrupt. However the following document, see also Fig. 96, indicates that already during his lifetime Edvard Scheutz had entertained the idea of raising money, by public subscription in connection with a donation to the Nordic Museum of the first engine:

"A Respectful invitation
There is in my possession the model of the calculating engine invented by my father and myself, which I built with my own hands between the ages of 16 and 22, that is to say during the period 1837-1843. Since I am not in a position to surrender the prototype in question, to the custody of some museum, without payment, I would hereby invite interested parties to enter beneath, the sum they would be prepared to subscribe towards the purchase of the prototype, *so that it, together with the*

drawings and documents belonging to it, might be preserved for the benefit of posterity. In this connection, I would like to mention that the Professors Er. Edlund and D. G. Lindhagen as well as D:r Hazelius — as the following statement shows — have declared that it would be desirable if the prototype were to be incorporated in the collections of the Nordic Museum.

I consider, therefore, that it is my duty to make this invitation, so that if a sufficiently large sum were to be subscribed, I would be in a position to make other inventions, which, due to lack of working capital, I have been unable to do.

Documents relating to the above mentioned engine and its history are enclosed for those interested.

Stockholm in December 1880

Edvard Scheutz"

Edvard's introduction was followed by a list where the subscriber could write his name, title and the amount subscribed. The first page contained a statement from the two professors and Arthur Hazelius:

"The undersigned hereby certify, upon request, that the calculating engine invented by Messrs. Scheutz, father and son, is the first complete one of its kind to be built, and is still unsurpassed despite the many efforts of prominent scientists and engineers abroad to do so. Since 1859, it has been used for statistical calculations at the Register Office in London, to the greatest advantage. Because of this, we believe that it would be entirely fitting if the first model of this machine which appears to belong to Engineer E. Scheutz, could be incorporated in the collections of the Nordic Museum, as a testimony to outstanding Swedish inventive capacity.

Stockholm 23 December 1880

| Er. Edlund, | D. G. Lindhagen, |
| Professor. | Professor." |

Erik Edlund was a Professor of Physics, with a special interest in engineering and technology. Daniel Georg Lindhagen was an astronomer. He had worked at the Observatory at Pulkova in Russia before taking up his position at the observatory in Stockholm. He was in charge of the production of the Almanac. Hazelius wrote:

"The undersigned hereby testifies that the model of the calculating engine invented by Messrs. G. and E. Scheutz, constituting as it does, an object of the greatest historical interest, would be received by the Nordic Museum with the utmost gratitude, as an adornment to its collections, were it to be offered for incorporation in these. I might also add that Mr. Scheutz, Engineer, has for the time being, deposited the above prototype in the museum, where it may be inspected during normal visiting hours, in the second annex, Number 79 Drottninggatan.

Stockholm, 28th December 1880.

Arthur Hazelius,
Director of the Nordic Museum."

The subscription invitation was dated the 22nd of December 1880 and Hazelius dated his statement the 28th of the same month. It is uncertain if the subscription took place or not. The document shows, nonetheless, that the significance of the invention of the first engine, and the need to preserve it for posterity, were well appreciated. On the 28th of January 1881, only one month after the subscription had got under way, Edvard Scheutz died. The engine was handed over to the Nordic Museum in July 1881 and it was eventually stored away and gradually forgotten.

The entry in the main index suggests that the engine was sold to the Nordic Museum by Carl J. Grafström for 50 crowns (2 pounds 15 shilling), by way of meeting outstanding claims on the estate. In the inventory of Edvard Scheutz, the engine was however valued at 500 crowns (27 pounds 9 shilling) – it was his most valuable possession. Thus even at the very last, the Swedish difference engine was a financial failure.

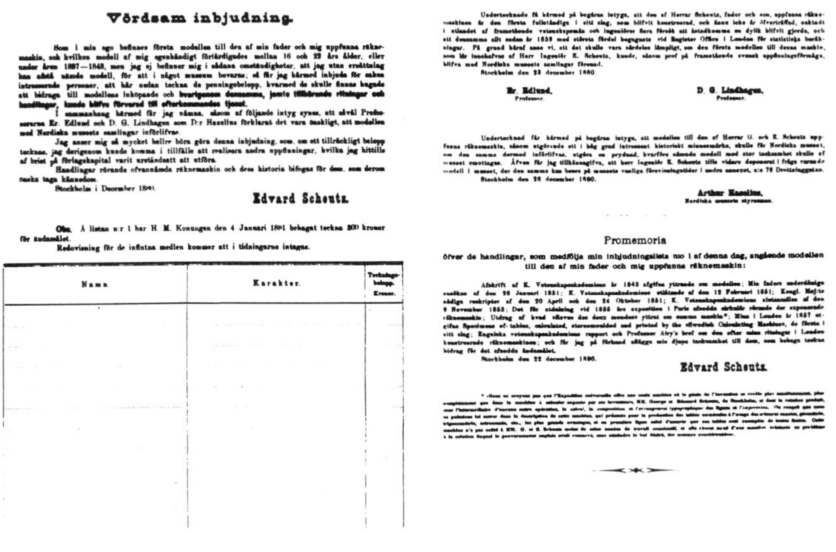

Vördsam inbjudning.

Som i min ego befinnes första modellen till den af min fader och mig uppfunna räknemaskin, och hvilken modell af mig egenhändigt förfärdigades mellan 16 och 23 års ålder, eller under åren 1837—1843, men jag ej befinner mig i sådana omständigheter, att jag utan ersättning kan afstå nämde modell, för att i något museum bevaras; så får jag härmed inbjuda för saken intresserade personer, att här nedan teckna de penningebelopp, hvarmed de skulle finnas hugade att bidraga till modellens inköpande och hvarigenom densamma, jemte tillhörande ritningar och handlingar, kunde blifva förvarad till efterkommandes tjenst.

I sammanhang härmed får jag nämna, såsom af följande intyg synes, att såväl Professorerna Er. Edlund och D. G. Lindhagen som D:r Hazelius förklarat det vara önskligt, att modellen med Nordiska museets samlingar införlifvas.

Jag anser mig så mycket hellre böra göra denna inbjudning, som, om ett tillräckligt belopp tecknas, jag derigenom kunde komma i tillfälle att realisera andra uppfinningar, hvilka jag hittills af brist på förlagskapital varit urståndsatt att utföra.

Handlingar rörande ofvannämda räknemaskin och dess historia bifogas för dem, som derom önska taga kännedom.

Stockholm i December 1880.

Edvard Scheutz.

Obs. Å listan n:r 1 har H. M. Konungen den 4 Januari 1881 behagat teckna 300 kronor för ändamålet.

Redovisning för de infintna medlen kommer att i tidningarne intagas.

Namn.	Karakter.	Teckningsbelopp. Kronor.

Undertecknade få härmed på begäran intyga, att den af Herrar Scheutz, fader och son, uppfunna räknemaskinen är den första fullständiga i sitt slag, som blifvit konstruerad, och ännu icke är öfverträffad, oaktadt i utlandet af framstående vetenskapsmän och ingeniörer flera försök att åstadkomma en dylik blifvit gjorda, och att densamma allt sedan år 1859 med största fördel begagnats vid Register Office i London för statistiska beräkningar. På grund häraf anse vi, att det skulle vara särdeles lämpligt, om den första modellen till denna maskin, som nu innehafves af Herr Ingeniör E. Scheutz, kunde, såsom prof på framstående svensk uppfinningsförmåga, blifva med Nordiska museets samlingar förenad.

Stockholm den 23 december 1880.

Er. Edlund, Professor. D. G. Lindhagen, Professor.

Undertecknad får härmed på begäran intyga, att modellen till den af Herrar G. och E. Scheutz uppfunna räknemaskin, såsom utgörande ett i hög grad intressant historiskt minnesmärke, skulle för Nordiska museet, om den samma dermed införlifvas, utgöra en prydnad, hvarföre nämde modell med stor tacksamhet skulle af museet emottagas. Äfven får jag tillkännagifva, att herr Ingeniör E. Scheutz tills vidare deponerat i fråga varande modell i museet, der den samma kan beses på museets vanliga förevisningstider i andra annexet, n:o 79 Drottninggatan.

Stockholm den 28 december 1880.

Arthur Hazelius,
Nordiska museets styresman.

Promemoria

öfver de handlingar, som medfölja min inbjudningslista no 1 af denna dag, angående modellen till den af min fader och mig uppfunna räknemaskin:

Afskrift af K. Vetenskapsakademiens år 1843 afgifna yttrande om modellen; Min faders underdåniga ansökan af den 28 Januari 1851; K. Vetenskapsakademiens utlåtande af den 12 Februari 1851; Kongl. Maj:ts nådiga reskripter af den 20 April och den 24 Oktober 1851; K. Vetenskapsakademiens slutanmälan af den 9 November 1853; Det för utdelning vid 1855 års exposition i Paris afsedda cirkulär rörande der exponerade räknemaskin; Utdrag af hvad »Revue des deux mondes» yttrat om samma maskin*; Mina i London år 1857 utgifna Specimens of tables, calculated, stereomoulded and printed by the Swedish Calculating Machine», de första i sitt slag; Engelska vetenskapsakademiens rapport och Professor Airy's bref om den efter mina ritningar i London konstruerade räknemaskinen; och får jag på förhand afägga min djupa tacksamhet till dem, som behaga teckna bidrag för det afsedda ändamålet.

Stockholm den 22 december 1880.

Edvard Scheutz.

Fig. 96 Edvard Scheutz' "Respectful invitation" of December 1880, which was intended to raise money by public subscription so that the engine could be handed over to the Nordic Museum in Stockholm. But only one month after the subscribtion had got under way, Edvard Raphael Scheutz died. The engine was stored away at the Nordic Museum and gradually it was forgotten. Original kept in the Nordic Museum. Photograph by courtesy of the Nordic Museum, Stockholm.

RESTORATION:

After a century in a repository, the Scheutz difference engine is now restored as far as possible to its original state. Restoration began on the 4th of January 1980 and was carried out by the furniture restorer at the Nordic Museum, Per Westberg, in cooperation with the present author.

When the cover was lifted for the first time, the engine was revealed to be in very bad shape. It was completely covered with dust and none of the mechanical parts could be moved. Several parts were broken or obviously missing. The cover was split right along the top, allowing dust to settle on the engine. In addition, the engine frame was at an angle to the base and both carriages had come adrift.

We decided to proceed very cautiously, and various experts were consulted regarding some details. Following their advice, we began by dismantling the engine into its larger constituent units − the printing unit, the calculating unit, the different shelves etc. Careful sketches were made and one unit after aother was taken apart, cleaned and then fitted together again.

The seizing up of the mechanical parts of the engine was in large measure due to oxidization, but also to the fact that the film of oil in the bearings had dried up and acted as a glue. The rust on the iron parts was confined to the surface and easily removed. Both the brass and iron parts were cleaned with watchmaker's fluid which restored them to their original state.

Nothing in the engine's "history" was changed. We refrained from replacing broken parts by new ones, and no attempt was made to repair scratches or fractured solderings. However, a number of constructive details, such as screws, nuts and the cord to the plumb weights, which were necessary if the engine was to hold together, were added. (These additions were marked.)

When each unit had been reassembled, it was lubricated with special oil, and adjusted so that it functioned properly. No steps were taken against corrosion, since it was presupposed that the engine in the future would be preserved in a dry, indoor, atmosphere. The engine frame and the wooden parts required only drying out but the split mahogany cover, which had previously been repaired very badly with sections of oak, was set right by Mr. Westberg.

Among the papers and books discovered along with the engine, there were none dealing with the engine's design. In the course of restoration however, the design and mode of operation of the engine gradually became clear, and many of the loose parts were reassigned to their correct place.

When the engine was first examined, the frame was skew on account of being lifted from the base. As a result, both carriages had come adrift. In addition, the handle had been turned, despite the fact that the engine had not functioned and at several places on the large gear wheel, the teeth had been torn off, see Fig. 25. Two spacing shims had been replaced in the reverse order. These mishaps must have taken place after the engine had been put on display at Drottninggatan, since it is highly unlikely that Edvard Scheutz would have allowed the difference engine to be exhibited in such a condition.

The drawbacks of the combination of wood and metal in a precision instrument such as a difference engine soon became apparent. The wood had warped so that many parts, intended to move freely, had locked. The slide had warped and locked onto the printing board. This was rectified by a thin layer of veneer. The warping of the base resulted in two rods, which were used to steer the upper carriage, being moved apart to such an extent that the carriage no longer could be moved. By introducing a new layer, the rods could be moved back to their original position, and were then able to function properly. The split on the outside of the case was also the result of warping.

The restoration work went on for two months and when it was completed, Georg and Edvard Scheutz' difference engine was restored to its original condition. However it was impossible to make it operational because the large gear wheel had been damaged. A hook in the numerator had broken off and a soldering had fractured. Furthermore it was impossible to print out the result of calculations because the lead types on the print wheels had oxidized to such an extent that they had partly disintegrated. These defects, combined with the effects of warping, made it impossible to operate the engine in the intended manner. It would merely increase the risk of further damage. Otherwise the engine, now on exhibit at the National Museum of Science and Technology in Stockholm, is in a sound condition.

Running between the black square rods of the frame are polished steel axles which contrast with the brass parts with their marks of Edvard's filing. Blue-grey lead parts, the plumb weights on their cords, the steel parts with a spatter of brass solder give the engine its unique "personality".

The engine has a great number of apparently unnecessary holes and marks etc., which show that father and son had proceeded by trial and error and that they changed the design on a number of occasions. The repairs which were carried out when some damage occurred, presumably during the making of a particular part, are also of interest, see Fig. 45-46.

The following objects were also discovered in the Nordic Museum:

A gilt framed drawing of Scheutz' second engine. It bears the text: "Machine à calculer par M.M.rs Scheutz père et fils, Stockholm", which suggests that it was taken and exhibited beside the engine at the Paris Exhibition in 1855.

Cliché or Stereotype plate obtained from matrix, calculated and printed by the first engine, see Fig. 39. Table for the function:

$f(x) = x^3 - 3x^2 + 90037x$ for x from 1 to 25.

This is in fact the cliché that was used to print the table shown in Fig. 28

and discussed on pages 148–149. It is thus particularly interesting to note, as appears from the next item, that both the wax matrix, the stereotype plate and the final product – the table – have been preserved.

Fragments of matrices. Some in wax, which were parts of a matrix of the above cliché, and some in lead, presumably used in testing to see if printing in lead was possible. (The impression is very shallow which means that the attempt probably failed because the types were insufficiently hard.)

Operating tools (2) for the calculating unit in the form of a slim rod with the ends bent at right angles like a hook.

Fig. 97 Per Westberg, furniture restorer of the Nordic Museum in Stockholm, with the first engine after restoration. Photographed by author.

Appendix 2

Distribution list

Copy of a handwritten distribution list, drawn up by Edvard Scheutz in consultation with Charles Babbage, for *Specimens of Tables, Calculated, Stereomoulded and Printed by Machinery* (London 1857). The original, which is to be found in the Nordic Museum in Stockholm, is dated 1857. The names on the list are reproduced as given and misspellings occur. Some names appear twice in the list. The reason for this appears to be that additions were made to the list, as the French version of *Specimens* was ready to be distributed in 1858. For further comments on this list, see p 208.

America:

The President of the United States
George Mifflin Dallas Env. Ex. in London
Professor B.A. Gould
John F. Rathbone
The Library of the Senate
The Library of the Congress
The Smithsonian Institution
The Military College West Point
The New York State Library
A.n Academy of Arts and Science
Cambridge Observatory
Am.n Association for Advancement of Science
Am. Journal of Science
Am.n Philosophical Society
Bowditch Library
William Bond
General Charles C. Andrews

England:

Her Majesty Queen Victoria
Prince Albert

The Prince of Wales
The Duke of Cambridge
The Duchess of Somerset
Sir Benjamin Hawes
I. K. Brunel Esq.re
Bryan Donkin Esq.re J.or
W. Wolryche Whitmore Esq.re
W. H. Fitton Esq.re M.D. F.R.S.
General Edward Sabine F.R.S.
Sir John Fr. W.am Herschel
R. H. Earl Granville
Earl Clarendon KG
Sir Edw. Geo. Lytton Bulwer Bart.
Charles Dickens Esq.re
W. M. Thackeray
Atheneum
Royal Artillery Library (Woolwich)
Royal Engineers Library (Chatum)
R. H. Sir George Lewis/Chancellor of Exch.
The Bank of England Library
The Governor of the Bank of England
The Dep.ty Governor
R. H. Sir Charles Wood Bart/Admiralty
Duke of Argyle
Marquis Lansdowne.
R. H. Sir Benj. Hatt/The Words of For...
R. H. Robert LoweEdw. John Cooper
R.d Doctor Robinson
Arch Bishop of Dublin Whateley
Sir Richard Berthell
R. H. Lord Campbell
R. H. Sir W. Maule
Pr. Aug. De Morgan
M. Faraday Roy. Inst.
Dr W.m Farr
Rowland Hill Esq.re Post Office.
The Library of the House of Lords
The Library of the House of Commons
Sir James Graham/Registrar General
The Earl of Ross
R.d Temple Chevalier Durham
Durham University Library
R. H. Lord Monteagle
E. J. Reed Esq.re (Editor of Mech. Magazine)
Pr. Lardner the Author of the Article on Calculating Machines in Edinburgh Review July, 1834.

John Fimbs Esq.re (Ill. London News)
Captain Sir John Franklin R.N. F.R.S.
P. M. Roget Esq.re M.D. F.R.S.
Ingram Esq.re M.P.
Brown Esq.re New Library Liverpool
R. H. Earl of Derby
R. H. Benjamin Disraeli
J. C. Cobbold Esq.re M.P.
Captain Douglas Galton R.E.
Sir E. Head Bart. Gov.r of Canada
Sir David Brewster F.R.S. etc, etc
Joshua Field Esq.re F.R.S.
Royal Society
Thomas Smythe Esq.re
Pr. W. Th. Thomson
Nath. Beardmore Esq.re
Lord Panmure
William Vandervalt Esq.re
Sir W.m Rowan Hamilton
Henry Donkin Esq.re
Thomas Donkin Esq.re
Piazzi Smyth Esq.re
Pr. Hind
Pr. Farley
Royal Astronomer G. B. Airy F.R.S.
R.d Maine
R.d Glaisher
R.d Godie
General Sir Fenwick William of Kars
R. H. Lord Wrottesley
C. Baldwin Esq.re
C. Whiting Esq.re
A. Deacon Esq.re
R. H. Lord Mayor of London
Society of Arts
John Lee Esq.re L.L.D. F.R.S.
Rear Admiral W.m Henry Smyth
Sir J. Macneil F.R.S.
R.d W. C. Williams M.A.
Cardinal Wiseman
J. Outhwaite Esq.re
Joseph Baxendale Esq.re
Royal Astr. Society
Royal Observatory (Greenwich)
Statistical Society
W. Simms Esq.re F.R.S.

James Watker Esq.re
Thomas Mayr M.D. F.R.S.
Thomas Lloyd Esq.re
General Sir John Fr. Bourgogne
R. H. Evelyn Denison
Pr. G. G. Stokes
Pr. W. H. Miller
Pr. C. Wheatstone
Pr. R. Willis
R.d W. Whewell D.D. F.R.S.
The Very R.d G. Peacock D.D. F.R.S.
Archbishop of York
Ven.ble Archdeacon Musgrave
Swedenborgian Society
Linnean Society
R. Stephenson Esq.re F.R.S.
C. Manby F.R.S.J. Rennie F.R.S.
G. Bidder
The Institution of Civil Engineers
Whitbread F.R.S. F.A.S.
The R.d J. B. Reade F.R.S.
C. R. Weld Esq.re
James Dundas Esq.re
The Royal Society of Edinburgh.
Frank Crossley
R. H. Lord Napier
Admiral Sir Charles Napier
General Sir William Napier
H. J. H. Lucien Bonaparte
H. Holiness the Pope Pius IX
Duke Welington
The Editor of Edinburgh Review
John Waterhouse Esq.re F.R.S.
Major General Wyld
Pr. Charles Babbage
Viscount Ockham the representative of Ada Countess of Lovelace.
William Gravatt F.R.S.

France

Emperor Louis Napoleon
H. J. H. Prince Napoleon
Prince Charles Bonaparte
Mr Le Minister de L'Instruction Publique
Mr Le Minister de la Marine
Antione Cesar Becquerel

382

Alphonse Marie Louis de Lamartine
Jean Baptiste Biot
Michel Chasles
Baron Charles Dupin
Jean Victor Poncelet
General Guillaume Piobert
Arthur Jules Morin
Claude Louis Mathieu
Urbain Jean Joseph Le Verrier
Paul August Ernest Langier
Claude Servais Mathias Pouillet
Joseph Liouville
Augustin Louis Cauchy
Jacques Babinet
Cesar Mansuete Despretz
Jean Baptiste Dumas
Henri Victor Regnault
Henri Hurean de Senarmont
Henri Milne Edwards
Isidor Geoffry Saint Hilaire
Jean Baptiste Elie de Beaumont
Marechal Jean Baptiste Philibert Vaillant
Hippolyte Philibert Passy
Michel Chevalier
Alexis Charles Tocqueville
Victor Consin
René Vilermeo
Fransvit Pierre Guillaume Guizot
Adolphe Thiers
Francois Mignet
Comte d'Argont
Louis Poinsot
Institut de France
Gustave de Beaumont
Pr. Geffroy
Pr. Louis Figuier (La Presse)
Foucault (Physicien l'Observatoire)
Yvon Villarceau (Astronome l'Observ.)
C. Danssy
Colonel Favit
Löjtnant Jonbert
L. de Fontaine Moreau
Edmond Texier (Siecle)
Mr. F. Didot
Mr. Bailleul

Sweden

Oscar I
Prince Charles
Prince Oscar
Prince Nicolaus
Baron Wrede
Georg Scheutz
B. Lilliehöök
N. H. Selander
C. A. Agardh
P. F. Wahlberg
Brinck
C. J. D. Hill
Ph. Meyer
Michaelson
C. Grafström
F. v. Rothstein
Vetenskapsakademien
Kongl. Bibliotheket
Upsala Universitet
Lunds Universitet
T. F. Berg
C. F. Bergstedt
J. W. Bergström
Crasselt
Eklund
Falkenholm
N. Grafström
L. J. Hierta
G. Lallerstedt
S. Lovén
P. Lundgren
B. O. Nycander
Amiral K. A. Virgin
Pehr Sparre
Ambjörn Sparre
P. A. Siljeström
P. E. Svedbom
J. G. Wahlström
F. Johns
Jean Bolinder
Molerins
D. G. Lindhagen
Linköpings Gym: Bibliothek
Göteborgs Navigations Skola

Consul Fahlman
Grefve Barck
Baron C. R. L. Manderström
G. Granström
A. Fr. Sandberg
J. Edv. Francke
Baron A. Hermelin

In Foreign Countries

Alexander Humboldt
Pierre Gustave Lejeune Dirichlet
E. Mitscherlich
J. Plana (Turin)
Jacob Steiner. Berlin
J. F. Enke (Berlin)
P. A. Hansen (Gotha)
F. W. A. Argelander (Bonn)
Ch. Hansteen Christiania
J. Liebig
General L. F. Menabrea
Amiral von Glasenapp
General Guillaume Henri Dufour
Comte Rodolphe de Appanye
Silvain van de Weyer
General W. F. af Oxholm
Comte Fialin de Persigny
Adoplhe Comte de Kielmansegge
Baron de Bentinck
Comte de Bernsdorff
Michet Comte Chreptowitsch
Marquis Emanuel Tapparelli dAzeglio
Baron Charles de Hochschild
Mussurns Bey
Monsieur Triecoupis
Alfred Comte de Reventlorr Criminet
Marquis Benso di Cavour
Consul General Charles Tottie
Consul General John Rapp
Comte Corte
Emperor Alexander II & Grand Duke Constantin
King Gredrik Wilhelm IV
Prince Fredrik Wilhelm
Emperor Francis Joseph & Archd. Maximilian
King George the Fifth
King Leopold

King Fredrik VII
King Victor Emanuel
King William the third

— — —

The Asiatic Society at Calcutta
The Calcutta Public Library
The Library Society of Bombay
The Royal Institution
The London Institution
The Royal Observatory at Breslau
The Observatory at Bologna
The Observatory at Brussels
The Observatory at Dorpat
The Observatory at Helsingfors
The Observatory at Kazan
The Observatory at Königsberg
The Observatory at Milan
The Observatory at Moscow
The Observatory at Napels
The Observatory at Nicolajew
The Observatory at Palermo
The Observatory at Poulkowa
The Observatory at Trevandrum
The Observatory at Vienna
The Observatory at Washington
The Imperial Academy of Sciences at St:Petersburg
The Imperial Academy of Sciences at Vienna
The Royal Academy of Sciences at Lisbon
The Collegio Romano Rome
The Royal Academy of Sciences at Berlin
The Royal Academy of Sciences at Munich
The Royal Society at Göttingen
The Royal Society at Naples
The University of Leyden
The Library at Berne
The Society at Geneva
The Society at Zurich

— — —

M. Tournie
M. Albert Bizonard
M. Blanchard

M.r. le comte Nils Barck

M. Lindeman

M. Pipeo

Madmoiselle Guemain

M. Monniot (brocheur)

M. Chichereau (cartonneur)

M. Moigno

M. Jarry La revue des deux mondes.

M. Edmond Texier

M. Bailleul

M. Didot

M. Mallet Bachelier

M. Terquem

M. Kovalek

M. Villermé

Institut imperial de France

M. Jean Baptiste Biot

M. Louis Poinsot

M. Gabriel Lamé

M. Michel Chasles

M. Joseph Louis Fr. Bertrand

M. Charles Hermite

Baron Charles Dupin

Jean Victor Poncelet

Guillaume Piobert

Arthur Jules Morin

Charles Pierre M. Combes

M. Clapeyron

Claude Joseph Mathieu

M.r Joseph Liouville

M. P. A. Ernest Langier

M. Urbain Jean Joseph Le Verrier

M. Herve Auguste Faye

M. Charles Eugene Delennay

M. Pierre Danssy

M. Antoine Cesar Becquerel

M. Claude Servais Mathias Pouillet

Jacques Babinet

Jean Marie Constant Duhamel

Jean Baptiste Elie de Beaumont

Irenee Jules Bienaymé

Jean Baptiste Philibert Vaillant

Cesar Mansuete Despretz

Leon Focault

Vice President de l'Institut Francaise

Villemain

Robert Fleury

H. Passy

Joseph Naudet

Lacroix Baudry

M. Barbier; M. Louis Figuier

Thomas de Colmar

M.r Bergeson

M.r Framblay

M.r Paulin

M.r Arsene Sue

M.r Duclos

Madame Jenny Lind Goldschmidt

Colonel Favé

Dr. C. Peters Astr. Prof. Altona

M. Dieterici Royal Statist. Bureau Berlin

M. Alexander Humboldt Berlin

M. Adam v. Burgh Vienna

M.r le baron de Czoernig Vienna

Baron Baumgartner

Doctor Haller Vienna

Professor Seligman Vienna

Docteur Maurice Haller Vienna

Dr. Stubenrauch Vienna

Dr. Riedet Vienna

M. Adolphe Luetelet Bruxelles

M. Xavier Heuschling Bruxelles

M.r Cabansky St:Petersburgh

M.r J. Steiner à Berlin

Professor Encke

Academie de Sciences à Berlin

Vetenskapsakademien i Bruxelles

– – –

Appendix 3

Berzelius' statement

Undertecknade, som på begäran tagit kännedom om en räkne- och tryckningsmachin, uttänkt af Auditören Herr Georg Scheutz och förfärdigad, samt till åtskilliga väsendtliga delar äfven uppfunnen, af hans son Edward Scheutz, Elev vid Kongl. Technologiska Institutet därstädes, få däröfver lemna följande yttrande.

Machinens allmänna ändamål är lösningen af samma problem, som åsyftas med den Engelska af Babbage konstruerade räknemachinen, nämligen att tabellariskt framställa och i stereotypmatriser aftrycka de successiva termerna i en arithmetiska serier. Den kan således begagnas för beräknandet af sådana tabeller, der differensen af någon viss ordning blir konstant. Den här ifrågavarande apparaten består af 3ne delar:

1.) Egentliga räknemachin. Denna kan visserligen ej behandla arithmetiska serier af lägre grad än den tredje, och ger ej fullständigt termer, hvilka skrifvas med flere än 5 siffror, men i machinens natur ligger icke något hinder, att utsträcka dess verksamhet till serier af hvilken grad som helst och med termer af så många siffror, som ändamålet fordrar. Härtill blir endast nödvändigt att anbringa flera machin-delar, lika med de redan befintliga, d. v. s. machinen blir till sin höjd och längd förökad; i sitt närvarande skick kan hon dock, under vissa förhållanden, gifva termer af till och med 10 siffror. De fem sista ge hon alltid riktiga, och, om termerna ej vore mycket hastigt kommer den 6te framställda siffrorna till venster om densamma, att följa först ökas med 1, eller möjligen att uti flera på hvarandra följande termer blifva konstant. På denna grund var med machinen förenad en annan inrättning, hvarigenom de felande siffrorna i termer större än 99999 voro ämnade att angifvas. I vår närvaro blefvo de särskilta termerna af machinen riktigt framställda för 5 olika, af oss uppgifna, serier af tredje graden. Härvid får anmärkas, att i den ena serien, om vars aftagande, gaf machinen icke de negativa termerna utan deras fyllnader i 100,000. Men om machinen ställes vid den term, der serien öfvergår från positiv till negativ, och man då inställer fyllnaderna här till vid det tillfället i machinen befintliga differenserna i stället för sjelfva differenserna, så framkomma de negativa termerna och

... utan deras fullmakter. — För machinens inställning fordras endast att känna så många termer, att den hvarandra differensen blir gifven.

2°) Tryckningsmachinen. Hvarje af räknemachinen gifven term framställes genom tryckta siffror, ordnade radvis tätt intill hvarandra som i en tryckt tabell, och raderna intryckas omedelbart uti någon lösare materia, tjenlig att deraf sedan taga galvanoplastiska eller stereotyp aftryck. Intryckningen sker med vanliga boktryckeri stilar, hvilka dock, i en större machin eller om fråga blefve att i koppar intrycka siffrorna, måste förfärdigas af stål eller annan härd metall, och raderna stå alla i samma vertikal kolumn och med mycken noggrannhet under hvarandra. Här har gjorda försök inpressade siffrorna i en tunn blyskifva.

3°) Numeratorn. Med tryckningsmachinen är förenad en annan apparat, som framom hvarje term trycker dess ordnings nummer.

Machinen hålles i rörelse genom vridningen af en vef, medelst hvilken man, utan vidare åtgärd, åstadkommer så väl sjelfva räkningen som siffrornas och radernas anordning och tryckning, och rymmes, oförändrad, i ett foder om 2 fots 8 tums längd, 2 fots bredd och en fot och 8 tums höjd. Ställd på ett bord, lagom stort till dess uppbärande; kan den tillika med bordet lyftas och flyttas af två personer.

Slutligen får anmärkas, att machinen, såsom endast modell, är förfärdigad utan tillgång till sådana mekaniska verktyg, som för en noggrannare metallarbetning äro nödvändiga, och kan således icke ega den fulländning, som en i större skala, för verkligt användande och under mera gynnande förhållanden utförd, kunde och måste besitta. Men i det ofullkomliga skick den redan är, har den dock förmåga att framställa resultater af ... ja klasser mathematiska formler, då, te variabla deri erhålla jemnt vexande bestämda värden.

Stockholm den 18 September 1843.

Jac. Berzelius
K. Vet. Acad. Secret.

N.H. Selander
Kongl. Vetenskaps-Academiens
Astronom, Professor

Lilliehöök
Kapt. Löjt., Lärare i Fysik
vid Marieberg. —

Bibliography

The guiding principle of my research has been always to examine the original source material (whether machine or document) and I am grateful that this has been possible. With the exception of a few letters, I have examined all the relevant sources used by those scholars who have, to a greater or less degree, dealt with the engines. In addition I have examined a great deal of source material which has hitherto remained unused.

In the course of the last twenty or so years, Charles Babbage, now often called "the grandfather of the digital computer" because of his later invention of the Analytical Engine, has attracted the attention of several scholars. The first biography, Maboth Mosely's *Irascible Genius: A Life of Charles Babbage, Inventor* (London 1964), has now been superseded by Anthony Hyman's work *Charles Babbage: Pioneer of the Computer* (Princeton, N. J. 1982). However neither of these books deals with the difference engine in a fully satisfactory way. Moreover, it seems to me that Hyman has presented Babbage's achievements with respect to the difference engine in too flattering a light. The best study of Babbage, as the inventor, is without a doubt Bruce Collier's unpublished dissertation, *The Little Engines that Could've: The Calculating Machines of Charles Babbage* (Harvard 1970). Babbage's role as a scientist is examined in detail in Walter Lyle Bell, *Charles Babbage, Philosopher, Reformer, Inventor: A History of His Contributions to Science,* which is another unpublished dissertation (Oregon State University 1975). Bell, like Collier, studied Babbage's difference engine project, albeit not in so thorough a fashion. Lastly there is the book by John Michael Dubbey, *The mathematical work of Charles Babbage* (Cambridge 1979) which however does not contain anything substantially new about the difference engine.

Going back to the 19th century, Charles Babbage's autobiography, *Passages from the Life of a Philosopher* (London 1864) provides a readable, if disorganized and partly unreliable, collection of recollections. Most of the printed material about Babbage's engines is to be found in his son, Henry Prevost Babbage's compedium, entitled *Babbage's Calculating Engines* (London 1889). Selections from these two books were printed with an introduction by Philip and Emily Morrison in their volume *Charles Babbage and his Calculating Engines* (New York 1961).

Interest in the Scheutz engines was reawakened by Raymond Claire Archibald's article "P.G.Scheutz, Publicist, Author, Scientific Mechanician, and Edvard Scheutz, Engineer, − Biography and Bibliography" published in *Mathematical Tables and other Aids to Computation* (April 1947). The article's indirect encouragement to further study prompted Uta C. Merzbach's exhaustive and pioneering monograph *Georg Scheutz and the First Printing Calculator* (Washington D.C. 1977), which is the only study hitherto, devoted to the Scheutz difference engines. Among the older printed sources, there is Carl Fredrik Bergstedt's biographical study in Swedish − "Georg Scheutz: Auditör, skriftställare och mekanisk uppfinnare" printed in *Lefnadsteckningar öfver Kongl. Svenska Vetenskapsakademiens efter år 1854 aflidna ledamöter* 2 (Stockholm 1878). It contains unfortunately a number of minor errors. The same is true of [Charles Babbage, Georg and Edvard Scheutz, William Gravatt], *Specimens of Tables, Calculated, Stereomoulded and Printed by Machinery* (London 1857), which presents a history of the Scheutz engines and describes their engineering and mathematical principles.

The following hitherto unused sources have been examined (abbreviations according to the list on page 8): Babbage's and Herschel's correpondence in RS (this has been studied by Hyman who was less concerned with the machines); the Scheutz correspondence in NM (100 pieces) and KB (40 pieces) including letters from Babbage and other documents; diverse documents and letters relating to Scheutz in RA, KVA, KTHB and SSA, TM, SFM; drawings, notations, "scribbling books" and Babbage's difference engine in SML and SM; the first Scheutz engine in NM, the second Scheutz engine in the Smithsonian Institution, Washington, D.C.; the third Scheutz engine in SM; together with various other printed sources which have hitherto not been noted.

English quotations have been reproduced verbatim. Where the quotations are translations of a language other than English, this has been done in a way which tries to capture the nuances of the original. In such cases as Edvard Scheutz' letters in English to Babbage, where the language is not always formally correct, the text of the original has nevertheless been retained.

The rates of exchanges used in this book have been taken from: *Sveriges Riksbank 1668−1924* 5 (Stockholm 1931).

Sources:

A. Unprinted material

1 Ph.D. dissertations

Bell, Walter Lyle, *Charles Babbage, Philosopher, Reformer, Inventor: A History of his Contributions to Science* (Oregon State University 1975)

Collier, Bruce, *The Little Engines that Could've: The Calculating Machines of Charles Babbage* (Harvard 1970).

James, Mary Ann, *The Dudley Observatory Controversy* (Rice University, Texas 1980).

2 Manuscripts

British Library, London, (BL:
Babbage's letters. (Add. Ms 37182—37201)
Babbage's manuscripts etc. (Add. Ms. 37202—37205)
Peel papers (Add. Ms. 40449)

Boston Public Library, Boston, (BPL):
MsE. 210

Royal Library, Stockholm, (KB):
Scheutz' letters (I. s. 10)
Papers regarding the engine (X279)
Autografsamlingen
Brevskrivararkivet (Ep, L)

Royal Institute of Technology, Stockholm, (KTHB):
Edvard Scheutz' travel report (MS3)

Stockholm University with the Library of the Royal Academy of Sciences (KVA):
KVA Protokoll
Bilagor KVA Protokoll
Letters

Nordic Museum, Stockholm, (NM):
Scheutz' letters and other documents

Public Record Office, Kew, (PRO):
Treasury (T.1, T.2)
Home Office

National Archives, Stockholm, (RA):
Kommerskollegie Huvudarkiv (DII, EXVII, Kammarkontorets årsberättelser)
Ericsbergsarkivets autografsamling
KTH arkiv (FIIbaa, CIIa, BI, Dla)
Utrikes Departementet
Skrivelser till Kongl. Maj:t
Ecklesiastik Departementet

Royal Society Library, London, (RS):
Herschel's letters (HS1, HS2)

Society of Business Archives in Stockholm, Stockholm, (SF):
Bolinders huvudbok

Science Museum Library, London, (SML):
Babbage's Scribbling Books etc.
Drawings
Notations of Babbage's and Scheutz' engines

Science Reference Library, London:
Patents (Babbage, Scheutz, Sparre and Deacon)

Stockholm City Archives. Stockholm, (SSA):
Allmänna BB:s födelsebok
BOU
Klara likbok
Storkyrkoförsamlingens lysnings- och vigselbok
Storkyrkoförsamlingens dopbok

National Museum of Science and Technology, Stockholm, (TM)
Teknologiska Institutet (966r)

Buxton, Harry Wilmot "The Life and Labours of the late Charles Babbage, Esq., F.R.S.". Microfiche copy of the original undated manuscript Buxton vol. 16−17, kept in the Oxford Museum of the History of Science.
Förteckningar och register över privilegia exclusiva och patent samt tillståndsbevis 1740−1865, Kommerskollegie Huvudarkiv, DII d:1: (RA).
Scheutz, Edvard, "Machin för beräkning och tryckning af matematiska tabeller. Af Edvard Scheutz", X279, (KB).
Scheutz, Georg, "Praktisk Differensräkning för Geometriska Serier", Bilagor KVA Protokoll 1842, (KVA).
[Scheutz, Georg], "Historical Sketch", X279, (KB).
[Scheutz, Georg], "Historique de la machine à calculer & imprimer les tables de mathematique, inventée par Mrs. George et Eduard Scheutz, père et fils", X279 (KB).
James, Mary Ann, *Commitment to Basic Research in Astronomy in Nineteenth Century Albany: A Paper submitted to the Second History Conference of Hudson Valley Colleges & Universities,* Bard College, 22nd October 1983.

B. Printed material

1 Newspapers, journals, proceedings
a. 19th century
Aftonbladet (1830−1860)
Anmärkaren
Anmärkarne
The Athenaeum
Argus
Argus den tredje
Comptes Rendus des Séances de l'Academie des Sciences (1800−1860)
Cosmos
Dinglers Polytechnisches Journal
The Edinburgh Philosophical Journal
The Edinburgh Review
The Illustrated London News
Illustrerad Tidning
L'Illustration. Journal Universel
Journal för Manufakturer och Hushållning (1825−1826, 1833−1834)
Journal of the Franklin Institute
Kungliga Vetenskapsakademiens Handlingar
Mechanics Magazine
Nature
Ny Illustrerad Tidning
Philosophical Transactions of the Royal Society

Proceedings of the Royal Society of London
La Propieté Industrielle: Journal Judicaire de L'Industrie
Le Siècle
Spegeln (1837–1838)
Svenska Industriföreningens Tidskrift (1834–1839)
Svensken: Illustrerad Veckotidning
Tidning för Näringarne (1840–1841)
Tidskrift för Byggnadskonst och Ingenjörsvetenskap
Transactions of the Society for the Encouragement of Arts, Manufacture, and Commerce
Victoria: Illustrerad Veckotidning

b. 20th century
Annals of the History of Computing
The Computer Journal
Grafiskt form
Historia Mathematica
Mathematical Tables and other Aids to Computation (1943–1959)
Nature
Photorin: Mitteilungen der Lichtenberg – Gesellschaft
Polhem: Tidskrift för teknikhistoria
Stockholmstidningen

2 Public documents

Hedervärda Borgar-Ståndets Protokoller vid Lagtima Riksdagen i Stockholm Åren 1850 och 1851 6 (Stockholm 1851), pp 155–157.

"Stats-Utskottets utlåtande, N:o 294", Stockholm, 31st July 1851, Bihang till Samtliga Riks-Ståndens Protokoll vid Lagtima Riksdagen i Stockholm Åren 1850 och 1851, fjerde samlingen, andra bandet, första afdelningen (Stockholm 1851), pp 14–17.

Protokoll hållna hos höglofliga Riddareskapet och Adeln vid lagtima riksdagen i Stockholm, åren 1850 och 1851 9 (Stockholm 1851) pp 247–248.

Högvördiga Preste-Ståndets protokoll vid Lagtima riksdagen i Stockholm år 1851 10 (Stockholm 1852), p 411.

Protocoll hållna hos vällofliga Borgare-Ståndet vid lagtima riksdagen i Stockholm åren 1850 och 1851 4 (Stockholm 1851), p 834.

Hedervärda Bonde-Ståndets Protokoll vid Lagtima Riksdagen i Stockholm åren 1850 och 1851 6 (Stockholm 1851), pp 185–186, 269–270.

"Stats-Utskottets memorial, N:o 328", Stockholm, 18th August 1854, Bihang till Samtliga Riks-Ståndens Protokoll 1850/51 fjerde samlingen, andra bandet, första afdelningen (Stockholm 1851).

"Expeditions-Utskottets Förslag till und. Skrifvelse N:o 189, Stockholm den 20 augusti 1851", Bihang till Samtlige Riks-Ståndens Protokoll vid Lagtima Riks-dagen i Stockholm Åren 1850 och 1851, tionde samlingen, första bandet, första avdelningen (Stockholm 1851), pp 514–515.

Swensk Författnings-Samling 1851 No 50, Kongl. Maj:ts och Riksens Ständers fastställda Riksdags-Ordning, Dat. Stockholm den 10 Februari 1810; Med de derefter, och sist wid Riksdagen i Stockholm åren 1850 och 1851, af Konungen och Riksens Ständer antagna förändringar. (Stockholm 1851), p 33.

"Kongl. Maj:ts Nådiga Proposition, N:o 51, Stockholm den 13 januari 1854", Bihang till samtlige Riks-Ståndens protokoll vid Lagtima riksdagen i Stockholm åren 1853–1854, första samlingen, andra afdelningen, första bandet (Stockholm 1854).

"Stats-Utskottets Utlåtande, N:o 136, Stockholm den 29 maj 1854", *Bihang till samtliga Riks-Ståndens protokoll vid Lagtima riksdagen i Stockholm åren 1853–1854,* fjärde samlingen, första afdelningen, andra bandet (Stockholm 1854).

Protocoll hållna hos högloflige Ridderskapet och Adeln vid Lagtima Riksdagen i Stockholm Åren 1853–1854 8 (Stockholm 1854), p 155.

Högvördiga Preste-Ståndets Protokoll vid Lagtima Riksdagen i Stockholm År 1854 5 (Stockholm 1854), pp 222–223.

Protocoll hållna hos vällofliga Borgare-Ståndet vid Lagtima Riksdagen i Stockholm åren 1853 och 1854 4 (Stockholm 1854), p 80.

Hedervärda Bonde-Ståndets Protokoller vid Lagtima Riksdagen i Stockholm Åren 1853 och 1854 5 (Stockholm 1854), p 303.

"Expeditions-Utskottets förslag till underd. Skrifvelse. N:o 64, Stockholm den 1 juli 1854", *Bihang till samtlige Riks-Ståndens protokoll vid Lagtima Riksdagen i Stockholm åren 1853–1854,* tionde samlingen, första afdelningen, första bandet (Stockholm 1854), pp 97–98.

"Riksdagsbeslut, §20, Nr 34, Stockholm den 1 juli 1854", *Bihang till samtliga Riks-Ståndens protokoll vid Lagtima Riksdagen i Stockholm åren 1853–54,* tionde samlingen, första afdelningen, andra bandet (Stockholm 1854), p 33.

Protocoll, hållna hos höglofliga Ridderskapet och Adeln, vid Lagtima Riksdagen i Stockholm år 1859–1860 1 (Stockholm 1859), pp 570–572.

– Vol. 9 (Stockholm 1861), p 343.

– Vol. 10 (Stockholm 1861), pp 58-59

Högvördiga Preste-Ståndets Protocoll vid Lagtima Riksdagen i Stockholm åren 1859 & 1860 7 (Stockholm 1861), p 540.

– Vol. 8 (Stockholm 1861), p 104.

Protocoll, hållna hos vällofliga Borgare-Ståndet, vid Lagtima Riksdagen i Stockholm åren 1859 och 1860 5 (Stockholm 1861), pp 370–371, 967.

– Vol. 6 (Stockholm 1861), p 152.

Hedervärda Bonde-Ståndets Protokoller vid Lagtima Riksdagen i Stockholm åren 1859–60 7 (Stockholm 1860), pp 566–567.

– Vol. 8 (Stockholm 1860), p 51.

"Kongl. Maj:ts Nåd. Proposition N:o 108", Stockholm, 30th March 1860, *Bihang till samtlige Riks-Ståndens Protokoll vid Lagtima Riksdagen i Stockholm Åren 1859 och 1860,* första samlingen, första afdelningen, första bandet (Stockholm 1860), pp 20–21.

Stats-Utskottets Utlåtande N:o 152", *Bihang till samtlige Riks-Ståndens Protokoll vid Lagtima Riksdagen i Stockholm åren 1859 och 1860,* fjerde samlingen, första avdelningen, första bandet (Stockholm 1860), pp 64–65.

– N:o 169, tredje bandet (Stockholm 1860), pp 3–5.

"Expeditions-Utskottets förslag till underd. Skrifvelse N:o 129", Stockholm, 18th September, *Bihang till Samtlige Riks-Ståndens Protokoll vid Lagtima Riksdagen i Stockholm Åren 1859 och 1860,* tionde samlingen, första afdelningen, första bandet (Stockholm 1860), pp 396–397.

– N:o 205, andra bandet (Stockholm 1860), pp 312–313, (325).

Johansson, J. (ed.), *Sakregister till Rikets Ständers Protokoll med bihang: för tiden från och med år 1809 till och med år 1866,* 1–2 (Stockholm 1892–1893).

Seth, Martin (ed.), *Personregister till Rikets Ständers Protokoll: för tiden från och med år 1809 till och med år 1866* (Stockholm 1935).

3 Books, articles, etc

A Brief Account of Bryan Donkin F. R. S. and of the Company he founded 150 Years ago (Chesterfield 1953).

"Académie des Sciences: Séance du 20 avril 1856", *Cosmos* 8, 1856.

Airy, Wilfred (ed.), *Autobiography of Sir George Biddell Airy*, (Cambridge 1896).

Allwood, John, *The Great Exhibitions* (London 1977).

Althin, Torsten, *KTH 1912–63. Kungliga Tekniska Högskolan i Stockholm under 50 år* (Stockholm 1970).

–, *1861: Teknikhistorisk rapsodi till Svenska Teknologföreningens hundraårs-jubileum* (Stockholm 1861).

Andersson, Tore, "Wibergs räknemaskin", *Daedalus* (1933).

–, "Första svenska räknemaskinen", *Daedalus* (1932).

Annals of the Dudley Observatory 1 (Albany 1866).

Archibald, Raymond Claire, *Benjamin Pierce 1809–1880* (Oberlin, Ohio 1925).

–, *Mathematical Table Makers,* Scripta Mathematica Studies 3 (New York 1948).

–, "P. G. Scheutz, Publicist, Author, Scientific Mechanician, and Edvard Scheutz, Engineer, – Biography and Bibliography", Raymond Claire Archibald and Derrek Henry Lechmer et. al., *Mathematical Tables and other Aids to Computation* 2, No. 18, April 1947.

Arrhenius, Svante, "Fabian Jacob Wrede", *Lefnadsteckningar över Kungl. Svenska Vetenskapsakademiens ledamöter* 5 (Uppsala 1920).

L'Art de l'Horlogerie, enseigné en trente lecons ou manuel complet de l'horloger et de l'amateur, d'aprés Berthoud et les travaux de Wuillamy, premier horloger du Roi d'Angleterre, Georges IV, (Paris 1827).

Article on the Scheutz engine, *Aftonbladet* 14, 1859.

[Babbage, Benjamin Herschel], *Babbage's Calculating Machine, or Difference Engine, A description of a portion of this machine put together in 1833 and now exhibited, by permission of the board of works, in the educational division of the South Kensington Museum, Science and Art Departement,* (London 1872).

Babbage, Charles, *A Comparative View of the Various Institutions for the Assurance of Lives* (London 1826).

Babbage, Charles, *A Word to the Wise; Observations on Peerage for Life* (London 1856).

Babbage, Charles, *The Exposition of 1851; or, Views of the Industry, the Science, and the Government of England* (London 1851).

Babbage, Charles, *Logarithmai 1 töl 108 000 ig* (London 1834). Translated by Karl Nagy.

Babbage, Charles, *Logarithmen der natürlichen Zahlen 1 bis 108 000* (London 1834). Translated by Karl Nagy.

Babbage, Charles, "Note sur la machine suédoise de MM. Schutz [misspelling by Babbage] pour calculer les Tables mathématiues par la méthode des différences", *Comptes Rendus Hebdomaires des Séances de l'Academie des Sciences* 41 (Paris 1855).

Babbage, Charles, *Observations Addressed, at the Last Anniversary, to the President and Fellows of the Royal Society, After the Delivery of the Medals* (London 1856).

Babbage, Charles, *On the Economy of Machinery and Manufactures* (London 1832), (London 1833), (London 1835).

Babbage, Charles, Paper on the Principles of Tools, for Turning and Planing Metals; extracted from Charles Holtzapfel, *Turning and Mechanical Manipulation*, vol. 2 (London 1846).

Babbage, Charles, *Passages from the Life of a Philosopher* (London 1864).

Babbage, Charles, *Reflections on the Decline of Science in England: and on Some of its Causes* (London 1830).

Babbage, Charles, *Table of Logarithms of the Natural Numbers, from 1 to 108 000* (London 1827), (London 1831).

Babbage, Charles, *The Ninth Bridgewater Treatise: A Fragment* (London 1837).

Babbage, Charles, *Traité sur l'economie des machines et des manufactures* (Paris 1833). Translated by Ed. Biot.

Babbage, Charles and Scheutz, Georg and Edvard, Gravatt, William, *Spécimen de tables calculées stéréotypées et imprimées au moyen d'une machine* (Paris 1858). Translation by Edvard Scheutz.

Babbage, Charles, Scheutz, Georg and Edvard, Gravatt, William, *Specimens of Tables, Calculated, Stereomoulded and Printed by Machinery* (London 1857).

Babbage, Henry Prevost (ed.), *Babbage's Calculating Engines, being a Collection of Papers Relating to them; their History, and Construction* (London 1889).

Babbage, Richard H., "The Work of Charles Babbage", *Proceedings of a Symposium on Large-Scale Digital Machinery*. The Annals of the Computation Laboratory of Harvard University 16 (Cambridge, MA 1948).

Bagge, Jonas Samuel, *Elementarkurs i Fysiken* (Stockholm 1835).

Baxandall, D., *Catalogue of the Collections in the Science Museum, South Kensington. With Descriptive and Historical Notes and Illustrations. Mathematics, 1. Calculating Machines and Instruments* (London 1926).

de Beauclair W., and Hauck, H. *Rechnen mit Maschinen* (Braunschweig 1968).

Bengtsson, Bengt, Malmborg, Emil and Nerman, Ture, *Typografiska Föreningen i Stockholm ett hundra år: Minnesskrift 1846–1946* 1 (Stockholm 1946).

Bergstedt, Carl Fredrik, "Georg Scheutz: Auditör, skriftställare och mekanisk uppfinnare", *Lefnadsteckningar öfver Kongl. Svenska Vetenskapsakademiens efter år 1854 aflidna ledamöter* 2 (Stockholm 1878).

Biografiskt Lexicon öfver namnkunnige Svenska män 1–23 (Uppsala and Örebro 1835–1857.

Bishop, Morris, *Pascal: The Life of a Genius* (New York 1936).

Björck, Henrik, "På de tillfälliga uppfinningarnas oroliga haf", *Polhem: Tidskrift för teknikhistoria*, No. 2, 1986.

Björklund, Hans, "Partigrupperingar i borgarståndet vid 1853/54 års riksdag", *Partiliv i ståndsriksdagen: Adel och borgare 1850–1865*, Acta Universitatis Stockholmienses 23, (Stockholm 1977).

[Blanche, August], "Georg Scheutz", *Illustrerad Tidning*, 29th January 1859.

Bohman, Nils (ed.), *Svenska Män och Kvinnor: Biografisk uppslagsbok* 1–8 (Stockholm 1942–1955).

Bolton, Henry Carrington, *A Catalogue of Scientific and Technical Periodicals: 1665–1895: Together with chronological Tables and a Library Check-List* (Washington, D.C., 1897–98).

Bool, Vladimir Georgievich von, *Apparatus and machines for mechanical execution of arithmetical operations: A description of design and an evaluation of calculating apparatus and machines* (Moscow 1896). Book in Russian. (I have examined this source which is listed in Archibald (1947) and in Merzbach's bibliography, but it does not contain any further information of interest.

Borgström, Ludvig, "Borgström, Ludvig: Sjelfbiographie", *Biografiskt Lexicon öfver namnkunnige Svenska män* 2 (Uppsala 1836).

Boss, Lewis, *Dudley Observatory. Annual Report of the Astronomer for 1877* (Albany 1878).

Brenner, Otto and Thimon, Gösta, *Uppsala Universitets matrikel 1695–1817: Register,* Acta universitatis Upsalienses 20 (Uppsala 1971).

Bring, Samuel E. and Kulling, Ernst Rikard, *Svenska Boktryckareföreningen 50 år: Kort historik över Boktryckeri-Societeten och Svenska Boktryckareföreningen utgiven med anledning av föreningens femtioårsjubileum: 1893–1943* (Göteborg 1943).

Bromley, Allan G., *Babbage General: The evolution of Charles Babbage's calculating engines*, Technical Report 272, November 1985, Basser Department of Computer Science; the University of Sydney (Sydney 1985).

Bromley, Allan G., "Charles Babbage's Analytical Engine, 1838", *Annals of the History of Computing,* vol. 4, No. 3, July 1982.

Buttman, Günther, *The Shadow of the Telescope: A Biography of John Herschel* (New York 1970).

Buxton, Dudley L. H., "Charles Babbage and his Difference Engines", *Transactions of the Newcomen Society* 14, 1835.

Byron, Noel, *Don Juan,* Canto X (1818–1824).

Castegren, Erik, *Riksbankens pappersbruk Tumba; Minnesskrift till dess tvåhundraårsjubileum 1955* (Stockholm 1955).

Catalogue of the Special Loan Collection of the Scientific Apparatus at the South Kensington Museum (London 1876).

"Charles Babbage: Died the 20th of October", *Nature,* No. 106, 9th November 1871.

"Cederborg, Fredrik", *Biografiskt lexicon öfver namnkunnige Svenska män* 3 (Uppsala 1837).

Claesson Rålamb, Åke, *En liten och kort Hand-Bok utaf Adelig öfning, att bruka wid många tillfällen. Till stor hjelpreda i Daglig Handel* (Örebro 1824, 1827).

Clerke, Agnes M., *The Herschels and Moderna Astronomy* (New York 1895).

Colliander, Elof (ed.), *Kungl. Svenska Vetenskapsakademiens skrifter 1826–1917: Register* (Uppsala 1917).

Commisioners of Longitude, *Table Requisite to be used with the Astronomical and Nautical Ephemeris* (London 1766).

The Compact Edition of the Oxford English Dictionary (Complete Text Reproduced Micrographically) 1, (New York 1975).

Comptes Rendus Hebdomaires de Séances de l'Academie des Sciences 7 (Paris 1838), pp 1031, 1056.

–, 42 vol. 1, (Paris 1856), pp 798–800.

–, 47, p 64.

Cotter, Charles H., *A History of Nautical Astronomy* (London 1968).

Dahlgren, E. W. (ed.), *Kungl. Svenska Vetenskapsakademien personförteckningar 1739–1915* (Uppsala 1915).

Daumas, Maurice, "Precision Mechanics", Charles Singer, E. J. Holmyard, A. R. Hall and Trevor I. Williams, *A History of Technology, Vol. IV, the Industrial Revolution c. 1750 to c. 1850,* (London 1958).

de Morgan, Augustus, "Mr. Babbage's Calculating Machine", *The Athenaeum,* 14th October 1848.

de Morgan, Augustus, "Table", Charles Knight (ed.), *The English Cyclopaedia: a Dictionary of Universal Knowledge* 7 (Arts and Sciences), (London 1861).

"Den Scheutziska Räknemaskinen", *Illustrerad Tidning,* No, 28, 21 st July 1855. (It is very possible that this article was written by Georg of Edvard, because it is written in a style quite similar to that of an article written in 1859. This latter article was written by them and it also had the same title "'Den Scheutziska räknemaskinen", *Aftonbladet* 17, 1859.

Dickinson, H. W., *Sir Samuel Morland: Diplomat and Inventor, 1625–1696* (Cambridge 1970).

Diehl, Wilhelm (ed.), "Lebensbeschreibung des Obristen und Oberbaudirektors, auch Direktors des Oberbaukollegs Johann Helfrich von Müller", published in *Hessische Cronik* 1–2 (1930).

Dubbey, John Michael, *The mathematical work of Charles Babbage* (Cambridge 1979).

Edlund, Barbro (ed.), *Lunds universitets matrikel 1732–1830* (Lund 1979).

"Edvard Scheutz roterande ångmaskin", *Illustrerad Tidning*, 16th February 1861.

Elvius, Petrus, *Tabula compendiosa logarithmorum sinum ad quadrantis gradus, eorumq; partes decimas, ned non numerorum absolutorum ab unitate ad 1000* (Uppsala 1698).

Enros, Philip C., "Cambridge University and the Adoption of Analytics in Early Nineteenth-Century England", Herbert Mehrtens, Henk Bos and Ivo Schneider (eds.), *Social History of Nineteenth Century Mathematics* (Boston 1981).

"Exposition universelle de 1855: L'exposition Suédoise au Palais de l'industrie", *Extrait du bulletin de la Revue des deux mondes* (reprint), original article printed on the 15th October 1855.

Exposition universelle de 1855, Rapports du jury mixte international (Paris 1856), p 405.

Farr, William (ed.), *English Life Table: Table of Lifetimes, Annuities, and Premiums* (London 1864).

Fletcher, A., Miller, J. C. P., Rosenhead, L. and Comrie, L. J., *An Index of Mathemathical Tables* 1−2, (Edinburgh 1962).

Forbes, Eric G., *Greenwich Observatory: The Royal Observatory at Greenwich and Herstmonceux 1675−1975* 1: "Origins and Early History" (1675−1835) (London 1975).

"Fosterländskt Bildgalleri CVII. Georg Scheutz", *Svenska Familjejournalen*, September 1883.

Fredriksson, Gunnar, Strand, Dieter, Hadenius, Stig and Gustafsson, Karl Erik, *Aftonbladet − en svensk historia* (Stockholm 1980).

Gallon, M. *Machines et inventions approuvées par l'Academie Royale des Sciences* 4, (Paris 1735).

Gardiner, William, *Tables de Logarithmes* (Avignon 1742).

Gilbert, K. R., *The Machine Tool Collection. Science Museum Catalogue of Exhibits with Historical Introduction* (London 1966).

Gingerich, Owen and Welther, Barbara, *Planetary, Lunar, and Solar Positions − New and Full Moons, 1650−1805* (Philadelphia 1983), reprint from the *Memoirs series of the American Philosophical Society,* Vol. 59S.

Giron August, "Lillehöök, Carl Bertil", Torsten Dahl (ed.), *Svenska män och kvinnor* 4 (Stockholm 1948), p 591.

Glaisher, James Whitbread Lee, (ed., Secretary of the Committee), "Report of the Committee on Mathematical Tables", *Report of the Forty-Third Meeting of the British Association for the Advancement of Science, held at Bradford in September 1873* (London 1874).

Goldstine, Herman, *The Computer: From Pascal to von Neumann* (Princeton, N. J. 1980).

Gould, Benjamin Aphtorp, *Reply to the "Statement of the Trustees" of the Dudley Observatory* (Albany, N. Y. 1859).

Grape, Ernst, *Enhetsportot och frimärket* (Stockholm 1955).

Gravatt, William, *Companion to the Barometer, Mountain Barometer Tables; Calculated and Stereotyped by Messrs. Scheutz's Calculating Machine No. 2 and Printed by Machinery* (London 1859).

Gårdlund, Torsten, *Industrialismens samhälle* (Stockholm 1942).

Hansson, Nils, "Reflektioner kring en fotografisk metod från år 1832 för bestämning av en orts meridian", *Värld och Vetande: Populärvetenskaplig tidskrift* 3 1960.

Hasselberg, Gudmar, *Rudolf Wall: Dagens Nyheters skapare* (Stockholm 1945).

Heckscher, Eli F., *Svenskt arbete och liv: Från medeltiden till nutiden* (Stockholm 1980).

Henriuqes, Pontus, *Skildringar ur Kungl. Tekniska Högskolans historia* 1 (Stockholm 1917).

Henry, Joseph, "Charles Babbage", *Annual Report of the Board of Regents of the Smithsonian Institution, showing the operations, expenditures and condition of the Institution for the Year 1873* (Washington, D. C. 1874).

Henry, Joseph, Alexander Dallas Bache and Benjamin Pierce, *Defence of Mr. Gould by the Scientific Council of the Dudley Observatory* (Albany 1858).

Herschel, John Frederick William, *Collections of Examples of the applications of the Calculus of Finite Diferences* (Cambridge 1820).

Herschel, John, (Chairman of the committee) "Report of the Committee appointed by the Council of the Royal Society to consider the subject referred to in Mr. Stewart's Letter relative to Mr. Babbage's Calculating Engine, and to report thereon − Feb. 1929" *Journal of the Franklin Insitute* March 1831.

"Herschel, Sir John Frederick William", Leslie Stephen and Sidney Lee (eds.), *Dictionary of National Biography* 26 (London 1891).

Heurgren, Paul Gerhard, "Greve Pehr Ambjörn Sparre; Ritade, graverade och tryckte de första svenska frimärkena", *Frimärkets dags årsbok 1945*.

Hierta, Lars Johan, *Biographiska anteckningar* (Örebro 1863).

Hobson, E. W., *John Napier and the Invention of Logarithms, 1614* (Cambridge 1914).

Hofberg, Herman (ed.),"Scheutz, Edvard", *Svenskt biografiskt handlexikon* 1 (Stockholm 1876).

[Hough, George Washington], *Report of the Astronomer in change of the Dudley Observatory. For the Year 1863* (Albany 1864).

Hughes, Thomas Parke, *Networks of Power: Electrification in Western Society 1880−1930* (Baltimore 1983).

Hutton, Charles, *A Mathematical and Philosophical Dictionary: containing an explanation of the terms, and an account of the several subjects, comprised under the heads, Mathematics, Astronomy and Philosophy, both natural and experimental* 1−2 (London 1795−1796), (London 1815).

Hutton, Charles, *Mathematical Tables: Containing the common, hyperbolic, and logistic logarithms, also sines, tangents, secants and versed sines, both natural and logarithmic. Together with several other tables useful in mathematical calculations. Also the complete description and use of these tables.* (London 1804), (London 1822), (London 1860).

Hutton, Charles, *Tracts on Mathematical and Philosophical Subjects; comprising, among Numerous Important Articles, The Theory of Bridges, Numerous experiments on the Force of Gunpowder, with Applications to the Modern Practice of Artillery* 1 (London 1812).

Hyman, A., *Charles Babbage: Pioneer of the Computer* (Princeton, N.J. 1982).

Indebetou, Govert and Hylander, Erik *Svenska Teknologföreningen 1861−1936, biografier* 1−2 (Stockholm 1837).

Interpolation Tables, used at the Nautical Almanac Office (London 1857).

Jacob, Louis, *Le calcul mécanique* (Paris 1911).

Jennings, Louis J. (ed.), *The Croker Papers: The Correspondence and Diaries of the Late Right Honourable John Wilson Croker, LL.D., F.R.S., Secretary to the Admirality from 1809 to 1830* 1 (London 1884).

Johnson, William A. (ed.), *Cristopher Polhem: The Father of Swedish Technology* (Hartford, Connecticut 1963).

"Jones, William", Sidney Lee (ed.), *Dictionary of National Biography* 30 (London 1892).

Joost, Ulrich and Schöne, Albrecht, *Lichtenberg Briefwechsel* 1−2 (München 1983−1985).

Kihlberg, Leif, *Lars Hierta i helfigur* (Stockholm 1968).

Kjellander, Rune G:son. "J. W. Bergström, mekanikus och daguerrotypist", *Daedalus* 1953.

Klemming, Gustaf Edvard and Nordin, Johan Gabriel, *Svensk boktryckeri-historia 1483–1883: Med inledande allmän öfversigt* (Stockholm 1883).

Klemming, Sven, *Gustaf Carl Fredrik Löwenhielm: Hovman – krigare – diplomat* (Stockholm 1956).

– (ed.), *Jöns Jacob Berzelius och Gustaf Carl Fredrik Löwenhielm: En brevväxling 1818–1847* (Västerås 1968).

Klipstein, Philipp Engel, *J. H. Müllers Beschreibung seiner neu erfunderen Rechenmaschine; nach ihrer Gestalt, ihrem Gebrauch und Nutzen* (Frankfurt and Mainz 1786).

Knight, Thomas, "On the construction of logarithmic tables", *Philosophical Transactions of the Royal Society 1817* (London 1817).

–, "Two general propositions in the method of differences". *Philosophical Transactons of the Royal Society 1817* (London 1817).

Krause, Rudolf, "Geschichte und heutige Bestände des Physikalischen Kabinetts in Hessischen Landesmuseum Darmstadt", *Naturwissenschaftlicher Verein Darmstadt e.V., Bericht 1963/64* (Darmstadt 1965).

Lacroix, Silvestre Francois, *An Elementary Treatise on the Differential and Integral Calculus* (London 1816). Translation and addition by Charles Babbage, John Herschel and George Peacock.

–, *Handbok i landtmäteriet: Innehållande första grunderna för jordsträckors mätning och kartläggning, äfvensom för afvägningar och rymdmätningar. Till tjänst för Landtmän och dem som icke förut känna Geometrien,* Bibliothek för konst, slöjd och tillämpad vetenskap (Stockholm 1832). An unsigned translation probably by Magnus Luttrop, arranged with an addition by Georg Scheutz.

–, *Traité élémentaire de calcul differentiel et de calcul intégral* (Paris 1802).

Landes, David S., *The Unbound Prometheus: Technological Change and Industrial Development in Western Europe from 1750 to the Present* (Westford, MA 1979).

[Lardner, Doinysius], "Babbage's Calculating Engine", *Edinburgh Review,* July 1834.

"Lardner, Dionysius (1793–1859)", *Dictionary of National Biography* XI (Oxford 1917).

Letters Patent, Specification of Georg Scheutz and Edvard Scheutz, Calculating Machines, A. D. 1854, No. 2216 (London 1855).

Liljecrona, Carl Wilhelm, *Bakom Riksdagens kulisser: C. W. Liljecronas dagbok under Riksdagen 1840–1841: Med inledning, noter och personregister af Gustaf A. Aldén* (Stockholm 1917).

Lindgren, Torgny, *Riksbankens sedelhistoria 1668–1968* (Stockholm 1968).

Lindroth, Sten, *Kungl. Svenska Vetenskapsakademiens historia 1739–1818* 1–3 (Uppsala 1967).

Lloyd, Alan H., "Mechanical Time-keepers", Charles Singer, E. J. Holmyard, A. R. Hall and Trevor I. Williams (eds.), *A History of Technology* 3 (New York 1957).

Losano, Mario G. (ed), *Scheutz. La Macchina alle differenze. Un Secolo di calculo automatico* (Milano 1974). A translation of Merzbach's work, together with translations of some wellknown documents on the engines (*Specimens,* Bergstedt, H. P. Babbage etc.).

Lundstedt, Bernard, *Sveriges periodiska litteratur 1645–1899: Bibliografi* 1–3 (Stockholm 1895–1902).

[Luttrop, Magnus], *Handbok i Svarfkonsten, innehållande fullständiga underrättelser om denna konsts alla delar*, Bibliothek för konst, slöjd och tillämpad vetenskap (Stockholm 1839).

Manning, Thomas, "New method of computing logarithms", *Philosophical Transactions of the Royal Society* 1806 (London 1806).

May, Kenneth O., *Bibliography and Research Manual of the History of Mathematics* (Buffalo 1973).

"Mécanique appliquée à la solution de problèmes mathématiques et autres", *Le Siècle*, 11th August 1858.

Meidinger, Heinrich, "Die Scheutz'sche Rechenmachine", *Dinglers Polytechnisches Journal*, 156, No. 4, 1860.

Merzbach, Uta C., *Georg Scheutz and the First Printing Calculator*, Smithsonian Studies in History and Technology 36, (Washington, D. C. 1977).

Metropolis, N. and Worlton, J., "A Trilogy on Errors in the History of Computing", *Annals of the History of Computing*, 2, No. 1, January 1980.

[Moigno], "Academie des Sciences: Séance du Lundi 12 juillet", *Cosmos* 13, 16th July 1858.

Montgomery, Arthur, *Industrialismens genombrott i Sverige* (Stockholm 1947).

Moore, Doris Langley, *Ada: Countess of Lovelace: Byron's Legitimate Daughter* (Southampton 1977).

Moran, James, *Printing Preses: History and Development from the Fifteenth Century to Modern Times* (London 1973).

Morell, Jack and Thackray, Arnold, *Gentlemen of Science. Early Years of the British Association for the Advancement of Science* (Oxford 1981).

Morland, Samuel, *The Description and use of two Arithmetick Instruments* (London 1673).

Morrison, Philip and Emily (eds.), *Charles Babbage and his Calculating Engines* (New York 1961).

Mosely, Maboth, *Irascible Genius: A Life of Charles Babbage, Inventor* (London 1964).

"Mr Babbage's Calculating Engine", *The Edinburgh Philosophical Journal* 9 (Edinburgh 1823).

"Mr. Babbage's Calculating Machine", *The Athenaeum*, 16th December 1848.

"Mr. Babbage's Calculating Machinery", *Mechanics Magazine*, 448, 1832.

Napier, John, *Logarithmorum Canonis Desciptio, sev Arithmeticarum Suppurationum Mirabilis Abbreviatio* (London 1620).

−, *Mirifici, Logarithmorum Canonis Constructio* (London 1620).

−, (Authore ac Inventore), *Mirifici Logarithmorum Canonis Descriptio* (Edinburgh 1614).

Neugebauer, Otto, *A History of Ancient Mathematical Astronomy* 1−3 (Berlin 1975).

Neugebauer, Otto, "Ancient Mathematics and Astronomy", Charles Singer, E. J. Holmyard and A. R. Hall (ed.), *A History of Technology* 1 (London 1954).

"New Calculating Machine", *The Illustrated London News*, 30th June 1855.

Newton, Isaac, *Philosophiae Naturalis Principia Mathematica* (London 1687).

Nilsson, Göran B., *Banker i brytningstid: A O Wallenberg i svensk bankpolitik 1850−1856* (Stockholm 1981).

"Obituary Notices of Fellows deceased": Bryan Donkin, *Proceedings of the Royal Society of London* 7, (London 1856).

"Obituary Notices of Fellows deceased": William Gravatt, *Proceedings of the Royal Society of London* 16 (London 1868).

"Obituary Notices of Fellows deceased": George Peacock, *Proceedings of the Royal Society of London 1859:*.

O'Byrne, William R., *A Naval Biographical Dictionary: comprising the Life and Services of every Living Officer in Her Majesty's Navy, from the Rank of Admiral of the Fleet to that of Lieutenant* 1–2 (London 1849).

[Olcott, Thomas, Rathbone John F. et. al.], *The Dudley Observatory and the Scientific Council. Statement of the Trustees* (Albany 1858).

Olsson, Hugo, "Något om Greve P. A. Sparres tryckmaterial samt redskap och maskiner för tillverkningen av skilling banco-frimärkena", *Postryttaren* 1954.

"On Machinery for Calculating and Printing Mathematical Tables", *The Edinburgh Philosophical Journal* 7, (Edinburgh 1822).

Panis, E., *Exposition de l'Industrie de toutes les Nations 1855: Catalogue Official* (Paris 1855).

Pemberton, John E., *How to find out in mathematics* (Sussex 1963).

"Per Georg Scheutz", Svensken: Illustrerad *Veckotidning*, 20th July 1894.

"Per Georg Scheutz" *Victoria: Illustrerad Veckotidning*, 12th April 1889.

Petrenko, A. K. and Petrenko, O. L., "The Babbage machine and the origins of programming", *Istoriko-matematicheskie Issledovaniia*, 24, 1979. (Article in Russian).

Randell, Brian, "A Mysterious Advertisement", *Annals of the History of Computing*, 5, No. 1, January 1983.

Randell, Brian, *The origins of Digital Computers: Selected Papers (Heidelberg 1973)*.

Regnier, D., *Article on the Scheutz engine, La Proprieté Industrielle: Journal Judicaire de L'Industrie*, 19th August 1858.

"Remarks on Calculating Machines", *Journal of the Frankling Institute* 60 (Philadelphia 1855).

Report of the Secretary of the Navy 1858 (Washington D. C. 1858).

Rivere, A., "Machine à calculer", *L'Illustration, Journal Universel,* 28th August 1858.

Rolt, L. T. C., *Isambard Kingdom Brunel; Engineer, visionary and magnetic personality, he transformed the face of England* (Reading 1982).

Rolt, L. T. C., *Tools for the Job* (London 1968).

Ronan, Colin A., *Astronomers Royal* (New York 1969).

Rosenberg, Nathan, *Perspectives on Technology* (Binghamton, N. Y. 1976).

"Roterande ångmaskin af Edvard Scheutz", *Tidskrift för Byggnadskonst och Ingenjörsvetenskap*, 1861.

"Roterande Ångmaskin af Edvard Scheutz" *Tidskrift för Byggnadskonst och Ingenjörsvetenskap*, 1863.

Rouse Ball, Walter W., *A History of the Study of Mathematics at Cambridge* (Cambridge 1889).

Sahlholm, Bo, *Mekaniska verkstadsbyggnader under 1800-talet: Den moderna verkstadsplaneringens ursprung*, Stockholm Papers in History and Philosophy of Technology 2002, (Stockholm 1978).

Sahlin, Carl, "Svenska Linbanekonstruktioner", *Daedalus* (1931).

Sandqvist, Inga Britta, "Tekniska tidskrifter före Teknisk Tidskrift", Nicolai Herlofsson, Svante Lindqvist and Erik Tholander (eds.), *Vilja och kunnande: Teknikhistoriska uppsatser tillägnade Torsten Althin på hans åttioårsdag den 11 july 1977 av vänner* (Uppsala 1977).

Schartau, Sigurd, "Eldsvådorna 1785 och 1790: Staden i början av 1800-talet", Ernst L. Hartman, C. O. von Porat, Algot Friberg och Robert Johansson (eds.), *Jönköpings historia* 4 (Jönköping 1921).

Scheutz, Edvard, *Vackra flickor finnas äfven i Sibirien: Lustspel i två akter* (Stockholm 1836).

Scheutz, Ernst Thor, *Biografiska anteckningar över släkten Scheutz till år 1923* (Kalmar 1923).

[Scheutz, Georg], "Flygande Skottkärror", *Journal för Manufakturer och Hushållning* 4–5, 1825.

[Scheutz, Georg] *Handbok för bleckarbeten*, Bibliothek för konst, slöjd och tillämpad vetenskap (Stockholm 1849).

[Georg Scheutz], *Handbok för så wäl enklare som mera konstig Blekning Winter- och Sommartiden, af Lin, Blånor och Lingarn, Drell, Hollandslärft, Bomullsgarn och Bomullstyger, Papper, Wax och Halm, gamla Böcker och Kopparstick, m m, i sammandrag* (Stockholm 1817) (Rare book, KB).

Scheutz, Georg, *Handbok i ritkonsten*, Bibliothek för konst, slöjd och tillämpad vetenskap (Stockholm 1832).

Scheutz, Georg, *Stockholm. Illustrerade utkast* (Stockholm 1860).

Scheutz, Georg, *Industriens Bok. Uppfinningarne och slöjderna. Skildrade från historisk och teknisk ståndpunkt* 1–2 (Stockholm 1860).

Scheutz, Georg, *Industriens Bok. Uppfinningarne och slöjderna. Skildrade från historisk och teknisk ståndpunkt* 1–2 Stockholm (1860–61). Second edition.

[Scheutz, Georg], "Insända Meddelanden och Uppsatser", *Svenska Industriföreningens Tidskrift*, June 1834, August 1835, July 1836, June 1837.

[Scheutz, Georg], "Kranpumpar: George Scheutz's Patent, af den 14 november 1825", *Journal för Manufakturer och Hushållning* 8, 1825.

Scheutz, Georg, *Nytt och enkelt sätt att lösa nummereqvationer af högre och lägre grader efter Agardhska teorien: För praktiska behof* (Stockholm 1849).

Scheutz, Georg, *Bihang till skriften: Nytt och enkelt sätt att lösa nummereqvationer af högre och lägre grader efter Agardhska teorien* (Stockholm 1849).

[Scheutz, Georg], "Om Babbages Räknemaskin", *Journal för Manufakturer och Hushållning*, November 1833.

[Scheutz, Georg], "Om konsten att uppfinna redskap och machiner: En vink för uppfinnare och användare", *Journal för Manufakturer och Hushållning*, June 1834. (Based on Babbage's *Economy*.)

[Scheutz, Georg], "Om Sug- och Presspumpars bruk, i åtskilliga slöjder", *Journal för Manufakturer och Hushållning* 8, 1825.

[Scheutz, Georg], "Om sättet att bese större fabriker eller manufakturanläggningar", *Svenska Industriföreningars Tidskrift*, March 1836.

Scheutz, Georg, *Portatif räknemachin i form af en liten bok: En tillämpning av John Nepers, Baron af Marchiston, Räknestafwar* (Stockholm 1834).

Scheutz, Georg, *Register öfwer Stockholms tidningar* (Stockholm 1819).

[Scheutz, Georg], Review of Beskow's *Har Sverige Publicitet och Publicister?*, *Aftonbladet* 145, 149, 155, 182, 185, 1840.

[Scheutz, Georg], "Scheutz, Georg", *Biografiskt Lexicon öfver namnkunnige Svenska män* 14 (Uppsala 1847).

[Scheutz, Georg], *Slägtvälde och idévälde, eller det som var och det som komer* (Stockholm 1840).

[Scheutz, Georg], "Slödjexpositionen i Stockholm 1834", *Journal för Manufakturer och Hushållning*, June 1834.

[Scheutz, Georg], "Strödda uppsatser uti industriella ämnen", *Svenska Industriföreningens tidskrift*, November 1835. (Based on Babbage's *Economy*).

[Scheutz, Georg], "Säkerhetsventil för ångpannor, som fritt medgifver minskning, men icke förökning, af den en gång för alla bestämda ångtryckningen", *Svenska Industritidningens Tidskrift*, September 1835.

[Scheutz, Georg], "Trollkammaren", *Aftonbladet* 195, 197, 1841.

Scheutz, Georg, *Vägen till naturens riken: En elementarbok i naturhistorien: För lägre läroverk och sjelfundervisning*, (Stockholm 1843).

[Scheutz, Georg], "Öfversigt af de egentligen industriella Staternas Patentlagar", *Tidning för Näringarne*, October 1836.

Scheutz, Georg and Edvard, *Machine à calculer, qui presénte les résultats en les imprimant elle-même. Inventée par Georges Scheutz & Edouard Scheutz, de Stockholm, Exposans* (Stockholm 1855).

−, "Vördsam Inbjudning", (Stockholm 1881).

Schrön, Ludvig, *Sjuställiga vanliga logaritmer för alla hela tal från 1 till 108,000 och för sinus, cosinus, tangenter och cotangenter för alla vinklar i qvadranten från 10 till 10 sekunder* (Stockholm 1868). Translation from German original by F. W. Hultman.

Schulze, Carl Johan, *Neue und erweiterte Sammlung Logarithmischer, trigonometrischer und anderer zum gebrauch der Mathematik unentbehrlicher Tafeln* 1−2 (Berlin 1778). Combined German and French edition.

Schütz, Fredrik, "Samuel Owen", *Daedalus* (1975).

The Science Museum: The First Hundred Years, (London 1957).

Seseman, Hans Jacob, *Multiplications- och Divisions-Taflas Intresse-Räkning à 6 Pro Cent om Året, som utwisar Intresset icke allenast för År, Månader och Dagar, utan för alla 360 Dagarna i Året, eller Större och Mindre Capitaler, så wäl uti Koppar och Silfwer, samt Specie-Mynt med sina fördelningar* (Stockholm 1811).

Sherwin, Henry, *Sherwin's Mathematical Tables* (London 1741).

Sinderen, Alfred W. van, "The Printed Papers of Charles Babbage", *Annals of the History of Computing* 2, No. 2, April 1980.

Smiles, Samuel, *Industrial Biography: Iron Workers and Tool Makers* (London 1863).

−, *Lives of the Engineers, with an account of their principal Works; comprising also a History of Inland Communication in Britain* 1−3 (London 1861).

Sommer, Morten and Müller, Wilhelm, *Italiensk Läsebok, med därtill tillhörande Ordbok och Språklära* (Stockholm 1819). Translation and addition by Georg Scheutz. (Rare book, KB).

"Specimens of Tables, Calculated, Stereomoulded, and Printed by Machinery", *The Athenaeum* No. 1545, 6th June 1857.

Stokes, George Gabriel, Wheatstone, Charles, Willis, Robert and Miller, William H., *Report on the Calculating Machine recently constructed by Mr. Donkin*, January 21st 1855.

Stål, A. D., (ed.), *Register öfver Kongl. Vetenskaps-Academiens Handlingar, ifrån dess början år 1739 till och med år 1825* (Stockholm 1831).

Sveriges Riksbank 1668−1924 (Stockholm 1931).

"Sällskapet Idun 1862−1903", Albin Hildebrand *Svenskt Porträttgalleri* 23 (Stockholm 1903).

Söderbaum, Henrik Gustaf, *Jacob Berzelius: Själfbiografiska anteckningar* (Stockholm 1901).

Taylor, Michael, *Tables of Logarithms of all Numbers, from 1 to 101 000; and of the Sines and Tangents to Every Second of the quadrant* (London 1792).

Tee, Gary J., "The Heritage of Charles Babbage in Australasia", *Annals of the History of Computing*, 5, No. 1, January 1983.

Terquem, Olry, *Handbok i algebra*, Bibliothek för konst, slöjd och tillämpad vetenskap (Stockholm 1832). Unsigned translation by Magnus Luttrop, edited and adapted by Georg Scheutz.

Thomée, Gustaf, *Nionde Bridgewater-afhandlingen. Aphorismer*, Bibliotek för Populär Naturkunnighet, Andra afdelningen 9 (Stockholm 1846).

Thuring, C. W., *Intresse-uträkning på Större och Mindre Capital efter 5 och 6 procent ifrån en dag till och med Ett År* (Örebro 1804, 1810, 1817, 1824).

Torstendahl, Rolf, *Teknologins nytta: Motiveringar för det svenska tekniska utbildningsväsendets framväxt framförda av riksdagsmän och utbildningsadministratörer 1810—1870* (Uppsala 1975).

Toynbee, William (ed.), *The Diaries of William Charles Macready 1833—1851* 1—2 (New York 1912).

Transactions of the Society for the Encouragement of Arts, Manufacture, and Commerce XXXVI (London 1818), pp 133—177.

Transactions of the Society for the Encouragement of Arts, Manufacture, and Commerce XLIII (London 1825), pp 138—142.

Tresca, M. (ed.), *Visite à l'Expostition Universelle de Paris, en 1855* (Paris 1855).

Trofast, Jan (ed.), *Brevväxlingen mellan Jöns Jacob Berzelius och Carl Palmstedt* 1—3 (Lund 1979, 1981, 1983).

Tucker, Robert *The Mathematical and Scientific Library of the late Charles Babbage, Dorset Street Manchest er Sq., To be sold by Private Contract* (London 1872).

Vega, Georg von, *Thesaurus Logarithmorum completus* (Leipzig 1794). Also with German text.

Venn, J. A. (ed.), *Alumni Cantabrigenses. A Biographical List of all known Students, Graduates and Holders of Office at the University of Cambridge, from the earliest Times to 1900*, 1, part two, (Cambridge 1940).

Virgil, *Aeneid*, II.

Vlacq, Adrian, *Trigonometria Artificialis: sive Magnus Canon Triangolorum Logarithmicus, Ad Radium 100000,00000, & ad dena Scrupula Secunda* (Gouda 1633).

Vogel, Kurt (ed.), *Das Bamberger Blockbuch, Ein xylographisches Rechenbuch aus dem 15. Jahrhundert* (Munich 1980). Fascimile edition.

Weber, Otto, "Ein 'Computer' des 18. Jahrhunderts", *Photorin: Mitteilungen der Lichtenberg-Gesellschaft* 3, (1980).

Webster's New International Dictionary of the English Language (Springfield, MA. 1949).

Weld, Charles Richard, (ed.), *A History of the Royal Society, With Memoirs of the President* 1—2 (London 1848).

—, *The Eleventh Chapter of the History of the Royal Society* 2, chapter XI (London 1848).

Westrin, Theodor, *Några bidrag till sällskapet Iduns historia: I anledning af dess 50-års jubileum* (Stockholm 1912).

White, John H. Jr., *The John Bull: 150 Years a Locomotive* (Washington, D. C. 1981).

Wiberg, Helgo, "Martin Wiberg, En svensk uppfinnare inom grafiska branschen", *Grafiskt forum*, No. 9, 1954.

Wiberg, Helgo, "Några av Martin Wibergs uppfinningar", *Deadalus* (1955).

Wiberg, Helgo, "Svensk gjorde första användbara sättmaskinen", *Stockholmstidningen*, 1st December 1954.

Wiberg, Martin, *Med maskin uträknade och stereotyperade räntetabeller jemte en dagräknings-tabell* (Stockholm 1860).

—, *Logarithmic-Tables. Computed and Printed by Means of his Calculating-Machine* (Stockholm 1876).

Wieselgren, Harald, "Georg Scheutz", *Ny Illustrerad Tidning* 25, 21 st June 1873.

Wieselgren, Harald, "Georg Scheutz † 1873", *Ur vår samtid: Femtio porträtt med nekrologer* (Stockholm 1880).

Wilkes, M. V., "How Babbage's dream came true", *Nature* 257, October 16, 1975.

–, "Babbage as a computer pioneer", *Historica Mathematica* 4, 1977.

Williams, F. J., "The Swedish Calculating Machine at the General Register Office, Somerset House", *Companion to the Almanac; or Year-Book of General Information for 1866* (London 1865).

Williams, M. R., "The difference engines", *The Computer Journal* 19, No. 1, 1976.

Williams, M. R., "The Scientific Library of Charles Babbage", *Annals of the History of Computing* 3, No. 3, July 1981.

Woodbury, Robert S., "History of the Lathe to 1850", *Studies in the History of Machine Tools* (Cambridge, MA 1972).

Woodcroft, Bennet (ed.), *Alphabetical Index of Patentees of Inventions: From March 2, 1617 to October 1, 1852* (London 1854).

Åkerman, Joachim, *Elementarkurs i Kemien* (Stockolm 1836).

Åkerstedt, Sven, "Frimärksleverantörerna", Sven Åkerstedt (ed.), *Handbok över Sveriges frankotecken* 1855–1963 (Karlshamn 1964).

Index of persons

412

The MIT Press, with Peter Denning as general consulting editor, publishes computer science books in the following series:

ACM Doctoral Dissertation Award and Distinguished Dissertation Series

Artificial Intelligence
Patrick Winston, founding editor
Michael Brady, Daniel Bobrow, and Randall Davis, editors

Charles Babbage Institute Reprint Series for the History of Computing
Martin Campbell-Kelly, editor

Computer Systems
Herb Schwetman, editor

Explorations with Logo
E. Paul Goldenberg, editor

Foundations of Computing
Michael Garey and Albert Meyer, editors

History of Computing
I. Bernard Cohen and William Aspray, editors

Information Systems
Michael Lesk, editor

Logic Programming
Ehud Shapiro, editor; Fernando Pereira, Koichi Furukawa, Jean-Louis Lassez, and David H. D. Warren, associate editors

The MIT Press Electrical Engineering and Computer Science Series

Research Monographs in Parallel and Distributed Processing
Christopher Jesshope and David Klappholz, editors

Scientific and Engineering Computation
Janusz Kowalik, editor

Technical Communication
Ed Barrett, editor